BURGHLEY
TUDOR STATESMAN
1520–1598

William Cecil, Lord Burghley

BURGHLEY

TUDOR STATESMAN

1520–1598

B. W. Beckingsale

MACMILLAN

LONDON · MELBOURNE · TORONTO

ST MARTIN'S PRESS

NEW YORK

1967

MACMILLAN AND COMPANY LIMITED
Little Essex Street WC2
also Bombay Calcutta Madras Melbourne

THE MACMILLAN COMPANY OF CANADA LIMITED
70 Bond Street Toronto 2

ST MARTIN'S PRESS INC
175 Fifth Avenue New York NY 10010

Library of Congress catalog card no. 67-19278

PRINTED IN GREAT BRITAIN

TO THE

MEMORY OF

WILLIAM LAURENCE BURN

HISTORIAN AND

MAN OF LAW

CONTENTS

ILLUSTRATIONS

PREFACE

When reviewing his father's life, Thomas, the eldest son of William Cecil, observed that it was 'a large field to gather flowers in'. In preparing this book I have peeped and botanised in parts of those very extensive acres and I have gratefully availed myself of the bouquets of learning plucked by such historians as Conyers Read, Joel Hurstfield, A. L. Rowse, Lawrence Stone and many others who have sought out Tudor roses. What I have gathered from their labours will be apparent to all who have been picking flowers in that particular field. Any weeds of error are of my own harvesting.

The first part of this book presents a short biography of William Cecil which is largely concerned with his political career. The second part deals with aspects of his character and achievements in government and politics and in the intellectual and social milieu mainly during his mature years in the reign of Elizabeth I. If together these parts make William Cecil seem a little more accessible and comprehensible to the student and general reader, this book will have achieved its object.

I thank all those who have helped me in my studies. I am most grateful to Lord Salisbury for his permission to visit Hatfield House and to consult the records of his family. I am much indebted to Dr Roy Strong of the National Portrait Gallery, who not only helped me greatly in collecting illustrations for this book, but also generously allowed me to see the results of his researches on the portraiture of William Cecil which are to be published in his *Catalogue of Sixteenth-Century Portraits in the National Portrait Gallery*. For financial aid I thank the Research Committee of the University of Newcastle upon Tyne, which gave me a grant to help defray the expenses of my visits to the British Museum and the Public Record Office. My most constant helper in authorship, as in all else, has been my wife, who gallantly undertook to produce the typescript.

In my use of William Cecil's surname and title I hope that I have achieved an acceptable compromise between consistent usage and the demands of chronology. In the pursuit of clarity I have employed throughout the title of the Duke of Alençon for Francis Valois, who became the Duke of Anjou when his brother surrendered that title upon ascending the throne of France.

Lastly I mention with especial gratitude the encouragement given to me by the late Professor William Laurence Burn, who read the typescript of this book. I offer this work to his memory in the belief that in his modesty and generosity he would have accepted the dedication.

B. W. BECKINGSALE

Newcastle upon Tyne
September 1966

Part One

CHAPTER I

Origins

IN August 1485 Wales was astir. Henry Tudor, Earl of Richmond, had landed at Milford Haven and was calling upon the Welsh to help him depose 'that odious tyrant, Richard', the Yorkist King. It seemed as if the prophecies of the bards that a British King would again sit upon the English throne were about to be fulfilled. Henry, with his Welsh blood and upbringing, promised to restore to the people of Wales 'their former liberties, delivering them of such miserable servitudes as they have long stood in'. The young usurper marched on and triumphed at Bosworth Field.

The torrent of these great events, swirling through the mountains of Wales, carried along with it many Welshmen. Those who dared to ride the dangerous current of rebellion might be swept as far afield as the Court of the new King of England, Henry VII. English courtiers thought that too many Welshmen had arrived in the English heaven. While England did not turn out to be the promised land that some desired, for others it was a land of opportunities. Among those who had followed the successful usurper from the borders of Wales was David Syssill or Sitsilt.

By taking advantage of yet another turn in the fortunes of the wars of Lancaster and York, David found favour with the new King. His treason against Richard III had not led to the horror of a traitor's execution or to death on the field of battle. He had shared in the Tudor triumph and he lived to settle and begin his family in England. His grandson William was to write his name as 'Cecil',[1] acquire the title Lord Burghley and become Lord Treasurer of England. David had taken a risk, but he had established the connection of his family with the Tudors. His own obscure part in the precarious beginnings of Tudor rule prepared the way for the great role which his grandson Lord Burghley was to play in the reign of Henry VII's granddaughter Elizabeth I.

David Cecil had left the home of his father Philip.[2] As a younger
son of a family of the small gentry on the Welsh Border he could
not hope for a share of the modest wealth which was destined to
be the inheritance of the eldest son, Richard. Thus it was that the
home of the Syssills or Cecils at Alltyrynys, with its green meadows
bounded by the pleasant streams of Honddu and Monnow, finally
passed into the hands of Richard's son. That branch of the Cecil
family was to continue in obscurity, tangled in the troubles of the
turbulent society in the marches of Wales. They lived on where the
Celtic influence was strong. But David took with him only his
memories of Alltyrynys in Ewyas and founded a new home in
eastern England.

By the time of this great change in his fortunes in 1485, David
Cecil was nearly thirty years old.[3] Of the early years of his life little
is known. He had acquired some schooling. But the best guarantee
that he could use his assets was a patron of influence. David may
have been with Henry Tudor at some time during the fourteen
years of exile on the Continent which preceded his return to
England. He may have fought at Bosworth Field. What is certain
is that he was in the service of one of his mother's most prosperous
relatives, Sir David Philips, who was a supporter of Henry Tudor
and was much favoured by the King's influential mother, Margaret
Beaufort. It was through Sir David Philips that David Cecil could
expect to obtain a reward for his support of Henry Tudor.

When Henry VII created his own personal bodyguard of some
two hundred chosen men, David Cecil was among them. David
must have been well trusted and have had the appearance and
reputation of a good soldier to have been made a guardian of the
King's safety in the first perilous years of the reign. To be a
Yeoman of the Guard was an honour which bore promise of
further favours. Henry VII was not likely to prove ungrateful for
such loyalty when rebellion was still stirring. Fortunately for
David Cecil he had committed himself to the King who was able
to end the civil wars and establish a new dynasty.

By the end of 1496, with the defeat of the conspiracy which
centred on the pretender Perkin Warbeck, Henry VII had finally
established himself. During the years since Bosworth, David Cecil

had also been settling himself in England. The weight of Sir David Philips' influence told in his favour and dictated where David should make his home. It was in the town of Stamford, where Lincolnshire and Northamptonshire meet on the river Welland, some ninety miles along the main route to the North from London, that David was given his opportunity. He took it.

In 1494 David Cecil was granted the freedom of the borough of Stamford. At about the same time he married Alice Dycons, a relative and most probably the daughter of John Dycons, who was thrice mayor of Stamford. Although he was a stranger from the far-off south-western edge of Herefordshire it had taken David barely a decade to break into one of those exclusive little oligarchies which ran the affairs of small towns all over England. Stamford was suffering a decline in its cloth industry.[4] Consequently it was susceptible to new wealth and open to buyers of property like David Cecil. Soon he was one of the 'upper twelve' of Stamford. He was to be mayor three times and three times a Member for the borough in the Commons.

David Cecil had responded to the challenge of new surroundings and to the resentment of a strange community. Like so many immigrants, he had made good. If his first marriage had helped to prepare the way for influence in Stamford, his second marriage to a local heiress, Joan Roos of Dowsby, was to give him the financial strength to sample the opportunities of the neighbouring district. Stamford stood where the forests of the Midlands met the fenlands of eastern England. In the undeveloped countryside with its tracts of woodland and fen lay potential riches for a man who could exploit them at a time of an increasing hunger for land.

In the second decade after Bosworth, David Cecil spread his interests beyond the boundaries of the town in which he was already a leading burgess. He became a commissioner of sewers in Lincolnshire, entrusted with the surveying of the dykes and waterways of the fens. He acquired a hold upon the keepership of Cliffe Park, part of the Rockingham forest. The keeperships of Whittleseamere near Peterborough, of the Duchy of Lancaster lands in the neighbouring counties and of the woodlands of Glatton and Holme became his.[5] With the profits of these offices and the power which they gave him to offer employment he became prosperous. His wealth derived now not only from property in Stamford, but also from the skilful management of land in the three counties of Northamptonshire, Rutland and Lincolnshire. David Cecil retained the outlook of the small gentry into which he had been born. He did not attempt to become a merchant or seek to organise local industry. Land and property provided his livelihood.

David's position was sufficiently substantial to survive the death of his patron Sir David Philips in 1506. He was one of the executors and took over some of his patron's offices, which was a tribute to his business acumen and trustworthiness.[6] When Henry VII died in 1509 David Cecil's prospects at Court were not ruined. As a Yeoman of the Guard he attended the royal funeral. He was present to enjoy the bounty of the new King. Henry VIII made him bailiff of the lordships of Essendine, Preston and Uppingham in Rutland and of Shillingthorpe in Lincolnshire. In 1513 he secured a pension of 12d. a day for life on his appointment as a Serjeant-at-arms.[7]

While preserving his own advantageous foothold at Court, David Cecil had also introduced his eldest son Richard[8] into that charmed circle. He had educated his son probably at Stamford Grammar School, but it seems he had not prepared Richard for the higher flights of ambition by sending him to a university or to the Inns of Court. For the old man the Court of the King was the place where men were made, and there he saw to it that his son obtained a post. In 1517 Richard Cecil appears as a Page of the Chamber in the Royal Household.[9] The close connection with the Tudors was thus maintained in the second generation.

It was to be expected that Richard's marriage would be arranged to strengthen the Cecil hold around Stamford. Jane, daughter of William Heckington of Bourne, was Richard's chosen bride. Jane was not yet twenty but she was already a widow and a worth-while match. In 1520, while his young wife was expecting a child, Richard Cecil, as a personal attendant of the King, had to accompany his master abroad to the Field of the Cloth of Gold where Henry VIII met Francis I.[10] Then, at Bourne, on 13 September

1520 Jane gave birth to Richard's son, William Cecil.[11] Three girls, Elizabeth, Margaret and Ann, finally made up Richard's family but William remained the only son. On him were fixed the hopes of his grandfather and father for the future of the Cecil family.

When William Cecil was old enough he was sent to a local school. The services of a priest or tutor in the household were not available for the education of the lesser gentry. Yet at this time even the greater gentry were beginning to send their boys to local schools in response to the demand that a gentleman should have a bookish learning. Eton and Shrewsbury were attracting aristocratic patronage. There was some complaint that the sons of the poor were being robbed of their places in the schools by the invasion of young gentlemen. In sending William to learn Latin his father was providing him with knowledge which was coming to be expected of the upper classes in secular society.

It appears that while William's parents lived at Bourne, his mother's home, he attended the grammar school at Grantham. As the school was some fifteen miles from his home it is likely that young William boarded at Grantham during the term time. When his mother and father moved to Little Burghley or Stamford Baron[12] on the southern outskirts of Stamford, William attended the grammar school in the town.

His days at school do not seem to have left any deep impression upon William. If he did suffer from his schooling as Thomas Cranmer claims to have done, losing 'much of that benefit of memory and audacity'[13] by ill-treatment, he has not left any note of it. In an age which the contemporary educational reformers claimed was too much devoted to the belief that sparing the rod would spoil the child, William survived, it seemed, without any mental or bodily scars. Later in life he expressed himself[14] against over-severity in whipping schoolboys, but whether he formed his opinion as the result of happy or unhappy experience at school cannot be said.

How far the character, training and abilities of his schoolmasters modified the discipline and enlivened the curriculum of his schools William was judge. They may have been amongst those schools

which used 'to read the Grammar alone by itself'.[15] That they
made William proficient in Latin grammar, which it was their
prime object to teach, is certain. What of the wisdom of the
Ancients the boy absorbed from his linguistic training depended
on William's sensitivity. He was a clever child and no doubt he
drew all that an immature mind might from the classical quotations
in the text-books. But the long school-days were not all of
William's childhood. At home there was much to learn.

As the young William grew up he had before him the example
of his grandfather David, who lived on until he was nearly eighty
and remained active until the end. In 1524 the old man had the
honour to entertain King Henry's bastard son, the Duke of
Richmond.[16] David reached the peak of local distinction when, in
1532, upon the death of Sir William Spencer, he was appointed
Sheriff of Northamptonshire. He was not too proud, however, to
badger Thomas Cromwell for a warrant for £100 to defray the
expenses of that costly honour. His last royal employment was on
a commission for Rutland which was inquiring into the value of
ecclesiastical and monastic revenues, in preparation for the
Dissolution of the Monasteries.[17] He undertook it in the year in
which he died, 1536. Death did not catch him unawares. For some
years arrangements had been made so that the offices and properties
which he had acquired would eventually pass to his son Richard.

David's will revealed that he had been prosperous since his
second marriage, for he was able to leave intact to his wife the
stock of plate which had been in her dowry and to add the bonus
of twenty cows and a bull. His bequest of two feather-beds to his
son Richard was a sign that he had enjoyed those luxuries which
only the well-to-do could afford. He left a black gown of cloth
lined with damask, a second-best gown, a doublet of 'satin streaked'
with a jacket, another doublet, a velvet jacket and green coats. It
was the wardrobe of a man of substance. For a man who had
provided well for this world his provision for the next was modest.
'I will that a priest shall sing a year at St. George's Church at
Stamford for my soul.'[18]

William Cecil's father Richard made steady advances in the
family fortune and consolidated the gains already made. His

acceptance as one of the rural gentry in his neighbourhood came in 1539 when he was made a Justice of the Peace in Northamptonshire. He continued to accumulate property. The time was favourable: the Dissolution of the Monasteries which began in 1536 had put a large amount of valuable land on the market. The lands were not cheap, but they were available. When he settled in Stamford, David Cecil could have had no notion that the conglomeration of monastic property in the town and neighbourhood would provide easy pickings for his son.

By persistence Richard got first the lease and then the possession of the Benedictine nunnery, the Priory of St Michael, in Stamford, nearly three hundred acres of land, a site in the town and the advowsons and tithes which had belonged to the priory. Two years after finally securing the nunnery he got a twenty-one-year lease of the White Friars, one of the four friaries in Stamford, and in the next year, 1543, he obtained a lease of the lands in Colley Weston which had belonged to Stamford priory.

Richard took a second bite at monastic lands, when Henry VIII died, by taking advantage of the scramble at Court to appropriate clerical wealth. The lordship and manor of Tinwell in Rutland, formerly in the possession of Peterborough monastery, was his greatest prize among other spoils which included properties in Holborn and in Essex and the manor of Ducketts in Middlesex, all of which had belonged to St Bartholomew's, Smithfield. He acquired also the larger advowson of Warfield in Berkshire of which he later disposed.[19]

Richard Cecil did not confine his attentions to monastic property. Like his father he had the knack of collecting at the Court grants and offices which, though small in themselves, constituted considerable wealth in aggregate. He was made constable of the castles of Maxey and of Warwick and bailiff of the manors and woods of Torpel, Maxey and Bourne. In 1542 he obtained the lordships of Nassington, Upton and Yarwell in Northamptonshire.[20] His chief acquisitions had been made with an eye to increasing the family properties and lands in and around Stamford.

While at Stamford and in the neighbouring counties Richard Cecil became a considerable personage, at Court he was content to

occupy a minor post. He rose slowly from Page of the Chamber to
Groom of the Wardrobe.[21] The post in the Wardrobe had certain
advantages. It brought him close to the person of the King. It
gave him the status and privileges of a courtier without making
any great demands upon his purse. There was wisdom in accepting
the limitations of his education and social standing.

While it demanded tact and efficiency Richard's post carried no
dangerous responsibility. He held the King's favour at the personal,
not the political, level. The King saw none of the ambitious side of
Richard's nature and did not thrust him into higher office. Richard
Cecil might attend the King at the Field of the Cloth of Gold or go
with six archers and six billmen to the siege of Boulogne,[22] but he
played no part which could implicate him in the success or failure
of the King's plans.

If Richard Cecil made no great mark at Court, he avoided
putting the family gains in jeopardy at a time when it was all too
easy for misplaced ambition to lead to ruin. He held the favour of
Henry VIII and was remembered like other faithful servants in the
royal will.[23] Although he was very close to all the hazards of the
King's matrimonial intrigues, he survived. He passed unscathed,
with profit even, through the shifts of religious and ecclesiastical
policy under Henry VIII and his son Edward VI. To be at Court
without danger and to snap up the unconsidered trifles without
difficulty suited Richard Cecil very well. He did not allow the
family connection with the Tudors to lapse. When his son William
was only eight years old, in 1529, Richard found a place for him in
royal service as one of the three Pages of the Robes.[24] In 1529 the
little niche which the Cecils had made for themselves at Court was
occupied by all three generations. Years later Richard's position in
the Wardrobe enabled the young William to visit Court and draw
the attention of Henry VIII. It was worth keeping a place warm at
Court.

When Richard died in March 1553 at his house in Cannon Row,
he was still only Groom of the Wardrobe, but the Cecil wealth
had grown and was intact. His son William was described as of
'gentle birth'[25] and had risen to the dangerous heights to which
Richard never attempted to climb. But William's success rested

upon the endeavours of David, the founder, and Richard, the consolidator, of the fortunes of this branch of the Cecil family.

The influence of the older generations upon William Cecil was long-lasting. His grandfather did not die until William was sixteen. His father lived until his only son was thirty-three. Jane, William's beloved mother, although blind, endured into a somewhat trouble-some old age and lived until he was sixty-eight. Throughout all those years William enjoyed his mother's affection. In her old age she could still weep for joy over his letters and insist upon treating as a holiday gown a dress which he sent her.[26] William could not easily escape the formative pressures of family behaviour and the filial obligations of an only son. He did not wish to escape. He was full of family piety and inherited something of the Celtic sense of kin. From his family upbringing he derived many of the charac-teristics which were to make him successful. The lessons which he learned in his boyhood crystallised into a platitudinous wisdom by his old age.

The public modesty and deference of men seeking to avoid the jealousy of those who watch them climb was ingrained in William. It paid David Cecil, the immigrant stranger, to maintain a certain humility in envious Stamford. Richard Cecil remained humble at Court. The family cultivated a tactful taciturnity which prevented a fatal slip of the tongue. The Cecils of Stamford had suppressed any tendency to Welsh eloquence. They lived cautiously and studied to avoid giving offence either to their betters or to their inferiors.

As self-made men, the Cecils had sought from Providence the approval for their successful lives which their fellow men might be more ready to grudge them. At the end of a particularly prosperous year in November 1506, David Cecil endowed a chantry at St Mary's, Stamford.[27] His direction that prayers were to be offered for Henry VII and the late Queen as well as for his own father, mother and wife projected his association with royalty into the next world. Nearly thirty years later Richard Cecil found that protestant doctrines were more relevant to the circumstances of his life. Men who rise in society find it easier, perhaps, to be sure of themselves as innovators than as the upholders of tradition.

In August 1535 Richard was sure enough of his convictions and
the mood of the government to defend openly in the church at
Stamford a sermon on Justification by Faith, preached by Richard
Quiaenus, against the attacks of two Dominican friars.[28] Just as
David Cecil had committed himself to a new dynasty, so Richard
defended the new doctrines. Richard was a good friend of
the radical Protestant, John Hooper, who became Bishop of
Gloucester.[29] The Cecils sensed the flow of the tide and they swam
with it. In William's home the discipline of worship and the
assurance of moral rectitude strengthened the family morale and
gave it confidence. The piety of the Cecils was not of that other-
worldly kind cultivated by the saints. It was that practical piety
which was good for business.

One loyalty in this world which William had known from early
childhood was to the House of Tudor. He never forgot the need
of good lordship and in his turn he pressed the lesson on his
younger son. Both David and Richard knew their royal masters
with that observant intimacy which is so much more vivid and
absorbing for the servant than for the master. David and his son
owed much to the Tudors. The material and personal links with
the royal family generated a loyalty in the Cecils which stirred the
Celtic blood that they shared with their patrons. William grew up
accepting that he must serve those who had been the benefactors
of grandfather and father. The fortunes of the Cecils and the
Tudors were clearly tied together. It was to be for his service to
her father and her brother that Elizabeth awarded a title to William
Cecil.[30]

In the affairs of public life the young William saw his elders
involved in the problems of local government. His grandfather
was mayor of Stamford for the third time when William was six
years old. As a boy of twelve William was the grandson of a
sheriff. He was the son of a Justice of the Peace when he was
nineteen. The intricacies of local affairs were part of the background of his home life. William glimpsed the wider world when
his grandfather went off to Parliament. He heard talk of the Court
in the family circle. His prudent father must have given him
instructions on how to behave when he attended the Court as a

Page. William was being made familiar at an early age with the way in which a man should conduct himself in commanding authority in borough and county and in humble service at the Court. A knowledge of the etiquette of social success was a valuable inheritance. William enjoyed that subtle dynastic training in the habits of power which can help to keep a family great.

In a similar way, by unconscious imitation and casual experience, the business of estate management, which was the most vital of family interests, passed into the mental grasp of the intelligent young William. His mother was, it seems, as shrewd as his father in gaining the pennies which added up to the pounds. How to estimate the potentialities of any piece of property or land and use it to the best advantage was a faculty readily acquired by a sharp son from such parents. The interests of the family ranged from David Cecil's share in the Tabard Inn at Stamford through the stewardships and keeperships of woods and marshes to the full possession of such a manor as that of Tinwell, which Richard bought. It was a time when children shared at an early age in the concerns of adult life.

Such were the advantages of disciplined living, social behaviour and worldly wisdom that William Cecil was given by his home. His upbringing gave him a grounding in the virtues and techniques required for successful social climbing. Among these virtues was a utilitarian respect for education as the ladder to higher social status and political eminence. Richard Cecil had seen the careers open to trained talents at Court and had the sense to realise that the time had now come to train the family talents in William. It was clear that places of authority and responsibility could be won by those with a university education and a knowledge of the law. Richard Cecil determined that his son should go to Cambridge. It was to be a preparation which would enable William to rise to a higher plane of royal service than that which any Cecil had yet reached.

CHAPTER II

University and Inns of Court

CAMBRIDGE was the university which served eastern England. It was natural that Richard Cecil should send his son there from Stamford Baron. At this time an increasing number of the children of the aristocracy were entering the universities. A cultural revolution was beginning, by which the gentleman was acquiring an education equivalent to that of the clerk. The New Learning was becoming fashionable among the leaders of the laity because it had become the necessity of the ruling class. The new standards in court life and in the conduct of government required men with the classical education prescribed by the humanists. The ecclesiastics with their canon law and scholasticism were being ousted from the highest government posts by the laymen with their common law and humanism. Sir Thomas More followed Cardinal Wolsey in the Chancellorship.

About 1490, when young Thomas Wolsey from Ipswich went to Oxford, the prospects of a career in the world of affairs as a churchman were still bright. But in 1535 the clerical future looked cloudy and confused. The doubt about the safety and wisdom of entering a threatened Church and the limited opportunities of an underdeveloped economy steered the ambitious into a training for the secular professions of law and medicine or for government service. There was no question of seeking to rise to greatness through the Church for William Cecil. He was fortunate to profit by the educational changes which put the highest posts in the royal bureaucracy into the hands of laymen. Once again the Cecils had caught the tide of change.

Cambridge was not an intellectual backwater.[1] The great humanist, Erasmus, had been there in cold rooms at Queens'. Thomas Cranmer, who had become Archbishop of Canterbury, had been a fellow at Jesus College. 'Little' Bilney of Peterhouse, one of the first protestant martyrs, had been burned at Norwich. The lessons of humanism and Protestantism were being thrashed out by the scholars assembled in the little fenland town. When young Cecil arrived there the validity of the papal supremacy was the current topic of debate.[2] New ideas eddied around Cambridge like the Cam in winter flood.

Academic opinions and beliefs could have mortal consequence. John Fisher, the Chancellor of the University, was put in the Tower along with Sir Thomas More in the year that William went up to Cambridge. Thomas Cromwell, the draftsman of the statutes which made the Royal Supremacy effective in England, became the new Chancellor of the University. The university stood all too close to the edge of the volcanic Court and shook with each convulsion of the royal will. Thomas Cromwell's commissioners stripped the university and college libraries of the books of the old learning. The colleges feared for their very existence when the Dissolution of the Monasteries began. William was not in an ivory tower.

When William Cecil came to this intellectual centre he was fourteen years old. It was not an exceptional age at which to enter university but it was as young as was normally acceptable. He entered St John's College in May 1535.[3] It was a fortunate choice of college because it placed William under the influence of a young and brilliant teacher of the classics, John Cheke.[4] For Cheke and his circle the relevance of the classics to contemporary life was obvious. They wrote in what they deemed to be a Roman hand and William Cecil learned his italic calligraphy from them.[5] They pioneered a new subject, Greek, at Cambridge. In 1530 John Fisher provided for lectures in Greek as part of the college teaching. The first Reader in Greek in the university, appointed in 1535, was Richard Croke, who justified the study of his subject by asserting its usefulness in the understanding of the sciences and in fitting men for public service. In 1540 John Cheke became the first Professor of Greek. William Cecil was reading the very latest subject when he studied Greek. He was not concerned with dead learning but with a most relevant and useful education for an active life.

It was clear at Cambridge that Cecil was a very able young man. He mastered Greek sufficiently well to be entrusted with some teaching. His progress was the result of hard work. It was said that he paid the college bell-ringer a little extra to wake him each morning at four o'clock so that he could gain an hour or so for study.[6] It was the practice to begin the day early in Tudor Cambridge. Yet, even where it was usual for scholars to be at work in the dawn, Cecil determined to be the early bird.

William evidently found scholarship to his liking. He acquired the habit and discipline of long hours of study, which lasted him all his life. His academic work seems to have supplied him with a genuine intellectual interest. In later life, when he was immersed in affairs of State, he could still enjoy learning for learning's sake. An interest in education, a love of books and an enjoyment of the company and friendship of learned men remained with him. He had in him the makings of a don. His friend Ascham remembered him as 'one of the forwardest young plants in all that worthy College of St John's'.[7]

Yet a life of academic study in Cambridge was not altogether suited to William's developing personality and talents. He could master Latin and Greek. But he showed little aesthetic appreciation of literature. The techniques of scholarship fascinated him because they gave him accurate information and increased his powers of persuasion. He could absorb all that he wished to know and keep the details clear in his mind. He could expound and argue in an orderly fashion. But while he possessed a vastly competent and capacious mind, he was not an original thinker. His genius, as his early rising shows, was the genius which is founded upon an infinite capacity for taking pains.

Once he had gained the technical mastery of his studies, Cecil's interest in the substance of classical literature was utilitarian. He wanted to learn the lessons of life from his reading. The ancient historians and moralists commented upon the life of action. It was typical of Cecil's attitude to the classics that in later life he could turn to Plato or Cicero for moral comfort in times of difficulty. His practical and utilitarian bent found encouragement in the humanist circle to which he belonged.

Cecil's teachers and friends rejected the life of studious retirement, the contemplative life. Richard Croke, Thomas Smith and
John Cheke all believed that the object of a university was to fit
men for the active life and in particular to train them for the
service of the King. Sir Thomas More had come to the conclusion
that it was his duty to counsel the King. Sir Thomas Elyot set out
a scheme of education for those who were to become governors
in the commonwealth. Inside and outside the university men were
coming to believe that the end of education was public service.[8]

So influential did the humanist educational ideals and small
stipends prove that many of the able scholars whom Cecil knew at
Cambridge left the university to play their part as the tutors and
secretaries, the counsellors and ambassadors of their Princes. John
Cheke taught Edward VI. Roger Ascham and William Grindal
taught the Princess Elizabeth. Thomas Smith became Secretary of
State. The result was that those who had been readers, professors
and fellows, lecturers and students at Cambridge when Cecil was
an undergraduate, were to be found at Court when Cecil entered
public life. It was to be a circumstance much in Cecil's favour. In
such an atmosphere it seems unlikely that the young Cecil ever
considered an academic career in Cambridge to the exclusion of
ambitions in the wider world.

The academic training which Cecil received was predominantly
a secular education. But it was inevitably affected by the religious
changes which were shaking Cambridge and were beginning to
stir the country. Cheke had edited a number of Chrysostom's
homilies.[9] Many who studied the New Learning felt the pull of
Protestantism. In the 'little Germany', established in the White
Horse tavern, which lay between King's and St Catharine's College,
the doctrines of Luther had been discussed. As yet only a few were
openly committed to all the main doctrines of Protestantism. But
the problems of religion could not be dismissed by thinking
scholars. The humanists at Cambridge had to come to terms with
the rival forms of Christianity. Cecil had no training as a theologian
but he had the intellect to follow theological argument. He was
not the sort of young man to experience a sudden conversion.
When his emotions overcame his caution they took a different

turn. Like most of his generation he was absorbing the new
religious doctrines piecemeal.

Those of the New Learning who were critical in so many ways
of tradition were susceptible to the new theology. The philological
approach of the protestant interpreters of the Bible and their
reliance on historical argument were attractive to the classical
scholars with whom Cecil mixed. Acceptance of the supreme
authority of the Bible came easily to those who studied the Greek
New Testament of Erasmus. Humanist historians stirred a
nationalism which expressed itself in obedience to the monarch.
The Reformers offered a justification of the authority of the Godly
Prince and of a Church in which the King was the Supreme Head.
The 'grudge against the clergy', made fashionable amongst
humanist intellectuals by Erasmus, was reinforced by the social
conscience of the protestant preachers. There was a place for the
educated layman in the protestant priesthood of all true believers.
The drift from Catholicism to Protestantism was simple for the
men of the New Learning. At Cambridge Cecil was carried along
by that drift and confirmed in favour of Protestantism.[10] The new
doctrines seemed more relevant than those of traditional Catholicism, both to his studies and to the political and ecclesiastical world
which Cecil found in the making.

Cecil came to Cambridge at that crucial time in the third decade
of the century when the humanist cultural revolution and the
religious reformation were being fused in England. His youth
coincided with the establishment of the norms in education and
religion which guided his world. He was fortunate in that his
experience and study at Cambridge enabled him to absorb the
formative ideas of the future.

At Cambridge William Cecil was exploring his mental capabilities but he was also discovering his emotional depths. In April
1565 a former fellow of Queens' College, Sir Thomas Smith, wrote
to Cecil of the regard in which Cecil was held by Catherine de
Medici. 'She liketh marvellous well', he continued, 'that you had a
son in your xiiiith or xvth year, for she hopeth therefore that her
son the King shall have a son as well as you in his xvith year and
thinketh you may serve for an example to the Queen's Majesty not

to contemn the young years of the King.'[11] The matter-of-fact way in which Smith wrote to Cecil makes it clear that he was referring to what he held to be a mutually well-remembered fact.

Yet the imputation of fathering a bastard was one which even the tactless Smith was most unlikely to make to a friend who had been recently grieved over his son's partiality to wenching. It was a subject calculated to embarrass Cecil at this time. Smith's reference to Cecil's precocious paternity came some thirty years after the alleged event. Smith may in all innocence or in the pursuit of diplomatic ends have antedated by some few years Cecil's first early marriage. He may have been utilising some undergraduate fiction or slander to persuade Catherine de Medici. Whatever the explanation of Smith's revelation, it seems odd that he should have so casually informed Cecil of it. What is more strange is that courtiers who would have taken it lightly did not record it as gossip, and enemies who would have taken it seriously did not use it to denigrate Cecil. If Smith was stating fact, he was guilty of broadcasting one of Cecil's best-kept secrets.

Young William seems to have escaped the consequences of his alleged paternity with unusual ease. No accusing mother or illegitimate son appeared to plague him in later life. If they were real, they conveniently disappeared, as well they might in such an age of mortality. Neither his family nor his college seem to have been perturbed. He retained the regard of his moralist friends and teachers. Yet those who accept Sir Thomas Smith's exposure of a secret are provided with a psychological clue to Cecil's character capable of considerable elaboration. But there remain other plausible explanations of Cecil's eminently respectable and controlled behaviour in later life.

However acceptable the evidence of the boy's frolic may be, it remains scant in comparison with the story of the young man's romance. When William Cecil fell in love, it was with the identifiable Mary Cheke. This young woman was the daughter of a former bedell of the University of Cambridge. She helped her widowed mother to run an ale-house in the town. Cecil's affection for Mary was certainly not stirred by any hope of riches. Her dowry was to be £40.[12] The best that could be said for her socially was that she was the sister of no less a figure in the university than the Professor of Greek, John Cheke. It was, perhaps, a recommendation which weighed heavily with the undergraduate lover, who had a great respect for his teacher. John Cheke was to be attached to the Court and given a knighthood, but neither this place of vantage nor this honour were his when Cecil formed his attachment to Mary.

From the point of view of the Cecil family a marriage to Mary Cheke was, on the face of it, the worst alliance that it had been called upon to accept for three generations. It did not help to consolidate the material foundations of the family. It opened no obvious avenue to influence outside St John's College. There is evidence that William's father disapproved.[13] It seems most likely that such a prudent father would not wish to see his only son jeopardise his fortune and his future by an indiscreet marriage to a girl who, however worthy, could not be regarded as a dynastic asset.

It may be that William's courtship of Mary Cheke explained his departure from Cambridge in May 1541. Perhaps Richard Cecil was hoping to cut short his son's romance. But William had already been at Cambridge for six years and was twenty years of age. Unless he was attempting to make an academic career for himself it was time for him to move. He was content to leave without a degree.[14] Such a disregard for academic formalities is not necessarily evidence that his studies were cut short. Young gentlemen were satisfied to have been at a college. The reputations which they made for themselves as students were well enough known in the small circle of men who had been educated at Cambridge.

Some three months after Cecil had left St John's for London he married Mary Cheke. The wedding day was 8 August 1541, when the bridegroom was not quite twenty-one.[15] It looks as if young William loved his bride. If the courtship of Mary had been designed to better his chances in the university by an alliance with John Cheke's sister, then William's removal from Cambridge would have meant its end. If his father's disapproval took the form of taking him from Cambridge and altering a will to his disadvantage, William had disregarded such signs of parental displeasure. The marriage was a love-match to William, but, no doubt, an indiscretion to his elders. The episode of William's first marriage might seem to indicate a lack of worldly wisdom in the young man. But the emotional strength which William showed over his love affair augured well. His youthful awareness of the deeper compulsions of human nature had not been dulled by discretion. He always retained that appreciation of human feeling which is essential for the politician who seeks to be a statesman. His first marriage is a reminder that later in life Cecil did not lack passion but that he controlled it.

Nine months after their marriage in May 1542 a son, Thomas, was born to William and Mary.[16] It is, perhaps, significant of the difficulties under which the young couple were living that the child was born in Cambridge. But whatever the trials and pleasures of the parents were, they were brought to a tragic end by Mary's death in February 1543.[17] It was not an unusual fate in the sixteenth century for a newly married husband to lose his wife, but that can have been small consolation to William Cecil. Mary died some months before she would have become socially acceptable as the sister of the tutor of Prince Edward. John Cheke was appointed to that post in 1544.

Meanwhile, upon his removal in 1541 from Cambridge to London, William Cecil had been at Gray's Inn.[18] The Inns of Court were becoming a finishing school for the sons of gentlemen who had no intention of becoming lawyers by profession. The Tudor peace had discouraged the rough justice of the riot and affray in the countryside and had led men to seek more frequently the arbitration of the courts. A successful man had to know how to defend himself and pursue his enemies in the courts of common law. Legal learning was likewise indispensable for anyone who wished to take part in government. Administration was largely carried out in judicial form. The organs of Tudor government were courts: from the High Court of Parliament to the petty sessions of the Justices of the Peace.

Residence at the Inns of Court gave young men a taste of life in London and enabled them to see and mingle with the great. William Cecil made use of his opportunities. Like Justice Shallow

he recalled later in life the mad days of his time as a student of the
law. One of the stories which he told was of how he regained his
losses at gambling. A hearer of the tale recorded it.[19] It ran:

that a mad companion of his, while he was thus at Gray's Inn
enticed him to play. Whereupon in a short time he lost all his
money, bedding and books to his companion; having never used
to play before.

And being afterwards among his other company, he told them
how such a one had misled him; saying he would presently have a
device to be even with him.

And he was as good as his word. For with a long trunk he made
a hole in the wall, near his playfellow's beds-head and in a fearful
voice spake thus, through the trunk: 'O mortal man, repent!
repent of thy horrible time consumed in play, cozenage and such
lewdness as thou hast committed or else thou art damned, and can
not be saved!'

Which being spoken at midnight, when he was all alone, so
amazed him as drove him into a sweat for fear.

Most penitent and heavy, the next day, in presence of the youths
he told with trembling, what a fearful voice spoke to him at
midnight, vowing never to play again. And, calling for Mr. Cecil,
asked him forgiveness on his knees, and restored all his money,
bedding and books. So two gamesters were both reclaimed with
this merry device, and never played more.

It was perhaps natural that the old and respected William Cecil
should represent himself as the innocent youth who had strayed
only once to the gambling table and that he should have moralised
the tale by claiming the reformation of his erring companion. The
way in which the old man told his story showed that he had lost
none of the skill of the young man who concocted the device to
recoup himself. The same psychological approach, the same
manipulation of morality is there in the event and its recounting.
Whether William was so innocent a gambler as he later suggested
is doubtful. He needed a quick loan of £50 on one occasion.[20]
With the shield of university discipline withdrawn it seems as if
Cecil was for a while susceptible to the temptations of London life.

The same intimate of Cecil who recorded the merry tale also
tells of how the young law student visited the Court in 1542 and

argued, much to their discomfiture, with two priests in the train of the visiting Irish magnate O'Neill. The argument came to the attention of the King, who called for the young champion of his cause and talked with him. Later Henry VIII called for his Groom of the Wardrobe, Richard Cecil, and instructed him to find some reward for his son. If Richard had not planned the whole incident, he gauged the reward for his son with finesse. William was granted the reversion of the office of *custos brevium* in the Court of Common Pleas.[21] It was the promise of a considerable income for the future. The combination of the father's knowledge of the plums of royal favour and the son's confidence in argument had secured a good start for William.

William profited by his father's position in the Royal Household. He was also to profit from the influence of his family in finding him a seat in the Commons during 1543.[22] At twenty-three a man of William's standing had to content himself with a borough seat. It is most likely that he sat for Stamford, which had been represented by his grandfather. It was good experience to see the Commons at work. It was in this Parliament that Henry declared, 'We be informed by our judges that we at no time stand so highly in our royal estate as in time of parliament. . . .'[23] William could not fail as a law student to see how important Parliament had become. His first experience in Parliament was a valuable introduction to the great themes of Tudor politics, religion and the succession.

Amidst these beginnings of public life William remade his private life. On 21 December 1545 he was married again.[24] If it was a marriage in which there was, at the start, more of family convenience than of affection, it was to grow into a working partnership which was cherished by both husband and wife. The nineteen-year-old bride was Mildred Cooke, the eldest daughter of Sir Anthony Cooke, who, being Governor of Prince Edward, was in the circle of academics at Court to which John Cheke, the brother of Cecil's first wife, belonged.[25] Mildred and her three sisters had been given the education of the learned lady of the Renaissance. It was the same classical education which was being given to the Princess Elizabeth.

William's second marriage was to help shape his life in many

c

ways. The Protestantism which his new wife had imbibed with
her New Learning was transmuted by her character and upbringing
into puritanism. Her influence was to develop the ascetic puritan
streak in Cecil's make-up. From the time of his second marriage,
whatever there was in Cecil of the headstrong romantic and the
careless gambler was to be suppressed. She fortified all that was
methodical, cautious and sensible in her husband. Cecil's duties
seldom parted him from his wife. What her moral support was to
mean to him Cecil showed, when she died after forty-three years
of married life.

His intellectual sisters-in-law, with their Court connections,
were to prove of greater value to William Cecil in making useful
marriage alliances than his own sisters, who were to wed comparatively obscure gentlemen. While the three Cecil girls in their
various marriages took the names of White, Cave, Smith, Wingfield
and Allington, the Cooke sisters allied with the Bacons, the Hobys,
the Killigrews and the Russells, families of consequence in public
affairs. Through his wife's sisters, Cecil was able to confirm and
develop connections which were valuable in political and
protestant circles.

William's own marriage immediately drew him closer to the
protestant-minded group of men who had charge of the education
of the heir to the throne. The circle of academics among whom
Cecil could now count a brother-in-law and a father-in-law was
high in the favour of the Prince Edward and of his uncle Edward
Seymour, Earl of Hertford. Thomas Smith was making a reputation for himself with the King's councillors. At a less exalted level
William's own father was in the King's favour. Such contacts
prepared the way for entry into the royal service. William Cecil's
opportunity came when the death of Henry VIII in 1547 caused
the leading men in the government to build up their own
followings.

By the age of twenty-seven it might be said that William Cecil's
apprenticeship was over. He had had a rather longer university
education than most young gentlemen. His residence at Cambridge
was only one year short of the seven years required for taking an
M.A. degree. His academic attainment was considerably greater

than that of the average layman. He had spent some years in the study of the law. Although he had not achieved a professional mastery of legal learning, he was conversant with the modes of argument and the procedures of the common law. He had served as a Justice of the Peace in Lincolnshire and had sat in Parliament. From his post as *custos brevium* in the Court of Common Pleas he was to draw an income of £240 per annum. His father had given him lands upon his second marriage.[26] William was enjoying a modest affluence. His prospects lay in his own abilities and in the friends which he had at Court.

Cecil was fortunate that his chance to embark upon a career in public service came when he was ready for responsibility. He had just entered upon what was accounted, at the time, middle age: from twenty-five to thirty-nine years of age. It was the time of life when, it was said, ambition replaced love as a strong motive in a man's life. But it was to be in the attainment of his ambition that he learned to love his second wife. If he was to keep up with his former peers at Cambridge it was time that Cecil joined them at Court.

Cecil's education was such that he might expect to be employed in the bureaucracy of the central government. But Cecil lacked two important qualifications for high office. He had not travelled abroad and he had had no military experience or training. Neither his health nor his disposition encouraged him to be a man of action. His attributes were not those of a courtier or a soldier but those of a scholar and administrator.

CHAPTER III

The King's Path

W HEN Henry VIII died the man who took over effective control
of the government was Edward Seymour, Earl of Hertford, the
uncle of the boy King Edward VI. Seymour acquired the dukedom
of Somerset and the title of Protector.[1] Through his protestant
and Court connections William Cecil secured a place in the
Protector's entourage. He already knew something of local
government, of Parliament and the Court but this was his first
chance to take part in the great affairs of State. Under the wing of
the ducal cock of the walk, Cecil could scarcely have anticipated
the dangers which this new phase in his life was to bring.

The lord whose good graces Cecil enjoyed was a difficult but in
some ways an inspiring character. He attracted the 'Commonwealth men', who cherished notions of an organic society in
which every man played his part and who sought to enforce social
morality as a cure for economic ills. Among the humanists and
reformers there were idealistic expectations of the new reign. To
the common people Somerset was the 'Good Duke'. But to the
nobles, above whom he raised himself as Protector, he appeared
less high-minded. The Duke's brusque manner, which was effective
on the battlefield, made him enemies in the Council. Like many good
soldiers he appeared in politics to be at once ruthless and naïve.

Ironically enough, it was upon Somerset's expedition to Scotland
in the late summer of 1547 that the unwarlike Cecil found himself
soon after he had joined the Protector's following. Lacking
military training, Cecil could not be a combatant. But he found
employment with the army as one of the two judges of the
Marshal's Court, in which he gave the Duke's notoriously firm
discipline the semblance of martial law. At the victory of Pinkie
on 10 September, Somerset's secretary won a reputation for
bravery and his steward won his spurs. All that could be related of

Cecil was a story of a narrow escape. It was said that 'one putting forth his arm, to thrust Mr. Cecil out of the level of the cannon, had his arm striken off'.[2] But if Cecil lost no limbs neither did he lose his head under fire. William Patten, using Cecil's notes on the campaign for his own account of the expedition, found them to be full and accurate.[3]

Having freedom 'to ride to see things that were done',[4] Cecil was well able to observe the conduct of the campaign and learn the problems of military administration and supply. This brief first-hand experience served as the practical basis for his future mastery of the logistics of warfare. The campaign also impressed upon Cecil the importance of relations with Scotland for the peace and security of England. When the victory at Pinkie proved futile the need for diplomacy as well as force was all the more apparent to him. His personal involvement in the expedition gave the young man his lifelong sense of the hazards and limitations of war as an instrument of policy.

While there were all these lessons to be pondered by Cecil, he had as yet no active part in the conduct or formation of high policy. Similarly in the Protector's moves to further ecclesiastical reformation, Cecil was a sympathetic follower rather than a protagonist. With a brother-in-law and a father-in-law teaching the King to be a Protestant, Cecil was attached to reforming circles at Court. Soon after his return from Scotland he contributed an introduction to *The Lamentations of a Sinner*, a pamphlet written by the Dowager Queen, Catherine Parr.[5] Like its author, the 'excellent queen', Cecil stressed the personal, not the social, consequences of repentance. He took it for what it was, an appeal 'to all ladies of high estate' to adopt quietly the biblical truths of Protestantism. His handling of Catherine Parr's exposition of faith revealed the problem of the Reformation for those in authority. It was how to encourage a religious change without stirring up social revolution.

Whenever Cecil's influence in religious matters came to light in Somerset's period of power, it was that of a man seeking to win the influential and to control the radical converts. With the Protector, Cranmer, Ridley and Sir Thomas Smith, he played a part in trying to induce Stephen Gardiner to accept new doctrines. But the Bishop of Winchester, who had vindicated the Royal Supremacy, defended traditional theology. His recalcitrance was to land him in prison late in 1547 and to lead to his deposition in 1551. A good lawyer, he was not to be outwitted like the two priests whom the young Cecil had routed at the Court of Henry VIII.

In January 1548 Cecil failed to entice Gardiner to accept articles which he had prepared. During May and June, Cecil made four attempts to induce Gardiner to accept his notes for a sermon. But the sermon, when delivered, ignored Cecil's directions. In his dealings with Gardiner, Cecil alternated the friendly approach of the 'private advice' of the Protector with browbeating of which Gardiner complained. The Bishop accused Cecil of ignorance about transubstantiation and at his trial in 1551 declared that Cecil's evidence was inaccurate. He was a match for Cecil. But for the moment it was Cecil who was on the winning side. He did not like the Bishop, who had attacked his teacher Cheke over the pronunciation of Greek.[6]

In June 1549 Cecil signed the council letter which prohibited Bonner, the Bishop of London, from performing private masses at St Paul's.[7] While he was ranged against the conservatives, Cecil did not support the extremists. When John Hooper,[8] a friend of his father, was made Bishop of Gloucester and rejected ecclesiastical vestments, Cecil put what weight he had against this puritan gesture. More anarchical than John Hooper were the Anabaptists who undermined both Church and State, as understood in the sixteenth century. Cecil was given the opportunity to deal with them in the summer of 1549, when he was made a member of a commission to inquire into Anabaptist heresies.[9] At about the same time he was made responsible along with Petre and Smith for examining all books printed in England before they were released for sale.[10] Cecil was clearly a trusted moderate.

The need to check extremism was in part the consequence of the repeal of the treason and heresy laws by the Parliament which had met in October 1547. Cecil's role as member for Stamford is not recorded. No doubt, he approved the measures which freed

Protestants from the threat of burning for heresy and execution for treason. Most certainly, the bait contained in the Chantries Act, which put more ecclesiastical land on the market, was nibbled by the Cecils.[11] The Uniformity Act of 1549 with its mild enforcement of a broad-based Prayer Book recommended itself to moderates. Cranmer's desire to hasten slowly satisfied Cecil.

Meanwhile the metamorphosis of catholic chrysalises into protestant butterflies continued. For some the process was speedy, for others it was painful and slow. Cranmer was feeling his way round the problem of transubstantiation. Ascham told Cecil what the men of his old college were thinking when he reported in January 1549 a debate on the Mass.[12] John Hooper wanted to slough off vestments; Hugh Latimer to break images. Men burst through the husk of tradition at different places. The doctrinal markings of Protestantism were visible on Cecil but he showed no hurry to shatter the old ecclesiastical cocoon. He was cautious about the new world into which some of his reforming friends were struggling with imprudent haste.

Having seen as a boy something of the Lincolnshire rising in 1536,[13] Cecil had no desire to see religion mix with social discontent again. Yet in the Protector's household the 'Commonwealth men' were urging social justice. Economic ills and moral wrongs were fused in the minds of those who were calling for action. Along with the diagnosis of economic maladies by John Hales went the condemnation of triumphant wickedness by Latimer. Cecil was in the midst of all this ratiocination and heart searching, but his involvement is not clear. He may have been sympathetic, but he was too moderate to be an active and positive supporter. His old friend, Catherine Duchess of Suffolk, found him lukewarm in religion.[14] It is unlikely that those dedicated to the restoration of economic morality found him any warmer.

Cecil's chief connection with Somerset's policy of protecting tenants, chastening avaricious landlords and suppressing self-interest was his appointment in the autumn of 1547 as the Duke's personal Master of Requests. Cecil was not an official of the Court of Requests but he watched over the business of that Court for the Protector. It was an unusual post and Cecil boasted that he was the first in England ever to bear the title.[15] The Court of Requests, known as the 'court of poor men's causes', had been used by Wolsey for administrative justice. The Protector, with Cecil as his watchdog, was likewise seeking to pursue a policy of curbing powerful landlords through that Court. The later accusation that Somerset had actually set up the Court in his own household was a tribute to Cecil's close supervision of proceedings. Once again Cecil's legal learning had stood him in good stead. He had administered martial law on a campaign and in the Court of Requests he showed a familiarity with civil law.

Such versatility and efficiency won Cecil in September 1548 the position of personal secretary to Somerset.[16] Just as he had contrived to be with the army and yet not of it so now he was with the government and yet in no official post. From his vantage point he learned not only the routine of administration, but also, as an intimate servant of the Protector, the methods of backstairs intrigue. It was a valuable schooling for a bureaucrat. He was courted by both the friends and enemies of his master, whose business he knew so well. As he later declared of one instance, 'that he being attendant on the duke's grace of Somerset, then protector, hath seen and heard the said complaints brought and presented in writing, and by mouth, to the said duke'.[17] While he watched, he became aware of a mounting opposition to the Duke.

The threat to the Protector came from John Dudley, who after a distinguished military career had become Earl of Warwick. Cecil had seen him in action on the Scottish campaign and had corresponded with him. It behoved anyone connected with the government to be on the best possible terms with John Dudley, who had all the ruthlessness of his notorious father, Edmund Dudley. The Earl of Warwick appreciated the value of Cecil and he was not above flattering so useful a servant.[18] In August 1549 he wrote to Cecil as a 'faithful friend' asking him to use his 'accustomed wisdom and good heart' on behalf of Northampton. Next to the Protector, Warwick had become the most powerful man in the Council.

It was unfortunate for Cecil that Somerset's authority was crumbling. The Protector had failed in Scotland and had antagonised France. The French King thrust him into war over Boulogne, a liability acquired by Henry VIII. Somerset's efforts at Church reform had frightened the Catholics and disappointed the protestant extremists. Yet he might have survived the diplomatic and religious difficulties if he had not undermined the trust of the aristocracy by two moves which seemed to threaten their wealth and safety. The execution of the Protector's brother, Thomas Seymour, following an act of attainder, disturbed the nobility by the spectacle of a great man being destroyed so easily with the aid of the Commons. The people were shocked by fratricide. The second setback to the acceptance of the Protector's sway was his mishandling of the social problem of agrarian unrest.

Somerset accepted that misguided mixture of economics and morality which combined a belief that the enclosure of land was the cause of higher prices, unemployment and scarcity of food, with the conviction that the conflict between landlord and tenant for the rising economic rent of land was a wicked outburst of avarice. He adopted the old and ineffective policy, put forward by John Hales, of setting up a commission to inquire into the extent of enclosures since 1485. 'Maugre the devil', he declared, 'private profit, self-love, money, and such like the devil's instruments, it shall go forward.'[19] The aristocracy obstructed the inquiries. This might have been the end of the matter had not widespread agrarian rioting swept across southern England in the summer of 1549.

If Somerset was to clear himself from the charge of having encouraged rural revolt, his only course was to quell rebellion by force. While Cheke and Cranmer denounced sedition, and Russell and Warwick crushed the rebels in the field, the Protector remained paralysed by the clash of his ideals with the reality of violence. Warwick's resolute action against the Norfolk rebels on the bloody field of Dussindale on 27 August 1549 won him the support of those disillusioned by the apparent failure of the Protector's nerve. By October, having played upon the catholic resentment of Somerset's Protestantism, Warwick was in a position to exert pressure. He was in conference with eleven malcontent councillors.

When Somerset became aware of the conspiracy against him, he

withdrew to Windsor, taking with him the King, the two
Secretaries, Sir Thomas Smith and William Petre, and two
councillors, Thomas Cranmer, the Archbishop, and William Paget,
his most loyal supporter. His panic appeals for support were
ignored by the military commanders, Lord Russell and Sir William
Herbert, the sheriffs, the justices of the peace and the Corporation
of London. Petre, sent to challenge the Warwick faction, chose to
join it. The situation was hopeless. Somerset was persuaded to
capitulate to the opposition on 8 October 1549. Two days later at
Windsor the Council with Cranmer and Paget in their places
agreed to commit Somerset to the Tower.

The only government official to suffer was Sir Thomas Smith.
He was deprived of his Secretaryship and imprisoned, not because
he had remained loyal to Somerset, but because his intolerable
manner had made him very unpopular. No one had sacrificed
himself for the Protector's sake. But the prominent members of
Somerset's household fell with their master. Thomas Fisher, a
former personal secretary of the Protector, Sir John Thynne,
Somerset's steward, Sir Michael Stanhope, the Duke's ablest
military supporter and a few lesser followers were imprisoned.
The only outstanding personal servant of the Duke to escape
immediate imprisonment was his secretary, William Cecil.[20]

In the negotiations between Somerset and the Warwick faction
Cecil had played no part because he was not a councillor or an
official of the government. Cranmer, Paget and Petre, who were
councillors and had been with Somerset, all retained their places.
But it was surprising that Cecil, who was not a royal official, but a
member of the Duke's household should have escaped being sent
to the Tower. His well-placed friends must have made some special
plea on his behalf. Perhaps Warwick already regarded him as a
likely candidate for royal office. It is difficult to guess how
Cecil dissociated himself or was dissociated from 'the principal
instruments . . . that the Duke did use in the affairs of his ill
government'.[21]

Cecil's respite was short. He was put in the custody of the Lord
Chancellor and by November he was in the Tower.[22] But the
councillors were not bent on destroying Somerset or his followers.

Cecil had influential friends in Petre, Cheke, Cooke, and the Duchess of Suffolk. On 25 January 1550 he was released with some of the lesser fry. He was bound by a recognisance for £1,000 to hold himself ready for questioning by the Council.[23] Of those of importance Cecil had been the last into the Tower and the first out.

It seemed that after little more than two years of experience in public affairs Cecil's career had been shattered. Yet Cecil himself showed no readiness to abandon the stimulus and interest of politics. He had tasted the spoils of office. Court life offered him broader intellectual horizons. Fortunately the Protector's fall had not been decisive. Recovery was possible. The lesson for Cecil was that, while good lordship was a necessity, it was not the only requirement for survival. The way in which Cranmer, Petre and Paget had clung to the upper ledges when Somerset fell, revealed that high royal office was the strongest hold to have upon the rock face of power.

In the spring of 1550 Cecil's prospects brightened. Somerset was released in February and back in the Council in April. Warwick had been unable to exploit his success in tumbling the Protector. The Council had been shy of pressing dangerous treason charges which set a precedent. The necessity was to reconcile Somerset and Warwick. It was Cecil's chance to play the political middleman, the honest broker. The role suited his talents and temperament. He tried to use the Duchess of Suffolk to dispel the hard feelings between the two great nobles.[24] Gradually relations between them improved. In May they were visiting each other and in June they entered into a dynastic alliance. Somerset's daughter Anne married Warwick's son Ambrose.

During this period of balance Cecil edged his way along the beam of faction to a place nearer the more stable fulcrum. By taking up a middle position Cecil won golden opinions. Ascham wrote of him, 'A young man it is true, but possessed of such prudence beyond his years, such learning and such moderation that the voice of all ascribes to him the possession of all those four excellencies which Thucydides says were blended in the Athenian Pericles. . . .'[25] More important than Ascham's flattery was the good opinion of Somerset and the calculating regard of Warwick.

In September Cecil reached his goal. He was sworn to the Council
and appointed alongside Petre as one of the two Secretaries of the
King.[26] Cecil began his career in royal office in the month in which
he celebrated his twenty-ninth birthday.

Cecil's new confidence in his position showed itself in negotiations for a house in Cannon Row, close to Parliament and the Law
Courts in Westminster. He put down £400 cash to secure an abode
convenient for a busy Secretary.[27] At the same time, he made plans
to settle his family close to the governmental capital. He leased the
old rectory at Wimbledon, an unpretentious manor house.[28] His
investment in property near London indicated that Cecil had
found the life that he wanted and that he anticipated some
permanency of employment. The Secretaryship added another
£100 a year to his income and gave him the opportunity to add
much more. There were more solid rewards to the office than the
wine which Sir George Somerset began to send him from Calais.
The forthright Duchess of Suffolk thought he was in a good
market.[29]

In his position as Secretary, Cecil was the servant of the King
and his Council, and not of one vulnerable patron. He had reached
the comparative safety of the royal bureaucracy, where loyalty and
efficiency preserved a man from the dangers of faction strife. In
the circumstances Cecil was very willing to play second fiddle to
the older and more experienced Petre. The seniority of the older
man was recognised formally by the precedence given to his name
in correspondence addressed to the Secretaries and effectively by
the tasks given to him. Cecil was left with the routine work.

Following his appointment Cecil toiled assiduously at the
business of government. His attendance at Council was regular
but his share in its deliberations is obscure. It fell to him to see
that some of its decisions were translated into administrative
action. Besides such work there was a large correspondence calling
for varied answers and action. Cecil's friends both in and out of
government sought his aid. The boroughs of Boston and Stamford
looked to his protection. He became Recorder of Boston. Thomas
Parry wrote to him about the affairs of his mistress, the Princess
Elizabeth, for whose lands Cecil became surveyor in 1550.[30] Cecil,

it seemed, was accessible to every worried dignitary and friend, every busybody and conscientious citizen. Much of his time was occupied in settling the individual cases of suitors.

In foreign affairs, a sphere of the prerogative which was normally a concern of the Secretaries, Petre took the lead and Cecil does not seem to have been noticed by the foreign ambassadors. Yet Cecil was not uninterested in foreign policy. A surviving part of a memorandum reveals that he saw the European situation as a struggle between Catholic and Protestant.[31] For him Charles V, kinsman of the Princess Mary, was the arch-enemy. He was pessimistic about the fate of English Protestants should the country become involved in war. Apart from the official papers on foreign relations Cecil's correspondence with diplomats was a source of information for him. He exchanged letters with a particularly able and well-educated group of Englishmen abroad.[32] Sir John Mason, a former fellow of All Souls and a protégé of Sir Thomas More, whose policy was to be friendly with 'the exactest lawyer and ablest favourite', wrote to Cecil from Paris, where he was ambassador to the French King, as did his successor, Sir William Pickering, a pupil of Cheke. From Germany Sir Richard Morison, one of Thomas Cromwell's propagandists from Cardinal Pole's group in Padua, sent the witty epistles which had earned him the nickname 'merry Morison'. Later John Hales and Roger Ascham went abroad and remained in touch with Cecil.

While Cecil was becoming well known among the educated laity of the ruling class, he was also on intimate terms with many of the leading reformers in the clergy.[33] John Hooper wrote to him from Gloucester. Ridley of London replied to Cecil's request for a gift of timber with the suggestion that Cecil might try begging for the Church as successfully as he begged for himself. Cecil was becoming something of a patron of ecclesiastics. William Turner, the puritan naturalist, had to soothe Cecil, who had taken offence at his efforts to obtain preferment from Somerset through other parties. But, if Cecil wanted a monopoly of clerical patronage and a share of episcopal wealth, he also shared Hooper's joy in the 'success and going forthward of God's Word'. Cecil helped Cranmer in his scheme to settle foreign reformers in England and was in correspondence with men like Peter Martyr, Bucer, Fagius and à'Lasco.

It was Hooper among the Bishops who lamented to Cecil about 'the price of things'. Amongst his diplomatic friends, Sir John Mason wrote to him of the serious price rise in England. From the City, William Lane, a merchant, called Cecil's attention to the coinage.[34] Since Warwick's first attack on Somerset, the campaign against enclosure, as the prime cause of economic ills, had been dropped and consideration was being given to currency manipulation. It was at this time that Cecil's interest in monetary problems, which contributed years later to the recoinage under Elizabeth, was aroused. The lessons which he learned from the attempts in 1551 to profit both from debasement and then from the establishment of a sound currency were not forgotten.

In the protective shadow of William Petre, Cecil's understanding of the problems of statesmanship was maturing. Foreign affairs, the reformation of the Church and the reform of the coinage were taxing his mind. As yet there was little opportunity for the new and junior Secretary to play an important role but he was already showing the makings of something more than a bureaucrat. But it was not easy for Cecil to scan the wider horizons of policy, when the political ground under his feet was beginning to quake with yet another shift in the strata of faction.

Beneath the surface of harmony between Somerset and Warwick intrigue was rumbling. Cecil was tempted to sound Warwick by complaining of Somerset's leniency towards his old antagonist Gardiner. Through a former servant of the Protector, Warwick let Cecil know indirectly in June 1551 that the Council was disturbed by Somerset's tolerant attitude to Gardiner and by his favouritism towards the catholic Arundel. In the accusation that Somerset was aspiring 'to have the self and same overdue an authority to the despatch and direction of the proceedings as his Grace had being Protector', there was an ominous revival of the charge made against Somerset in October 1549. What sincerity there was in Warwick's plea to Cecil to warn the Duke to reform his ways Cecil had to judge. The loyal Paget advised Somerset to watch his step. The rift in the Council was opening. Warwick's praise of Cecil as 'a faithful servant and by that, most witty councillor unto the King's Majesty and his proceedings' was reassuring.[35] Cecil could count on a line from Warwick and a grip upon royal office to steady him, if Somerset was caught in another avalanche.

By autumn Warwick's insinuations against Somerset had worked upon the Council and the King. Somerset's illness in September gave Warwick his chance. On 7 October Sir Thomas Palmer came to Warwick with a story of how Somerset and the Arundels had planned to raise the country and assassinate Warwick and Northampton. As Palmer disclosed more details, the smoke thickened and men began to see the fire of conspiracy.[36] The evidence was calculated to make the nobility distrust Somerset, to rouse the Protestants against the catholic Arundels and to alarm the City of London by alleging that the Duke had schemed to cause a rising among the apprentices in the capital. During these manœuvres against Somerset, Petre had been ill and Cecil bore the full burden of work until Petre returned on 28 October. In the thick of the faction strife, Cecil knew all the details of the struggle and was well aware of how things were going.

On 11 October at Hampton Court, Warwick was invested with the dukedom of Northumberland. Dorset became Duke of Suffolk; Wiltshire, Marquess of Winchester; Sir William Herbert, Earl of Pembroke. Among the four men knighted was William Cecil.[37] Northumberland was buying support. It was not hard to obtain. At Somerset's first fall no one had felt ready to make any sacrifice to support him. Now, two years later, Somerset had failed to inspire any greater loyalty.

That 'Cecil carried himself even to both'[38] was recognised by Somerset and Warwick. Just as Warwick had used Cecil as a go-between in the previous June to warn the Duke, so on 14 October, Somerset, suspecting conspiracy against himself, sent for Cecil. The posture of official impartiality which Cecil had taken up made him the agent of both sides in the struggle for power. Yet there was the ominous detachment of Pilate in his reply to Somerset's questions about the accusations against him. He told the Duke that 'if he were not guilty, he might be of good courage;

if he were, he had nothing to say but to lament him.'[39] Two days after Cecil's interview with the Duke, Somerset and those who were named as his fellow conspirators were sent to the Tower.

It was Cecil's task to justify the accusations against Somerset to the Spanish ambassador, but it was also his problem to justify to himself the role which he had played in his former good lord's downfall. His friends agreed that Cecil could not be expected to share in the results of the Duke's political ineptitude. Sir William Pickering congratulated him on being 'found undefiled with the folly of this unfortunate Duke'. Pickering's answer on 27 October to Cecil's explanation of his part in the affair reflected the line of Cecil's self-defence.[40] Pickering wrote, 'The King's path, which you have taken to travel in, is the right line that leadeth to that life that is most laudable; and although sometimes a terrible tempest do trouble the traveller in that trade, yet the incomparable comfort of an uncorrupt conscience cannot be so stirred with no storm to scare out of that way, but holdeth fast by the firm faith that he hath found in God, to be relieved at length for his truth's sake.'

Cecil had evidently found his trade as servant to the King. It was the current political morality of humanist and reformer. In solving the problem of who might interpret the boy King's will Cecil had wrestled with his conscience and had decided that Northumberland was the guide to the King's path. In November material comfort came to the new knight in a grant of lands from the King.[41] Whether the grant, like the knighthood, was Northumberland's reward for his desertion of Somerset or a recompense for loyal service to the King was left for Cecil to decide. If some were cynical about his motives, others were well satisfied that he had acted rightly. Sir Henry Sidney, who was knighted at the same time as Cecil, found his fellow knight 'a most rare man both for sundry singular gifts of nature, learning, wisdom and integrity'.[42]

CHAPTER IV

The Problem of Obedience

WHILE Somerset lay in the Tower, Northumberland rapidly asserted his leadership in the government. Using the royal authority as his stalking-horse, he captured power. With the majority of his fellows Cecil was committed to Northumberland. The destruction of the balance of faction, with the fall of Somerset, had also destroyed the middle way. Cecil's only hold upon office lay in his readiness to serve Northumberland. Knowing his own part in making Northumberland master, he could not escape the consequences. If Somerset had proved impossible to follow, Northumberland was to prove difficult to serve. After Somerset was condemned by his peers in December and finally executed in January 1552, there was no choice but to accept the dominance of Northumberland.

In the political world of the new régime Cecil could find little comfort. A sharp rise in prices caused social and economic havoc. Public morality and administrative efficiency were deteriorating. Petre once lamented to Cecil that 'we leave fishing for the souls of men and fish again in the tempestuous seas of this world for gain and wicked Mammon'.[1] Cecil did not rise above his colleagues in office. The scope for his initiative in administrative reform was small. It was Petre who tried to reorganise the Council to stimulate the administration. Cecil remained absorbed in routine work and ready to accept government as he found it. Yet in the problem of religious reform Cecil was showing concern. In the establishment of a Godly Reformation and in the coming of age of the young Josiah, Edward VI, lay hope for the future.

The reformers were able to take advantage of Northumberland's inclination to radical religious change. While he was still taming his conscience over his part in Somerset's fall, Cecil was appointed to a commission charged with the overwhelming task of bringing

D

the canon law into harmony with the common law.[2] Cecil's part in
its inconclusive proceedings is not known, but the fact that he was
nominated along with Sir Thomas Smith and Doctor May as one
of the civilians on the commission reveals that his competence in
civil law was accepted. The legal approach to reform was to be
expected from William Cecil, but he also became involved in
theological discussion.

During November and December at meetings held in Cecil's
house in Cannon Row and at Richard Morison's home, the
significance of the Lord's Supper was discussed.[3] Assuming the
role of chairman, Cecil began the first disputation with a plea for
freedom of speech without ill consequences for any speaker. His
object was to guard his friends Cheke and Grindal. These debates
were far from being a dilettante recreation. Luther had shown that
a change of theology lay at the root of radical reform. To search
out the implication of doctrine was a necessary step towards
establishing a truly Protestant Church in England. Cecil and his
friends were sounding opinion and testing the foundations of their
own beliefs. Less pleasant for Cecil were the practical results of
these theological explorations, which meant dealing with the
conservative Catholics. He was involved in the trial of Gardiner
and the bullying of the Princess Mary, who persisted in celebrating
the Mass.[4]

In the spring of 1552 Cecil was busy with constant attendance at
Council and in Parliament. On 23 January, the day after Somerset's
execution, Parliament began. Cecil sat for Stamford. It was the
first Parliament in which he had sat as a royal official. As a
Secretary he had a certain prominence among the borough
members. He carried Bills to the Lords. A Bill on enclosures was
referred to him after its third reading. Such are the scraps of
evidence about Cecil's activities as he began to deal with Parliament
from the position of a councillor.[5]

When summer came, the routine of court life was broken by
Northumberland's departure for the Border and by a royal
progress. On 19 June Cecil hurried to Stamford to greet
Northumberland, who had promised to take a cup of wine with
Richard Cecil at the door of his house. The Duke's formal gesture

to Cecil's father was a mark of favour which Sir William was anxious to acknowledge by his own presence. After the Duke's visit Cecil spent some time calling upon friends in the neighbourhood of his father's house. He went to Boston, of which he was Recorder. On 20 July he rejoined the travelling Court and took over from Petre.[6]

While Northumberland and Petre were absent Cecil became better known to the King. But he did not enjoy the intimacy with the young Edward that his friends Cheke and Barnaby Fitzpatrick shared. As a Secretary he had drafted letters and written some memoranda. In September 1551 he had written on foreign affairs. A year later he was writing on the imperial alliance and the prospects of establishing markets in England to rival Antwerp. As Edward's interest in matters of State grew it was inevitable that he should look to Cecil for information and advice. At this time Cecil's reputation as a councillor seemed to lie in foreign and economic affairs.[7] The progress was not the round of pleasures for Cecil which his friends pictured. Cecil was not well. Hooper warned him, 'Your health is not the surest, favour it as ye may.' Cecil dreamed of getting away 'to the Baths' to ease his gouty legs.[8]

The wearying conditions of the progress were not the only tax upon Cecil's health: he was disquieted about the extremism of Northumberland's religious policy. The gradualism of Archbishop Cranmer suited Cecil but irritated the Duke. Cecil warned Cranmer that there were insinuations about the accumulation of archiepiscopal wealth. Cranmer responded to the financial goad which Northumberland applied and in September produced the Forty-two Articles. Cecil and Cheke were asked for their opinion upon the Articles. Cecil, it seems, was satisfied. But the Duke threatened to appoint the fiery John Knox as Bishop of Rochester in order to provide 'a whetstone to quicken and sharp the Bishop of Canterbury'.[9]

It was clear that Cecil followed the middle way in religion. Moderation was not merely a matter of practical expediency for Cecil, but an approach which had positive virtues. It reached back to the Erasmian tradition, cultivated by Thomas Cromwell, and to the teachings of the Cambridge humanists. Cecil was thus prepared to support Cranmer, despite the Duke's impatience. It was significant that Cecil's first doubts about Somerset's behaviour in the previous year had been over the former Protector's policy towards Catholics. Now he found Northumberland's religious policy ill-advised. The last act on the progress which Cecil performed was concerned with a minor manifestation of the great religious problem. He mediated in a quarrel between the Provost and Fellows of Eton and secured the deletion of superstitious statutes from the school rules.[10] There could be no escape from the surge of the Reformation.

Before the Christmas celebrations were over the Secretary was involved in planning the date and agenda for the next Parliament. He arranged for his nominees to sit for Stamford and Grantham but he did not put himself up for election.[11] There seems to be no political or religious calculation in Cecil's abstention from the Parliament which passed the Bill of Uniformity, imposing the second Prayer Book. As a friend of Cranmer and a councillor Cecil knew of the more forthright protestant doctrine of the new Prayer Book and of the wider penalties for non-attendance set out in the second Act of Uniformity. The demands of the Secretaryship upon his health and time, rather than any considerations of policy, seem to be the reason for Cecil's absence from the Commons in the spring of 1553.

The Uniformity Act was a triumph for Cranmer and the moderates like Cecil. Northumberland accepted it, although John Knox contrived to insert in the Prayer Book the Black Rubric which prohibited superstitious kneeling. Cecil's support of Cranmer did not bring him into disfavour, for in April he was made Chancellor of the Order of the Garter. The compliment paid to his 'gentle blood' was, no doubt, a greater consolation to Cecil than the annual fee of 100 marks. He fussed about altering the liveries of his retainers to show his new honour and about his own robes. In May Petre, replying on behalf of the Duke to Cecil's inquiries about arrangements for the next session of the Order, expressed doubts about the date of the meeting.[12] The reason which he gave for his doubt was the state of the King's health.

It was ominous information. Cecil was absent from Court from the last week in April. It was his first respite from state business for many months and he was attending to his own affairs. His father, Richard Cecil, had died in March. There were family matters to expedite. But his withdrawal from the Court revealed how exhausted Cecil was. He fell sick. He was too ill to respond either to Petre's revelation that his own 'affection homeward' was growing or to the devious letter from Northumberland, which praised Petre's devotion to duty and added 'Others we have whose sort you are well acquainted withal that neither earnest zeal or consideration of time can scarcely awake them out of their wonted dreams and smoothly winketh all care from their hearts.' Whether the Duke was identifying Cecil with the hard-working servants of the crown or hinting that he was malingering was for the invalid to decide. But subtle ambiguities could not cure Cecil any more than the herbal pork broth prescribed by Lord Audley.[13]

Northumberland wanted Cecil back at Court in what he called 'these most careful days'. The immediate worry over the King's health eased, however, as Edward appeared to recover. But Cecil was still not fit for service. He remained away convalescing. The genuineness of Cecil's illness was recognised by the acceptance of the fact that he could not return to his duties and by the appointment of his friend and relative Sir John Cheke to take his place as Secretary.

When at last on 11 June Cecil returned to Court, Cheke stayed to share the burdens of the Secretaryship with Petre and Cecil. But, if the extra help lightened Cecil's load of work, it could not lessen the increasing political tension. It had become evident that the King was doomed to die. By the will of Henry VIII and the current Succession Act, Mary Tudor was successor to the throne. His respect for legality and his loyalty to the house of Tudor disposed Cecil to accept the prospect of a catholic Queen. A disputed succession carried with it the threat of civil war. But the restoration of papal authority, the re-establishment of Roman doctrine and the dominance of Hapsburg interests which might result from Mary's accession were not encouraging. The dilemma involved not only Cecil's personal fate and that of his monastic

property, but also the future of the Church of England and of the
political independence of the realm.

If a legally plausible plan could be devised which would deny
Mary the throne and establish in her stead a protestant candidate
without endangering the domestic peace, it might prove a temp-
tation to Protestants to support it. Such a scheme was Northumberland's preoccupation. The Duke had everything to win or lose.
His problem was to carry with him the Council and the country. On
21 May he married his son, Lord Guildford Dudley, to Lady Jane
Grey, the King's cousin and the representative of the Suffolk claim
to the throne which was recognised in the Succession Act. Lady
Jane would be the perfect instrument to perpetuate the power of
her father-in-law, if she could be brought to the throne by
excluding the claims of Mary and Elizabeth.

By the time Cecil returned to the Court the design of Northumberland's plot was clear. The device by which Mary and her sister
were to be set aside was a declaration by the dying King that Lady
Jane would be his successor. Having discussed Lady Jane's
marriage and the royal declaration with his servant Roger Alford,
Cecil was not ignorant of the gravity of the situation. His
misgivings about the Duke's plot became widely known. In
anticipation of the consequences of his opposition, he took certain
precautions. Contrary to his usual custom he carried arms. It was
arranged that there would be small pickings if he were arrested on
any charge leading to forfeiture. Money, plate and papers were
removed from Cannon Row. Conveyances were made of lands,
leases, part of his moveables and even of his clothes. He prepared
to leave the country. But, on the advice of Cheke, who, like a good
humanist urged him to fortify his resolution by reading Plato, he
stayed. Socrates, Cecil claimed, persuaded him to remain and obey
the law.[14]

Having just recovered his physical strength, Cecil found that
his moral fortitude and political courage were being put to the
test. It is significant that he appeared in Council at the time when
the legality of the King's declaration on the succession was to be
considered. He put his name to the letter summoning the chief law
officers of the Crown to give legal form to the royal testament.

Knowing the law and its officers, Cecil anticipated strong opposition to the Council's request.[15] Legal resistance to Northumberland might well split the Council, which was far from unanimous in support of the Duke. Cecil showed his sense of political opportunity by returning to the Council when there seemed a chance of defeating Northumberland by lawful means.

Cecil's judgement proved right. The King's legal officers, refusing to set aside the Succession Act, which subordinated the Suffolk claim of Lady Jane to the claims of Mary and Elizabeth Tudor, declared that 'if any of them set their pen to devise the instrument, he was *ipso facto* traitor'. They argued that Statute could only be changed by Parliament. But Northumberland used his own threats and the royal command to break the resistance of the lawyers in three bitter meetings. 'With sorrowful hearts and with weeping eyes' the lawyers agreed on 15 June to prepare the necessary legal instrument when the King promised to call Parliament.[16]

Two days before, when Northumberland had called the Chief Justice of Common Pleas a traitor and had offered to fight in his shirt any man in that quarrel, Cecil had realised that Northumberland was not to be baulked. The Duke's revenge, if he won the day, upon those who had opposed him seemed certain. 'Being well strengthened in mind by Christ', William Cecil wrote a farewell letter to his wife and entrusted it to Nicholas Bacon.[17]

The letter to Mildred resulted, as Cecil wrote, from 'a long consultation betwixt God and my conscience'. When communicating with his wife religious idiom came naturally to him as the vehicle of sincere emotion. He urged her to study the Scriptures and not to mourn him since he would die in the 'faith of the Gospel'. His instructions for the education of Thomas were that he was to be sent to a university and then be trained as a lawyer or, failing that, as a merchant. For himself there was no self-pity. His concern was for his wife and son. His only vanity was a desire to leave a good name. He asked that his friends should be told that he was accepting death to save his conscience. His closing words showed the inviolability of the religious mind which can regard inevitable fate as a matter of choice. 'Seeing great perils threatened upon us by the likeness of the time', he wrote, 'I do make choice to avoid the peril of God's displeasure.'

If the sentiments of Cecil's letter may be interpreted as those of the man whom he wished to be rather than those of the man he was, it must be allowed that in the face of death he rose to what he aspired to be before his wife with enviable sincerity. To sustain such a mood in public before hardened men was more difficult. But Cecil continued to make his resistance known and he hoped that his consent to the alteration of the succession would not be expected or required. The councillors, believing that there was safety in numbers, summoned him to sign the instrument. Northumberland put forward Shrewsbury and others to persuade Cecil, who, much to his surprise, found himself being treated with consideration and respect. Finally it was arranged for the King to intervene and upon the royal command Cecil was the last of the councillors to sign.[18]

Cecil's reluctant surrender came only when it seemed that the royal prerogative and statute law would be reconciled in a future meeting of Parliament. His behaviour had revealed the conflict of authorities and loyalties which was the predicament of his generation. As a lawyer he accepted the sovereignty of statute law. As a subject he gave his obedience to the King. His personal loyalty was to the house of Tudor. His protestant conscience turned to the Bible when he wrote to his wife in expectation of death. Seldom did all the demands of royal prerogative, parliamentary statute, dynastic allegiance and God's Word coincide. To decide which was paramount in each circumstance was the problem which Cecil had tried to solve. To stand by the succession of the catholic Mary looked like the abandonment of his protestant hopes. Yet it satisfied the law, his loyalty and his obedience and was not inconsistent with the mysterious ways of Providence.

For all his Plato and the Gospel, Cecil was neither philosopher nor saint. He wavered between flight and open opposition, between cowardice and courage. His hope was not to be put to the test. The motive of self-preservation so strong among his colleagues affected him. But Cecil was too much of an intellectual to succumb to instinct without agony of mind; too aware of religious truths to surrender without pangs of conscience. That he did not pay with his life for his opposition to Northumberland was the result of the Duke's subtle policy rather than of any efforts by Cecil to save his own skin. To Northumberland the acquiescence of a man with a high reputation for integrity was worth while.

Having obtained authority for Lady Jane Grey to succeed Edward, Northumberland had no intention of perpetuating the high-minded mood of opposition. He had implicated all those whom he wished to drag with him. It was now time to allow anti-climax to ease the tension. The government continued as before. Cecil remained in his post as Secretary. There was no victimisation of opponents by the Duke. The real test, as Northumberland knew, would come when the King died. Then it would be all or nothing.

The Duke did not have long to wait. On 6 July 1553, only a fortnight after the Great Seal had been set upon the instrument to alter the succession, Edward died. For the events which followed Cecil had no responsibility and he did his best to avoid, as far as he was able, being involved in Northumberland's moves. On the King's death the great nobles acted in secret and did not allow the Secretaries to attend their first meeting in Council. Such an exclusion suited Cecil but he did not escape having to take an oath of allegiance to Lady Jane Grey. But, when he was appointed to draw up the proclamation of the new Queen's accession, he argued that it was a task for the Queen's attorney or solicitor. The proclamation made on 10 July in London was the work of Mr Throckmorton, a Master of Requests, 'whose conscience', as Cecil noted, 'was troubled therewith.'[19]

On the day on which Lady Jane was proclaimed Queen, Cecil and Petre were engaged on the delicate mission of informing the imperial ambassador of Edward's death and the new succession.[20] It was doubtful if Charles V would recognise anyone but his kinswoman Mary Tudor as Queen of England. Northumberland's actions were endangering not only the domestic peace of the realm, but also the relations of England with the Emperor. Cecil's employment with Petre revealed that both men were still acting as

Secretaries. It was clear that it was going to be difficult to withdraw
from Northumberland's service as long as he had any use for the
reluctant Secretaries.

Meanwhile Mary was taking action. She wrote to the Council
asserting her right to the throne. The answer of the Council argued
that Mary was excluded by her illegitimacy. Once again Cecil
escaped the task of drafting a compromising document. He
'avoided the answer'. He also 'eschewed the writing of the Queen's
Highness' bastard' in a letter. Cecil was denying Northumberland
his skill as an author of official documents. His passive resistance
took the form of abstaining from drafting any of the 'public
letters to the realm'. For such purposes Cecil had virtually ceased
to act as Secretary.[21]

Cecil was not the only man to be reluctant to be dragged along
in the dangerous wake of Northumberland. Only the Duke's
powerful presence held the Council together. But, when supporters
gathered round Mary and it became clear that she would have to
be met with force, the Duke had to make the choice between
remaining to dominate the Council or marching out in person to
take the rival Queen. Having failed to persuade Lady Jane's father
to lead a force against Mary, Northumberland, despite his distrust
of the councillors, decided to attempt to make Mary surrender by
marching towards her refuge at Framlingham. The Duke's withdrawal from London gave his opponents the opportunity which
they had helped to contrive. In failing to secure the person of
Mary Tudor on the King's death, Northumberland had made his
most costly mistake.

In London the great nobles, Bedford, Arundel, Shrewsbury,
Pembroke and Cobham, began to intrigue. Efforts were made to
take control of Windsor Castle and the Tower. The imperial
embassy was persuaded to stay in England. By 19 July the
conspirators were sure enough of themselves to arrange for the
proclamation of Mary Tudor as Queen. Cecil and his friends Petre
and Mason were in no position to lead in these manœuvres, but
they did all they could to help the nobles and to frustrate
Northumberland's plans.

In the week between Northumberland's departure and the

proclamation of Mary's succession in London, Cecil was again torn between leaving the country and facing the consequences of the dangerous politics in which he was involved. His papers and such money and plate as he had by him were moved and divided between the house of his servant Sere and that of a Mr Nelson. His man, Roger Alford, prepared two hide-outs, one at his mother's house and another at Nelson's house in Essex, which was close to the Thames. Cecil even went so far as to convey his lands to his son Thomas. It was a move which his legal friend Gosnald thought risky since Thomas might not play the game. The precautions would prove useful either in the event of Northumberland's triumph or if Cecil failed to make his peace with a successful Mary. Cecil did not blind himself to the eventualities which he feared most.[22]

While ready to slip out of England if the situation became too desperate, Cecil played what part he could in the intrigues of the succession crisis. He used his influence in Lincolnshire and Northamptonshire to prevent military aid being given to Northumberland. The hundred men whom he might have raised at Wimbledon were prevented from joining the Duke's army. He was determined that neither he nor his tenants should fight against a Tudor. On the disposition of more important forces he claimed to have had an influence. 'I practiced with the Lord Treasurer to win the Lord Privy Seal', he stated, 'that I might by the Lord Russell's means cause Windsor Castle to serve the Queen; and they two to levy the west parts for the Queen's service.' It was risky work. Cecil, with a safe-conduct from the Marquess of Winchester, operated under an assumed name. He approached Arundel and Lord Darcy and passed to Petre the news of their willingness to join in the move to put Mary on the throne. At Lambeth Cecil had horses ready which would have enabled him 'to have stolen down to the Queen's Highness', Mary Tudor.[23]

When the proclamation of Mary was made, Cecil did not have to steal down to the Queen: he was despatched on official business by the Council to meet Mary, who was progressing to London after the collapse of Northumberland's power. The meeting with Mary at Newhall in Essex was a delicate task for the protestant

Secretary. Not since his youthful encounter with the awesome
Henry VIII had Cecil faced a mature monarch who personally
wielded the royal authority. Arundel and Paget had prepared the
way and it seemed that Mary had accepted the professions of
loyalty which they had given her on behalf of the Council. But a
letter of the Council to Northumberland, which had been
intercepted by Mary's supporters, had made it appear that Cecil
'had armed horsemen against her'. Nevertheless Cecil's reception
by Mary was friendly. His sister-in-law, Lady Bacon, had inter-
ceded for him. He was, no doubt, relieved to hear that Mary had
called him 'a very honest man'. His submission to the Queen was
accompanied by an explanation of his actions in the whole affair of
the succession.[24]

The explanation was the work of a skilled advocate who knew
how to put his case. It is the evidence for the part which Cecil
played in Northumberland's plot. It has never been discredited,
but twenty years later it was corroborated by the recollections of
his servant Roger Alford. The bare factual relation of events and
the circumstantial detail enhance its credibility. It was tainted
neither with rhetorical heroics nor with abject sycophancy. His
simple plea was that the Queen would discriminate between him
and the 'others that have plainly offended', and between him and
those who were more free to 'show their duties to their Sovereign
Lady'. Having heard Cecil's version of his acts, Mary might well
have felt that she had some justification for declaring him to be a
very honest man. If the Queen's notoriously weak judgement was
at fault, it must be admitted that she was not the only one to be
deceived. Cecil had made a good showing and no one came
forward to challenge him.

When Cecil met the Queen later at Sir William Petre's house at
Ingatestone in Essex, he was the first of the councillors to be
allowed to kiss the Queen's hand.[25] For the moment Cecil was
safe. If he had been justified in fearing the consequences of his
opposition to Northumberland, he was allowing his pessimism to
get the better of him in anticipating danger from Mary. Since the
deposition of Richard II in 1399 the majority of trained bureaucrats
had remained in office throughout the plots and intrigues which

had attended the change of dynasties and the sequence of succession. Mary depended on administrators like Cecil to maintain the continuity of government at a critical time. William Petre continued to serve Mary as Secretary and there was no political reason why Cecil should not also retain his post. The new Queen had been in no position to build up a party of her own and she was obliged to accept the services of the men who had worked for Northumberland. The main reason for Cecil's survival of Northumberland's downfall was not any exceptional pliancy or cunning on his part, but the same training and experience which had previously recommended him to Northumberland when Somerset fell. Survival was the normal fate of the skilled bureaucrat.

The role of William Cecil in the reign of Edward VI does not appear to justify any knowing appraisal of him as a masterly Machiavellian. Because of his power to hold friends and his talents for administration he suffered only a temporary set-back when Somerset was first deposed. The learned and able Sir Thomas Smith had lost the Secretaryship because he could not keep his friends. Like Thomas Cromwell's, Cecil's power lay not in name, connections or wealth, but in personal abilities. Northumberland and Somerset had agreed to his appointment as Secretary. At Somerset's second fall Cecil had felt qualms of conscience but everyone was agreed that Somerset was not worthy of any personal or political sacrifice. Among his contemporaries Cecil seemed over-scrupulous. Under Northumberland he had dared to stand with the law officers of the Crown against the alteration of the succession. If he had contemplated flight, he had also been prepared to face death. His surrender to Northumberland had been under royal duress and he had continued to show opposition. Finally he had faced and convinced Mary of his honesty.

In the political world William Petre had been Cecil's mentor. In religion Cecil had found himself in friendly sympathy with Thomas Cranmer. The moderate men attracted him. His reputation was that of a hard-working administrator and a moderate politician of more than usual integrity. Circumstances had limited his opportunities to show constructive statesmanship. By the age of thirty-three years he had made for himself a successful career in royal government. It was, perhaps, typical of his conscience and of his moderation that he was prepared at this juncture to withdraw quietly from public life.

CHAPTER V

In the Wilderness

AFTER he had made his peace with Mary, Cecil retired from the government. His early biographer makes it clear that Cecil declined to serve a catholic Queen for the sake of his religion.[1] No doubt religion was the substantial reason for Cecil's withdrawal. Mary's return to the imperial alliance and the predictable conduct of domestic affairs, still largely in the hands of his old colleagues and friends, gave him no grounds for political objection to the new régime. Cecil might well have continued in office as Petre and Paget did had he been the complete time-server. By not accepting high office Cecil was in his moderate way showing a measure of disapproval for the new Queen's faith.

Retirement from the Council lessened the chances of becoming involved in friction over religious matters and removed altogether any responsibility for ecclesiastical policy. To Cecil there was all the difference between conscientious active support of the religion of the Queen and the legal acceptance of her authority. He believed that it was the lawful duty of the subject to show outward conformity to the religion of the Prince. He was ready to 'serve her at large as a private man, rather than to be her greatest counsellor'.[2] The need for obedience to the powers that be was taught by all the most respected authorities of the time. It was Cranmer and Cheke, not Cecil, who were inconsistent in rejecting Mary's rule.

There was no encouragement to resist the Queen either in current political thinking or in Protestant attitudes. Doctrines of resistance were born later of the frustration of exiles but they were not countenanced at Mary's accession. In the country at large Mary had been accepted as the rightful and divinely sanctioned candidate for the throne. If she were to restore Catholicism and the authority of the Pope, it would be interpreted by many

Protestants as the work of Providence. It would be represented as a punishment by God for the way in which the Protestants had misused the opportunities which the Lord had given them in Edward VI's reign. The chastening had to be endured. Obedience to Mary or exile were the two solutions to the predicament which confronted Protestants. Cecil as usual found a middle way. He combined obedience and withdrawal. His retirement was not into foreign exile but into the political wilderness.

It was preferable to retire on his own terms rather than to await expulsion at the Queen's pleasure. He must have heard from his friends who were present of how Mary, as a Princess, had commented upon the Council's instructions prohibiting her from celebrating the Mass, 'Ah! good Mr. Cecil took much pains here'.[3] But in the summer of 1553 Mary, far from working to expel Cecil, was sounding him on his willingness to serve her. Had Cecil made a determined effort to stay in the government it seems likely that he would have succeeded as well as his former colleagues. Cecil's abilities were respected at Mary's Court. He resisted later appeals for his return from two such champions of Catholicism as Cuthbert Tunstall and Reginald Pole. There was a rumour that Cecil might follow Petre if the old Secretary retired.[4] Sir William was ready to take his place in local government and to undertake more important business on occasion. He did what he deemed to be his duty in carrying out the responsibilities of his degree but he would do no more.

Upon his reputation and his behaviour as a private man his safety rested. He was no longer in a position to defend himself at Court. It was a position which all important men attempted to avoid. By retiring from the government, he guarded himself from involvement in policies which he did not approve, but, at the same time, he made himself more vulnerable to the intrigues of those with authority. There was a risk in leaving the government. It was not a simple guarantee of safe rural seclusion in which to enjoy the fruits of office gathered under Edward VI. Cecil knew that he would have to walk delicately.

The strain of the last few months of Edward VI's reign may, for the moment, have disposed him to look with favour upon the life

Mr Secretary Cecil

Sir William Petre

of a country gentleman. But, for the sake of a life of ease Cecil would not have shirked the difficulties of working for Mary or with Gardiner, who was now restored to favour. He found high office too satisfying to abandon it for any but the most serious considerations. He had dared in the past to return to the Court from the Tower. In his years of experience he had learned that patience was a political virtue. Perhaps he had the prescience to withdraw so that he might return at a more favourable juncture. In this mortal world it was possible that before long the Princess Elizabeth would ascend the throne.

Whatever the cause of Cecil's relinquishment of the Secretary-ship, it seems likely that it was largely for reasons of his own. He had survived the last days of 'the Great Devil, Dudley'. Providence might be tempted too far. Cecil went quietly. There was no open conflict, no recrimination, no heroics. He managed his retirement with great discretion. Both Mary and Cecil were satisfied. The Queen did not listen to Cecil's enemies or seek to persecute him in any way. She treated him in accordance with her opinion of him as 'a very honest man'.[5]

It was as a councillor that Sir William attended the funeral of Edward VI on 8 August 1553. He gave up his Secretaryship later in that month when Sir John Bourne took his place alongside Sir William Petre. In September he was asked to surrender the seals and register of the Order of the Garter. Only the duties of his father's post in the Wardrobe, which he had carried on since Richard Cecil's death, remained to link him with the Court. When Sir Edward Dymoke, anxious to be ready for Mary's coronation on 1 October, asked for various items of his ceremonial outfit as the Queen's champion, Cecil proved stricter than his father about authorisation for issuing the 'stuff'. The aggrieved champion was still complaining two months after the coronation about his failure to receive what he wanted.[6] Cecil knew that lesser officials have to be sticklers about warrants if they wish to avoid reprimands from their superiors. He was not going to lay himself open to any charges of laxity.

On 6 October, amongst the earliest recipients, Cecil was granted a general pardon by the Queen. Mary's trust in him was further

E

displayed by his continued inclusion in the Commission of the
Peace for Lincolnshire and in the confirmation of his office of
Commissioner for Sewers in the same county.[7] He had not been
humiliated or reduced in county society. By the end of 1553 he had
settled down to a life which was less busy and more free of great
responsibility than he had known since he had been appointed
Somerset's Master of Requests some six years previously.

Sir William, no doubt, counted his spiritual blessings at the
daily prayers which were said in his household in the morning. He
certainly enumerated his material blessings. He kept strict accounts
of his household expenditure and drew up lists of his lands and
offices.[8] His administrator's appetite for detail showed in his
private affairs. Out of office, he could expect no further rewards
for service and he lacked the opportunities to make the profitable
acquisitions of those in the know. Under Mary he deemed it wise
to make no purchases of monastic lands. But his surveys of his
property must have been reassuring.

His properties constituted considerable wealth. He had recently
inherited the estates and emoluments of his father. His inheritance
had made it materially easier to retire. But under Edward VI he
himself had done well. He later recognised it as his heyday. While
serving Somerset he had been able to purchase over £2,000 worth
of chantry properties and lands situated at Corby, Hungerton,
Wyvell and in Stamford itself. Northumberland's rule had proved
even more profitable. Early in 1551 he bought a monastic property,
the manor of Bromley in Middlesex. Later in that year he had a
gift of lands worth an annual value of just over £150. It consisted
of a string of manors, Achurch, Bereham, Deeping, Stowe,
Thetford and Thorpe along with the reversion of two other
manors and the advowsons and rectories of Lynwood and St
Mary's, Stamford. At the end of 1552 he was ready to buy the
house of the Austin Friars in Stamford and the manor of Barholme
in Lincolnshire. In March of the next year he acquired an advowson
for the rectory of Clennog. In June he made his last great purchase
of Edward's reign when he bought from the Crown for £687 6s. 6d.
in cash a number of small parcels of Lincolnshire chantry land.[9]

Sir William had not strayed from the family policy of building up control of property in Stamford and the surrounding counties. He went one step further than his grandfather and father in establishing influence in county society, when in May 1553 he obtained a wardship. Arthur Hall had lands in Lincolnshire and it was of this minor that Sir William secured the right of custody and marriage. His ward came to live under his care at Wimbledon.[10] Apart from grants assigned upon the lands of a ward, there were profitable dynastic bargains to be made. It was Cecil's first venture in a complex legal game which engaged his interest in land, money and family politics. The time was to come when he would be Master of the Court of Wards in charge of the destinies of many heirs and heiresses of the nobility and gentry.

Under Mary if he could not increase his lands he could improve them and their yield. In the first year of her reign he took stock in a list entitled 'A brief value of my land'. He had his eye on the profits to be made from his sheep, his timber and leather. Applying his academic training to the practical problems of farming, he made detailed notes on how to plant elm trees and sow oats. He compiled tables of the different weights and measures in use in the markets. Prices of commodities were carefully noted. He believed that one could save a penny in every four by buying at the right time in the right market. He found it cheaper still to feed his household on home-grown corn and cattle.[11]

While land was the safest investment and remained the massive core of Sir William's fortune he was ready to try other ways of making money and investing. He had made a modest start in the market of wards, run by the Crown to exploit its ancient feudal rights. He also began to try his luck in foreign trade. Under Northumberland's patronage and pressed by the slump in Antwerp, merchants were beginning to look for new markets. The new joint-stock organisation, being tried by far-ranging trading companies, gave Cecil his chance. For 1553 he noted, 'I delivered to the society of the Adventurers into Russia £25'. His investment in the Muscovy Company was enterprising. There were few investors who were not merchants. It must have been profitable, for under Mary he put more money into the venture. In 1556 he invested £45. Commerce was a speculative business, but

Cecil continued his interest in the Russia trade and eventually became the oldest charter member of the company.[12] Far safer was his stock of plate to which he continued to add. It was no doubt charitable of him to buy a silver vessel from his exiled father-in-law.[13]

On such wealth his household at Wimbledon lived well but with moderation. It was Cecil's opinion that men should live within their means 'rather plentiful than sparing, but not costly'. It was his rule that a quarter of a man's total income should be reserved for extraordinary expenses and that of the remaining three quarters, committed to routine expenditure, not more than a third should be spent upon hospitality, the running of the household and entertainment.[14]

Sir William kept a considerable establishment: a priest, a schoolmaster, a tailor, butler, cook and a host of other servants. Twenty-eight badges and liveries had to be provided. The principal members of the household were Sir William, his wife, his son Thomas, his sister Margaret and his wife's sister Elizabeth Cooke. There were also Arthur Hall, the ward, and John Stanhope, a young gentleman. They lived in material comfort with recreations and treats. William, his wife, his son and the ward did some shooting. In the Armoury were two long bows, one 'for my own shooting the other for my wife'. At a sale of the wardrobe of Anne of Cleves William bought his wife some dozen lots including regal gowns of red cloth of gold, of cloth of silver, of purple velvet. William listed his own apparel, which was extensive. He ran up a tailor's bill for himself and Thomas. For his own pleasure he bought books. He undertook some building at his mother's home at Stamford Baron. There were celebrations for the marriage of his sister Elizabeth to Robert Wingfield. All Cecil's moderation could not disguise the affluence in which he lived.[15]

It was a home of decorous and disciplined living. The pious and thoughtfully contrived domestic routine mirrored the harmony of the affectionate relationship between William and his wife. Whatever the physical or psychological explanation, it was not until her husband's retirement that Mildred Cecil, after nine years of childless marriage, became pregnant. The daughter, Frances, delivered in April 1554, survived only a few hours. But hope of an heir there now was. In December 1556 at the house in Cannon Row another daughter, Anne, was born. Sir Anthony Cooke, as father-in-law, sent his congratulations and the hope that it would be a son next time. But little 'Tannikin' became the cherished favourite of her father. Both parents were ready to sacrifice social invitations in order to watch over their precious infant. William made every effort to care for his wife, and Philip Hoby thought that he had been as good a nurse to her as William could have wished her to be to him. It is evident that Cecil and his wife understood the nature of marriage.[16]

Family life was rich, if not happy in a facile way. But, if a judgement can be made on subsequent behaviour, Thomas Cecil was the least happy member of the family. He was fourteen when Anne was born, and he was, perhaps, unsure of the affection of his stepmother and of his father, who tried to find the middle way between 'foolish cockering' and 'overstern carriage' in bringing up his son.[17]

In his retirement Cecil kept most of his friends and was on good terms with his relatives. Sir Nicholas Bacon and Sir Thomas Hoby were his brothers-in-law through their marriages to his wife's sisters. William Paget and John Mason, who were now enjoying Mary's favour and were rising at Court, were in his circle. Walter Mildmay, the Exchequer official, was also friendly. Sir William was acquainted with those out of royal favour, like Lord John Grey, uncle of Lady Jane Grey, who asked him to act as godfather to his child. He managed business affairs for the Countess of Bedford while her husband, Francis Russell, was abroad with the army. He was still Surveyor to the Princess Elizabeth. He knew and mixed with important people who were both in and out of favour with the Queen. He so conducted his personal relationships that they embarrassed neither himself nor his friends. Perhaps his most unexpected acquaintanceship was that with Cardinal Pole. A mutual interest in Christian humanism and a mutual respect, it seems, drew these men together.[18] From such men Cecil could have learned all he wished to know about the politics of the day. But Cecil studiously avoided becoming involved in the issues of the reign.

If he was careful to keep his relationships with those whom he knew in England on a purely social or strictly business plane, he was equally cautious about his dealings with all those who had gone into voluntary exile rather than accept Catholicism or live at home without royal favour. Among the exiles was Catherine, Duchess of Suffolk, who had always tried to spur Cecil to greater efforts for the Reformation. Sir Anthony Cooke, while he was abroad, remained friendly and grateful towards his son-in-law. Richard Morison died in Strasbourg and Cecil received an appeal to help his widow. John Hales and Thomas Lever, 'Commonwealth men' of Somerset's time, were exiles. Of all those whom Cecil knew it was John Cheke who proved the bitterest and expressed his fears that Cecil would abandon his faith. Cecil received some hard words from his old Cambridge teacher.[19] Perhaps the pupil remembered that he had learned from Cheke in the past to obey the King and not to rebel for religion's sake.

The moral pressure which Cheke tried to put upon Cecil had no effect. The reformers had taught obedience and passive acceptance of authority. Cecil stood by that teaching in the hope that the Lord would, in His own good time, restore to power the men whom He was chastening. Sir William was not a theologian like his friend Thomas Cranmer. The Archbishop felt the dilemma posed by the conflict between obedience to God in religious belief and obedience to his anointed royal servant. He wavered, and then made the choice against obedience to the Queen. Cecil knew of his death at the stake. The burning of heretics under Mary made an impression on him as it did on all who were Protestant at heart. He made a note in his sparse diary of many such burnings. He avoided comment. The only hint of shock was the addition to his note on the total of burnings for 1554 which ran 'whereof many were maidens.'[20]

Sir William was too much of an intellectual, too knowledgeable about doctrine, to dodge the problem of religious conformity and cynically admit that he found it more convenient to serve Mammon than to serve God. While he stayed at home and conformed he was maturing those thoughts on the claims of Church and State which he was to expound later. If they were not the inspiration of zeal, they were intellectually respectable. So when Cecil received the sacrament of the Altar and made his offering at Wimbledon Church at Easter 1556, he could feel assured that he had the sparks left in him, 'as in a fire well raked up, to light a candle or raise a fire in a convenient time'.[21]

Meanwhile Cecil did as his Queen demanded. Her requests for his services were few, but in November 1554 he was a member of the party sent to welcome Cardinal Pole. The humanist Cardinal had opposed Henry VIII and had retired to Padua, where he had played his part as a reformer of the Roman Church and had created an Erasmian Academy for young English scholars. His return to England, at first delayed by the cautious counsels of Charles, who wanted no rival to his influence, was a step towards reconciliation with and reform of the Roman Church in the Queen's realm. If his enemies hoped that Cecil would take the chance while abroad to bolt or compromise himself with exiles, they were disappointed. In company with Paget and Sir Edward Hastings, Cecil visited the Imperial Court at Brussels and escorted Pole back to Westminster. The excursion, which lasted eighteen days, was Sir William's first visit to the Continent.[22]

Cecil must have acquitted himself well on the trip to Brussels. His efficiency and obvious abilities made an impression on Pole. Six months later he accompanied the Cardinal in some secretarial capacity on a very important embassy to Calais where English, French and Imperial representatives met in a vain attempt to make a peace between Hapsburg and Valois. The conference of diplomats met on 23 April but before their deliberations were complete Cecil had left on a tour of the Netherlands. In three weeks he covered 250 miles and visited such towns as Gravelines, Dunkirk, Nieuport, Bruges, Ghent, Alost, Brussels, Louvain, Mechelen, Antwerp, Lille and Ypres. Whether the tour through the commercial and industrial Netherlands was on his own initiative is not known. But busy as he was he did not forget to buy presents — a hat each for the children.[23]

After 1555 Cecil was not employed again in diplomacy. Mary's marriage to Philip of Spain had removed the flexibility and the initiative from English foreign policy. It was as a local magnate that Cecil emerged again into high politics by standing for the Parliament which met on 21 October 1555. It was the fourth of Mary's Parliaments. Cecil had not attended the previous three, although he had no doubt exercised his usual influence at Stamford and Grantham. In this autumn Parliament Cecil sat as a Knight of the Shire for Lincolnshire, which meant that he had the respect and support of the gentry in that county. Sir William was no longer content with a borough seat, which carried less prestige in the House. He was somewhat reluctant to take his place in Parliament. The pressure for him to attend may have come from his friends in the government. He may have felt it necessary to his local standing to accept the acclaim of the gentry, which was the vital factor in an election. Perhaps he found it difficult to suppress his appetite for politics and felt the urge to intervene in what promised to be a troublesome Parliament.[24]

A mood of disillusion had spread amongst the protestant political nation. Active measures were being taken against heretics. The Queen had failed to produce an heir and the Tudor succession was being threatened by suggestions that Philip or some Hapsburg nominee should be named as successor. It was the opinion of the French ambassador that only the heavy rains of the summer had prevented an uprising. By the time Parliament met it was being rumoured that the discontented Protestants had been using their influence at elections to return those who were disaffected in the matter of religion. It was no wonder that Cecil was not eager to be involved.

Once in Parliament, however, Cecil found himself being used by the government. Early in November he had the task of consolidating two Bills designed to check enclosures. Such legislation had been dangerous to handle in Somerset's day but now Cecil was able to do his job and see his Bill go through its readings without opposition. His legal expertise was employed to deal with a Bill entitled 'The Bill of Divers Statutes and Laws'. A similar Bill had come to nothing early in the session but the new Bill, referred to Cecil, was successful. A third Bill on First Fruits and Tenths introduced in the Lords was passed to Cecil for redrafting before it was presented to the Commons.[25] It looks as if his friends in the government were using Cecil as a stalking-horse to outflank the opposition. Members would accept from a known and respected moderate what they would not accept from time-servers or extremists.

If such was the hope of the Council, it was in the end to be disappointed. There was strong opposition to the Bill on First Fruits and Tenths. Its proposal that the Crown should renounce its right to this ecclesiastical taxation did not recommend itself to laymen. Having already shown their determination not to pay the taxes which the Queen was demanding of them, they were not prepared to see the burden of clerical taxes shifted to their own shoulders. Cecil spoke in the debate. From what is known of his attitude to the wealth of the Church it seems likely that he did not speak in favour of the Bill.

As the Parliament proceeded Cecil himself seems to have become infected with the antagonism that was being shown to the Queen's measures. When on 28 November a Bill, which required all those now abroad to return or forfeit the revenues of their lands, was introduced, Cecil opposed it.[26] The Bill was aimed at the protestant exiles, amongst whom was Cecil's own father-in-law. But it touched property rights. Here was a legal issue, which could be fought without mentioning doctrine. It was a matter in which every propertied man had an interest. Just as he had opposed Northumberland upon a point of legality, so now he made a stand against Mary on the property rights enshrined in common law. Cecil's attack on the Bill won him the admiration of the group of discontented gentlemen who met at Arundel's, near Tower Bridge, to discuss their grievances.

These men, amongst whom were Sir Anthony Kingston, Sir William Courtenay, Sir John Pollard and a number of others, mostly from the West Country, pressed Cecil for a meeting. He agreed to have them to dine with him on condition that they did not discuss 'any matters of Parliament'. Cecil was ready to ingratiate himself with this informal opposition, but he insisted upon meeting his guests socially and not for political purposes. Nevertheless politics were discussed despite the host's protestations for which he no doubt had good witnesses. The dinner party did not go unnoticed and the leaders of the opposition were arrested and committed for trial. Cecil was summoned to appear before his old friends Paget and Petre. It is perhaps not surprising that he was able to persuade them to listen to his explanation before they committed him. 'And upon their hearing the circumstances he cleared himself and so escaped both imprisonment and disgrace.' It was fortunate for Cecil that Stephen Gardiner had died a few days previously. The death was recorded in Cecil's diary.[27]

It was the first and last time that Cecil showed any detectable resistance to the government under Mary. Whenever his feelings and interests could be given the neutral shape of legalistic justice, he was apt to be carried away by his own skill in pleading. His own comment on his performance was, 'I spoke my opinion freely which created ill feeling towards me. But it is better to obey God than men.' His conscience endorsed the doings of his lawyer's intellect. Even John Cheke took Cecil's action in Parliament to be a sign that his erstwhile brother-in-law was not altogether a lost soul.[28]

For the rest of the reign Cecil lived quietly. As a Justice of the Peace in Lincolnshire he was commended by the Council for his part in dealing with the spreaders of seditious and false rumours. He was put on a commission in the following year, 1557, to inquire into charges against a tenant on a Northamptonshire manor.[29] The relief from strain and from the exacting work of government was no bad thing for Cecil in those vulnerable years of a man's life between thirty and forty. Many of those who have grown old with distinction in office have had such a period of retirement in middle age. There was time for meditation in the political wilderness. Cecil never lost the hope that one day he would regain favour and power; that in the providential pattern of history there would come a time when he might serve without conscientious conflict both God and his Prince. In his diary Cecil wrote, 'Queen Mary reigned five Years, five Months and twenty-two Days.'[30] He had been counting the days.

While Cecil was content with the obscurity of the life of a country gentleman, Mary in the public arena of the Court was ill and unhappy. As the Queen's health declined and the policies which she pursued ended in disaster for herself and her country, it was inevitable that the ever-present problem of the succession should grow more acute. Just as Mary had been the rightful heiress at Edward's death so now Elizabeth Tudor was accepted as the successor. Mary's accession had driven Cecil into retirement. When Elizabeth came to the throne, there might well be the opportunity for Cecil to serve her as he had served her brother.

CHAPTER VI

Return to Power

By the early autumn of 1558 it had been clear that Mary's days were numbered. Men were quietly preparing for the new reign. On Elizabeth were centred the hopes of all those who had seen their ideals and ambitions thwarted by the accession of Mary. The reformers were hoping to begin where they had left off at the end of Edward's reign. Few doubted that Elizabeth would restore Protestantism. The Marian exiles were ready to return. Patriots looked for an opportunity to throw off the Hapsburg yoke and avenge the loss of Calais. Speculation and stock-taking had begun.

Among the many who were prepared to give advice to Elizabeth was William Cecil. The prospects of his acceptance by the Princess were good. For a dozen years, perhaps even longer, he had known the heiress to the throne, who was now twenty-five. It was fortunate for Cecil that Elizabeth could have heard only good of him in the household of Catherine Parr, from her tutor, Ascham, and from her cofferer, Thomas Parry, who cultivated Cecil both as a distant relative among the cousinage of the Welsh Border and as an immediate asset.[1] Under Somerset, Elizabeth had found it useful to be able to call upon the services of the Protector's Secretary. When she was fourteen she had signed one of her characteristic little postscripts to Cecil 'Your Friend, Elizabeth.'[2] In July 1550 she attached him to her service by making him her Surveyor. The Tudors had always found the Cecils to be reliable men.

Cecil was eager to ingratiate himself with the grand-daughter of the family benefactor, Henry VII. He was ready to help the Princess, second in the line of succession, to approach the Protector. As her Surveyor he applied himself to the care of her properties and estates. During Mary's reign they exchanged letters on business matters to which the Princess contrived to give a personal touch. But Cecil had not been moved by any rash personal loyalty to spring to Elizabeth's aid when she was involved in the proceedings against Thomas Seymour which ended in Thomas' execution for treason. Cecil would not have won Elizabeth's thanks for any indiscreet move to rescue her. She saved herself by her own discretion and it was a quality which she admired in others.

Under Mary, Cecil was not in a position to help Elizabeth in political affairs. As a private man he continued to serve her as Surveyor. But the plots and the conspiracies woven around Elizabeth passed without implicating Cecil. Elizabeth, the involuntary figurehead and focus of intrigue, always tried to clear her servants and remained loyal to them. Cecil knew what constituted legal evidence and proof and, although his enemies were suspicious, no political involvement with Elizabeth could be substantiated. Cecil did not make things difficult for the Princess by conspiring against the Queen. Like Elizabeth he was concerned to survive and wait upon time.

To a less disenchanted Princess, Cecil's obedience to Mary might have seemed like disloyalty to herself. But Elizabeth understood the part which Cecil played under Mary: she had played the same role. To her, Cecil's determined acceptance of the duties of a subject and of the Tudor line of succession were powerful recommendations. It was simple reasoning for one so subtle: that the man who felt it his duty to obey Mary was all the more likely to be Elizabeth's devoted servant, when she became Queen. Of his business abilities she had proof in her own affairs. Educated by the same Cambridge circle they were like-minded in many of their assumptions. From the learning which they shared they drew similar conclusions about the conduct of political and religious matters. Yet another recommendation for Cecil was that he had had experience in high office without being associated with the disasters of Mary's reign. When Mary died Elizabeth was as eager to call upon Cecil's services as he was to give them.

Cecil had the power to inspire trust in women. Catherine, Duchess of Suffolk, had written to him some years before on his appointment as Secretary to Somerset, 'I am content to become

your partner . . . and I will abide all adventures in your ship, be
the weather fair or foul. . . .'³ Although he once said that 'there is
nothing more fulsome than a she-fool',⁴ he had a genuine respect
for intelligent women. He was enough of a humanist to admit
their intellectual equality and enough of a puritan to accept them
as spiritual equals. For them he was not a man with whom to fall
in love, but a practical, reasonable, and, as Mary Tudor had said,
'a very honest man' who knew how to solve the problems of the
world. It was one of the advantages of having married Mildred
Cooke that he was conditioned to a relationship with a strong-
minded, intelligent, self-controlled woman who had an academic
education to match his own. It prepared him for understanding
Elizabeth Tudor.

That understanding, already established, was confirmed in the
last weeks before Mary's death. Already, on 10 November, a day
before Mary finally accepted Elizabeth as her successor, Philip of
Spain's ambassador, de Feria, had heard that Cecil was likely to be
Elizabeth's Secretary and that, although a heretic, he was a wise
and prudent man.⁵ A few days later Cecil was sounding the Lord
Chancellor, Nicholas Heath, Archbishop of York, about his
attitude to the coming changes.⁶ On 17 November 1558, Mary
died and on the same day Elizabeth was proclaimed Queen in
Parliament. Three days later, at the first of her Council meetings
in the Palace of Hatfield, the new Queen appointed Sir William
Cecil to be a privy councillor and her principal Secretary.⁷

How well Elizabeth had read the character of the man she was
appointing was shown by the words which she addressed to him.⁸
'This judgement I have of you,' she said, 'that you will not be
corrupted by any manner of gift and that you will be faithful to the
state, and that without respect of my private will you will give me
that counsel which you think best and if you shall know anything
necessary to be declared to me of secrecy you shall show it to
myself only. And assure yourself I will not fail to keep taciturnity
therein and therefore I charge you.' She acknowledged his much
cherished reputation for integrity without denying him the
rewards of service. In her belief that he would be faithful to the
State she had detected that political principle which he had tested

in the reign of Edward VI. He had learned it as a politician and he sought as a Christian humanist to reconcile it with his conscience. The appeal to disregard her private will was made to his respect for the common law and the conception of kingship which it enshrined. The demand for and promise of secrecy was the way to penetrate his inscrutable discretion and introduce some intimacy into what evidently appeared to the Queen as the detached legalism and idealism of his approach to politics.

Cecil had done well, amidst the dangerous whirlpools and eddies of the political stream, to be in a position to snap up the Secretaryship. But it was Elizabeth with her skill in fishing for men's souls who had caught him. Of the seven new councillors whom Elizabeth appointed in her first year Cecil was the ablest. Next in ability was his brother-in-law, Sir Nicholas Bacon.[9] Cecil was no novice or stranger among the councillors. He had served with the majority of them in Edward's day. His reputation amongst them was made. The opportunity for him to play a leading role was great.

At the first meeting of the Council on 20 November Cecil showed that he had not lost his touch in retirement. He was ready with a comprehensive list of measures to be taken to ensure the quiet assumption of power by the new Queen.[10] It contained measures to secure the legal continuance of the central and local government and of the judiciary; to take over the centres of military power in London and on the coasts; to close the ports; to impose a moratorium on dealings in foreign exchange; to inform the Pope and the Emperor, Spain, Denmark and Venice of Elizabeth's accession; to continue peace negotiations with France; to send a commission to Ireland and to arrange the funeral of the late Queen and the coronation of the new Queen. It ended: 'To consider the preacher of St Paul's Cross, that no occasion be given by him to stir any dispute touching the governance of the realm.'

This list of largely routine practical measures touched upon the military, diplomatic, legal, economic, ceremonial and propagandist foundations of power. It reflected the wider problems which faced the new Queen. Paramount among them were the negotiation of peace with France, the establishment of sound finance, the settle-

ment of ecclesiastical jurisdiction and religious doctrine and last,
but not least, in the Queen's eyes, the coronation which would
make her an anointed Queen. In the efforts to solve all these
inter-related problems Cecil was to play a part.

In foreign affairs, a Secretary's province, Elizabeth pushed
Cecil forward to screen herself from the importunate ambassadors.
To de Feria it seemed that Cecil was the man who did everything.[11]
The Secretary was familiarising himself with the situation. The
hope of English diplomacy was to regain Calais, which Mary had
so recently lost. But, as Elizabeth had no effective forces, the only
way of persuading France to restore Calais was to use Spanish
influence. It was in the interest of Philip of Spain to maintain
Elizabeth's goodwill and to see that the French did not gain
control of England. The proclamation in France of Mary Queen
of Scots, the daughter-in-law of Henry II, as Queen of England
was a measure of the French King's ambition. It was for Cecil and
his mistress a question of using Spanish suspicions to counter
French hopes.

In late November 1558 Cecil was already absorbed in this
tortuous and delicate business. The firm stand over the restoration
of Calais, which, it was hoped, would draw Spanish support,
called forth the advice of Cecil's old friend, John Mason. He
urged Cecil not to sacrifice the best possible terms of peace by
bluffing over Calais 'as though they had the French at commandment'.[12] He need not have worried. Cecil knew when to climb
down but meanwhile he was wringing what advantage he could
from the balance of power between Spain and France. A direct
approach by the French through Lord Grey, a Calais prisoner
released for the purpose, called out his caution. 'It seemeth
necessary,' he wrote, 'neither so to like it nor so to follow it, as
thereby any jealousy shall arise in the heart of the King of Spain.'
He went on to suggest that all things done in Mary's time 'since
the war began be as it were revoked and put out of memory' by
the French King. Thus, without referring to Calais, Cecil, in the
politest of terms and amidst expressions of goodwill and peace,
gave no ground.[13] But the opening for further discussion was
carefully preserved. Meanwhile Dr Wotton was to reassure Philip

Mildred Cecil

Lord Burghley in a Procession of the Knights of the Garter

of Elizabeth's friendship. Such diplomacy was to continue into the spring of 1559 before any results were achieved.

Meanwhile at home the preparation for the Queen's coronation was being pressed forward. The Archbishop of York, Nicholas Heath, who, after the death of Reginald Pole, Archbishop of Canterbury, might have been expected to crown the Queen, refused to take part in the coronation ceremony. The services of Oglethorpe of Carlisle were obtained. On 16 January 1559, only eight weeks after the accession of the Queen, came the coronation day. Sir William Cecil was in the great procession to Westminster Abbey. Behind the scenes Cecil had already done something to ensure the smooth performance of the ceremony. He had carefully gone over the coronation service himself. He wanted no ill-omened incidents to mar the day. All the great nobility played their part. The problem was to find a co-operative ecclesiastic among the Marian episcopate. It was, therefore, Cecil himself, as an officer of State, who at the right moment stepped forward to hand a copy of the coronation oath to the bishops. Cecil had found a place for himself in the ritual of the making of the Queen.[14]

A week after the coronation Elizabeth's first Parliament met.[15] It was a significant session, for the Queen was expected to make known her plans for a religious settlement. It was an issue which meant much to Cecil. He had been busy discussing the restoration of Protestantism with his friends. It had been suggested just before Christmas that a committee should be set up to consider a revision of the Prayer Book. His dilemma was that men like his father-in-law, Sir Anthony Cooke, who had now returned from exile, were concerned above all with the doctrine for which they had suffered. They wanted an unequivocal declaration of protestant faith. But the Queen, at this stage, wanted only the essential minimum of ecclesiastical change: the royal supremacy. Those with political sense realised how difficult the situation was. The bold adoption of protestant doctrine might well wreck the peace negotiations with France, offend Spanish susceptibilities and prepare the way for a civil war of religion in England. Men with experience of affairs like Armagil Waad and Nicholas Throckmorton urged caution.

F

There is little doubt that Cecil was in favour of doctrinal change. The problem was the pace at which the reform should be made. In the Parliament Cecil sat for Lincolnshire.[16] As a Knight of the Shire and the Queen's Secretary, Cecil was in a position to play a leading part in the Commons. But it was a hard task for those whom the Queen expected to lead the House to induce the Commons to accept as sufficient the Supremacy Bill which was put before it. The Bill secured the royal supremacy but did nothing to satisfy demands for liturgical and doctrinal change beyond allowing communion in both kinds. The influential protestant minority in the Commons, led by Sir Anthony Cooke and Sir Francis Knollys, did all they could to introduce amendments and supplementary Bills on doctrine. In the Lords the Marian bishops voted against the Bill.

During the debate on that important Bill, Cecil was subjected to the pressure of his old friends and his father-in-law for doctrinal amendment. His duty to the Queen was to support the Bill as it stood. From the reports of the Spanish ambassador it seems that Cecil was true, as usual, to his duty as an obedient minister. At a crucial moment, when the Bill was about to be passed in the Commons, Cecil upset the last efforts to oppose it. With the skill of an experienced parliamentarian he created a wrangle which diverted the House and made the opportunity to pass the Bill. It looks as if even Knollys, the Queen's puritan cousin, who had been one of the ringleaders in the efforts to force doctrinal change was somehow persuaded to join Cecil in the last heave to secure the passage of the Bill.[17] Through Cecil, Elizabeth had used Parliament for her own purposes.

If Cecil had done as the Queen wished in Parliament and had helped to secure acceptance of the Supremacy Bill, it did not mean that he had abandoned his protestant friends or aims. But, as the Queen's Secretary, Cecil was hardly in a position to join in trying to force the Queen's hand in her first Parliament. The Commons was too public a stage for such action on Cecil's part. But outside Parliament Cecil was actively engaged in the campaign to establish Protestantism.

Cecil, with his experience of the theological debates of Edward

VI's reign and his knowledge of Cranmer's work, was both able and willing to talk with the laymen and clerics who 'were indeed urgent from the very first that a general reformation should take place'. He was connected with most of the notables of the reforming party in one way or another. Knollys and Bedford were fellow councillors. Sir Thomas Smith was an old friend. The Marquess of Northampton, William Parr, had commissioned him to write the preface to his sister's devotional work. Bacon and Cooke were his relatives. He knew most of the divines either through their connection with Cranmer or Cambridge. Of the former exiles, Cox, Scory and Jewel had all been close to Cranmer; Horne, Pilkington and Sandys were all St John's men; Aylmer was a friend of Ascham; Whitehead and Grindal had taken part in the debate on the Mass over which Cecil had presided in 1551. Among those divines who had not been in exile, Parker, Guest, May and Bill had all been well known in Cambridge.[18]

It was significant that those reformers with whom Cecil worked were those who were influenced primarily by Cranmer. They were the moderate men. Even the former exiles were mostly men who had stood by Cox at Frankfurt and had upheld the Prayer Book of 1552. Cecil could understand and sympathise with a protestantism which grew from English roots. He could accept the Second Prayer Book and the Forty-two Articles. Like the Queen, he did not wish to have any dealings with the reformers who insisted upon the full Calvinist discipline of Geneva. The clerics whom he trusted most were those who had remained in England and who were not tainted with continental extremism. His own conception of reform was the restoration of what had been achieved under Edward VI.

With the more moderate reformers Cecil planned, while the last stages of the debate on the Supremacy Bill were proceeding, the next step in the campaign to re-establish Protestantism in England. The scheme, in which Cecil had a hand, was to stage a public disputation in English between nine Catholics and nine Protestants upon three issues.[19] The points for debate were the use of vernacular in church services, the right of provincial churches to their own liturgies and the absence of biblical justification for a sacrificial interpretation of the Mass. Cox, Whitehead, Sandys, Grindal, Horne, Aylmer, Jewel, Scory and Guest were named as the protestant champions. The disputation was approved about 20 March and held under the chairmanship of Nicholas Bacon before the Lords and the Privy Council on 31 April. The debate was a fiasco, but the result seemed to the Protestants to fulfil their intention of discrediting the Catholics.

Meanwhile the situation had developed in favour of the reformers. Shortly after the plan for the disputation had been approved, the Queen changed her mind about dissolving Parliament. She did not accept the Supremacy Bill which was ready for the royal assent on 22 March. Instead she prorogued Parliament for an Easter recess. Cecil and his friends were now reaping the results of his hard work in foreign diplomacy.[20] A treaty with France had been concluded on 19 March. It was no great triumph in itself. Calais had not been restored. But neither the Queen nor Cecil had ever had any real hope that it would be. A face-saving clause preserved the English claim to Calais on precarious terms. At this juncture the significance of the peace was that it removed one of Elizabeth's objections to the open adoption of Protestantism. The Queen no longer feared the effect on negotiations with France and Spain of being a heretic.

It had also become clear that the passage of the Supremacy Bill was a Pyrrhic victory. Since the Marian bishops refused to accept the royal supremacy, Elizabeth found herself without an episcopate to run the Church. The Easter recess was required in order to recruit bishops from among the Protestants. The Queen knew the views of the reformers. Cecil had seen to it that Cox, Whitehead, Parker and others had preached before her.[21] The price of their support would be some concession to their demand for doctrinal change, which could be made law in the next session of Parliament. A bargain between the Queen and the reformers had to be struck.

Cecil knew that, while the Queen was reluctant to go beyond the Prayer Book of 1549, the reformers regarded the Prayer Book of 1552 as the starting point for revision. The hope of compromise lay between the First and Second Prayer Books of Edward VI: closer to the Second than to the First Book. In order to confine the discussion to these limits it was necessary to make the Prayer Book of 1549 the basis of amendment. Like every competent Secretary, Cecil sought to dictate the scope of negotiations by a wise choice of agenda. He put the Prayer Book of 1549 to the reformers for their comments. Guest informed him of their views.[22] The 'new service' which resulted could now be met by an advance towards the Prayer Book of 1552. Cecil had judged the power of the Queen and the reformers, and he had engineered a resolution of forces which brought the point of equilibrium inside the Cranmer tradition between the Books of 1549 and 1552.

The part which Cecil played in securing a compromise brought down on him the scorn of his old friend, the Duchess of Suffolk, newly returned from exile and full of zeal.[23] Later in his own life he was to wonder about the 'mingle-mangle' he had helped to construct.[24] But in 1559 it required Cecil's sense of practical politics to prevent an administrative breakdown of the Church or, what was worse, a drift towards fanaticism and civil war over religion. Cecil had rallied enough support for his compromise to isolate the fire-eaters on either wing and to provide a respectable episcopate. The Prayer Book described in the Uniformity Bill, which went before Parliament after the Easter recess, was the Book of 1552 with revisions looking back to the Book of 1549, not forward in the manner of the Frankfurt amendments urged upon the Queen by the moderate Marian exiles.

The ground had been well prepared. The Uniformity Bill was passed without difficulty in the sitting after Easter. But even now an attempt was made to persuade the Queen to refuse her assent. De Feria was aiding and abetting a few die-hards at Court to influence the Queen. Cecil was 'earnest with the Book'.[25] While de Feria was trying to discredit him, Cecil counter-attacked by encouraging the production and playing in London of comedies guying Philip of Spain.[26] Skilled as he was in the intrigues of the Court, he did not neglect the importance of the popular feeling in the surrounding city. The Uniformity Bill received the royal assent.

The Act of Supremacy and the Act of Uniformity provided a base from which to deal with religious and ecclesiastical problems.

As a lawyer Cecil knew that there was still plenty of scope for change in the interpretation of the Acts. The Queen pleased the conservatives when she approved a rubric in the newly authorised Prayer Book which preserved the traditional ornaments and vestments. Cecil was not averse to the rubric but he was able to help soothe the more advanced reformers in his draft of the Injunctions.[27] These instructions on ecclesiastical practice and conduct were more in keeping with protestant expectations. The rubric and the Injunctions were symptoms of the tensions in the Church, which were to grow when it became clear that the settlement of 1559 was not a first instalment of reform but the Queen's final concession.

With the Church settlement of 1559 the insular Protestantism, which Cecil had learned in Cambridge and from Cranmer, was established. He had not been fired by personal experience of exile and of the reformed churches on the Continent. He had an exclusively English experience of reform. He thought of himself as a member of a minority in seeking to spread the faith of the gospel. The Reformation appeared to him as a revolution from above, led by the intellectuals at Court and dependent on the Prince. The results of the bargain of 1559 were consonant with Cecil's experience and beliefs. He was proud to boast to the Spanish ambassador that he had brought about the Church settlement in England.

In all these dealings Cecil had appreciated the force of political convenience. The very nature of the settlement was the fortuitous product of contrary forces rather than the fulfilment of a pre-conceived plan. But it would be wrong to conclude that political convenience was all that concerned Cecil. The settlement met his religious and conscientious requirements. He was neither the extreme heretic whom the Catholics saw nor the lukewarm supporter whom the zealous reformers chided. He was not the purely secular statesman depicted by later historians. He stood on that religious *via media* which led through the English sixteenth century from Erasmus to Hooker.[28]

That Cecil accepted the Church which had eventuated in 1559 may be seen from the recommendation which he made to

Elizabeth upon the appointment of the Archbishop of Canterbury. Cecil supported Matthew Parker, the man most likely to preserve the compromise.[29] Parker's experience of Cambridge Protestantism was deeper than Cecil's. He had seen Bilney burn. He had been in the Boleyn household. But he had not been in exile. In helping to persuade Elizabeth to make the reluctant Parker her first Archbishop of Canterbury, Cecil did much to ensure that the moderate insular Protestantism with which he had grown up would survive.

At home the Elizabethan Church looked like a *via media* between the extremes of Rome and Geneva, but abroad England was reckoned to be in the protestant camp. Catholics were not to be persuaded either by Elizabeth or by Parker that the Church of England differed but little from the Church of Rome in its beliefs. Cecil's religious convictions were not wholly shaped by considerations of foreign policy any more than they were wholly moulded by domestic political persuasions. While he was worried by the possible consequences of Protestantism upon England's relations with the continental Kings, he worked for the faith of the gospel and for the rejection of the Pope. The peace with France was welcome, but it had done little to remove the threat of French ambitions. Ahead lay the prospect of difficult diplomacy.

In the spring of 1559 three of the important items on Cecil's list of measures had been achieved. Elizabeth had been crowned. Peace with France had been concluded. The Church settlement had been made without disturbance to the government of the realm. Cecil was also involved in trying to secure the financial foundations of the throne. In Parliament he had put before the House the problem of the Queen's foreign debts.[30] In February he had joined a commission to look into ways and means of restoring the debased coinage. He was discussing methods of currency reform with Paget and Parry.[31] Cecil was proving his worth. The essentials were being tackled. Strong in the trust of the Queen, her Secretary was making his views felt over a wider range of affairs and with greater effect than ever before in his career.

CHAPTER VII

Laying Foundations

DURING all the preoccupations of the first months of the new reign, Cecil had kept his eye upon Scotland. His first-hand knowledge of the Border and of Scotland, which he gained under Somerset, had been widened by his study of Border problems under Northumberland, whose personal interests had been in the North.[1] Cecil's earlier experience of the importance of Scottish affairs was to prove valuable. The turn of events was to make Scotland the focus of all the major themes of European politics. The rivalry of Hapsburg and Valois, the strife of Catholic and Protestant, the dynastic intrigues which determined the succession to the throne came to centre upon the only foreign country which had a land frontier with England. From the earliest days of Elizabeth's reign Cecil had been concerned to strengthen the Border.

It was clear that trouble was brewing in Scotland. Mary Queen of Scots was married to the Dauphin, Francis, and had a claim to the English throne. The dynastic alliance of France and Scotland might well be used to enforce the catholic Mary's right to succeed to the English Crown. French influence in Scotland was strong. Mary Guise, the Regent, supported by the most influential and militantly catholic family in France, ruled Scotland with the aid of French troops. The only threat to the catholic French hegemony in Scotland came from the rebellious nobility. They looked to England for support. In January and February 1559 they sounded Sir Henry Percy on the attitude of the English. The experienced Scottish statesman Maitland wanted to arrange a meeting with Cecil. It was too early for Cecil to take the initiative. The peace with France and Scotland was not signed until 19 March and not until 31 May was the Treaty of Upsettlington concluded, which dealt with all the points not covered by the Treaty of Cateau-Cambrésis.

During March and April, Cecil's policy began to take shape.

Maitland came to see him.[2] Knox, the Calvinist prophet from Geneva, wrote to Cecil as to a sinner and revealed to him God's will.[3] Unwelcome in England, Knox returned to Scotland in May. His zeal fired the Lords of Congregation into positive rebellion. By mid-June Cecil was informed that the Scottish nobility were ready to set forth God's word. They were planning to draw Elizabeth into their net by proposing her marriage to the Earl of Arran. Then Kirkcaldy assured Cecil that the Scottish nobles could deal with the Regent, Mary Guise, unless she called in reinforcements from France. He went on to ask Cecil whether the English would intervene if a French army landed in Scotland.[4] Then Knox demanded an interview with Cecil.[5] The Scots were making the pace.

The torrent of persuasion from Scotland and from men on the Border for an open commitment did not sweep Cecil off his feet. A secret reply through Sir Henry Percy, which expressed sympathy and hinted readiness to give aid, was all the answer that Cecil gave.[6] He would only see Knox if he came in secrecy. But behind this diplomatic reticence Cecil was well aware that the fire in Scotland must be kindled 'for if it be quenched the opportunity will not come again in our life time.' The persuasive voice of Throckmorton, ambassador in France, urged him to seize the chance of stifling French influence in Scotland.[7] His despatches hinted that, if the French were successful in Scotland, their next target would be the English throne.

The favourable opportunity to break the French hold in Scotland was being wasted because Cecil would not move until he had some clear idea of the plans of the Scottish lords, who, for their part, were unwilling to say how far they would go until they knew the extent of English support. Although Cecil saw the importance of action, he was countering vagueness with vagueness. The Scottish lords and Knox pleaded again for a plain answer. No progress was being made. Cecil in his caution was overtaken by events.

The comparatively simple situation, in which the Lords of Congregation and the Regent were the two counters in the game, suddenly became more complex. In July Henry II was killed in an accident at a tourney and Francis II with his wife, Mary Queen of Scots, ascended the French throne. Philip II negotiated a marriage with the French royal family. These events meant more immediate French interest in Scotland and in the English succession at a time when the restraint of Spanish suspicion had been removed. Cecil, who had been too cautious to act in the Scottish frying-pan, found himself in the fire of Guise and Valois ambitions. The international repercussions of any move in Scotland were now apparent.

Elizabeth came to the rescue. While the Earl of Arran on his return from the Continent was hiding in Cecil's house in Cannon Row[8] and the Scottish lords were hoping that the Earl might marry Elizabeth, the English Queen conducted a lively courtship with the Archduke Charles. The Queen's sudden quickening of interest in a Hapsburg Archduke was intended to neutralise the Franco-Spanish dynastic alliance. Cecil favoured the match.[9] What was a temporary expedient to Elizabeth looked to her Secretary like a permanent solution of the problem of exercising influence indirectly but effectively on the Hapsburgs.

Now clearly enmeshed with England's continental relationships, the Scottish problem could no longer be isolated. Cecil, who was bearing the burden of dealing with Scotland almost on his own, sought action at last. On the day on which Elizabeth, in a letter drafted by Cecil,[10] denied to the Regent any knowledge of English dealings with the Scottish rebels, money for the rebels was sent North. Sir Ralph Sadler, an old friend of Cecil, was put in charge of secret liaison with the Scots on the Border. Confident of his policy, Cecil drew up a substantial memorandum to impress the Queen.[11] In justifying intervention in Scotland Cecil dismissed the objection that England was supporting rebels, by asserting the historic English overlordship of Scotland. The 'right of this superiority' obliged the English Crown 'to defend the liberties, the laws, the baronage and people of Scotland from oppression' and bound it 'in honour and conscience to defend and protect the realm of Scotland against the French'. He charged this legal right and duty with emotion by building up a picture of French aggression and treachery. He pointed out that France, having made settlements with her neighbours, was free to act in Scotland

and that, having overcome the weak opposition of the Scots, would attempt to control England.

His plan to defeat French designs was to finance the Scots so that they could keep an army in the field. To garrison the Border and passively wait for the French to attack would cost far more than to maintain an active Scottish army. It would be difficult to raise an army either of foreign mercenaries or of English troops. If a large French army did land in Scotland, then would be the time 'to stir all good English bloods'. In the meantime, the best solution was to subsidise the Scots. Cecil's plan had the merit of being simple and of sounding economical. Its deliberate rejection of active armed intervention by the English made it attractive to the Queen.

Satisfied that the thin end of the wedge of English aid to Scotland had been driven across the Border, Cecil tried to take a few days away from Court in September. He went off to Stamford, where he could see how his rebuilding of his mother's house was progressing.[12] It had been a hard summer of work. He had not been well in August. Throckmorton urged him to watch his health and wrote 'your long sitting and writing do you no great pleasure in that behalf.'[13] Cecil needed a rest but he arranged to have his trusted Sadler's letters directed to him so that he could keep himself informed on affairs in Scotland. After a brief respite he was back at Court.

During the autumn the situation in Scotland did not improve. The French were making military preparations. Cecil was beginning to realise that money would not be enough to help the Scots. Without artillery the Scots could not effectively besiege Leith. 'Some not liking the progress of religion; some not so angry with French good fortune as I am', he noted, were opposing his policy.[14] There was little enthusiasm for a policy which might lead to the establishment in Scotland of the strict Calvinism advocated by the much distrusted Knox. Cecil's task was to ensure that enmity to France was stronger than antipathy to Genevan discipline in religion. It was understandable that Knox was less favourably regarded by many than Mary Queen of Scots. But Cecil was able to keep the money flowing northwards.[15]

In November a defeat of the Scottish lords jolted Elizabeth into taking stronger measures. Munitions were to be supplied to the rebels. Norfolk was to take charge of the forces on the Border and ships were fitted out. The Queen had reluctantly been drawn into taking military measures. They were precautionary moves. Maitland came to negotiate in secrecy. The problem of Scotland had become urgent and important. It was aired before the whole Council.

While the majority of councillors were prepared to take defensive precautions on the Border and even provide clandestine aid to the rebels, there was a general unwillingness to face up to the possibility of open war with France and undisguised support of the Scots. Cecil did what he could to save appearances. On his advice[16] the Lords of Congregation posed as the loyal subjects of their Queen Mary, anxious only to protect her from French oppression. In December came news of the sailing of French reinforcements for Scotland and of a projected attack upon Eyemouth a few miles north of Berwick. William Winter, with a force of fourteen ships, was sent to intercept French aid, but he was to act on his own initiative and admit no official orders. On the brink of open war the Queen and the Council hesitated.

Opposed by his own brother-in-law Nicholas Bacon, by his friends Parry, Petre, Wotton, Mason, and by old Winchester and Arundel, Cecil finally carried the Council and persuaded it to advise the Queen that it was 'best to avenge there great wrongs', inflicted by France, 'now in time while a small power and treasure may do it'. The necessary diplomatic, military and financial measures were outlined. Cecil was advocating a quick preventive campaign.[17] Having won the support of Council, Cecil was now faced with a rejection of his recommendations by the Queen. In the last days of December, Cecil wrote 'with a sorrowful heart and watery eyes' to the Queen. So sure of his policy was he that he asked to be relieved of any further responsibility for Scottish affairs. 'I cannot with my conscience give any contrary advice' he wrote. Tactfully and humbly he made it clear that he was still ready 'to serve Your Majesty in anything.'[18]

Cecil had not yet learned to trust the Queen's judgement. He was not prepared to modify his recommendations. Elizabeth managed the resolute Cecil. The solution was that, provided nothing was done as an open act of war, Cecil could carry on with all the measures he thought fit. The Queen was ready to bluff a little longer in the hope that the French would also draw back from open hostilities. Philip of Spain might see that it was not in his interests to allow France to dominate Scotland and menace England. Cecil was back in the game. In the spring his friend Throckmorton, in his despatches, was underlining French weakness and urging belligerence. Meanwhile the Queen had gone so far as to make it known that if a clash were to be avoided French troops must be withdrawn from Scotland. But diplomatic exchanges with France dragged on to no purpose.

When at last Elizabeth was convinced that time was not on her side she agreed to war. On 22 March 1560 orders went to Norfolk to invade, 'and with the aid of the Scots to expel such forces of Frenchmen as are there'. Cecil took the precaution of sending a long justification of the Council's advice on armed intervention to Elizabeth.[19] He wanted no royal rejection this time. As a gesture to the Queen's reluctance to open war a proclamation was issued in English, French and Italian which maintained that Elizabeth was at peace with France and Scotland and that her quarrel was only with the 'insolent claims and titles' of the House of Guise.[20] The proclamation was not all humbug: it served to stir up the faction strife in France.

Following the English invasion of Scotland the diplomatic activity increased. Philip's envoys were urging peace, suggesting Spanish intervention to end the civil war in Scotland and wavering over their support for France. Cecil was deep in the negotiations with them. He tried to divide his Spanish opponents by playing off the economic interests of Antwerp, with which the Spanish representative from the Lowlands was concerned, against the dynastic interests of the Hapsburgs, which were de Quadra's province.[21] Elizabeth was meanwhile sounding the Regent on peace terms. But the English army was being built up in Scotland. In early May the first important objective, Leith, was attacked. The result was a resounding defeat for the English.

'God trieth us with many difficulties', wrote Cecil. It was not only the mysterious ways of Providence which depressed him. The Queen vented her disappointment over the defeat upon Cecil. 'I have had such torment herein with the Queen's Majesty' he confided to Throckmorton.[22] In an effort to get a decision the army was strengthened and at the same time an agreement was reached with the French King over starting peace negotiations. Cecil's set-back resulted from the fortune of war and the Queen's disappointment. He was soon to bring his policy to a triumphant conclusion.

On 21 May the two chief French negotiators, Randan and the Bishop of Valence, arrived at Elizabeth's Court. The Queen had already appointed her commission, of which Cecil and Wotton were the principal and most experienced members.[23] Newcastle upon Tyne was the agreed rendezvous for all parties to the peace talks. This location had the advantage of obviating interference by the Queen but it removed Cecil from his place near the Queen where he could use his persuasion and prepare Elizabeth for the final terms. He was pessimistic. 'What will follow of my going towards Scotland, I know not, but I fear the success, *quia* the Queen's Majesty is so evil disposed to the matter; which troubleth us all,' he commented.[24] Meanwhile he settled down to analyse the situation and deduce what were the essential terms for English interests in any treaty.

'Rubbing on betwixt health and sickness' and doubtful of loyal support at Court, Cecil set out on 30 May for the week of arduous riding through rain and dust to Newcastle. 'I content myself with service' he wrote. His venture required a strong sense of public duty. The instructions which he carried from the Council left nearly every point to his and Wotton's discretion. He needed self-confidence to face such responsibility. 'If I may do good, I shall be glad:' he wrote, 'but this is so difficult, as I rather despair.' When, after the diplomats had moved to Edinburgh, negotiations began, there were days of frustration and the strain of hard bargaining. 'We can get nothing but with racking and straining; and we have it inwards; they always will steal it away in penning and writing,' was what he and Wotton reported to the Council.[25]

The situation however developed in Cecil's favour. The Regent, Mary Guise died. Philip of Spain suffered a defeat at Tripoli. France herself was having domestic troubles. Cecil knew how to exploit the difficulties of his enemies. He won the confidence of the suspicious Scots. With considerable diplomatic artistry he shaped a treaty. On 6 July 1560 Cecil and Wotton were able to write to the Queen, 'we have on all parts signed, sealed and delivered our treaties, that is to say, betwixt us and the French, and betwixt the French and the Scots; so as we be gone as far as writing can conduct us to peace.'[26]

The Treaty of Edinburgh was a tribute to Cecil's sense of what was practical in politics. He had won considerable advantages from an indecisive campaign. French troops were withdrawn and key fortresses demolished. A government of native Scots was established. Francis and Mary were to abandon the style and arms of England and Ireland. England and France were pledged to non-intervention in Scotland. Cecil may have cherished the hope of his old master, Somerset, of forging the union of England and Scotland but he had been content to win Scotch amity rather than pursue a dream. He left the guarantee of liberty of conscience to the Scots undefined. The ideal solutions had not been allowed to wreck the practical business of peacemaking. The result appeared to Lord Robert Dudley to be 'for us a perfect peace'.[27] The powers of discretion with which Cecil had been vested had been well used.

Cecil's diplomatic achievement had prevented Scotland from becoming another 'Savoy'. A *point d'appui* for Hapsburg–Valois rivalry had been removed from England's border. The withdrawal of French troops from Scotland helped to insulate England from the immediate pressures of continental politics. If Cecil had been slow to act in taking advantage of the 'stir' in Scotland he had nevertheless been one step ahead of the Council and two steps ahead of the Queen in the development of policy. In the event, the timing dictated by the Queen had been effective. But the direction of policy had been set under Cecil's guiding hand. The terms of the Treaty of Edinburgh had been Cecil's own triumph and upon it were to rest whatever hopes there were that England might pursue an independent foreign policy.

Whatever satisfaction Cecil felt was soon dispelled by the Queen's belated demand for the restoration of Calais and a massive indemnity. Whether the Queen had misjudged the situation or had been persuaded by Cecil's enemies to upset the negotiations cannot be known. Cecil was deeply depressed and he returned after an absence of sixty-three days to London to count the cost to his own pocket.[28] His only consolation was that the Queen's wild proposals had come too late to wreck his treaty. But he was to be disappointed by Elizabeth's failure to develop the goodwill which the treaty had created in Scotland and by the refusal of Mary Stuart and her husband to ratify the treaty.

Cecil's more immediate concern was the Queen's behaviour towards her Master of Horse, Robert Dudley. During the nine weeks in which Cecil had been away from Court the scandal of the Queen's infatuation for Robert Dudley had grown. It appeared as if the Queen, on whom he had so often pressed the need for marriage, was ready to find ways and means of making Robert Dudley her husband. Cecil had seen Northumberland try to take the throne for his son Guildford, now it was his younger son Robert who was near the throne. It seemed that the Queen herself had lost sight of the national interest. Cecil decided to withdraw from government. 'God send her Majesty understanding what shall be her surety'.[29] He was frustrated by the unfair competition of the handsome Robert in giving political advice to the Queen. Just after the success of his first big diplomatic mission Cecil found the Queen dissatisfied and unwilling to listen to him. He began to contrive to pass the Secretaryship to the ablest man who could take his place, Nicholas Throckmorton.[30] On questions of calculated policy, he was prepared to fight it out with the Queen, but when the personal emotions of the Queen were involved he knew that he was powerless. There was no advice he could give to a sovereign who failed to treat marriage as a serious political affair.

By early September Cecil had let his friends know his feelings. On 11th of that month he decided to make one last desperate bid to shake the Queen into a realisation of the magnitude of the scandal in which she was involved. He chose to confide in the Spanish ambassador, de Quadra, and begged him to try to persuade the Queen to remember her duty to herself and her people and not to throw herself away in marriage to Dudley. De Quadra was told in forthright terms that Robert Dudley was conspiring to oust Cecil from the Secretaryship, that Lord Robert intended to marry the Queen and that the country would not tolerate the marriage. Cecil declared that he would retire, even if it meant a spell in the Tower. The Queen had no regard for foreign Princes and thought that she had no need of their support. She was deep in debt and had ruined her credit in the City. Cecil's final revelation to the ambassador was that there was a plot to kill Dudley's wife.[31]

The indiscretions of those who were in disgrace were not new to the ambassador. But such calculated disloyalty, with its suggestion of rebellion and its criticism of the Queen's character and action, was new for Cecil. What he said to the Spanish ambassador was, if disclosed, sufficient to wreck his future unless the Queen did alter her policy and decide not to marry Dudley. It must have been in the risky hope of such a change that Cecil had sought to reach the Queen indirectly through de Quadra and to shock her deliberately. If he could get through to Elizabeth's political sense, he felt confident that he would win and re-establish himself in royal favour.

Cecil was fighting for his political life. But he did not safeguard it by accommodating himself to the Queen's wishes or by currying favour with Lord Robert. He took the risk of trying to assert his own influence because he believed that it was necessary for the good of the Queen and her realm. Egoism and jealousy were no doubt there among Cecil's motives but, unlike his opponents, he could gear the unadmitted forces of his personality to a rational appreciation of political ends and find an outlet for his emotions in appeals to the Almighty for aid.

Cecil had been right in his belief that it required some deep shock to bring the Queen back to her senses. He had gambled much on his reading of the Queen's character: on the assumption that the affair with Dudley was a temporary infatuation not in keeping with her royal conception of herself. He had tried to administer the shock himself. But the blow which shattered the love dream was the death of Amy Robsart, Lord Robert's wife.

G

Within a few days of Cecil's disclosure that there was a plot to kill her, Amy Robsart was found dead at the bottom of a steep staircase with her neck broken. Elizabeth could not afford to nourish the suspicion that she was an accessory to murder or to convict herself in the eyes of her people and of Europe by marrying Robert Dudley. The death of Amy Robsart was Cecil's good fortune. It shook Dudley's hold upon Elizabeth and opened the way for Cecil's return to influence with the Queen. In guarded and ambiguous terms the shaken Dudley, 'as it were in a dream', wrote Cecil an odd little note of conciliation, 'I thank you much for being here; and the great friendship you have showed towards me, I shall not forget.'[32] In that cautious overture there was an admission that Cecil was still strong.

Amidst all the unsettling anxiety over the Queen's behaviour towards Dudley, Cecil was contributing to another solid achievement in securing the new régime. Early in September the commission on the restoration of the coinage, on which he was serving, produced a plan. The scheme was launched by a proclamation on 27 September. It was a success in that it caused a minimum of panic, removed the economic disability of a debased currency and made a handsome profit of £45,000 for the Crown. The smooth execution of the recoinage owed much to Cecil's administration. He was also a member of the commission appointed to supervise the Mint while the base money was being converted. Above all, Cecil knew the necessity of maintaining public confidence. He was responsible for a reassuring explanatory pamphlet on the need for the recoinage.[33] To have planned and carried through such an operation without serious disturbances was a considerable achievement.

For Cecil the commissions dealing with the planning and execution of the recoinage provided valuable experience. He had taken an interest in currency since the days of Northumberland and he had been the man to put the statement of the Queen's foreign debts before her first Parliament. He was a personal friend of the two most technically competent financial experts on the commission, Sir Thomas Gresham, a merchant with a flair for handling international finance, and Walter Mildmay, who was soon to be Chancellor of the Exchequer and who had been trained by the great reformer of the financial administration, the Lord Treasurer William Paulet, Marquess of Winchester. From such men Cecil learned the technicalities of high finance.[34]

It was the combination of administrative expertise in financial matters and the appreciation of finance as an important factor in statesmanship and diplomacy that was one of Cecil's strengths. Although in the Scottish campaign he had been the advocate of large expenditure, it was not because he did not understand, at this stage of his career, the limitations of royal finance. His justification of the immediate cost was on the ground that it would be more expensive to delay the necessary action. When he wrote to the Queen in the midst of his negotiations in Edinburgh, he bitterly attacked the corruption over army pay and pointed out that he would have been able to get better terms if her 'coffers were full to maintain but one year's war'. In the event of a failure in his efforts for peace, he assured Elizabeth that 'there be many ways to offend your enemy withal, without great charge'.[35] He was always aware of the limits imposed by the availability of hard cash.

That Cecil's financial sense was not lost upon the Queen was shown by the first substantial gesture of her renewed confidence in him, which she made after the autumn crisis of the affair with Dudley. He was given the Stewardship of Westminster and on 10 January 1561 was made Master of the Court of Wards and Liveries.[36] The bestowal upon Cecil of the control of the financial court which dealt with the feudal profits of the Crown was a particular mark of favour and trust. On her accession Elizabeth had given the Mastership to her old servant Thomas Parry. His death had created the vacancy which Cecil was now called upon to fill.

For Cecil the appointment was the most lucrative that he had yet acquired. It could be made to provide an income as great as that which many a gentleman drew from his lands. The granting of wardships, the control of the lands of wards, the arrangement of marriages, the appointment of the officials of the Court, the settlement of family disputes, the education of the wards constituted a complex of patronage and influence which penetrated the most influential sector of society. The dynastic interests and property rights of the nobility and gentry still made up the better half of domestic politics. Cecil's responsibility for the education of wards gave him the chance to practise those ideas about the education of the ruling class which were such a large part of the credo of a humanist. Later in his life the Mastership was to involve his dynastic ambitions and entangle his family with the most noble of his wards.

In 1561 enough of the potentialities of his newly acquired office were apparent to Cecil to give him renewed confidence in his relationships with the Queen. His thoughts of retirement were banished. He was even prepared to carry on the Secretaryship single-handed, declaring 'his ability for execution of many offices without other aid'.[37]

CHAPTER VIII

In the Political Thicket

AFTER little more than two years in the Queen's service, Cecil
had apparently strengthened his hold upon important offices. But
he had not altered his relationship with the Queen. It pleased her
to trust him. He could not command that trust. Elizabeth's will
remained beyond capture. All that Cecil could do was to give his
best advice and hope that it satisfied the Queen. If he was to keep
royal regard and all that it brought to him, Cecil had to go
cautiously and carry the Council with him. He did not stand alone
as a sole adviser. In June 1561 he had to admit, 'I am overruled in
it with the opinion of the more.'[1]

The way ahead was full of anxieties. Dudley had not ceased to
intrigue and his schemes involved an increase in Spanish influence
and a restoration of Catholicism. The Church which Cecil had
helped to establish was threatened. The Treaty of Edinburgh was
still unratified by Mary. That dangerous woman had become a
widow in December 1560, free to return to Scotland and give her
hand where she would. Elizabeth was still unmarried and the
succession problem was unsolved. While the great issues of public
life pressed upon Cecil, he had to bear the disappointment of his
ambitions for his son Thomas and the suspense of Mildred's
pregnancy.

It was not until April 1561 that Cecil was able to strike a
damaging blow at Dudley, who, by inducing the Queen to accept
a papal nuncio and to consider representation at the Council of
Trent, hoped to win Spanish and catholic support. De Quadra, the
Spanish ambassador, was helping him. It looked as if Cecil was
friendly. In March Cecil had agreed to try to persuade de Quadra
to obtain Philip's approval of the Queen's marriage to Dudley.
But he contrived to make the match dependent not only on Philip's
agreement, but also on its acceptance by Parliament. De Quadra

did not see through Cecil's subtle obstruction and allowed himself
to be led on by the Secretary's willingness to keep the negotiations
alive over English participation at the Council of Trent.[2] With
rumours of a catholic restoration growing stronger, de Quadra
was sought out by the hopeful English Catholics.

When it looked in April as if Elizabeth was ready to admit the
papal nuncio, Cecil unmasked a catholic plot. Sir Edward
Waldegrave, one of Mary's former privy councillors, was made
the scapegoat but de Quadra was implicated. Sharp protestant
reaction ruled out the admission of the nuncio. De Quadra realised
his mistake in trying to use Cecil. 'I could not negotiate through
any other', he lamented. Cecil had avoided open opposition to
Dudley on the emotional issues which made the Queen defend her
favourite, but had struck at him on the tender subject of religion.
Cecil's triumph was confirmed in May by a strong statement from
the Council rejecting the nuncio and questioning the validity of
the Council of Trent as a General Council.[3]

The satisfaction over a protestant victory was enhanced for
Cecil by the birth of a son in May. Cecil felt free to risk Thomas
abroad. Travel was indeed the only solution to Thomas' education.
At nearly twenty Thomas showed no aptitude for learned studies.
'I mean not to have him scholarly learned but civilly trained'.
Cecil wrote. He comforted himself with the thought that Thomas
would not undermine his health with hard studies. When Cecil
sent him off to France on 29 May 1561 under the tutelage of
Thomas Windebank, he had misgivings about his son's behaviour
for he gave Thomas some advice. It consisted of a programme of
daily devotions which might have taxed the strictest puritan. An
earthly father was clearly putting his responsibilities upon a
heavenly Father. Behind these injunctions lay Cecil's frustration in
his relations with Thomas.[4] Yet Cecil could hardly have anticipated
the constant annoyance and grief which his son was to cause him
until the prodigal's return in January 1563.

The chronicle of Thomas' escapades and extravagances in his
own and his tutor's letters made bitter reading for Cecil. The
death of his lately born infant son after a few months of life added
to the misery which he felt over the conduct of his heir. In his

grief he wrote that he would rather have lost Thomas by an honourable death than to be troubled by him in such ways.[5] His harsh words were a measure of the despair of his outraged love and pride. While Cecil contended with his private sorrows he had to grapple with the tasks of public life.

When Thomas set out in the early summer of 1561, the statesman had much to absorb him. The problem created by Scotland and its Queen still nagged. The widowed Mary Queen of Scots might remarry or return to Scotland. Her efforts to marry Don Carlos, the idiot son of Philip II, had mercifully failed, largely through French opposition. Cecil's chief worry was that her return to Scotland would upset the protestant settlement there. In March 1561, after much non-committal diplomacy over the projected marriage of the Earl of Arran to Elizabeth and over the possible courses open to Mary, he formulated his policy.

In the Queen's name Cecil let the Scots know that the amity between 'England and Scotland is grounded upon Unity and consent in Christian Religion'. He supported this declaration by painting a picture of strong backing on the Continent for Elizabeth and the protestant faith. He urged the Scots, while they were free from French influence, to accept the English alliance and to persuade 'their sovereign either to marry at home in her own country or else not to marry without some great surety of them which ought to succeed'. Cecil set out a programme based on a safe succession and the protestant religion for the pro-English party which feared foreign rule and Catholicism.[6]

If Cecil had hoped that the conditions for an English alliance would make it difficult for Mary to return to Scotland, he was to be disappointed. In April he learnt that Mary was bent on return to Scotland. His calculated politics were of little avail against Mary's intuitive sense of how to get her own way. In July Mary requested a safe conduct. Its refusal by Elizabeth was resented in Scotland and threw Cecil on to the defensive.

Fortunately for Cecil, it was at this difficult juncture that Elizabeth chose to do him the honour of dining with him in the house which he was building in the Strand.[7] It was a mark of favour which reassured Cecil on the eve of awkward dealings with

Mary. He needed the royal reassurance, for Dudley and de Quadra were still influential and since their defeat over the admission of the nuncio had become less friendly.

Soon after the Queen's visit, Cecil found himself drafting a reply to the soft answer with which Mary had met the wrath of Elizabeth's refusal of a safe conduct. Mary, anticipating that the objection to her return would not be sustained, and disregarding inspired rumours that the English would intercept her sea voyage, had set out. She landed at Leith on 19 August. Maintaining the initiative, Mary conciliated most of her influential subjects, except John Knox, who claimed to be able to recognise craft in a woman when he saw it. Towards the English she was stubborn and refused to ratify the Treaty of Edinburgh because it excluded her succession to the English throne. In September Elizabeth declared that she would name no successor.

Cecil found no joy in the impasse between the rival Queens. He could offer no constructive policy. Maitland, the Scottish Secretary, could elicit nothing from him but 'brief dark sentences'.[8] By November Cecil found flatterers advising the Queen. De Quadra was still badgering Elizabeth to send a representative to Trent. Throckmorton urged Cecil to negotiate with de Quadra and use the opportunities for mischief. But de Quadra had been bitten once. By December Cecil had sunk into further gloom. He wondered if he had any credit with the Queen. Complaining of the cost of office, he lamented that he had been forced to sell his first office, Keeper of the Writs in the Common Pleas, and £150 worth of land. 'I do only keep on a course for show, but inwardly I meddle not, leaving things to run in a course as a clock is left when the barrel is wound up,' he wrote.[9] The death of his infant son and the waywardness of Thomas were, perhaps, paralysing his will. To add to his woes the succession problem had become more threatening. The secret of Lady Catherine Grey's marriage to the Earl of Hertford was out. Lady Mary Lennox was proposing her lanky son Lord Darnley as a bridegroom for Mary Queen of Scots. It was for Cecil a winter of discontent.

As 1562 drew on Cecil slowly recovered his relish for affairs. Gradually he succumbed to Maitland's pressure for a meeting

between Elizabeth and Mary. The ratification of the Treaty of
Edinburgh and the confirmation of a protestant settlement in
Scotland were the objectives which persuaded him of the value of
the royal meeting when he came to weigh the situation in the
summer. But in July, after Cecil had drawn up a safe conduct for
the Queen of Scots, Elizabeth decided to postpone the conference
with Mary.[10] Affairs in France had made an understanding with
Mary less urgent.

The threat of civil war in France lessened the likelihood of a
resurgence of French influence in Scotland. As early as 1560 Cecil
had seen the advantages to be gained by the religious divisions in
France. Then he had written, 'Profitable it is for the time to divert
the enemy by procuring him business at home.'[11] Cecil had kept
himself informed about the developing conflict between the rival
houses of Guise and Navarre and the growing bitterness between
Huguenot and Catholic. His policy had been the negative one of
weakening the enemy. But Cecil was developing a constructive
approach. His hope was that a protestant France would provide
England with a continental ally.

If progress was to be made with his plans on the Continent, it
was necessary for Cecil to break the pro-Spanish influence of de
Quadra and Dudley at home. He bribed de Quadra's secretary to
reveal his master's despatches.[12] Their contents shocked Elizabeth
and disillusioned Dudley. At one blow he had discredited de
Quadra and turned attention to France. Cecil exulted in his
personal triumph over the outraged Spanish ambassador. He had
won a duel of wits but his real achievement was on the level of
diplomacy. When in April 1562 civil war broke out in France,
Cecil was able to interest Elizabeth and Dudley in fishing in these
troubled waters.

Elizabeth's envoy, Sir Henry Sidney, was sent to France on
28 April. Cecil had drafted his instructions.[13] The intention was to
offer English mediation, to threaten participation in the event of
any foreign intervention and to stake a claim to any rewards which
might be wrung from French weakness. It was a bid to take a hand
in the internal affairs of France and a warning to Spain not to
intervene on behalf of the Guise. Sidney's mission was ineffective.

But Cecil seized upon the hope put forward by Throckmorton that the Huguenots might be ready to admit English garrisons to Calais, Le Havre and Dieppe. In June Cecil had his agents in these vital ports but their letters were discouraging.[14] As yet there was no opening. By July Cecil was considering the subsidising of German mercenaries to aid the Huguenots.[15]

When in the middle of that same month it was clear that there was little hope of peace in France, Elizabeth decided to make naval and military preparations to intervene in France should it become necessary. Cecil appraised the situation. He foresaw that a collapse of the Huguenots would put the Guise in power and that they would invite Philip II to crush the house of Navarre, to aid their kinswoman, Mary Queen of Scots, in taking the English throne and to induce her to seal a dynastic alliance with Spain by ceding Ireland to Philip. He expected the Council of Trent to condemn all heretic princes and urge invasion of their lands by the catholic powers. He predicted a catholic revolt in England to aid foreign attack. None of these dire consequences of a papist victory in France could be averted by appeasing the 'Guisans'. This gloomy vision of the future convinced Cecil of the need to be ready for war in France and of the dangers of failing to support the Huguenots.[16]

The summer brought no decisive action. Cecil's dark anticipations of a Guise victory were not fulfilled. As preparations proceeded Cecil became more and more aware of the financial and administrative burdens which military measures would involve. Dudley, setting the pace, had become the champion of armed intervention. Cecil was content to work at the administrative level and leave to others the responsibility for policy at this dangerous juncture.[17] His part was to ensure that the military and financial arrangements were sound. Being in a position to count the cost, Cecil had no desire to be regarded as one of the chief backers of operations in France. He had spoken before of intervention in France as a 'bottomless pit of expense'.[18]

Yet, when the time came, Cecil accepted the Queen's decision 'to preserve the miserable state of her poor neighbours in Normandy with the buckler of her defence'. Concerning the sending of troops to Le Havre and Dieppe, Cecil noted, 'herein both justice and policy shall maintain our actions; for as for Calais, by means the French have broken the treaty with us, we may be bold presently to demand it, and if thereof arguments shall arise I think the Queens Majesty need not be ashamed to utter her right to Newhaven as parcel of the Duchy of Normandy.' His legal conscience was further soothed by the reflection that 'nothing is meant here on our part to make any invasion but to enter quietly into these places, which by law of arms we may considering we take none of them by force.'[19] Cecil could only approve of a just war.

Early in October when the treaty with Condé, the Huguenot leader, had just been concluded and all attention was fixed on France, the Queen fell ill. Panic at the prospect of the Queen's death from smallpox jolted domestic politics to the fore. Cecil was in Council arguing about the succession. But conflict over the claims of Lady Catherine Grey, the Earl of Huntingdon and Mary Queen of Scots was not resolved before the Queen's rapid recovery. Elizabeth's reaction to the shock of illness was to beg the Council to name Dudley Lord Protector of England. When her plea was rejected, she brought Dudley into the Council on 20 October.[20]

Cecil, who had seen the initiative in military policy pass to Dudley, whose brother Ambrose commanded the expeditionary force, was prepared for the moment when Dudley would enter the Council. When that moment came, Cecil restored the balance of faction. At the same time as Dudley was sworn as a privy councillor so was Thomas Howard, Duke of Norfolk. The Duke's appointment was a triumph for Cecil, who had recommended him.[21] Opposition to Dudley's pretensions to marry the Queen had first brought Norfolk, Sussex and Cecil into alliance. The loose-knit factions of Elizabeth's Court were taking shape. Cecil, the bureaucrat, was connected with the circle of nobles who opposed Dudley, the royal favourite.

Amidst all the work of diplomacy, occasioned by the war, Cecil found the opportunity to destroy his old opponent de Quadra and neutralise the effect of Spanish protests to the venture in France.

De Quadra became involved in a city affray and was accused of harbouring a murderer. Cecil went further and accused him of protecting traitors and causing disaffection amongst Catholics. His campaign of vilification was successful.[22] In January 1563 Elizabeth asked Philip either to stop de Quadra from plotting or to recall him. The long personal and political struggle between Cecil and de Quadra had at last been won by Cecil.

During the autumn of 1562 Cecil was busy organising the supply of troops to France. He pieced together the reports on shipping, recruitment and military stores to provide a picture of the requirements for the operations in terms of transport, men, materials and money. While he could exercise some control over the logistics of war, he found it less easy to dictate the diplomacy and fortunes of the campaign. The English forces had to be withdrawn from Rouen and Dieppe. Cecil was ill when on 15 November the Council debated whether to try to hold Le Havre and, after much wrangling, decided to stand fast in that port.

'We are fully bent to keep Newhaven, by God's grace, against all France', wrote Cecil expressing the desperate determination of the Council to save something out of the French venture. He wavered between the optimism of hoping to see Calais surrendered for Le Havre and the pessimism of wondering whether the war ought to be continued. In December, when the protestant leader, Condé, was captured at Dreux, it seemed to Cecil that 'except the Almighty God shew his arm and power this web is undone and new to begin'. When Coligny rallied the Huguenots, Cecil took new heart and was all dedication to the cause of true religion. Such was his mood for Coligny, the foreigner; but to Sir Thomas Smith, the new ambassador in France, he mingled his spiritual joy with harsh political calculation. 'Let them understand,' he wrote of the French, 'that if accord and peace will not grow by treaty and reasonable speech which hitherto the Queen's Majesty hath used, her Majesty must and will seek her own by further means, that shall more miscontent them than anything yet enterprised.'[23]

Even as things seemed to be taking a turn for the better, the long dreaded agreement between the Huguenots and the Dowager

Queen, Catherine de Medici, took place. Upon receipt of this news in March 1563 Cecil acknowledged, 'I know the worst which is by stout and stiff dealing to make our own bargain.'[24] Somehow the liability of the garrison in Le Havre had to be turned into an asset.

Meanwhile the cost of war had necessitated the assembly in January 1563 of a Parliament which was to last until 10 April. Cecil sat as a knight for Northamptonshire. He knew that the purpose of the Parliament was for taxation but he knew that, after the shock of the Queen's illness, the question of the succession would be raised. 'I think somewhat will be attempted to ascertain the realm of a successor to this crown but I fear the unwillingness of her Majesty to have such a person known will stay the matter', was Cecil's justified prediction. On the committee which petitioned the Queen about the succession, he had a hand in abortive schemes to give Parliament the right to name the next monarch on the Queen's death and to limit the choice of successor to certain families. Cecil in the Commons and Norfolk in the Lords were giving the lead in finding a settlement which would preclude Dudley from coming closer to the throne. They continued to advise the Queen to marry the Archduke Charles. But Elizabeth was not to be caught and she prevaricated. In the end Cecil was content to admit, 'The matter is so deep I cannot reach unto it.'[25]

The state of religion was another issue which the puritan extremists in the Commons were not likely to allow to go unnoticed. Fortunately, puritan efforts to reform the practice of the Church were concentrated in Convocation. In the Commons they were aimed at the Catholics. Cecil discovered that the puritans found 'nothing sharp enough against the Papists'. Cecil wanted stricter enforcement of existing laws rather than an increase in penal legislation against the Catholics. His most practical contribution was to support a Bill for the better payment of clergy in poor parishes. The Bill failed because the reformers were not prepared to pay for the better-educated clergy whom they were demanding.[26]

At this stage of his career Cecil felt, like so many of the reformers of his generation, that the established Protestantism must be conserved. To meet the Catholic attack he had commissioned

John Jewel in 1561 to write his *Apology for the Church of England.*
Cecil's sister-in-law, Lady Bacon, translated it from Latin into
English. Of the Marian bishops in prison Cecil had written, 'More
will or must follow *ad terrorem.*' In his battle with de Quadra he
had not spared the Papists. It was with the leaders of the established
Church rather than with the puritan extremists that he found
himself in sympathy. He was intimate with Parker, the Archbishop
of Canterbury, who confided in him his feelings about Elizabeth's
sharp reproofs over nonconformity in services and her petty
persecution of the wives of the clergy.[27] In the absence of an
ecclesiastic in the Council the clergy turned to Cecil to fight their
battles and win them favours. Cecil was an important figure in
Church patronage.

The chief task which Cecil, as the financial spokesman of the
government in the Commons, had to perform was to obtain a
grant. On 20 January he made 'an excellent declaration of the
great charges defrayed by the Queen's Majesty'. Cecil was in
constant touch with the old Lord Treasurer and with his contemporary Mildmay so that he was well briefed on financial
matters. The grant, Cecil argued, was necessitated by the foreign
situation, which he blamed upon the King of Spain and his
support for the Guise. The result of his arguments, as he proudly
announced, was 'a subsidy and two fifteenths ... as big as ever
any was.'[28]

Cecil's share in the economic and social legislation was marked
neither by the mind of a master planner nor the penetration of an
economist. He could not allow the 'toleration of usury under ten
per cent' and he helped to defeat a Bill which proposed such
toleration. He supported Bills against enclosures and against
gypsies. He was the author of a law to prohibit the sale of foreign
cloths. Over the major piece of economic legislation in that
Parliament, the Statute of Apprentices, Cecil was more enthusiastic
than well-informed. He was obviously not following its progress
through the Commons and he did not grasp its wide significance.
On 27 February, while the Commons were still amending the
Bill, he wrote, 'There is also a very good law agreed upon for
indifferent allowances for servants' wages in husbandry.' His

keenest interest was in measures to create a reserve of mariners and increase English shipping. He argued for fish days, free export of fish, restrictions on foreign competition in fish markets and on shippers using foreign vessels to import woad and wine. Cecil was conservative in economic affairs and proposed traditional remedies.[29] His purposes were naval, fiscal and moral rather than economic.

Cecil's labours in Parliament had been heavy. 'I am so fully occupied,' he wrote, 'to expedite matters in this Parliament that I have no leisure almost to attend to any other things.'[30] When Parliament was prorogued on 10 April 1563, he was free to give more time to the political aspects of the war in France. It was a depressing summer. Cecil had believed that Le Havre could be held until some reasonable bargain could be struck. But the plague and French attacks forced the garrison to surrender on 29 July. His only comfort was that the operation which had been Dudley's opportunity was also the favourite's failure. The war had at least drawn the Queen and Dudley away from Spain and had identified them with the protestant cause.

While the eyes of the statesman were fixed upon France the hopes of a father were set upon a long awaited son. Robert Cecil was born on 1 June 1563.[31] When William Cecil's expectations of his eldest son had been so recently disappointed, the birth of another son was particularly welcome. Yet it can hardly have seemed likely that the delicate baby, Robert, would become the support which his father desired and the founder of a second Cecil dynasty.

Turning from the domestic scene Cecil was relieved to find that, when the war in France was over, the Guise were not in power. The 'politique' Catherine de Medici did not, however, intend to give Elizabeth easy terms in a peace treaty. Cecil set down his thoughts upon French affairs in October. Negotiations were complicated because of the incompatibility of Elizabeth's two ambassadors, the belligerent Throckmorton and the stolid Sir Thomas Smith. Cecil felt that negotiations should be stopped unless Throckmorton were freed from restraint or another ambassador accepted. He insisted on the reassertion of the terms

of the treaty of Cateau-Cambrésis, providing for the English claim
to Calais. Partly because the rival ambassadors were literally at
daggers drawn no progress was made. Cecil, who sympathised
with Smith, suspected that his old confidant Throckmorton was
playing Dudley's game. Faction at home was stultifying diplomacy
abroad. Finally the treaty of Troyes in April 1564 had to be
accepted. Out of it Elizabeth gained nothing but 120,000 crowns,
a fraction of the cost of the war. To Cecil and his fellow councillors
the Queen 'showed much misliking'.[32]

The peace marked no pause in Cecil's labours. He wrote to
Smith, 'My fortune is of all others worse. By this peace you and
other ministers take some rest, but this being come, I have no less
business'. The war in France had led to trouble with the Regent of
the Spanish Netherlands over the depredations of English priv-
ateers and had imposed an unnatural inaction on Anglo-Scottish
relations. Both these matters now had to be taken up with a new
burst of diplomacy. But more immediate was a domestic worry.
'Unfortunately', Cecil wrote, 'is happened here a troublesome
chance, occasioned by John Hales, who is found to have first made
and procured books in defence of the Earl of Hertford's marriage,
and likewise in approbation of the title of the succession for the
Lady Catherine.'[33]

The Queen resented Lady Catherine Grey's candidature for the
succession. Hales went to prison and Lady Catherine left her
father's custody. Cecil was deeply embarrassed by the Hales affair.
He knew all the principal culprits well. At the end of April 1564 he
complained, 'And yet am I not free from suspicion.' It was
rumoured that Dudley was playing upon that suspicion to oust
Cecil. Upon investigation by Cecil, Dudley and Northampton, it
was disclosed that other intimates of the Secretary were involved.
Nicholas Bacon, with whom Cecil's relations were strained over a
row in Council, was implicated and virtually banished from Court.
Cecil had determined to 'go upright, neither *ad dextram* nor *ad
sinistram*'. In November he could write with more assurance,
'I have been also noted a favourer of my Lady Catherine's title,
but my truth therein is tried and so I rest quietly; I am and always
have been circumspect to do nothing to make offence.' Cecil's

confidence in his own integrity had brought him through unscathed.[34]

During this scandal Cecil had been manœuvring to counter the reprisals, taken against English piracy, by Margaret of Parma, the Regent of the Spanish Netherlands. In November 1563 the Regent had imposed an embargo on English trade with Antwerp. Cecil had anticipated such a move by opening negotiations with the Countess of Friesland back in March of that year, when first complaints had come from the Low Countries. He obtained access for English merchants to Emden and in May 1564 the first fleet of the Merchant Adventurers put in at that port. By thus breaking the hold of Antwerp upon English trade Cecil had strengthened his hand and he went on to stop imports from Antwerp in June. Philip of Spain came to the rescue of his Regent by sending de Silva to England as ambassador in order to restore trade relations between London and Antwerp. Cecil and the new ambassador got on well and by the end of the year an agreement was reached.[35]

This sharp economic tussle focused attention upon the problems of the country's greatest export industry and the trade in cloth. Cecil received plenty of advice on their solution. His own assessment showed that he usually subordinated strictly economic considerations to those of social and political security. As a land-owner and investor in the Russia Company he had an eye for commercial advantage, but there was little of economic individualism left in him when he considered, as a statesman, the good of the realm. He disliked the concentration of trade in Antwerp which put English trade at the mercy of Spain, drained England of bullion and filled it with unnecessary luxuries. Loss of customs on cloths would be compensated by an increase in revenues from wool exports. The growth of the cloth industry he saw as a drain upon manpower to the detriment of food production and urban crafts. It had increased the numbers of small irresponsible merchants and of the clothworkers who were 'of worse condition to be quietly governed than husbandmen'. Cecil tended to accept as salutary the reduction of activity in the cloth industry brought about by the recent embargo.[36]

Social and economic ills seemed to Cecil to be within the reach

H

of well-tried remedies. He found it less easy to prescribe for the
political and religious convulsions which might follow upon
either the marriage of Mary Queen of Scots or of Elizabeth. The
emotions and wills of two such women were not easily directed.
Yet on their marriages rested the religious future of the two
kingdoms and the pattern of alliances which would go far to
determine the degree of independence which England would
enjoy. To bring royal emotions and political calculations into
harmony was a delicate task.

After the postponement of the meeting of the two Queens in
mid 1562, Cecil and Maitland maintained relations. For over a
year the two Secretaries fenced with their accustomed verbal
caution. Cecil pursued the objects which he had sought in the
Treaty of Edinburgh. 'The settling of the gospel of Christ and the
dissolution of anti-Christ' as he put it to Maitland in August 1563
was for him of paramount importance. He sought for 'whatsoever
may either unite the hearts of the people of this isle together in one
or preserve them from discord and hatred' and for 'whatsoever
might make the accord betwixt our two sovereigns'. Cecil's pious
principles covered a tangle of intrigue.[37]

Cecil came to accept Elizabeth's proposal to marry Mary to
Dudley, whom she created Earl of Leicester for the purpose. It
had the advantage of royal approval and it set upon the Scottish
throne a protestant Englishman, attached to Elizabeth, instead of
a politically powerful foreign prince for whom Mary was searching
Europe. If it threatened the prospect of Leicester's return at
Mary's side in the event of Elizabeth's death, its more immediate
effect was to remove Cecil's rival and the Queen's suitor. By the
end of 1564 Cecil was supporting Leicester's candidature for
Mary's hand. 'But to say truth of my knowledge in these fickle
matters, I can affirm nothing,' he wrote in December.[38]

Nothing was certain about Elizabeth's intentions for her own
marriage except that Leicester seemed to have been discarded for
the moment. Upon the Emperor Ferdinand's death in August
1564, Cecil opened negotiations again with the Archduke Charles.
As the autumn drew on there was a possibility that Cecil himself
would be sent on the mission. But he had been ill in September

and his wife's plea about his health seems to have stifled the proposal. Cecil had no desire to be out of the country and leave his rivals to take control of affairs.[39] But with Mary's obvious determination to find a husband filling the Court with speculations, it was an auspicious time to stir Elizabeth's thoughts on matrimony.

While Cecil had been involved in the dynastic affairs of Queens during 1564 he was also playing the dynast in his own family circle. At Easter he was objecting to the proposed marriage of his sister-in-law, Catherine Cooke, to Sir Henry Killigrew, a well-known supporter of Robert Dudley, Earl of Leicester. In July Mildred Cecil gave birth to a daughter in the new London house in the Strand. Cecil's family was growing. There were now three surviving children of his second marriage, Anne, Robert and Elizabeth. Then in August Cecil clinched the proposal for his son Thomas, who was now twenty-two years of age, to marry Dorothy, second daughter and co-heir of John Nevill, third Lord Latimer, and Lucy, daughter of Henry Somerset, Earl of Worcester. The marriage took place in November. If at the end of 1564 Cecil's political hopes were still frustrated, one of his great social ambitions had been realised.[40] The Cecils were allied to the great nobility.

CHAPTER IX

The Succession Predicament

In 1565 the matrimonial prospects of Elizabeth and of Mary Queen of Scots remained Cecil's principal preoccupation. Such prospects covered the issues of foreign policy and the question of religious settlement in England and Scotland. Both Queens complicated the problem of their courtships by finding new suitors. Mary found Lord Henry Darnley more attractive than Leicester. Elizabeth responded to French proposals on behalf of the boy King Charles IX as well as to the advances of Charles of Austria.

Cecil's first task was to prevent Mary's marriage to the catholic Darnley, who, as the son of Henry VIII's niece, Lady Margaret Douglas, and of the Earl of Lennox, had enough Tudor blood and Scottish influence to make him as politically acceptable to Mary as he was physically attractive to her. It was well known that Darnley's mother was determined to marry him to Mary and it had been a mistake on Elizabeth's part to let him visit Scotland. Darnley had arrived in Scotland at an opportune time, when deadlock over Leicester's chances had been reached. Mary would not take Leicester without an assurance of her right to succeed to the English throne.[1] Neither Elizabeth nor Cecil would give the assurance which would focus catholic hopes and intrigues upon Mary.

As summer came Mary showed every sign of having fallen in love with Darnley. While Leicester secretly encouraged the match, Cecil led the opposition to it.[2] He drafted the firm instructions to Throckmorton, whom Elizabeth sent as her ambassador to Scotland in May. He rallied the councillors, except Leicester and three others, to sign a declaration opposing the marriage. In June, when he weighed up the situation, he made explicit his fears about the catholic plots which he expected to follow a declaration of

Mary's right to the English succession. Catholics who were ready to set Mary on the throne in place of Elizabeth, he declared, would scheme to kill the English Queen and would spread propaganda in the North and stir up border incidents and rebellions. He feared Scottish alliances with France and Spain. The less precipitate, who were concerned to see Mary follow Elizabeth, would, he suggested, do all that they could to ensure that Mary had an heir and that Elizabeth had none. Cecil saw Mary as the champion of Catholicism and dreaded a war of succession inspired by religion.[3]

The measures for which he won Council's approval in June were put to the Queen. There were to be preparations for invasion on the Border and a show of force. Lady Lennox was to be put under restraint and her son and husband were to be recalled from Scotland. Catholic sympathisers were to be watched and removed from responsible posts. Some favour was to be shown to Lady Catherine Grey as a rival to Mary for the succession.[4] But, on 29 July, before Elizabeth had decided to act, Mary married Darnley.

Just as Darnley's arrival in Scotland had complicated the problem of Mary's marriage, so Elizabeth's readiness to negotiate with France on a marriage with Charles IX made Cecil's efforts to win her favour for the Archduke Charles more complex. Through the spring of 1565 Cecil played the Queen's diplomatic game of setting France and the Hapsburgs in rivalry for her hand. Competition might speed the Hapsburg suit. Cecil did not take the French proposal seriously. But there was danger in it. It became a means by which the French hoped to wreck the Austrian match. Even more dangerous was the way in which domestic faction began to divide on the French and Austrian negotiations.

Leicester, confident that there would be no marriage with Charles IX to exclude his own hopes, gathered about him a pro-French faction. De Foix, the French ambassador, and Throckmorton were the leading spirits. Cecil countered by gaining support for the Hapsburg marriage from de Silva, the Spanish ambassador, and from two great nobles, Sussex and Norfolk, who distrusted Leicester as a francophil parvenu. Elizabeth liked to govern by faction. Between 1564 and 1566 faction intrigue reached a dangerous intensity on occasion. Cecil watched the divisions at Court with care. He had long experience of such rivalries.

Skilled as Cecil was in handling faction, he did not, as the Queen did, encourage it.[5] He posed as a royal servant detached from partisan commitments. He stressed above all his loyalty to the Queen and, when she visited him in Stamford in 1566, he enjoyed the chance to demonstrate that loyalty outside the clash of court politics.[6] Yet Cecil was committed and he knew how to pursue his ends through the tangle of personal and social prejudice, family feuds and conspiracies which enveloped the main religious and political issues. His skill lay in conciliation and the maintenance of tolerable personal relationships. It was no part of his game to exacerbate rivalries. In 1565 Cecil prevented Throckmorton from becoming a privy councillor, but in the following year he was reconciled to Throckmorton. Nevertheless it was Cecil's old friend Sir Ralph Sadler who entered the Council.[7] Cecil disliked violence in domestic politics and took no part in the clash between Sussex and Leicester in 1566 when the two nobles paraded their retinues. It was when the Council was united behind him that he could best persuade the Queen.

Through the summer of 1565 Cecil fought the pro-French faction in his efforts to clinch the negotiations with the Archduke Charles. Norfolk and Sussex spoke for Cecil's policy. On occasion even Leicester pretended to favour the Austrian match. The Queen played the situation but would accept no conditions until she had seen her suitor. The Emperor would not send Charles until his conditions had been accepted. Cecil could find no way to break the stalemate and as the autumn passed into the spring of 1566 his hopes began to wane. He justified his support for the Archduke by contrasting him with Leicester.[8] He saw Leicester as a debt-ridden, factious noble, whose reputation was tarnished by the circumstances of his wife's death and who was like 'to prove unkind or jealous of the Queen's Majesty'. In the Archduke he saw a royal Prince who would bring the requisite honour and birth to his position and who would protect an isolated England with a Burgundian and Spanish alliance against France, Scotland and the

Pope. Such a comparison might satisfy Cecil but it did not satisfy the Queen.

Meanwhile the political harvest of Mary's marriage proved full of tares. Elizabeth was threatening open support for the rebels in Scotland. Secret help she did give. But it was clear that any full-scale attack upon Mary would bring her the support of France. There was consultation between Cecil and the French envoys, and talk of sending Cecil and a French envoy to Scotland. There were recriminations between the Queens. But there was little action. Leicester and Throckmorton were game for a fight. But Cecil, who had been all for a show of force, was chary of becoming involved in armed intervention. By October he was emphasising the costs and dangers of undertaking a war. He tempered his attacks upon Mary and even ceased to labour the religious issue. He began to argue that the best way out of the situation was for Elizabeth to marry and make an open declaration on the succession. Finally Cecil was glad to report that the Queen had decided to give only diplomatic support to the rebels 'to use all good mediation, by outward countenance to relieve them, but to do nothing that may break the peace'.[9]

In the event Elizabeth gave little encouragement of any sort to the Scottish rebels and ostentatiously declared that she would not 'maintain any subject in any disobedience against the prince'. The protestant Scots looked to Cecil. They hoped that he might be the leader of a commission which it was proposed to send to Scotland. But the proposal failed. Cecil had obtained peace but not on the conditions for which he had hoped.[10] The support of Protestantism in Scotland, for which he had struggled so long, was virtually abandoned by the end of 1565. Elizabeth had no intention of driving Mary into the arms of her enemies.

The removal of English pressure allowed the Scots to disintegrate. Cecil was soon aware that violent plots were hatching in Mary's Court. The Queen of Scots' encouragement of Catholicism was provoking her protestant subjects. Darnley was proving intolerable as a King and as a husband. In March 1566 Darnley sought to assert himself by murdering Riccio, Mary's Italian secretary. With courage and craft, the pregnant Queen turned the

tables upon her hated husband and, having regained control,
guarded against English intervention by being friendly to
Elizabeth. While Mary's friendship was welcome to Cecil, he did
not like the way in which Irish rebels and papal agents continued
to haunt the Scottish Court. More dangerous was the swing of
influential opinion in England in favour of Mary. The birth of her
son in June was a further recommendation of Mary to those who
were beginning to accept her as the next Queen of England.
Norfolk, Pembroke and Leicester were said to be her supporters.
Even Cecil commended himself to Mary when she invited him to
the christening of the royal heir. He did not attend but Mary wrote
to tease him about his efforts to induce a gentleman named
Rokesby to spy upon her.[11]

The growing strength of Mary as a candidate for the English
throne made it seem all the more imperative to Cecil to decide
Elizabeth's marriage and determine the right of succession. The
future hung upon the thread of Elizabeth's life. Cecil wanted some
sure basis for the future. When in September 1566 the recall of
Parliament was necessitated by the financial needs of the Crown,
Cecil knew that the opportunity to press the Queen on the matter
of the succession had come. His planning for the session disclosed
nothing but the preparation for taxation, the reform of certain
legal practices and a note on a Bill to deal with apparel. But at a
Council meeting in September the succession was discussed. Cecil
considered that the best tactics were to try to settle the Queen's
marriage first, and if that failed to try to obtain a declaration of
who was to be successor. Of the two requirements he felt that the
royal marriage might prove the easier to accomplish.[12]

Cecil found the Commons in a militant mood over the succession.
Early in October pamphlets attacking the Queen and Cecil for
refusing to allow the matter of the succession to proceed in
Parliament were scattered in London.[13] In the Commons Cecil had
evidently put his duty to the Queen before his desire for action on
the question which so roused the Commons. Later in the month,
Norfolk boldly requested the Queen to allow the Lords to debate
the succession. The Queen refused. In the Commons Cecil tried to
press on with the financial business. His account of the Queen's

charges was challenged.[14] Worse still, the Commons took the opportunity to exploit the power of the purse. They decided to treat the succession and the subsidy together. Neither Cecil nor any other councillor was able to satisfy the House with assurances that the Queen intended to marry and that supply should precede the redress of their grievances.

Cecil, on the committee to prepare the terms of the subsidy, tactfully kept the royal demand down to some £220,000. He was also a member of a joint committee of Lords and Commons which petitioned the Queen on the succession. Meanwhile Norfolk took the lead for the Lords and headed a deputation to the Queen. He met with a sharp rebuff. Cecil was still ready to maintain his arguments for royal action on marriage and for naming a successor. But when on 5 November the Queen met the joint committee of Lords and Commons, she rejected Cecil's advice and the petition of Parliament.[15] She declared her intention to marry for the purpose of having children but refused to name a successor until she judged the time convenient. She upbraided the Lords and Commons for their unruly behaviour in the matter and reminded them of the royal will. 'I am your anointed Queen. I will never be by violence constrained to do anything,' she declared. She would exercise her prerogative at her own discretion when the time was ripe. 'For it is monstrous that the feet should direct the head,' was her parting shot.[16]

After the royal ban on further discussion of the succession was announced in the Commons, Cecil had the task of making the Queen's bitter words more palatable. Paul Wentworth then raised the question as to whether the Queen's prohibition of debate was an infringement of the privileges of the House. Elizabeth's answer was to send for the Speaker and forbid him to permit the subject to be raised again. Cecil guided the discontent of the Commons into a petition on freedom of speech.[17] But Elizabeth forestalled its presentation by lifting her ban. The royal concession satisfied the injured dignity of the Commons and for the moment the succession was allowed to depend on the royal promises.

When it came to drafting the subsidy Bill, however, Cecil found that the Commons wanted a preamble which registered the

Queen's promises on marriage and her commitment to announce her successor at a convenient time. The final draft made clear the parliamentary disapproval of the royal reluctance to act. The Queen was outraged at the attempt to bind her with niggling legalities. Her angry reaction caused the preamble to shrink into an expression of gratitude for the Queen's determination to arrange the succession.

While the battle of the puritan-led Commons to force the Queen's hand over the succession dominated the session for Cecil, there was other business in which he was interested. He took part in defeating a Bill to abolish restrictions on the sale of French wines. He expressed his hostility to enriching France with English bullion in exchange for wine. He resisted any increase in the number of taverns, which were notorious centres of discontent among the vulgar people. He pointed out that wine ousted the native beer and ale and decreased the demand for home-grown grain. He countered the argument about encouraging shipping through the wine trade by insisting that increased fisheries would foster as many ships and more experienced mariners. His suspicions about foreign trade were still strong.[18]

On the subject of religion the proceedings of Parliament were a disappointment to Cecil. A Bill on apparel which he supported failed. Under the guise of a sumptuary law he had hoped to obtain legislation on standard ecclesiastical vestments. He was supporting Archbishop Parker and the Queen in their insistence upon uniformity in the use of clerical vestments against the puritan attack upon the 'livery of Anti-Christ'. But the Queen preferred to leave the odious responsibility for enforcing uniformity in religious practice and doctrine with the bishops. Thus Cecil was disappointed again when the Articles of Religion failed to gain statutory sanction.[19] For the moment the Queen had no wish to stir the puritans or offend the Catholics by her support for legislation on ecclesiastical matters.

The strain of serving the Queen and Commons, of suppressing his sympathy with the demands of the Commons in order to maintain his obedience as a royal servant, had told upon Cecil's health. His gout raged and he withdrew from parliamentary sessions in November. Cecil was ready to persuade the Queen through Council but not through the Commons. But his policy on the succession was well known and he was laid open to charges of inciting the Commons to resist the Queen. When the Queen taxed him with these charges in Council, he denied them and successfully refuted them to her satisfaction. Yet, when he came to consider the achievements of Parliament, he made a sorry list of things undone. His failed hopes were betrayed by a note that neither the Queen's marriage nor the succession was settled. The legal reforms had not been made. Uniformity of doctrine had not been given statutory authority.[20]

For the future Cecil saw difficulty in collecting the subsidy, although the Queen had reduced it by a third. He anticipated renewed trouble over vestments and uprisings among the malcontents in the summer. The cost of suppressing the Irish rebellion had to be met. Abroad the dispute over Calais with the French was due for settlement under the terms of the Treaty of Cateau-Cambrésis in 1567. The revolt in the Netherlands called for a reappraisal of policy. Sunk in gloom and tortured by gout, Cecil drew a pessimistic picture of past failures and future difficulties.

In the spring of 1567 came news of extraordinary happenings in Scotland. Darnley was murdered in February. Mary was under the spell of Bothwell, the reputed murderer of the King. Cecil's reaction was to hope to lay hands upon James, the heir, who was now, despite his infancy, the most significant guarantee of the future. Killigrew, Cecil's brother-in-law, went to Scotland as Elizabeth's ambassador. Murray called on Elizabeth on his way to France. Kirkcaldy begged Elizabeth to aid the rebellious nobility to overthrow Bothwell. The situation was developing too fast for Cecil. 'Scotland is a Quagmire, Nobody seems to stand still,' he wrote on 23 April. But two days later he had an agenda ready for Council. He was concerned that the murderers should be brought to trial, that Mary should be made to understand the public verdict on her actions and that she should be prevented from marrying Bothwell. He was anxious to obstruct any alliance between Scotland and France and to stop any attempt to change the established religion in Scotland. Finally he demanded redress for incidents on the Border.[21] Cecil's objectives were clear. The means to accomplish them were less obvious.

Events went on apace. Once again Mary fulfilled Cecil's worst fears and allowed herself to be carried off by the newly divorced Bothwell in a romantic blending of rape and marriage. The outraged Scottish nobles demanded English aid in their rising. But before Elizabeth decided upon action they had defeated Mary and Bothwell and held the Queen of Scots in prison at Lochleven Castle. The rebellious treatment of Mary seemed to Elizabeth to be an intolerable affront to royalty. She demanded Mary's release. Cecil cared little about Mary's fate. With his memories of how Mary had been spirited away to France as a child, he was anxious above everything else to secure the custody of James before the French kidnapped him. Fear of the French haunted him. 'They fish with hooks of gold, and we but with speech,' he complained.[22]

Cecil saw the need to eliminate Bothwell by a divorce, a trial and the confiscation of his lands. Equally essential to a settlement was the binding of Mary by the Scottish Parliament to the succession of James and the maintenance of Protestantism. He put his hopes in restoring Murray to the Scottish scene. But his policy was hampered by Elizabeth's unacceptable insistence on Mary's freedom.[23] The success of the rebels had filled Elizabeth with a dread that Mary would be executed. At the end of July 1567 the rebellious lords secured Mary's abdication and determined to crown James and establish a regency government. Elizabeth blamed Cecil 'that nothing was thought of for her to revenge the Queen of Scots imprisonment and deliver her'.[24]

In her frustration Elizabeth was contemplating war on behalf of an injured Queen. Cecil's readiness to accept the situation, to send an ambassador to James and to trust Murray to prevent a further deterioration of the situation enraged Elizabeth. Cecil was in disgrace and the Queen was turning to Leicester. Cecil feared 'the likelihood of the loss of the fruits of six or seven years of negotiations with Scotland'.[25] The great aim of his foreign policy from the beginning of the reign had been to secure a friendly and protestant Scotland. Now it seemed as if all his work was threatened by the Queen's determination to free Mary. Cecil endured the Queen's disfavour and maintained his position. Once before he had resisted the Queen on Scottish policy when he was a newly appointed Secretary in 1560, now as her most experienced adviser he was ready to stand firm in August 1567.

Elizabeth refused to deal with the regency government, subsidised the wavering supporters of Mary and began to sound French opinion. Fortunately the French were too absorbed in the prospect of renewed civil war to take an interest in Scotland. Murray, who had become Regent, was providing good government in Scotland. He carried on a friendly and unofficial correspondence with Cecil. The situation was turning out better than Cecil had dared to hope. He was waiting now to resume a firm line with Scotland.

Cecil had been able to pursue a more positive policy in France in 1567. Admittedly the claim to the restitution of Calais or compensation which was due under the Treaty of Cateau-Cambrésis was a futile diplomatic exercise. But Cecil had expected nothing and was not perturbed at the French refusal to make any gesture. More significant was the part which Cecil hoped to play in the civil war in France. He and the majority of the Council were ready to give support to the Huguenots. But Elizabeth resisted giving aid to rebels in France just as she refused to aid them in Scotland. Her memories of the costly failure in France during 1563 made her proof against the lure of easy profits. The second civil war was over in March 1568 before Cecil could persuade the Queen to ally herself with the French Protestants. But by the end of the year he had drawn the Queen to the edge of open war on behalf of the Huguenots. Cecil did not wish for a declared war but he presided over a thriving trade in munitions with their stronghold, La Rochelle. England was uncommitted but was giving what aid she cared to supply.[26] This was the sort of situation which pleased Cecil best.

With regard to Spain, Cecil was becoming aware in 1567 that there were two dangerous points of contact with the great catholic power. The more dangerous of these appeared to be the Netherlands, where Alva appeared with a powerful army to suppress rebellious nobles and Calvinist riots.[27] The strategic

consequences of a powerful Spanish force in the neighbouring
Low Countries seemed more sinister to Cecil than the deterioration
of the Antwerp money market and trade of which his friend Sir
Thomas Gresham was always reminding him. The other contact
with Spanish interests lay over the ocean in the West Indies.[28]
When in the summer of 1567 Hawkins was preparing a naval
expedition, de Silva had shown a threatening concern about its
destination. He warned Cecil not to allow Hawkins to go to the
Caribbean. The object of the voyage was to intrude upon
Portuguese Africa. Cecil was involved in the diplomatic preparation for the voyage and had informed the King of Portugal that
the English rejected the papal sanction of the Portuguese possession of Africa. But the plan for Africa fell through and when
Hawkins sailed in early October his plan included a call in the
West Indies.

    In the next year 1568, relations with Spain grew less friendly.
Cecil made the most of the insult to his Queen when Philip
expelled the English ambassador Dr Man. In September the
gentlemanly de Silva was replaced by the bellicose de Spes as
Philip II's ambassador. Meanwhile Hawkins was drawing near to
his disastrous clash with the Spaniards at San Juan de Ulloa in the
West Indies. Cecil's cultivation of anti-Spanish feeling at Court
revealed a change of attitude towards Spain.[29] Now that France
was debilitated by civil war, his reliance on Spain for support
against France was not so necessary. He was beginning to realise
that the most pressing danger to England lay in the Netherlands.

    His new sense of the Spanish threat was not altered by the
strange turn of events in Scotland in 1568. Mary escaped from her
prison, put up a fight, was defeated and fled to England. The
arrival of the Queen of Scots in England posed problems. Cecil
advised against offending the Regency government by treating
with her as a Queen. He concluded that she must be isolated from
the outside world while her part in Darnley's murder was
investigated. But for the future he admitted that there were
dangers either in holding her in England or in allowing her to
return to Scotland or to enter France. If she were guiltless of her
husband's murder she might be restored in Scotland upon

confirming the Treaty of Edinburgh. If guilty, she might be allowed to reign jointly with James under the rule of the Regent until James came of age. He believed that Elizabeth must take the initiative in dealing with Mary because of Mary's claim to the English throne and the need to preserve the Protestantism and friendship of Scotland. Meanwhile he urged Elizabeth to reassure the French of her good will to Mary and to warn them off meddling in Scotland. His fear of France was great. Cecil expected that Mary, whether guilty or innocent of murder, would have to return to Scotland. For the moment he was content to see that she was under guard.[30]

Elizabeth's professions of friendship continued, but for a royal sister in distress her feelings cooled. Cecil, it seems, was allowed to encourage Murray to destroy Mary's supporters in Scotland. When Murray sent copies of the Casket Letters which incriminated Mary, the only official response which he received from Cecil was that Elizabeth hoped to reconcile Mary with her subjects. Somehow Murray must have been made aware that what Cecil wrote was very different from what he thought Mary's fate would be.[31]

The attitude of the Council to Mary hardened. It now recommended a more secure hold upon Mary by moving her from Carlisle to Tutbury. The Queen of Scots was not to be given aid, restored to her throne or allowed to leave England before her trial. Elizabeth was to be apprised of the issues between Mary and her subjects. But the Council's advice was unwelcome. Both Queens had to be won to accept the necessity of a trial. Cecil was ill for a few days in July but he played his part in persuading Elizabeth and manœuvring Mary. The juggling of words led both Queens to believe that, whatever the issue of a trial might be, Mary would somehow be restored to the Scottish throne. It suited the royal rivals to pretend that there was some possible compromise ahead. Cecil, convinced of Mary's guilt, made no such pretence to himself. 'It is not meant, if the Queen of Scots shall be proved guilty of murder to restore her to Scotland . . . nor yet shall there be any haste made of her delivery until the success of the matter in France and Flanders be seen,' he wrote. For Cecil, Mary's case had important bearings on international diplomacy and he had had second thoughts about Mary's return to Scotland.[32]

The hearing of evidence against the Queen of Scots began at York in October. But the investigation was moved to Westminster when Elizabeth heard the alarming news that Norfolk was ready to solve the problem of Mary's future by marrying her. 'The Queen's Majesty is now at the pinch so careful for her own surety and state as I perceive the Queen of Scots shall not be advanced to greater credit than her cause will serve,' was Cecil's satisfied comment upon Elizabeth's reaction to Norfolk's dangerous proposal. In November Cecil was put on the commission before which the Casket Letters were disclosed. But Mary withdrew her commissioners and refused to answer the charges against her. Elizabeth was content to have the evidence of Mary's guilt demonstrated. The proceedings ended in December.[33]

The result of the trial was inconclusive. But it was now harder than ever to release Mary or to contemplate her restoration. Mary accused Cecil of plotting to marry one of his daughters to the Earl of Hertford and secure the succession for him. Her wild charges showed that she recognised the part which Cecil had played in frustrating her own schemes for the succession. For the moment there was nothing to do but to hold the discredited Queen of Scots at Tutbury. Cecil might well have anticipated further trouble with the royal prisoner, but at the end of 1568 he had the satisfaction of having won another round against that dangerous woman.

The spectacular escapades of the Queen of Scots had not been the only important events of 1568 for Cecil. The spread of Protestantism to France and the Low Countries influenced his thinking. The potentialities of protestant revolt in France and Flanders were leading Cecil to a new view of European politics. From the beginning of Elizabeth's reign the Treaty of Edinburgh had been the focus of his diplomacy. He had relied on Spain as the check upon France. Now Spain was on the offensive in the Netherlands and France was debilitated by civil war. The practice of supporting protestant revolt which had worked in Scotland must now be applied on a grander scale to sap the energies of

catholic France and catholic Spain. The time for a reappraisal of
English diplomacy had come. Cecil was beginning to accept more
fully that European politics must be seen in terms of an ideological
struggle between Protestantism and Catholicism.

CHAPTER X

Challenge and Vindication

THE year 1569 began with an opportunity for Cecil to pursue his policy of discouraging Spain in the Netherlands. Ships carrying bullion for Alva and his army were forced by storm and pirates to put in at Plymouth and Southampton in December 1568. It could be argued that the money, lying in English ports, was still legally in the possession of the Genoese bankers who were shipping it and that it might be borrowed from them. The nice legality involved and the chance of a financial windfall appealed to Cecil. On his advice Elizabeth decided to replenish her treasury and deprive the Spanish army across the North Sea.[1]

The Spanish ambassador took it as a hostile act. By 3 January he had jolted Alva into confiscating English goods in the Netherlands. Fortunately Alva regretted the reprisal before the alarmed English government made a conciliatory gesture. He opened negotiations. The economic sting of Spain had been drawn. Following the precedent set by Cecil in the negotiations with Emden in 1564, the Merchant Adventurers had found an alternative to Antwerp in Hamburg and all was arranged for the spring fleet to sail for that port. To Cecil it seemed that England possessed the levers for economic pressure. 'We have ordered to shut up all passages,' he wrote on 6 January, 'and it is thought they will repent, for England oweth Antwerp £100,000 more than it hath. And I think a great richness is now in our ports. . . .' The Council was disposed 'to make a good bargain for England upon these hasty attempts'.[2]

The clash with Spain led Cecil to crystallise his ideas in 'A Short Memorial of the State of the Realm'.[3] He saw the principal menace as being the 'recovery of the tyranny of the Pope' through the support of the 'two great Monarchies' of France and Spain with the Queen of Scots 'as instrument' for their plans. He set out the factors in favour of the Queen of Scots against the weaknesses of

120

Elizabeth, who was without husband, children or allies and whose realm was enfeebled by a long peace, want of trained soldiers and sailors, 'soft and remiss government', lack of armaments, weak frontiers, rebellion in Ireland, little treasure, a poor nobility, and wealthy parvenus 'which are unmeet for service'. The troubles of Elizabeth's foreign enemies which permitted her survival seemed nearly at an end. Of the Queen of Scots he thought that even 'the fame of her murdering her husband will by time vanish away'. His broad survey included comments on the Ottoman Empire. His review of relations with France and Spain confirmed that they were hostile. There was substance in most of Cecil's points.

Having built up his gloomy picture of impending perils, Cecil set out the remedies. All depended on the Queen, 'the only physician, without whom neither remedies can be ministered nor perils avoided'. The Queen's marriage he left in the hands of God. Against the 'exalting of the tyranny of Rome' he suggested an alliance with the protestant Kings of Denmark and Sweden and the Princes of Germany which would bring pressure upon the Emperor. He placed no reliance on the old Burgundian alliance. The religious rebels 'which are persecuted with violence for this quarrel in France and the Low Countries would be comforted not to desist from their natural defence'. Protestants were to be supported in Scotland.

At home 'the laws and ordinances for religion would be earnestly executed'. No one in England must be allowed without royal consent 'to maintain, avow or allow' the cause of Mary Queen of Scots. Some settlement of the succession was required. In the North watch was to be kept and any sign of sedition suppressed. Finally, 'if by any good means, whilst these inward troubles are in France, any advantage could be taken to recover Calais, it were a device happily employed'.

In his survey Cecil chose to represent the leadership, policy and morale of the kingdoms and principalities of Christendom in terms of conflicting religious beliefs. The political struggle was simplified into the opposition of a protestant cause to a papal tyranny. But he insisted that 'the admitting of small aids and remedies' is no more to be neglected of a good Governor than it is 'of a Captain or

Master of a Ship, the having in readiness, and the using of the smallest tackling or meanest and simplest instrument in a Ship, which considered of itself, is many times not worth listing up, but in time of service found very necessary'. It was this combination of moral interpretation, broad vision and the eye for practical detail that made Cecil a formidable statesman.

Cecil's consideration of the balance of power between Catholicism and Protestantism abroad was not unconnected with the balance of faction at home. Cecil's policy, shaped in ideological terms, meant the abandonment of the old reliance upon the Hapsburgs and Spain. The collapse of negotiations with the Archduke Charles, the seizure of the bullion and the consequent insulting confinement of de Spes seemed to confirm that Cecil had made a major change in diplomacy. The change appeared provocative and dangerous to those who saw politics primarily in national and dynastic terms. Cecil, grasping the significance of her power in the Netherlands, anticipated a clash with Spain. The old nobility distrusted Cecil's new policy.[4] The balance of faction began to swing against Cecil.

Added to the disagreement over foreign policy was a growing resentment of Cecil's control of home affairs. In 1566 Cecil had noted of Leicester, 'He shall study nothing but to enhance his own particular friends to wealth, to offices, to lands and to offend others'.[5] This was now the charge against Cecil. His patronage and his hold over the Council and the Queen obstructed the influence of the nobles. Any difference over policy revealed to his opponents the extent of Cecil's power. It was easy to brand him as an upstart and a heretic according to the prejudice or conviction of his detractors.

When Norfolk drew close to Leicester, Cecil was in real danger. From the Scottish wars onwards the Secretary had always cultivated Norfolk, the most powerful and exalted of all the old nobility.[6] With Norfolk and Sussex on his side, Cecil was able to counter the influence of Leicester. But over the treatment of Mary Queen of Scots and his attitude towards Spain Cecil's greatest noble supporter was drifting into opposition to him.

In February Cecil discovered that a group of the nobility,

including Leicester, Norfolk, Pembroke, Northampton, Arundel and the old Lord Treasurer, the Marquess of Winchester, were conspiring to bring about his downfall. Norfolk, seeking Spanish friendship, was in touch with de Spes, who welcomed the chance to defeat Cecil and end the deadlock over trade with the Netherlands. The nobles hoped to catch Cecil, as Thomas Cromwell had been caught, by arresting him in Council and striking a minister who had already fallen.

Elizabeth was impervious to the gestures and hints of the disgruntled nobles. They lacked the nerve to act. Cecil, steadfast in his trust in God and his Queen, clung to his office and royal favour. Gradually the tension subsided. Sussex played the peacemaker. On 9 June he wrote to the Secretary of 'the good and hearty reconciliation' which existed now between Cecil and Norfolk.[7] Cecil had shown some flexibility and understanding of the Duke's views on Spain. Each had agreed that the other was 'void of private motives' and concerned only with the good of the Queen and the realm. Cloudy and poisonous personal emotions had been strained out and the stuff of civilised politics remained.

The intimate political life of the Court would soon have become intolerable and violent, if the Queen had not exercised her iron restraint and if Cecil had not sought to keep the issues at the level of arguable policies and to avoid personal vendettas. Cecil was able to keep his friends across the lines of faction. In February, while Leicester was scheming against him, Cecil was discussing with one of the Earl's supporters, Sir Henry Sidney, the chances of a marriage alliance between Sidney's son, Philip, and his own precious daughter, Anne. Cecil had young Sidney in his house.[8]

In May there was another example of how Cecil sought to take personal conflict out of domestic politics. As Master of the Court of Wards, he had made it his business to give evidence in person concerning the validity of the Duke of Norfolk's claim to Dacre lands. Admittedly it was Cecil's opportunity to ingratiate himself with the Duke and at the same time to sow dissension between the Duke and the Dacres with their Northern following.[9] But it was characteristic of his conciliatory technique in politics that he took the chance not only to win the Duke's favour, but also to preserve his reputation for giving impartial justice. Nobody at the time challenged Cecil's interpretation of the evidence. Cecil was in a position to harm his opponents and he could have easily pushed his relationships beyond the limits of reconciliation. His behaviour lowered the temperature of domestic politics.

The friendship with Norfolk, renewed in the summer, carried with it an unwelcome confidence. Norfolk disclosed to Cecil that he had not given up the plan to marry Mary Queen of Scots which Elizabeth had told him to abandon in the previous October. Norfolk was deaf to Cecil's advice to tell Elizabeth of his intentions to persevere with his wooing of Mary. Cecil's choice was either to betray Norfolk or to hoodwink the Queen. On the merits of Norfolk's matrimonial plan Cecil did not commit himself. He wanted to be uninvolved in a quarrel between the Queen and her greatest subject. In August he wrote, 'I wish myself as free from the consideration thereof as I have been from the intelligence of the devising thereof'.[10] Cecil busied himself with administrative detail during that difficult summer. But it was not mere chance that he reviewed the military strength of the realm and pondered on the means of creating a sworn association for the defence of the Queen and the established Church.[11]

As the summer wore on Elizabeth learned of Norfolk's persistence with his marriage plans. She began to test the nerve of the nobles and took her opportunities to make clear her disapproval. Cecil wanted the plan to be brought into the open, where it would become politics and not conspiracy. In September the Queen at last confronted Norfolk and he fell back on a demand for a meeting of Council. When on 15 September, Cecil heard from the Duke that he had decided that he 'must bear all overthwarts with patience', it was clear that the Queen's will was prevailing.[12]

Norfolk's patience did, however, run out. On 21 September he withdrew to Kenninghall in the heart of his country. There he struggled miserably to decide on whether to lead a rebellion or to obey the Queen. Cecil urged him to use 'that humble and affectionate mind towards her Majesty our sovereign that always you have in all such conferences manifested to me.'[13] Leicester too sapped the Duke's resolution with calls for a return to Court.

Norfolk's nerve failed. He went to the Tower. Arundel, Pembroke, Lumley and Throckmorton were arrested. All those, except Leicester, who had conspired against him in the spring, Cecil now saw discredited. The collapse of his opponents had come about through the strength of Elizabeth's and the weakness of the Duke's will.

The French and Spanish ambassadors credited Cecil with having engineered the downfall of his enemies.[14] It was a flattering misconception of Cecil's political skill. Cecil, like Sussex, had disengaged himself from a dangerous situation. He had walked delicately and he had left no incriminating footprints beyond the border of loyalty to his Queen or to his noble fellow councillor. Cecil was not seeking to destroy the nobility. It was no advantage to Cecil to remove the man who could be used to balance Leicester in Council. He recommended to the Queen that Norfolk should be found a wife to prevent a marriage to Mary. He added, 'I cannot see how his acts are within the compass of treason'. Had Cecil been either personally vindictive or socially prejudiced towards the Duke, he might well have found it easy enough to stretch the limits of treason. Of Mary he did not hesitate to write to Elizabeth, 'The Queen of Scots is and shall always be a dangerous person to your estate.'[15] He suggested that she would be least dangerous in prison, married to Bothwell and openly convicted of murder.

With Norfolk in the Tower the troubles of 1569 were not at an end. The Earls of Northumberland and of Westmorland, who had earlier promised Norfolk armed support, were summoned to Court by Elizabeth to test their loyalty. Upon rumours of revolt in the North, Cecil, who always kept an eye on the border country, sounded Sussex, the President of the Council of the North. It appeared to be a false alarm until on 13 November, Sussex, unable to make Northumberland and Westmorland respond to the Queen's command, declared them rebels. The rebellion in the North which Cecil suspected might one day break out in favour of Mary Queen of Scots and her catholic faith was a reality.

Cecil, who had seen in Edward's day the need to act firmly against rebellion feared the worst and prepared for the worst. He planned the mobilisation of armies large enough to suppress a

country-wide uprising of Catholics and to deter foreign interference. The trusted Hunsdon and Sadler were sent North. As the
army to guard the Queen, the army to control the West and the
army to be sent North assembled, even the military men protested
that the forces were excessive. But Cecil encouraged a massive
demonstration of loyalty and force. He sent his son Thomas and
his ward, the Earl of Rutland, to the Border for military experience.
But the Earls did not make a stand and ignominiously withdrew
to Scotland. On Christmas day Cecil was able to write, 'the vermin
be fled into foreign covert.'[16]

The revolt of the Northern Earls had been a shock. Cecil
considered stern means of punishment which the age expected.
He wanted to make the rebels pay for the cost of the countermeasures. 'It were a pity', he wrote, 'but some of these rascals
were hanged by martial law, but for the ruler, would be taken and
attainted, for otherwise it is doubtful how the Queen's Majesty
shall have any forfeiture of their lands or goods.'[17] But Cecil had
more on his mind than the hundreds of misguided men who loaded
the gallows in the North: he was searching for the clues which led
to Mary Queen of Scots and the Spanish ambassador.

In 1570 the Border and Scotland remained the focus of interest
for Cecil. The last fling of northern revolt under Dacre was
crushed by Hunsdon. Sussex struck across the Border at the
refugee Northern Earls and their supporters. In January the
Regent had been assassinated and Scotland was falling into
disorder. The Queen seemed to wish to restore Mary in order to
achieve a settlement in Scotland, but the Council supported James
as the figure-head of English influence. Cecil remained in the
background and it was his brother-in-law, Nicholas Bacon, who
expressed the opposition of the Council to government by Mary
in Scotland. The division between the Queen and the Council was
deep. Elizabeth was impressed by the threat of foreign intervention
in Scotland, which looked real in July, and she opened negotiations
with Mary despite Bacon's forthright resistance. Cecil and Mildmay
were called upon to deal with Mary. While the Queen of Scots
accepted all concessions and gave no guarantees, Cecil made
himself agreeable. During the autumn his interest was in extending

the negotiations and allowing Mary to overreach herself. But Elizabeth's firmness forced Mary to accept her terms. The next stage was to put these terms before the young King's party. Cecil remained convinced that nothing could come of the Queen's support for Mary. 'Surely, few here amongst us,' he wrote, 'conceive it feasible with surety.'[18]

Just as the negotiations with Mary were in part a consequence of the revolt of the Northern Earls, so was the publication of a papal bull, excommunicating Elizabeth and deposing her. During the early summer, when Cecil learned of the bull, he began to write a defensive pamphlet which he did not complete. The bull confirmed his suspicions of the tyranny of the Pope and of the loyalty of the catholic laity in England, who were now absolved from their oath of allegiance to the Queen. But the bull did, by stressing the political implications of Catholicism, invite political retaliation. Cecil saw that the bull was indeed a weapon against the Catholics, since, as he pointed out, it 'induceth necessarily the party to be criminal of treason.'[19] Cecil liked legal weapons and from 1570 onwards he was well equipped to strike at Catholics.

Another legacy of the troubles of 1569 which remained to be settled was the treatment of the imprisoned Duke of Norfolk. Cecil was instrumental in getting the Duke released from the Tower and restored to Kenninghall during the summer plague season in London. Norfolk was in no position to do further harm. He might still be helpful to the Secretary to balance the factions at Court. Perhaps Cecil, knowing of the Duke's continued correspondence with Mary Queen of Scots, was hoping to give enough rope for the reckless pair to hang themselves.

While the survival of the greatest noble title in England, that of the Dukedom of Norfolk, was thus in some doubt, Cecil became the latest peer of the realm. On 25 February 1571, the Queen in her Presence Chamber at Westminster, with all due ceremony, pronounced him first Baron Burghley. Cecil had reached the social and honorific peak of his career. The Queen had recognised his past successes and had confirmed her trust in him. His ennoblement was a reward for long service to the Crown.[20] To those who had seen him incapacitated for long periods by ill health in the winter of 1570–1 his title must have appeared as the prelude to retirement.

When Throckmorton died in the month of Cecil's honour, Cecil himself had said, 'he doth but lead the way to us'. Walsingham had felt that Cecil's burden must be lightened and had spoken to him of finding some way 'so to use your service as you may long serve'.[21] Few would have guessed that Cecil, with his grey beard and his gout, was only half way through his career.

In the social hierarchy Cecil had climbed high. He rounded off the personal success of the year with the marriage of his favourite daughter, the fifteen-year-old Anne, to a de Vere, the seventeenth Earl of Oxford, his former ward.[22] The marriage took place on 19 December in the presence of the Queen at Westminster Abbey. Lord Burghley had turned down Philip Sidney and the Earl of Rutland. He had made the match with the most brilliant of the young nobility. The marriage proved too good to be true. The parental miseries which Cecil had once endured over his son Thomas were now about to be renewed by the unhappy marriage of his daughter.

Cecil was not prepared to retire in a blaze of glory as Lord Burghley. In the year of his elevation to the peerage he was as fully immersed as ever in his secretarial duties. He urged procrastination over any settlement with Mary and took up the proposal that Elizabeth might marry the Duc d'Anjou because it drew French interest away from Mary and Scotland. An alliance against the Pope and Philip II and the prospect of ensuring peace at home and in Ireland seemed to Burghley to be the advantages which outweighed the dangers in the latest matrimonial venture which attracted the Queen. Burghley instructed his protégé Walsingham as ambassador in France to make light of the difficulties over religion and play the Queen's game. But he did not favour Walsingham's advocacy of a plan put forward by the French King to form a grand alliance against Spain. In following the royal initiative in the Anjou affair, Burghley had abandoned the vision of a protestant cause and was playing for limited dynastic and national stakes in opportunist diplomacy. Both he and Leicester, whom the Queen had made her prime agents in the Anjou negotiations, revealed their position when they confessed that, 'As for the inward intention of her Majesty in this case, we cannot certainly give you to understand more than it pleaseth her to utter.'[23] Their admission was not diplomatic discretion: it was true.

At home his title did not lessen his role as the Queen's manager of Parliament. When Parliament met in the spring of 1571, protestant anger over the papal bull made it lively with puritan attempts to attack Catholics and secure further reform of the Church. The new lord kept a close watch on proceedings in both Houses. He fostered co-operation between the Lords and the Commons. It appears that he gave support to a Bill to impose the religious test of attendance at Communion upon Catholics.[24] Elizabeth vetoed the Bill. But it was small wonder if Burghley showed sympathy with the puritans in the Commons as the details of the Ridolfi plot became clear to him.

Ridolfi had acted as the imaginative weaver of a conspiracy which involved Norfolk, Mary Queen of Scots and de Spes in a scheme to rouse catholic revolt at home and invasion from abroad. Burghley's unravelling of the plot revealed his readiness to meet unscrupulousness with ruthlessness. He got wind of the schemings by placing an agent of his in prison with a courier of Bishop Ross, Mary's chief adviser. He personally interrogated and then sent to the rack the courier who had been hoodwinked into dangerous disclosures. The confessions obtained implicated Ross and the Duke of Norfolk. To catch the big fish, Burghley used his trusted friends, Sadler, Smith, Mildmay and Wilson. Ross confessed everything and so Norfolk was trapped. De Spes was shown to be involved and was expelled.[25]

Norfolk could not be exonerated of treason again. But Burghley took no personal part in the interrogations of the Duke and at his long delayed trial sought only to establish that the evidence was correct. It was Lord Cobham who on this occasion derived advantage from Burghley's partiality for the nobility.[26] Burghley connived at Cobham's suppression of evidence in the early stages of unmasking the Ridolfi plot. Torture was reserved for lesser men. Gentlemen and nobles were treated as befitted their degree. It was the code of the age. When finally the end came for him,

Norfolk rose to the occasion. He put his children into the care of
Burghley. It was a considerable tribute.

While Norfolk showed no resentment towards the man with
whom and against whom he had worked, there were those who
were ready to claim that Burghley had deliberately sought the
downfall of Norfolk. Two of the Duke's men tried to devise a
plot against Burghley's life. But it was an affair of small men with
big ideas and it resulted in the execution of the two leading spirits.[27]

The disclosures of the Ridolfi plot persuaded the Queen that
Mary could not be restored and inclined her to accept Burghley's
policy for Scotland. During the winter of 1571-2 Burghley
elaborated his plans for a settlement in Scotland. James was
accepted as King and Mar as Regent. Every effort was to be made
to compose the civil strife. Burghley was ready to offer lenient
treatment to the Marian party. Even the diehards, Kirkcaldy and
Maitland, were to be spared and given compensation.[28] The
settlement of Scotland remained the nearest and dearest object of
Burghley's diplomacy.

As always a policy for Scotland became entangled with
diplomacy towards France. The French King was holding up a
treaty with England while he tried to get favourable terms for
Mary Queen of Scots. Elizabeth had switched her courtship to
Alençon, Anjou's ugly younger brother, and her most skilled
diplomats, Smith, Killigrew and Walsingham, were busy trying to
turn the Queen's romantic gesture into a formal alliance. But
Burghley, more concerned with ending the embargo on the
Antwerp trade, was negotiating with Spanish agents. In order to
obtain the best terms, he took the *rapprochement* with Spain slowly.
Thus early in 1572 both France and Spain were seeking a settlement
of differences with England.[29]

These negotiations were suddenly suspended when the Queen
fell ill in March. Burghley's part in affairs lapsed when he in his
turn fell sick in April. The Secretary appeared to be near to death.
The Queen came in person to see him.[30] But like the Queen,
Burghley did not give up easily and he recovered. Both illnesses
had important effects: the Queen's brought about the calling of a
Parliament for May and Burghley's persuaded him to give up the

Secretaryship. The Lord Treasurer's death in March presented an opportunity for advancement.

The Treaty of Blois with France was signed while Burghley lay in bed. Its terms were those, however, for which he had worked. The treaty was defensive, both parties agreeing not to assist each other's enemies. There was no grand alliance and no positive aggressive aim which would commit England to war. The signatories were to arrange peace in Scotland. Mary Queen of Scots was excluded. An agreement for an English staple in France was in the nature of a threat to Antwerp rather than a serious economic proposal. Burghley had some justification for his pious hopes of the treaty, which were that 'first the Glory of God and next the two realms and princes may long see the fruits thereof'.[31]

Burghley was less happy about the results of the Parliament which had been summoned in the shadow of the Queen's illness and met on 8 May. Its purpose was to deal with Mary Queen of Scots. A joint committee of the two Houses, in which Burghley was an influential member, recommended that either Mary be executed for her crimes or excluded from the succession. Elizabeth, much to the disappointment of the Commons and of Burghley, chose to consider exclusion. Burghley was in poor health and he had to be carried to Parliament and to see the Queen. He grumbled in confidence about the blame laid upon 'inward Councillors' for the Queen's weak decision upon Mary. Elizabeth's safety and all that was maintained by her existence seemed to Burghley to depend on the extinction of Mary.[32]

Just before Parliament had met, Burghley had been installed as a Knight of the Garter. He was clearly destined to succeed Winchester as Lord Treasurer. The Secretaryship passed to his old friend Sir Thomas Smith in June. On 15 July he became Lord Treasurer. His latest honour was celebrated by entertaining the Queen at his latest mansion, Theobalds. The new office made him responsible for the finances of the realm and greatly extended his patronage. But his personal participation in the work of the financial courts was only as great as he cared to make it. He was now freed from the detailed administrative tasks of the Secretaryship. But it was clear that he still carried out that part of the

Secretary's duties concerned with matters of high policy. Smith
was older than Burghley and, as a confirmed misogynist, was
quite unable to deal with the Queen. In Smith, Burghley had a
friend who could not possibly challenge his influence with the
Queen. 'I am not discharged from my ordinary care', was his
satisfied understatement. For Elizabeth, when she was in a good
mood, he had become 'our Principal Councillor'.[33]

Burghley would have found it hard to limit himself to financial
affairs in the summer of 1572. With the capture of Brill by the Sea
Beggars, whose rebel fleet manned by Calvinist refugees Elizabeth
had expelled from English ports in April, the revolt against Spain
in the Netherlands had been strengthened. Burghley feared that
the French Huguenots might seize the chance to intervene in the
Low Countries. In June he recommended that diplomatic
soundings should be made in the Dutch ports and among the
German protestant Princes. He was ready to counter French
intervention by assurances of English aid to Alva on condition
that Spain would restore the liberties of the United Provinces and
content herself with a nominal suzerainty. He predicted that if the
French established themselves in the Netherlands 'our sovereignty
upon the Narrow seas will be abridged with danger and
dishonour'.[34]

The arguments of Leicester and Walsingham for using the
French to support the Calvinist rebels in the Low Countries did
not appeal to Burghley. He was not enthusiastic for a protestant
alliance which would put France in place of Spain in the Netherlands. He abandoned the ideological politics of the balance
between Protestant and Catholic for the power politics of the
balance between France and Spain. But he was ready meanwhile
to insure England against both the 'great Monarchies' by allowing
English volunteers to pour into the Netherlands to aid the
protestant rebels.

The position in the Netherlands complicated negotiations for
the Alençon match and for the settlement with Alva. The English
volunteers upset Alva and his reaction alarmed Elizabeth. At the
same time Elizabeth checked the pace of her matrimonial negotiations by dwelling upon the ugliness of her French suitor. In July,

Burghley found the Queen 'very irresolute in these Bas Country matters.'[35] But the event which shook the surface of affairs into dangerous confusion was the Massacre of St Bartholomew's Eve in August.

'These French tragedies with blood and vile murders cannot be expressed with tongue to declare the cruelties ' wrote Burghley of the death of Coligny and the widespread slaughter of the Huguenots. Such religious violence, he feared, 'may come hither and into Scotland for such cruelties have large scopes'. The Massacre unmasked the ruthlessness of catholic France and revealed the menace of the papal tyranny before protestant English eyes. The focus 'for such cruelties' in England was Mary Queen of Scots.[36] The Queen, Burghley and Leicester plotted to return Mary to Scotland for execution by the Regent. Burghley instructed Killigrew upon his secret mission to the Regent. 'You may give the said party some likelihood to think that if there were any earnest means secretly made by the Regent and the earl of Morton to some of the lords of Council here to have her delivered to them' he told Killigrew, 'it might be at this time better than any time heretofore, brought to pass that they might have her, so as there might be good surety given that she should receive that she hath deserved there by order of Justice.'[37] The Scots did not accept that justice should be done.

Burghley put the navy in a state of readiness and connived at English volunteers crossing to the Huguenot stronghold, La Rochelle. He intrigued with important Calvinist refugees and with Alençon, who, nervous about his position in France, was ready to come to England. To the French King he conveyed the English shock at the Massacre and a demand for the punishment of the culprits. But Burghley could see that Elizabeth, after due expressions of horror, was prepared to accept the French explanations of the Massacre and keep the alliance which had been gained by the Treaty of Blois.

Mistrust of France, roused by the Massacre, made Burghley more willing to settle with Spain. An agreement in October with Alva was not ratified, because of rumours of further slaughter of Protestants. But the chance of settlement was too good to miss and Burghley steered the Council to improve relations with Alva. Burghley's terms were accepted on 1 January 1573. The embargo was lifted after four years. The political importance of the agreement was that it was aimed at removing the flash-points of hostility between Spain and England. Both sides agreed not to aid rebels or pirates against each other and to banish those of each other's subjects who gave offence in religious matters.[38]

By the end of 1572 Burghley had also reached agreement with France and saved the situation in Scotland. The armistice between the Marian party and those around the Regent and the King, which extended until 1 January 1573, looked like breaking down when the Regent, Mar, died in October. Burghley gave his advice and Morton became Regent. The armistice, arranged under the Treaty of Blois, was confirmed.

The four years which ended in 1572 had seen great changes in William Cecil's social rank, in his offices, and in his policies. At fifty-two he was now a noble with children wedded to aristocratic families. From the Secretaryship he had been elevated to the Lord Treasurership. To the Queen's trust in him he had now added her more intimate confidence. He had achieved an equality with Leicester in that he now touched the Queen's affection as much as he appealed to her self-interest. He was paired with Leicester in the most vital and secret of the Queen's inner counsels. Burghley had come closer to the Queen in his apprehension of the virtues of the negative and the ambiguous in diplomacy.

CHAPTER XI

Principal Councillor

THE settlements of 1572 with Scotland, France and Spain shifted
the emphasis of the political problems confronting the English
government. The King's party, established in Scotland, would
have to be watched and controlled. The treatment of the desperate
Queen of Scots became a more urgent question. Confidence in the
Treaty with France, undermined by the Massacre of St Bartholomew, had to be restored despite the moving background of civil
war and changes of King upon the French throne. The agreement
with Spain, while it reopened trade with Antwerp, made relations
with the Dutch rebels all the more delicate. These emergent
difficulties called for Burghley's experienced counsel.

During the spring of 1573 Burghley urged the Queen to send
forces to overthrow the last resistance to James VI. He parried
French efforts to dissuade the Queen from action. In April after
her usual attempt to make time solve her problems, the Queen
took Burghley's advice. English guns were sent to batter
Edinburgh Castle. Thomas Cecil, unknown to his father, had
slipped off to Scotland to see the final defeat of Mary Stuart's
party.[1] The summer saw Burghley involved in negotiations for
the marriage of Elizabeth to Alençon, brother of the French King.
While he was personally in favour of the match, he had given up
trying to control the matrimonial diplomacy of the Queen and
was content to follow as he might the game which she played with
all the fickleness of a coy mistress.[2]

In France the perils of religious strife were frightening. At home
Burghley looked at signs of the progress of Catholicism among the
influential gentry with foreboding. The challenge of presbyterian
puritanism was becoming apparent. The *Admonition to Parliament*
published in the last session had brought up the whole question of
Church government and reform. Behind the pamphlet by Field

and Wilcox lay the teaching of Thomas Cartwright. In 1570 Burghley had played Pilate over Cartwright and had allowed the University elders, led by Whitgift, to expel him from his professorship and fellowship. But in 1573 it was no longer possible for Burghley to wash his hands of what had become a movement among the puritan clergy and their powerful lay patrons to abolish the episcopate and develop a presbyterian system within the Church of England. The settlement of 1559 was being attacked and it did not need Parker's complaints to alert Burghley to the democratic implications or 'popularity' of Calvinistic ecclesiastical organisation.[3]

In the autumn of 1572 Burghley had already reviewed the weaknesses of the established Church in the face of this attack.[4] He could not and did not deny the need for reform. His dilemma was that he had a sympathy with the puritan programme in so far as it was concerned with stricter Sabbath observance, better financial and educational provision for the lower clergy and a greater emphasis on preaching and pastoral duty, but he could not accept the extremists' rejection of the Prayer Book and the episcopate. The appeal of Calvinism to the younger generation was not shared by Cecil, who had reached the limits of change with Cranmer. It was Leicester and Walsingham who took on the leadership of the new and well-organised presbyterian puritanism. Burghley found himself along with Parker on the defensive, guarding what seemed akin to popery in the eyes of extremists.[5] When he addressed the Justices of the Peace in October 1573, he characteristically fell back on a legalistic rather than a religious defence of the Church. He stressed the need for uniformity and the duty of obedience to the Supreme Governor.[6]

By the end of the year Burghley was again in ill-health. The continued control of the Secretaryship over Thomas Smith's head and the worry of embarrassing rumours about his son-in-law, Oxford, had taxed his strength. The appointment of Walsingham to a Secretaryship in December was well timed. The stricken Burghley was relieved at last of the daily weight of affairs. As Lord Treasurer, he was still entangled in financial business and he kept his influence in ecclesiastical matters. He was far from being retired. The Queen found the able Walsingham too much of a puritan and too impetuous to trust as she had trusted Burghley, and she was quick to seek the older man's advice when grave issues arose.

But Burghley's great reputation attracted constant attack. In 1573 he was concerned by the denigration of himself and his brother-in-law perpetrated in the *Treatise of Treasons*, published in Louvain in 1572, and in an abridged version which came out in the following year.[7] These anonymous pamphlets by catholic refugees tried to establish a picture of Burghley as a base-born 'new man', dedicated to abasing the nobility and to enriching himself and increasing his power at the expense of the Queen. He was accused of being an atheistical Machiavellian who was leading the people into heresy. His treatment of Mary Queen of Scots was represented as undermining the authority of Elizabeth. He was branded as a provoker of Spain and an advocate of anti-papal national sovereignty. It was also claimed that he imposed heavy taxes, was corrupt in the Court of Wards and encouraged the immigration of foreigners. Yet the same Burghley who could hoodwink a nation was accused of being 'a hen . . . Chiefly for his hennish heart and courage.'[8] A pattern of attack upon Elizabethan policy had been established and with a few changes could serve against Leicester.[9] Burghley was right in seeing that this mixture of moral indignation and xenophobia, of religious condemnation, social prejudice and personal abuse was good propaganda. It proved an enduring indictment of Burghley for those who lamented the protestant foundations of Elizabethan England.

Throughout most of 1574 Burghley was in bad health. The removal of the compulsions of routine made it easier, perhaps, for Burghley to surrender to the gout. He took more interest in the building of Theobalds, where the Queen came to see him in May.[10] But he kept his political attention on France. The imminent death of Charles IX made Burghley eager to strengthen Alençon, the Queen's suitor, as leader of the opposition which might check the ambitions of the heir to the throne, Henry of Anjou, King of Poland. The accession of Anjou was expected to bring about a restoration of the Guise power with a renewal of catholic militancy and interest in the cause of Mary Stuart. In the summer Burghley met the French and Spanish envoys. He demonstrated friendship for France in the hope of preserving the alliance and amity towards Spain in case the French *entente* collapsed.[11] His prestige and charm did something to disguise English doubts about which way to jump and enabled Elizabeth to hold off Leicester and Walsingham, who were clamouring for action to support the Huguenots in France. As the year drew to its close the Secretaries, Smith and Walsingham, began to lament Burghley's relapse into diplomatic inactivity.[12]

In the new year Burghley made an effort to tackle more detailed business and to keep in close touch with Walsingham. Elizabeth called him in to advise on the awkward situation which had arisen as a result of the success of the Sea Beggars. These Calvinist rebels had re-established themselves in the Netherlands all too effectively and their blockade of the trade with Antwerp was nullifying the Queen's arrangement with Spain to reopen commerce with the Netherlands. The blockade fouled relations with William of Orange, the rebel leader, and with Requesens, the Spanish Governor. Burghley drafted instructions for the diplomats but his ill-health still dominated his activities.[13]

In August Burghley decided to go to Buxton to take the waters of the spa recently made fashionable by the Earl of Shrewsbury. The change had a tonic effect. Burghley rode out each day, ate well and entertained. But the visit to Buxton involved him with its patron. He had to fend off the Earl of Shrewsbury's proposal for a marriage alliance between the Talbots and the Cecils. Equally embarrassing were the rumours which accused Burghley of having visited the Earl in order to enter into an intelligence with his charge, Mary Queen of Scots. The attempts to discredit Burghley with Elizabeth failed.[14]

In the autumn of 1575 Burghley returned with more gusto to consider the changing situation in Europe. Anjou had become Henry III and was not displaying the hostility which Elizabeth anticipated from her disappointed suitor. Alençon was with the Huguenot faction and his aid was being sought by William of Orange. Burghley put down his thoughts in October.[15] He regarded effective French or Spanish control in the Netherlands as inimical to English interests. His solution was either openly or secretly to aid the rebels until they had established their ancient rights, reducing Spanish influence to a nominal suzerainty, or to accept the rebels as subjects of the Queen. Before commitment to either course he suggested a legal investigation into the rights of the rebels and the claims of Spain, a survey of the military requirements of intervention and an inquiry into the support which the Queen was likely to receive, if she aided the rebels until the Spaniards were ready for mediation. It was a proposal which had all the usual ingredients of Burghley's statecraft. It was flexible, practical and legalistic.

Elizabeth decided to try mediation. Burghley controlled the diplomatic approach to Orange, Requesens and Philip II.[16] The reactions were disappointing. Orange threatened to resort to the French for aid if there was any further delay in action by Elizabeth. The Spaniards remained rigid in their attitude to the rebels. For Burghley the choice between mediation and intervention was becoming clearer. He worked out the financial and military requirements of supporting Orange and was considering the tactics of an expeditionary force. Carefully suppressing any religious appeal to the Queen, he tried to coax her with appreciations based on considerations of power politics. But neither the presentation of the national interest by Burghley nor the declaration of the needs of the common cause of Protestantism by Leicester and Walsingham altered the Queen's preference for mediation. Burghley had the task of dealing with the Spanish and Dutch envoys in England. Despite his efforts to put to them the Queen's conciliatory attitude, the Spaniards believed that Burghley was for aiding the rebels, and the Dutch thought that his object was to withhold support from them. The price of his loyalty to the Queen was misunderstanding.

While Burghley shielded the Queen from any commitment over the Netherlands the months passed. At home the spring Parliament of 1576 met. It was Mildmay who managed the Commons. Burghley in the Lords seems to have played no great part.[17] His attention was focused on foreign affairs. Events were leading towards hostility to the Dutch rebels. Their blockade of commerce with Antwerp and piratical attacks upon English shipping made Elizabeth's policy of mediation seem futile. Burghley's son-in-law, Oxford, had been the victim of piratical attack in the Channel.[18] But it was in response to the Queen's demand for action against William of Orange and not on behalf of Oxford that Burghley began to explore the possibilities of joint action with Spain, of armed protection for English merchantmen and of the diversion of trade to English markets as a means of defeating the Dutch blockade.[19] But the political, financial and practical objections to these proposals persuaded Burghley to suggest to Elizabeth that she left the suffering English merchants to work out their own arrangements with the Dutch while she concentrated upon negotiations with Orange to end depredations on English trade. By midsummer the Queen's anger had cooled and her readiness to meet force with force had changed to a willingness to resort again to diplomacy. Friendly relations with Orange were restored.

It was as well that Elizabeth had taken Burghley's advice, for Orange increased his influence in the Netherlands. The death of Requesens in March had created an opportunity for leadership by Orange and, when in the autumn Spanish troops mutinied, he was able to unite the Netherlands. The sack of Antwerp by Spanish soldiers in November was followed by the Pacification of Ghent which put the United Provinces behind Orange in an effort to restore the old privileges and expel the Spanish army. The new strength of Orange invited support. Henry III and his rebellious brother Alençon were ready to support resistance to Spain now that it arose from the Netherlands as a whole and not from two of its provinces. Elizabeth could not afford to be outbid. In December she sent a large subsidy to Orange. But she also approached the newly appointed Spanish Governor, Philip II's ambitious half-brother, Don John of Austria, with offers of mediation. Burghley set out the instructions for both moves.

In his domestic life the year 1576 had held much bitterness for Burghley. Not since the keenly felt disgrace of Thomas Cecil's behaviour in France had scandal touched the family. Now rumour had it that the child of Lady Oxford, born in July 1575, was no daughter of the Earl.[20] The rumour worried Burghley and enraged his son-in-law. When Oxford returned in April 1576 from a tour on the Continent, he refused to see his parents-in-law and his wife. Misunderstanding grew. Oxford persisted in disowning his wife until July, when, under pressure from the Queen, he agreed to provide for her separate maintenance. It was six years before Oxford was reconciled to his wife, but all his life he attracted scandal and was involved in scrapes. The only consolation which Burghley gained from that disastrous marriage came to him in his old age from the guardianship of his daughter's three girls. At the end of 1576 the misery of his daughter, the grief of his wife and his own discomfiture were still fresh.

With all these emotions locked within him, Burghley watched the greater tragedies and comedies of politics. A new act began in February 1577. Don John won over the Estates with the Perpetual Edict, promising the evacuation of Spanish forces from the Netherlands. Elizabeth saw hope for her cherished belief that the solution to the problems in the Netherlands lay in the maintenance of the nominal suzerainty of Spain in order to exclude French influence, satisfy the rebels and put Spanish communications at the mercy of the English fleet. But in Council, Leicester's desire to support the rebels prevailed. Burghley was won over to Leicester's view when Don John recalled Spanish troops and Orange prepared for resistance. The initiative was passing to Leicester and Walsingham. Burghley was content to let his recent control of foreign affairs lapse.

In July he planned to take his 'old crazed body' to Buxton.[21] With him he took his son Thomas and his son's friend Roger Manners. Although Walsingham dutifully informed Burghley of affairs, the August holiday was evidently intended to be a break from politics. Burghley was careful to avoid any contact with Mary Queen of Scots, who claimed to have won over Leicester on his visit to Buxton earlier in the summer. Burghley went for the waters. He does not seem to have cared greatly for the Derbyshire countryside. He once commiserated with Bess of Hardwick for living at Chatsworth 'amongst hills and rocks and stones'.[22] He preferred the controlled nature of his gardens.

Back at Court in September Burghley found his friend Grindal
heading for trouble with the Queen. On the death of Parker in the
spring, Burghley had put forward Grindal for the Archbishopric
of Canterbury. He regarded Grindal as a good administrator and a
firm anti-papist. But the new Archbishop's belief in 'prophesyings',
Bible study groups for the clergy and on occasion for the laity
also, as a means of educating the clergy ran counter to the Queen's
suspicion that 'prophesyings' were occasions for puritan sedition.
Puritans were making use of 'prophesyings' as presbyteries. When
the Queen decided to prohibit them, Grindal refused in a most
tactless manner to pass on her order. Burghley's unfortunate
nominee had gone too far and within six months the Queen had
sequestered his see. Burghley tried to find a formula for reconciliation but failed.[23] The lapse of archiepiscopal control over the
Church gave the puritans an opportunity to increase their hold
within the Church. It was a situation which favoured their patron
Leicester.

Meanwhile events in the Netherlands during the winter and
into the spring of 1578 made it difficult for Elizabeth to decide
how to maintain the peace, the trade and the ancient privileges of
the United Provinces. In the autumn of 1577 Burghley had picked
up the diplomatic threads and by December he set out the pattern
of his argument.[24] The designs of Don John to subjugate the
Netherlands, to invade England, to marry Mary Stuart, and to
threaten England's trade with the Continent seemed to Burghley
to outweigh any objections to giving aid to the rebel Dutch. He
was for immediate intervention. Leicester and Walsingham
supported more openly the arguments for protestant solidarity
against the catholic powers. Don John's victory over the Estates
in January made the need for action urgent. In March Elizabeth
made her decision. With her usual indirectness she agreed to
subsidise Duke Casimir of the Palatinate and his mercenaries to
campaign in the Netherlands on behalf of the rebels. Burghley put
her decision to the Council and out of caution considered the
requirements of an English expedition.[25]

While William of Orange waited for Duke Casimir to muster
his troops, Alençon offered him French help. In May the fear of a

French take-over in the Netherlands roused Burghley to suggest an immediate mission to the Low Countries to prevent French intervention, and a show of mobilisation at English ports to reassure the Dutch that England would act.[26] If the Estates did not reject Alençon's offer, Burghley was prepared to threaten joint action with the Spanish and the Duke Casimir to impose a peace. But, when the mission, led by no less a diplomat than Walsingham, was ready to depart, its instructions were reduced to a mild plea to Orange to see that Alençon did not make himself too powerful in the Netherlands. The Queen had been told by Alençon that he had no designs to establish French control in the Netherlands and that he would consult her on all his actions. These assurances had prompted Elizabeth to believe that the best way to deal with Alençon was to reopen marriage negotiations with him. Meanwhile the mission in the Netherlands had been frustrated in its efforts to mediate once again by the unacceptable terms for agreement put by the Estates to Don John. Walsingham was urging the sending of funds to the rebels. Burghley had been careful not to commit himself to the Queen's latest changes of policy. But in June Elizabeth turned to him to find a solution to the situation created by the failure of the negotiations in the Netherlands and the demands for money. The Queen was angry and vented her wrath on her old councillor, who patiently bore the brunt of her rage. He persuaded her to make further loans and with some difficulty he negotiated them.[27]

In August Elizabeth, having some doubts about Alençon's protestations of obedience, suggested to the Estates that Alençon should be asked to withdraw from the Netherlands. When she failed to support this request with any promise of English aid, Burghley took the opportunity to tell her that she would be blamed if France annexed the Low Countries, because she had made no offer of help as an alternative to French forces.[28] The Queen offered to send an army. Her change of mind came too late. Alençon and the Estates had reached agreement. The English mission tried desperately to obtain peace before the terms of the French agreement with Orange became effective but Orange responded by raising his demands for English help. The Queen refused to commit herself on such a scale. Burghley was in sympathy with the disheartened Walsingham in the Netherlands. He joined with Leicester in attempting to persuade the Queen to send both money and an army. He continued to hope that the Queen would see reason in the way that he saw it. She did not. She returned to the hope that Alençon could be manipulated by matrimonial strings.

By October Burghley was feeling the strain of a busy year. He had taken over the Secretary's duties while Walsingham was in the Netherlands. In July he had been on progress with the Queen. Yet, in the midst of it all, he had demonstrated his mental alertness by presiding over a three-hour disputation, conducted by a delegation from his University of Cambridge which had come to pay its respects to sovereign and chancellor at Audley End.[29] Now in the autumn he retired from Court. He took the opportunity to review the Queen's debts in Ireland and to ponder over the shift of events caused by the death of Don John.[30] But he was free from the pressure of proximity to the Queen.

The prospects of a return to Court were, however, lightened for him by Leicester's secret marriage to Lettice Knollys, widow of the Earl of Essex and daughter of Sir Francis Knollys. While the marriage strengthened Leicester's ties with the puritans and his father-in-law, the Treasurer of the Household and relative of the Queen, it could not but weaken his hold upon the affections of the Queen. Burghley was relieved that the marriage meant an end to a match with the Queen and the beginning of Leicester's need of his friendship. Meanwhile the Queen herself was becoming more than politically involved in the prospects of a marriage to Alençon. Her age and the blow of Leicester's defection conspired to turn dynastic manoeuvre into emotional fantasy.

In January 1579 Alençon's favourite, Simier, arrived to conduct the courtship of the Queen. His master's ineffectual campaign in the Netherlands had made the wooing a more worth-while adventure. Simier, whom Elizabeth nicknamed 'le singe', had a romantic repertoire which impressed the Queen more than it did her official negotiators, Burghley, Sussex, Leicester and Walsingham. They willingly acquiesced in the Queen's demand to

see Alençon in person. At the end of March, Burghley returned
to the old problem of the succession in memoranda on the
proposed marriage.[31] The justification of the marriage was the
need for an heir. On the advice of physicians and in trust of God's
blessing, Burghley was prepared to believe that the Queen might
bear a child without danger. The prospect of a French catholic
consort he found less easy to accept. Yet Alençon's record with
the Huguenots was not bad. If the Queen was ready to take the
risk, Burghley was ready to support the marriage despite his
mistrust of the traditional enemy, France.

Finding Burghley, of her principal councillors, the most
favourably inclined towards the match, the Queen relied upon
him to put the case before Council. In April the Queen asked the
Council to consider what situation would arise if she decided not
to marry Alençon. Burghley argued that the Queen's failure to
marry would lead to continual and costly rebellion on behalf of
Mary Queen of Scots, the catholic heir. A settlement of the
succession by the Queen's marriage would discourage the Pope
and the French and Spanish Kings from supporting Mary Stuart
and from plotting in Ireland and Scotland. The alternative to
dynastic alliance with France would be a rigorous policy of
enforcing uniformity in religion and building up military strength
at home while supporting rebels in France and the Netherlands,
and making pensioners of the Scottish King and nobility. Burghley
stressed the financial and military strain of such a policy. He
left little doubt that the marriage with Alençon was to be
preferred.[32]

Burghley's arguments suited the Queen. Arrangements went
ahead for a secret visit by Alençon. He arrived in mid August for
twelve days of courtship. On Alençon's arrival the Lord Treasurer
was away on a trip to Northamptonshire with his friend and
neighbour, the Chancellor of the Exchequer, Sir Walter Mildmay.[33]
On the Council's instructions they took the opportunity to look
into the puritan extremism which was rampant in the county town
and to meet the notorious Paul Wentworth, who championed the
puritan cause in the Commons. They seemed to have had some
success in quietening the extremists. A more congenial side of the

outing was a visit to the house of another neighbour, Sir Christopher Hatton. Burghley went to see Holdenby House with an architect's eye and he complimented Hatton on the new building which Hatton had modelled on Burghley's Theobalds. When Burghley returned to Court he found the Queen and Alençon philandering in a way which provoked the puritan courtiers and the citizens of London.

The violence of the puritan reaction expressed itself in a pamphlet by John Stubbs, which cost him and his printer a hand each in a memorable exhibition of royal justice and emotion. The old hatred of France had asserted itself and it was reinforced by fears that a marriage with a French prince would mean a catholic restoration in England. The Queen had not bargained for such vehement popular feeling. She defended herself but she began to have doubts about the wisdom of sacrificing the love of her people for the love of Alençon.

Early in October the Queen decided to test the opinion of Council. Burghley continued to argue in favour of the match.[34] He rehearsed the fears which he had expressed in the previous April of the dangers of catholic risings at home and foreign intervention on behalf of Mary Stuart if Elizabeth did not seize the chance to settle the succession by marriage. He again painted the picture of the grim suppression of discontent in England and heavy commitments to continental Protestants as the alternative to the dynastic alliance. When the Council remained unimpressed he stressed that the Queen had made up her mind to marry. But as spokesman of the deputation to the Queen he had to admit that there was no unanimity in the Council and that all that he could advise was for the Queen to see her councillors individually. Elizabeth was angry and her pride was hurt by the assumption that she would surrender to pressure for a catholic restoration. The councillors yielded to the Queen's obvious emotion and offered to give 'all our assents in furtherance of this marriage'. Elizabeth refused the hollow gesture and defiantly replied that she did not think it meet for Council 'to declare to us whether she should marry with Monsieur or no'. Negotiations for the match were continued but the final conclusion was postponed. By the end of 1579 Burghley sensed that the Queen was no longer serious about the emotional side of the matrimonial diplomacy.[35]

In September of 1579 Burghley had had his fifty-ninth birthday. During the previous six years he had become more preoccupied with his ailments. He had been more ready to go to Buxton and leave the Court. In 1579 his chief supporter in the early years under Elizabeth, Nicholas Bacon, his brother-in-law, died. Burghley's age prompted him to look after himself and try to postpone his own end. Yet on occasion he was tempted to make the most of his days. He sometimes showed an unusual pleasure in dining well. His expenditure upon building and furnishing his houses became more lavish. Knowing that his future must be shorter than his past he had reached the age of reminiscence.

It was only in comparison with his previous role in government that Burghley had appeared recently to be less concerned with the business of the State. He was still vastly more active and important than many other councillors. His attendance at Council and in the courts over which he presided was remarkably good whenever he was not totally incapacitated by gout. But he had become a reserve engine rather than the permanent driving force of the government. He was brought into action when the Queen needed extra power to deal with emergencies. The younger men too turned to him. When in 1577 the authority of Morton began to crumble in Scotland, the English agents there began to write to him as well as to Walsingham. It was still worth while to consult old Nestor. If his replies were becoming prolix, they had lost none of their pertinence. To foreign observers it seemed that the Lord Treasurer dominated the government. Burghley's treatment of the Queen was becoming more resigned and subtle. She was ready to admit that no other prince in Christendom had such a counsellor.

CHAPTER XII

Closing the Ranks

THE Earl of Northumberland declared that Burghley had been such a courtier all the summer of 1580 that he would not like to have to answer that the old man would be free of gout in the ensuing winter.[1] Burghley's attendance at Council and renewed activity were in response to the challenge posed by a combination of aggressive papal diplomacy, Jesuit missions and the growth of Spanish power following the annexation of Portugal. The menace of Catholicism intensified, not only in England, but also in Ireland and Scotland. The balance between Spain and France, pivoting on the course of affairs in the Netherlands, now swayed under Spain's added strength. The ultimate problem was to decide whether England's safety lay in placating Spain or in supporting France.

Early in 1580 Burghley was still arguing for the Queen's marriage to Alençon and sounding the French upon joint action to prevent Philip II from taking Portugal. But by midsummer, when he feared involvement in the civil wars of France, he was urging Elizabeth to drop her suitor. But Elizabeth took the advice of the majority of her Council and maintained correspondence with Alençon. In the autumn Burghley ceased to argue and was prepared to accept whatever resulted from the royal matrimonial diplomacy. He was ready to praise Alençon in order to preserve French friendship, but a growing appreciation of the value of trade with the Netherlands and of the power of the united Iberian Empires made him less ready to put all his trust in an alliance with France.[2]

His cool reception of Drake, who returned in July from his circumnavigation of the world, showed how anxious Burghley was becoming not to provoke Spain. From the beginning of Drake's voyage in 1577, Burghley, who had been excluded from its planning, was hostile to the project. The execution of Thomas

Doughty, Burghley's self-confessed agent on the expedition, had created further ill feeling.[3] When Elizabeth insulted Philip II by knighting Drake and injured the Spanish King by retaining Drake's booty, Burghley was depressed. He could see neither political advantage nor legal justification in such wanton provocation.

Burghley was keenly aware that a settlement in the Netherlands depended on Spanish good will. While Elizabeth fêted Drake, Burghley pondered over the situation in the Low Countries. Despairing of any arrangement with Philip II, he urged the Queen to outbid Alençon, who was striving to win over William of Orange by offering his personal assistance in the Netherlands. While underlining the cost of such a bid and the need to gain the support of the English nobility and Commons, who would have to bear the burden, Burghley seemed ready to support English intervention in the United Provinces.[4] But Elizabeth clung to the hope of using Alençon to check Spain.

If Burghley found that over the negotiations with Alençon, the reception of Drake and the policy in the Netherlands, he had to trust in God's good purposes rather than in those of the Queen, in the work of the Pope and the Jesuits he could detect the hand of the Devil. The offensive of the Counter-Reformation was striking the British Isles. The Jesuits, Campion and Parsons, arrived in England in June to revive the catholic faith. Gregory XIII identified, once again, Catholicism with treason in the protestant mind by issuing his explanation of the bull of 1570. The papal support for an invasion of Ireland by trouble-makers, which had been threatening since the adventurer Stucley had first offered his services to the Pope in 1571, now materialised. The rebel Desmond, Fitzmaurice Fitzgerald, entered Ireland along with the redoubtable opponent of the English Church, Nicholas Sanders. In Scotland, Esmé Stuart with his Guise and catholic connections arrived in September 1579 and was establishing himself in the favour of James VI. Burghley sent out proclamations against the Jesuits and the Desmond leader and demanded naval action against the rebels in Ireland. He strengthened the Border.[5]

The need to check Catholicism had already caught Burghley's

attention in 1579 and the events of 1580 made more severe action against the laity and the missionaries imperative. Since 1574 the seminary priests, trained at Douai, had been entering England and preventing Catholicism from dying for want of priests. Added to his fears about the influence of the catholic laity was Burghley's anger at the success of the seminaries, the 'seditious seedmen and sowers of rebellion', and of the Jesuits.[6] The Privy Council began to take action in 1580 against the revival of Catholicism.

In 1581 Parliament met 'to make provision of laws more strict and more severe to constrain' Catholics 'to yield their open obedience.'[7] Burghley took a close interest in the proceedings. The measures taken were in accord with the proposals of the bishops. The fine for recusancy was raised to £20 per month and heavy penalties for slandering the Queen were imposed. The financial pressure was upon the catholic gentry, of whom Burghley was most suspicious. It met Burghley's demand for a weapon against those who could be socially influential and politically dangerous.

Meanwhile Burghley was concerned with hunting down the Jesuits, particularly Campion, who declared that he came to preach the faith and not as a political agent of the Papacy. When Campion was captured, there followed a disputation, torture and trial, which ended in his conviction for treason under the statute of 1352. The impression of a religious martyrdom was left with too many Catholics. Burghley had not been in full charge of stage-managing the treatment of the Jesuit, but he took control of the propaganda which followed Campion's death.[8] It proved a difficult task to brand the martyr as a traitor.

Seeing the hand of Philip II behind papal diplomacy and the missions, Burghley swung to the French alliance in 1581. In April French commissioners with proposals for the marriage of Alençon and Elizabeth arrived to a festive and costly welcome by the Queen in a newly constructed banqueting hall and by Burghley in his house in the Strand. Negotiations, designed to save the Queen's dignity and buy time, proceeded until June, when the disgruntled commissioners left. Burghley too was tired and he withdrew from the Court, suffering from a cold.[9]

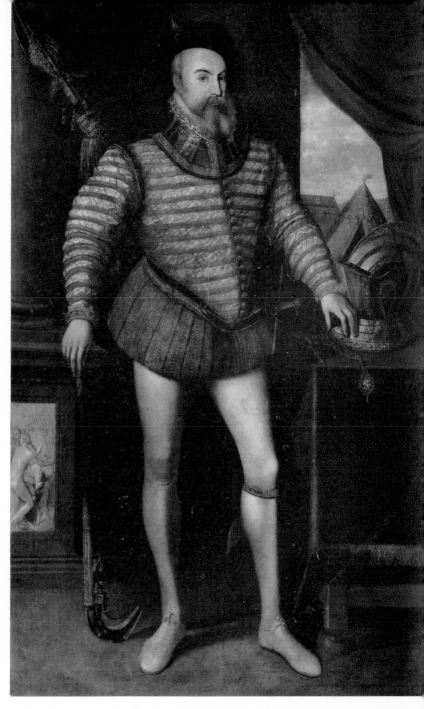

Robert Dudley, Earl of Leicester

Lord Burghley riding his mule in his garden

When Burghley returned to active politics in July, he tested the French King's friendship by suggesting that Drake with French aid should seize the Azores on behalf of the Portuguese pretender, Don Antonio.[10] The fact that England would not be officially involved and that no treaties would be violated by helping Don Antonio to take possession of what was still Portuguese territory made the venture palatable to Burghley. The French King proved less susceptible to legal niceties and refused to challenge Spain under such transparent cover. By August the plan was dropped, much to the disappointment of the militant followers of Leicester.

Meanwhile Elizabeth determined to stir the embers of the French marriage proposals once again. While Burghley performed the Secretary's duties at home, Walsingham was sent to France. Walsingham's efforts failed to obtain a political treaty before a marriage. Yet, when Henry III, tiring of the never-ending courtship, refused further support to Alençon, he gave Elizabeth the opportunity to control Alençon by the lure of gold rather than by royal nuptials. The old Lord Treasurer, by the risky procedure of sending bullion in the saddle-bags of couriers, delivered Elizabeth's first subsidy to Alençon more cheaply and more quickly than the skilled financier Horatio Palavicino thought possible.[11]

The successful transfer of the subsidy did not disguise from Burghley the diplomatic failure to win a firm alliance with France. Paying Alençon to fight Spain in the Netherlands seemed to be a poor insurance. Experience of negotiations with the French Prince, who came to England in October, did not convince Burghley that Elizabeth was backing a winner. By the end of the year Elizabeth wished to be rid of her guest and Burghley was contemplating a *rapprochement* with Spain. Yet, when Alençon finally departed in February 1582, Burghley seems to have taken little interest in continental diplomacy. Elizabeth was content to drift with only an occasional pull at the rudder. The cumbrous movements of the gigantic Spanish Empire seemed to provide an eternity of immunity.

Burghley's interest turned to Scotland. Since Esmé Stuart, now the Earl of Lennox, had contrived the downfall of the Regent

L

Morton in June 1581 there had been a cessation of diplomacy with
England. Jesuits were at work north of the Border. When the
Ruthven raid brought James under the control of men more
friendly to England in August 1582, Burghley was eager to
improve relations between the neighbouring kingdoms. He
learned from Sir George Cary, the son of his old friend, Hunsdon,
of the reception of attempts to influence James through his
mother and of the efforts to foil French diplomacy.[12] But by the
end of the year little progress had been made in winning the young
King of the Scots.

Meanwhile in his own household Burghley had the joy of seeing
his daughter Elizabeth married to William Wentworth in February
1582 and the sorrow of seeing her made a widow in the following
November, when plague carried off her husband. His grief over
the death of his amiable son-in-law was sharpened by the contrast
of Oxford's brawling life. The Queen's condolences came through
Hatton, who wrote, 'My good Lord, cast off this woe, let it not
touch your heart in which the wisdom of this world and state hath
found her seat for so many years, to God's glory, the Realm's
safety and your mortal renown.'[13] The old statesman was not
permitted to remain off the public stage in the wings of personal
emotion.

In the new year there were many parts for Burghley to play,
from the good angel in the tragi-comedy of the blackmail case,
involving Sandys, the Archbishop of York, who had been found
in bed with an innkeeper's wife, to the wealthy benefactor in the
winning of the Scotch King. In the first delicate matter Burghley's
'great and wise proceedings' saved the Archbishop's reputation,
gained pardon for his tormentor and pleased the Queen.[14] In
bringing a happy ending to this scandal Burghley had acted in his
most humane and tolerant manner. With no less understanding of
human nature he agreed to the proposal to win the Scottish hearts
of James and his nobles with English gold.[15]

Through these affairs Burghley was struggling against gout. In
April he was again stricken with grief when his newly widowed
daughter followed her bridegroom to the grave. Once more the
Queen rebuked him for indulgence in sorrow. When Burghley

appeared hurt by her harsh reminder of his duties, she wrote to
'Sir Spirit', 'But I have of late seen an *ecce signum*, that if an ass kick
you, you feel it too soon.' After the royal humour came the balm,
'God bless you and long may you last.'[16] Elizabeth visited the
bereaved parents at Theobalds in May.

Burghley obeyed the advice in his sovereign's letter: 'Serve
God for the King and be a good fellow to the rest.' Yet those to
whom he enjoyed being a good fellow were leaving the scene. Sir
Thomas Smith had gone. Burghley's constant supporter Sussex
died in 1583. Mildmay was soon to follow. While Burghley proved
able to establish relations with some of the younger men, like
Hatton, who had become Vice-Chamberlain, it was not so easy to
hold his own against Leicester and Walsingham.

Burghley's second thought about the wisdom of pensioning the
Scots and his fears that the purchase of unreliable allies would
offend the French were swept aside by the Leicester faction.
Burghley wished to use the Queen of Scots to influence her son.
When in June James shook off his advisers and, in August, turned
to Arran, Burghley suggested sending an envoy to discover
Scottish intentions.[17] His advice was taken and Walsingham left
for Scotland with Burghley's instructions. James did not prove an
easy fish to catch. Elizabeth began to think of treating with Arran.
Walsingham's mission proved ineffectual.

If the Secretary failed to land his catch in Scotland, at home his
agents netted Throgmorton in September. Burghley shared in the
dismay at Throgmorton's revelations of Jesuit plottings in
Scotland and of the scheme for the Duke of Guise with papal and
Spanish support to invade England, foment a catholic rising and
set free the Queen of Scots. The plot, implicating the Spanish
ambassador Mendoza and Mary Stuart, weakened Burghley's hope
of Spanish friendship and strengthened his distrust of the Scottish
Queen. The dangers to Elizabeth's life and realm were underlined
by the discovery in October of Somerville's plan to assassinate the
Queen.

To meet these threats Burghley recommended a determined
drive to destroy catholic influence. He made plain his attitude to
Catholics in his pamphlet, *The Execution of Justice in England*, which

was published in 1583.[18] It looked back to the execution of
Campion, and its argument that Catholicism was being put to
treasonable uses seemed to be confirmed by the Throgmorton
plot. The questions, propounded by Burghley, asking why
missionaries came in disguise, what weight Catholics gave to the
bull deposing Elizabeth, whether the Pope could authorise
rebellion and to whom Catholics would give their allegiance in the
event of an invasion of England at the behest of the Pope, were
hard to answer.

Where political Catholicism was concerned, Burghley was
ruthless because he was fighting for the survival of the realm. He
was prepared to argue on matters of faith. In 1582 the notable
recusant, Sir Thomas Tresham, had corresponded with Burghley
on matters of doctrine and had thanked him for his arguments,
'so balanced with magistrate-like indifference and justice and so
full fraught with honorable courtesy, divine precepts, Christian
charity, . . .'.[19] Burghley was charitable to many recusants who
were patently more concerned with salvation than with politics.
He may have imputed treason to Catholics who were innocent of
political intentions, but those Catholics who found Burghley 'a
very monster' were guilty of imputing their religious fanaticism to
a patriot concerned with politics.

Burghley was in Council when in January 1584 it expelled
Mendoza for his part in the Throgmorton plot. This hostile
gesture to Spain made it necessary to secure England's 'postern
Gate', the Border. Burghley was gracious to James VI and to his
captive mother. They in their turn hoped to use him. In the spring
Mary was thanking Burghley for his advice and wishing that she
might follow it. But Burghley's conditions for aid were high. He
wanted Mary to apologise for past misdeeds, to denounce former
plots and renounce future conspiracies, to ratify the Treaty of
Edinburgh and to desist from publicly insisting on her right to
succeed Elizabeth. He wanted to be judge of when it was opportune
for Mary to seek a share in the government of Scotland. He
demanded that hostages, the Scottish Parliament and the King of
France guaranteed Mary's good behaviour. While Burghley was
pondering over these demands, James informed him that he had

heard of his 'careful and bent good will' towards his royal person.[20] But, when James sent his envoy in October, it was Walsingham who handled the negotiations and Burghley who advised a reduction of the pension demanded by James.

While relations with Scotland improved, the situation in the Netherlands took a turn for the worse. The death of Alençon in June and the assassination of William of Orange in July left the Dutch rebels and the protestant cause without a leader. Elizabeth had to decide whether to take over the vacant leadership. When the problem came up in Council in early October, Burghley wrote a memorandum.[21] He saw that it was necessary to oppose Philip II, who, if he were allowed to triumph in the Netherlands, would turn upon England. But he did not disguise the magnitude of the military, financial and commercial strain of confronting Spain. To meet the cost, the control of cautionary ports in Holland and Zeeland and the close supervision of expenditure and taxation would be required. Diplomatic and military preparations would have to include securing Scottish friendship, inducing the King of Navarre and the Duke Casimir to undertake diversionary campaigns, attacking the Indies by sea, winning over more of the United Provinces and the employment of mercenaries for home defence. The morals of the people would have to be sustained by more fervent religious instruction and the better administration of justice.

Those who were more optimistic than Burghley could not escape the logic of his sober assessment. The decision depended upon whether 'the great peril and danger' of not intervening appeared greater than the 'many difficulties' which 'were remembered to depend upon succouring' the Dutch. To the 'martial men', Burghley seemed to be among those 'inclining to the Spaniard's party, degenerate and faint hearted cowards'.[22] But Burghley's robust pessimism could accept the worst without flinching. When the militant Leicester won from Council the momentous decision to fight Spain in the Netherlands, it was the measures, proposed by Burghley, which were undertaken in preparation for war.

The assassination of William of Orange which had persuaded the Council to go to war created panic amongst those eager

Protestants who were already shocked by the Throgmorton plot.
Burghley could not deny his sympathy with the keenest anti-papal
element in the country. When Whitgift, Grindal's successor as
Archbishop of Canterbury, began attacking puritan noncon-
formists, Burghley protested. He listened to the anti-episcopal
arguments put before him by men like old Sir Francis Knollys
who accused the bishops of acting as petty popes. He studied the
ex officio oath which had become Whitgift's weapon in the Court
of High Commission for striking down those who failed to
observe uniformity in religion.[23] But, despite Burghley's disapproval, Whitgift, secure in the Queen's favour, continued his
campaign for rigid ecclesiastical discipline. Strangely enough it
was Walsingham who achieved a compromise over the treatment
of the erring puritan clergy which satisfied both Burghley and
Whitgift.

Burghley's emotions rather than his intellect were also engaged
in the plan to protect the Queen's life which was put forward in
October 1584.[24] The scheme was a Bond of Association which
created a league amongst the gentry, bound by oath to put to
death any person who claimed the throne as a result of the
assassination of Elizabeth. It was a warning to Catholics that Mary
Queen of Scots or any other catholic candidate would not be
allowed to gain the throne 'by such devilish means'. But it was a
dangerous device since it sanctioned civil war. It lacked the legal
safeguards which usually characterised Burghley's work.

In the grim month which saw England committed to war in the
Netherlands and the protestant gentry committed to the Bond of
Association, Burghley found one reason for pleasure. His son,
Robert, returned from the Continent, where he had distinguished
himself by his good behaviour and the work which he had done
for Walsingham. Robert, at twenty-one years of age, was showing
promise. His father had called him back to England to take a seat
as Member for Westminster in the Parliament which was to meet
in late November.[25] Burghley was preparing Robert for a political
career.

The Parliament, after a long Christmas recess from 21 December
to 4 February, lasted until 29 March. They were embarrassing

sessions for Burghley. Statutory force for the Bond of Association was not obtained but, in the modified scheme which did become law, any person was to be tried if there was proof that he was involved in an attempt on Elizabeth's life. A trap had been set for the Queen of Scots. Burghley's hopes of a regency council to determine the succession in the event of Elizabeth's death were disappointed. The puritans in the Commons involved Burghley in a quarrel with Whitgift during which Burghley criticised the quality of the clergy and declared that in one diocese 'the greatest part of them are not worthy to keep horses'. But the Queen protected the Archbishop by forbidding the discussion of clerical affairs and vetoing ecclesiastical Bills, including one on Sabbath Day observance which Burghley supported in the Lords. A Bill to continue the fish days which Burghley had instituted in 1563 failed. Legal reforms, touching fraudulent conveyances and the liabilities of wardship, which had Burghley's backing, were nullified. Finally Puckering, in the closing address to the Queen, omitted from the outline, given him by Burghley, the reminder to the Queen that she was responsible for Church reform.[26]

Burghley's loyalties had been divided during the Parliament between the need for Church reform and obedience to the Queen, who sheltered Whitgift. His efforts to take the initiative through the Lords had roused resentment in the Commons. But what made that session the nadir of his parliamentary career was the behaviour in the Commons of one of his agents, William Parry.[27] In his role as agent provocateur, Parry advertised his sympathies for the Catholics by opposing legislation against the Jesuits. In the Christmas recess it was revealed that he had been double-crossing Burghley and had been engaging in a plot to kill the Queen. Burghley had to endure the spectacle of Walsingham raking over the discreditable details of the way in which Parry had hoodwinked his employer.

The ill will, created by the Parry plot, between Burghley and Leicester and the further estrangement of Walsingham by his belief that Burghley was obstructing his suit for a farm of customs were symptoms of a deeper opposition over the approach to war in the Netherlands.[28] In the early months of 1585 Walsingham manœuvred to win French help in resisting Spain. Meanwhile he persuaded Elizabeth to agree to take the Dutch under her protection on condition that cautionary ports were occupied by the English. Burghley had not involved himself in these moves but in March, shortly after the Queen had come to an agreement with the Dutch, he attacked the policy of intervention.[29]

Burghley played on the Queen's dislike of rebels, of Calvinists and of 'popularity' in opposing an alliance with the Dutch, whom he represented as a divided and untrustworthy people, leaning more to France than to England. Open support for rebels against their lawful lord stuck in Burghley's legal throat. He argued that the cost of war would ruin England's trade and the Queen's revenues, that war would not bring political stability in the Netherlands and that it would lead to direct conflict with Spain. On the brink Burghley's caution asserted itself and he recommended drawing back. He wanted the Queen to conclude a firm alliance with Scotland, preserve her resources for defence and sit tight. The Treasury men could not contemplate the expenditure demanded by war.

Meanwhile Philip II's diplomacy and military activity was altering the situation on the Continent. The Holy Catholic League, led by Guise, won over with Spanish help the French King and made the Huguenot leader, Henry of Navarre, a suppliant for Elizabeth's help. Early in August, Antwerp fell to Parma. English merchantmen were seized in Spanish ports. Elizabeth was responding to the increasing pressure. Renewed offers were made to the Netherlands. A firm treaty was settled in July with James VI, giving him a pension and the tacit expectation of the succession. Consideration was given to subsidising German princes to come to the rescue of the Huguenots. The events which were provoking the Queen to action forced Burghley to think again about the need to resist Spain.

From June onwards Burghley negotiated with the Dutch.[30] He refused all offers of sovereignty over the rebel provinces. The terms at issue were the securities which could be given to the Queen and the scale of English financial and military effort. By August a treaty was agreed and English troops committed. Having taken the irrevocable step, Burghley was ready to prosecute the war to the utmost. He even encouraged Drake to sail for a raid in the Caribbean before Elizabeth could have second thoughts.[31]

At home Burghley tried to close the ranks. He wanted a better understanding with Leicester and Walsingham, whom he suspected of having filled the Court with accusations against him. He repudiated the charges of opposition to aiding the Dutch, of corruption and of monopolising patronage and policy-making. By covertly circulating letters through his agent Herle he publicised his defence.[32] A catholic pamphlet, *Leicester's Commonwealth*, attacked Leicester at this time, by coincidence, for the very faults for which he blamed Burghley. Using his sister-in-law, Lady Russell, to gather Leicester's grievances, Burghley wrote to his accuser declaring that he bore him no enmity and asking for an end to all ill will. Leicester replied by denying responsibility for the attacks on Burghley. Whatever Burghley thought of the reply he was content in such a grave political situation to accept Leicester's gesture of friendship for the future.

It was as well that Burghley had attempted to reduce the tension between himself and Leicester, for after some hesitations the Queen decided to send the Earl to the Netherlands as Commander-in-Chief. Lingering doubts about Burghley's resistance to the war remained, but in October his agreement to the appointment of his son Thomas as governor of Brill committed him personally to the campaign. Upon his departure in December, Leicester asked for Burghley's support during his absence. Replying, Burghley wrote, 'And for the advancement of the action, if I should not with all the powers of my heart continually both wish and work advancement thereunto, I were to be an accursed person in the sight of God considering the end of this action tend to the glory of God, to the safety of the Queen's person, to the preservation of this realm in a perpetual quietness wherein for my particular interest both for myself and my posterity I have as much interest as any of my degree.'[33] When Burghley claimed to be moved by his religion, his loyalty to the Queen, his patriotism, his dynasty and his rank, Leicester had less cause to fear that personal rancour would prevail.

Open, if undeclared, war with Spain was a grave step. It was to be the turning point in Elizabeth's reign. During November as he lay in the grip of gout at Theobalds, Burghley pondered once again the state of the realm. He set out the mood of the people and the measures required to sustain it.[34] He wrote with an unwonted optimism as if bracing himself for the great trials ahead. He pictured a loyal and godly people, enjoying peace and prosperity and 'therefore earnestly bent to all services for her Majesty's safety'. To preserve religion by reform of the clergy and the enforcement of uniformity on the laity and to maintain equitable justice and taxation were the methods by which 'the former good things afore mentioned are likely to continue for her Majesty's safety, honour and greatness'. When there was no turning back from the precipice of war, Burghley obviously believed that it was to the benefit of all to display a robust faith in the people. But if his trust in the steadfastness of the people was genuine, he had his doubts about the intentions of the Queen. 'I am greatly discouraged with her lack of resolutions', he wrote to Leicester in December 1585.[35]

CHAPTER XIII

Adversary of the Queen's Adversaries

THE war in the Netherlands was more effective in destroying the reputation of Leicester than that of the Spanish army. The Earl's assumption in January 1586 of the governorship, which implied an English claim to sovereignty, enraged Elizabeth. Her object was to restore the liberties of the Netherlands but maintain the nominal suzerainty of Spain. Burghley assured Leicester, 'I have already and shall not desist to oppose myself, with good and sound reasons to move her majesty to alter her hard opinion.'[1] He remained true to his promise not to intrigue against the absent Earl. If financial stringency forced upon Leicester a defensive and ineffectual campaign, he could not blame the Lord Treasurer, who, commenting on the Queen's policy, noted, 'an old rooted opinion that she hath, that all this war will be turned upon her charge, by the backwardness in payment by the States'.[2]

The only legitimate complaint which Leicester could make was of the doubt cast on England's good faith by the feelers for peace being extended towards Parma, the Spanish commander. Such feelers were unofficial and depended in part upon the enterprise of Italian merchants, who made it their business to mislead both Elizabeth and Parma in the interests of a peace which would restore profitable commerce. Burghley encouraged this casual means of testing Spanish intentions.[3]

While personal relations with Leicester, the administrative requirements of the war in the Netherlands and negotiations with Parma absorbed Burghley in the first half of 1586, from August onwards he gave his attention to Mary Queen of Scots. After the Parry plot Burghley gave up any hope of conciliation with Mary. He had been instrumental in arranging for stricter surveillance of the royal captive. Despite her protests Mary was now at Chartley under the suspicious puritan eye of Sir Amias Paulet. Walsingham was scrutinising what Mary believed to be her secret correspondence. The hope was of discovering evidence of her plotting against Elizabeth's life so that Mary might be brought to trial under the statute of 1584. It was in August that Burghley learned from Walsingham of the Babington plot and of the letter which incriminated the Queen of Scots.

The amateur conspirators were important because they had drawn from Mary the treasonable sanction for their scheme. Burghley's interrogation elicited from them enough to convince him that the blow would 'fall upon their mistress betwixt her head and shoulders'.4 He did not attend their trial but he ensured that they suffered the full pains of a traitor's death. When hanging was the punishment for petty theft it was understandable that the most heinous of all crimes should be held to merit some greater deterrent.

Meanwhile, Burghley arranged for Mary to be moved to Fotheringhay Castle and planned her impending trial with detailed care. Despite the waverings of Elizabeth, whose royal instinct was to resist the trial of a Queen, Burghley held firmly to the requirements of the statute. In September under his direction the trial began. Mary refused to admit the jurisdiction of the Court. Burghley asserted the validity of the royal commission set up to try the Queen of Scots. In the end 'this Queen of the Castle', as Burghley called her, condescended to answer the charges.5 Mary soon perceived whose resolution lay behind the continuance of the trial. She said to Burghley, 'Ah! You are my adversary.' Burghley proudly and truthfully replied, 'Yes. I am the adversary to Queen Elizabeth's adversaries.'6

Elizabeth, worried at the prospects of the reactions in Scotland and France, refused to allow sentence to be pronounced. Burghley disguised the royal hesitation by adjourning the trial until the end of October, when, at last, Mary was condemned 'with one full assent' by the commissioners. Burghley still feared 'more slackness in her Majesty than will stand either with her surety or with ours'.7 His fears were to be amply justified.

In the hope of spreading the responsibility for putting Mary to death, Elizabeth summoned Parliament. The session, which began in October, lasted until 2 December and was largely occupied with the case of Mary Queen of Scots. Burghley in the Lords, and Hatton in the Commons found a sympathetic audience for their arguments. Both Houses petitioned for the execution of the sentence. Elizabeth continued to procrastinate and prorogued Parliament without having given any firm commitment. It was some comfort to Burghley when a few days later the sentence against Mary was proclaimed.

The struggle to give the proclamation effect now began. Burghley, in an attempt to alienate French support for Mary, had already revealed her reliance upon Philip II. He now sought to prevent French intervention by rigging the Stafford plot, which effectively disrupted relations with the French King.[8] As Burghley closed one loop-hole after another, Elizabeth tried in vain to induce someone to take the law into his own hands and do away with Mary. Finally on 1 February 1587, Elizabeth signed the warrant for execution and entrusted it to the Secretary, Davison, who had recently been appointed to share Walsingham's work. When the final legal instrument against Mary passed into his hands, Burghley acted 'without delay to do execution upon her'.[9] He met eleven of his fellow councillors, obtained their collusion concerning the instructions which he gave to Beale to carry to Fotheringhay Castle, where everything was ready. Mary was executed on 8 February.

Elizabeth's pent-up emotions and fears burst forth when the deed against Mary was done. The offending councillors were summoned to justify their action. Burghley was questioned twice. But Davison was the obvious scapegoat.[10] He suffered imprisonment and retirement on full pay. Elizabeth had to shake off the guilt of spilling royal blood and convince Europe that she had been tricked into the execution of Mary by her councillors. The necessary but unpleasant act which diplomacy forced upon the Queen had its own emotional strain. Burghley had been Mary's adversary. He had pursued his quarry to the end. Before Elizabeth could feel sure of herself again Burghley had to suffer.

Six months of unremitting concentration upon the case of the Queen of Scots were followed for Burghley by four months of exclusion from Court and the royal favour. Attacked by gout and depression, Burghley carried on during this period his routine work in the Council and courts, but he took no part in the parliamentary session during February and March. He directed the propaganda in justification of the execution of Mary. He gave support to the spoiling raid which Drake carried out in April against the assembling Armada at Cadiz.[11] He continued to serve the Queen.

Although he vigorously defended his part in securing the removal of Mary, whom he regarded as the greatest threat to domestic security, Burghley sometimes feared the worst for himself. He recalled the tag, *Indignatio principis mors est*.[12] He had crossed the public will of the Queen but the knowledge that he had not transgressed the law and that he had not blundered in his political judgement sustained him. He knew that he was not serving a tyrant but a monarch under the law. Burghley argued that the Queen had been forced 'not to deny to her people justice for the public peace of the realm'.[13] He noted that the Queen's reluctance to assent to Mary's execution before members of Parliament was 'much to their grief'.[14] For once the champion of the royal prerogative spoke for the political nation. If he had employed subterfuge to save the Queen from her own hesitance, he had acted as a lawyer and a parliamentarian, not as an unprincipled persecutor of Mary Stuart.

As it became clear that the consequences in Scotland and France of Mary's death were not as violent as Elizabeth feared, she began to speak less harshly of Burghley. His judgement was being vindicated. A focus of intrigue had been removed. As he had said, 'It was thought fit to remove the cause that the effect might cease.'[15] By June 1587 Burghley was once again in favour. With Leicester absent in the Netherlands and his friends Whitgift, Buckhurst and Cobham newly appointed to the Council, Burghley found his influence restored and strengthened. Walsingham, disillusioned by Leicester's failure to lead his military commanders and his allies, was turning to Burghley.

There was business to be done. At home a slump in the cloth market induced Burghley to suspend the privileges of the Merchant Adventurers and try the expedient of free trade. For more than a year he had been considering the commercial perils and opportunities involved in the Netherlands campaign. He had been writing to Leicester about the problems of trade and currency in the Low Countries.[16] The value of foreign commerce was impressing itself upon Burghley when it appeared to be threatened with disruption.

In France the uneasy alliance of the King with the Guise forced Henry of Navarre to beg Elizabeth for help. Burghley advocated and tried to provide the subsidies required by the Huguenot leader and to finance German mercenaries for his relief. It was a difficult task. The mercenaries were unreliable. But more serious was the unreliability of Sir Edward Stafford, the English ambassador.[17] This relative of the Queen and protégé of Burghley succumbed to gambling and the wiles of the Spanish diplomat Mendoza. He was disclosing all that he knew to the Spaniards. It was valuable information to Philip II, who was working to paralyse France so that the Armada campaign could proceed without fear of French intervention.

Drake's attack upon Cadiz in the spring had succeeded in postponing sea-borne attack upon England but 'the scope of all these great preparations of powers and treasures' in Spain was clear.[18] Burghley worked to mobilise the nation. The military preparations were his added burden, for Walsingham was ill. In October there was an invasion scare. To Elizabeth, despite all the intelligence to the contrary, it seemed that there was still time for diplomacy to ward off the impending blow. Burghley was ready for talks with Parma. 'I cannot hold my peace where peace will be lost' he had noted in September.[19]

The war against Spain in the Netherlands was proving in-effective. Burghley, having urged Leicester's return to his command in June, found himself ready in the winter to acquiesce in the recall of the unsuccessful Earl. Discredited in all eyes except those of the Queen, Leicester returned early in December 1587. The recall of the royal favourite made no difference to Burghley's objectives. He continued the preparations for a diplomatic mission to Parma but at the same time he insisted upon religious freedom as the condition for any peace in the Netherlands.[20] When the mission was ready to set out in February 1588, it included Robert Cecil who had persuaded his father to allow him to gain experience of diplomacy.

In the spring of 1588, while both his sons were abroad, Burghley was grieved by the death of his mother. Her existence had been one of the emotional props of his life and a link with the days of his childhood. The Queen grudged Burghley the luxury of genuine sorrow and hurried him back to her own service.[21] In June Burghley lost his daughter Anne. The void left by her death was to be filled for him by her three young daughters. But the concerns of public life provided a distraction and an anodyne when there was sadness in private life.

The negotiations with Parma were an attempt to buy time. Burghley knew that the power of Philip II was 'larger than any other monarch of Christendom'.[22] The great Armada was concentrating. The trial of strength could no longer be evaded. It was a moment for which Burghley had long been preparing. If his protestant heartbeat quickened and his puritan spirit sought strength in prayer, his political intellect calculated the odds. Stripped of continental bases, England had to be defended in her moat and maritime shires. The long vulnerable coast line made home defence an urgent preoccupation for cautious men, like Burghley, who had learned the difficulties of trying to defend England at long range by attack in France, on Spanish possessions and on the ocean. Although on occasion his religion tempted him to dream of the final defeat of all papal principalities and powers, he was too well aware that England's independence derived from her ability to play upon the rivalries of France and Spain to wish for the total abasement of either. From the early days of Elizabeth's reign he had built up England's strength against the day when the mutual restraint of France and Spain would fail and one would be free to strike at England.

In 1552, his memorandum noted: 'A consideration to be had of the Admiralty for the state of the King's Majesty's ships.' Thirty-

The Trial of Mary Queen of Scots. Lord Burghley is indicated by number two in the sketch.

Lord Burghley presiding over the Court of Wards

six years later he wrote, 'Her Majesty's special and most proper defence must be by ships.'[23] In the intervening years he had encouraged shipbuilding and the supply of naval stores, armament and personnel. Hawkins, the champion of the ocean-going fighting ship, who had been appointed to the Navy Office in 1578 was Burghley's choice. The Lord Treasurer had fought corruption in naval administration and had set up a commission to investigate the state of the navy in 1585. He had made it possible for Hawkins to provide the best warships in Europe. Elizabeth recognised Burghley's contribution to the creation of her formidable fleet by appointing him a Deputy Lord High Admiral. It was Burghley's forecast of a defensive campaign to keep the fleet in home waters which was adopted by the Queen when the Armada came.[24]

On land Burghley took an interest in the organisation and equipment of the shire levies, the second line of defence. Frequent musters allowed him to assess the numbers and readiness of the army. He was concerned to keep adequate forces at home despite the calls of campaigns in Ireland and the Netherlands. In the year of the Armada he was responsible as Lord Lieutenant for the levies, some 8000 men, in three of the eastern shires. He showed an interest in firearms and an appreciation of the role of artillery.[25] His share in ensuring that there were trained troops to meet an invasion was considerable.

With so many martial men at Court and in Council Burghley had to struggle to influence strategy. Like the Queen, he did not altogether trust the potentialities of an ocean-going navy. 'The enemy shall not be able to land any power where her Majesty's Navy shall be near to the enemy's Navy', he wrote.[26] But, if he failed to anticipate the future role of sea power, his preference for a defensive attitude was grounded in practical politics. The force of his arguments lay in his grasp of the political end of military power, in his appreciation of the administrative problems of war and in his control of finance. In 1588 he wrote, 'Of necessity there must be money.'[27] As a statesman Burghley's view of warfare was not confined to the scene of battle: it embraced the material and the spiritual resources of the nation.

While Elizabeth made magnificent appeals to the patriotic

M

loyalty of her subjects, Burghley considered the foundations of morale. His public appraisals of England's power were optimistic. He heartened the Justices of the Peace, upon whose religious loyalties he had asked the Bishops to report in 1587. He could not dismiss from his legal mind the sanction for catholic disobedience contained in the papal bull of 1570. He was nervous about the effect of the execution of Mary Queen of Scots upon the influential catholic laity. Lists of recusants were made. Recusants from overseas were required to take the oath of Supremacy. In January 1588 the Council ordered that stubborn papists were to be imprisoned and more amenable catholics were to be watched by the clergy. Burghley intended to forestall catholic rebellion, which had been part of every popish p ot for so long.[28]

Whenever Burghley thought about the safety of England his mind turned to the Border. His first great act of statesmanship had been the Treaty of Edinburgh. In 1588 James VI, now twenty-two years of age and showing himself an effective King, had to be beguiled in the hour of England's peril. Burghley could entice by diplomacy: he could not afford to deter by force. William Ashley, the English ambassador, made brave promises. James was too canny a Protestant to act against England in favour of Spain but he had an eye for a bargain. However unreal the diplomacy was in Scotland, all that mattered to Burghley was that James should not mistake where his interest lay at this critical moment.[29]

Another vulnerable part of the Queen's dominions was Ireland, where it was suspected that the Armada might land. Burghley was regarded as an expert on Irish affairs. Campion had thought of him as a patron for his history of Ireland. Burghley read about Ireland and studied his maps and Irish pedigrees. Like most Englishmen, he found the Irish a 'savage people' beyond the Pale where there was a veneer of English ways. But among Irishmen he was able to find an intimate friend like Nicholas White. He tended to treat the clan feuds like court factions and he supported the Ormondes, while Leicester backed the Desmonds. He hoped to anglicise the Irish leaders and wished to educate the sons of the Irish gentry in England. In his patronage of the Church in Ireland, of Trinity College, subsequently the University, Dublin, of which he became Chancellor late in life, he took the opportunity to place good Protestants. His interest in Irish affairs was keen. Even in his old age the news of Tyrone's surrender was sufficient to bring him to Court from his sick-bed.[30]

Reports on the financial, judicial and political affairs of Ireland were constantly before Burghley. He had to weigh conflicting statements. He was on good terms with the English governors, especially Sir Henry Sidney, through whom he exercised patronage in offices in Ireland. The Queen's servants in Ireland looked to him, as did English ambassadors abroad, to protect their private and public interests at Court. They looked to him to provide them with the necessary money, troops and supplies. He watched them to detect corruption. His administrative expertise was applied to the problems of colonial settlement. He contributed to the attempts of the Earl of Essex and of Sir Thomas Smith to plant colonies in Ireland. His concern with Irish mineral wealth and trade arose from his desire to make Ireland an asset. The fact that it was a liability vitiated Burghley's hopes of peace and good government. The need for economy made him too ready to relax his efforts for pacification whenever there was a lull in the endemic turbulence of the clans. But he had been the champion of strong measures against Shane O'Neill in the fifteen sixties.[31] Fortunately after the suppression of the Desmond rebellion in 1583 the masterful Sir John Perrott became Lord Deputy. His iron rule and velvet compromise over the problems of land tenure provided peace until 1597. It was as well, however, for the fate of English power in Ireland that the Armada was directed to the task of bringing Parma's troops from the Netherlands rather than to the invasion of Ireland.

By the time that the Armada arrived off the shores of England in mid-July 1588, Burghley had done his best to ensure that England was sound in morale, defended by adequate forces and secure from her Irish subjects and northern neighbour. The defeat of the Armada was the work of the navy. The rest of Burghley's work was not put to the test. The victory might have been more crushing had Burghley spent more upon naval preparations. There had been shortages of powder and shot but not serious enough to affect the issue. Burghley was justified by that principle of war which demands economy of effort. He had judged the expenditure on the Armada campaign to the finest margin.[32] Burghley stands well in comparison with the statesmen of any age who have had to budget for war. The English victory established not only the fame of England's seamen, but also that of the Queen and of her great councillor.

Just as the Pope looked enviously upon the heretic Queen so did his enemies look upon Burghley. It was admitted that 'he is so experienced and grounded, with so deep a judgement, as his piercing eye foresees and looks into all accidents and sequences that may prejudice or further his purposes and intentions in any matter he takes in hand, or is to be handled in government of the realm, and practised and followed against any other state'.[33] When Leicester died in September 1588 his reputation faded but Burghley lived on to enjoy the admiration of Europe.

The laurels upon his brow did not blind Burghley to the need to take advantage of the victory. He took steps to round up Spanish survivors in Ireland and he used their stories to reveal the magnitude of the Spanish disaster. He produced propaganda pamphlets stressing England's power and exposing Spanish claims and pretensions. With satisfaction he recorded the loyalty of the catholic laity. Even in his exultation he remembered his maxim that 'to spend in time convenient is wisdom. To continue charge without needful cause bringeth repentance'. He pressed so hard for a speedy demobilisation that Hawkins thought his service was 'hell'. He applied economy not only to national finances, but also to his own resources when he refused the Queen's reward of an earldom on the grounds of being unable to bear so costly an honour.[34]

Elizabeth saw in the defeat of the Armada 'the beginning, though not the end of the ruin of that King', Philip II.[35] The need to press home the advantages of the victory was apparent to the English commanders. Burghley watched over the evolution of a plan to destroy the remnants of the Spanish fleet, to capture the treasure fleet and to establish Don Antonio, the Portuguese pretender upon his throne: all with the aid of English volunteers and the Dutch. As usual Burghley, 'the Purse', had financial misgivings.[36] He was worried by the effect of such ambitious schemes upon the war in the Netherlands. He did not let his doubts mature in open opposition. When the Portugal Voyage set off under Drake and Norris in April, it promised to be a decisive blow at Spain.

Meanwhile Parliament met in February. Burghley pushed young Robert Cecil forward as a knight for Hertfordshire by asking the Sheriff for his 'favourable allowance to favour his son'.[37] In the Lords, Burghley supported the Queen's determined assertion that it was her prerogative to reform the administration by acquiescing in the suppression of two Bills to reform the Exchequer and purveyance. If he agreed with the object of the Bills, he preferred to humour the Queen. He lost through the Commons a Bill which attempted to penalise private appropriation of military equipment and stores by men and officers.[38] Any limitation of the spoils of military service did not appeal to the Commons. Burghley's continuous fight against corruption in the army suffered a setback.

In dealing with ecclesiastical matters which were brought up, despite the Queen's warning not to meddle with religion, great tact was required. The Martin Marprelate Tracts, issuing from a secret press, were pouring ridicule upon the Bishops. Puritan wits had been sharpened and episcopal tempers frayed. In such an atmosphere Burghley had to deal gently with a Bill against pluralism. He made a show of support, while turning the tables upon the reformers by pointing out that pluralism was often the only way of providing with 'a competent reward' the preachers whom the puritans were demanding.[39] After an airing of arguments in debate, the Bill quietly disappeared in response, no doubt, to royal wishes. The last gesture of Parliament was a patriotic show of loyalty and a call for a declaration of war upon Spain. To regularise such an open attack upon Philip II as the Portugal Voyage would appeal to Burghley's sense of legal requirements.

In April a few days after Parliament ended, Burghley's wife died. The loss of Mildred's moral support was a hard blow. The women who had meant most to him, his mother, 'Tannikin' and

Mildred, were now all gone from his life. He had the courage to look to the future of his son Robert and of his grandchildren. The routine of his great household proceeded smoothly under the care of his devoted servants, led by his faithful steward, Thomas Bellot. Public life still demanded his attention especially as Walsingham was ill. A week after Mildred's death Elizabeth summoned Burghley from Theobalds to give his counsel.[40]

The failure of the ambitious Portugal Voyage, which brought disgrace to Drake, posed a problem of international law for Burghley. The Spanish fleet had not been destroyed, the treasure fleet had not been intercepted, the march on Lisbon had ended in disaster, but the English forces had captured Hanseatic merchantmen, bound for Spain with stores. The German merchants protested. In July the Council justified the confiscation of munitions of war from the non-belligerents. Robert Beale, for whose legal knowledge Burghley had a high regard, was commissioned to make a public declaration of England's right to seize contraband. Burghley himself began, but did not finish, a paper on the subject.[41] The least that could be done was to insist on the legality of the only successful action in the riposte to the Spanish Armada.

In the summer of 1589 Burghley was also occupied with Scottish and French affairs. James VI was peeved that he had not taken better advantage of the Armada campaign to gain concessions from Elizabeth. In the spring he began a flirtation with the Scottish Catholic leader, the Earl of Huntly. Elizabeth was duly worried. When James turned on the erstwhile favourite, he found it easy to persuade Elizabeth and Burghley to send him money for the campaign which ended Huntly's influence at the beginning of May. With English money in his pocket James contemplated marriage. Elizabeth refused his request for personal advice on the choice of a bride but in private agreed with Burghley and Walsingham that a match with the sister of Henry of Navarre would break Scottish ties with Guisan France and bring Protestants together. James, like his merchants, favoured marriage to the Danish Princess. By August Elizabeth had blessed the Danish proposal and Burghley was buying a wedding gift of plate on her behalf for the payment of which he had to wait. Burghley suffered some anxiety while the King was abroad fetching his bride but the caretaker government did well.[42]

It was a sign that deep political change was taking place when Burghley indulged in wide visions of the future. In July he was considering the need of a 'confederacy' against Spain and the Turk 'as all Christendom may sing on universal peace'.[43] The alliance, based on common hostility to mighty empires, was to include the principal partners, England, France, Denmark, Scotland, the German Principalities and such Italian states as Venice and Florence. Burghley was reading the future in the light of James VI's marriage and the unexpected turn of events in France.

The Duke of Guise and his brother had been assassinated and Catherine de Medici had died in December 1588. Henry III, after failing to take over the leadership of the Holy Catholic League, was in alliance with the protestant heir to the throne, Henry of Navarre, and was turning to England for support. Burghley had some cause for speculation but, soon after his dreams of a grand alliance to keep the peace, Henry III was assassinated and the rift between Catholic and Protestant in France prevented the national acceptance of Henry of Navarre as King. Faced with civil war, Henry IV looked for English help. Burghley helped to persuade Elizabeth to give the struggling Henry IV money and troops. Bickering with Elizabeth and Henry IV about the scale and purpose of financial and military aid to France became the substance of diplomacy with France for the rest of Burghley's political life.[44]

The same sort of problem dominated relations with the Dutch. After the Armada the commitment of England to the war with Spain was apparent and the Dutch no longer feared to offend their ally. Burghley and Walsingham busied themselves during the autumn of 1589 in reducing English political and military involvement in the Netherlands. Burghley stood firmly by the Treaty of 1585 and would have favoured withdrawal had it not been that occupation of the cautionary ports was the only guarantee of the repayment of English loans.[45] The continuance of their trade with Spain and their commercial rivalry with England was beginning to make the Dutch irksome allies.

As the year closed Burghley faced his first Christmas in forty odd years without Mildred. Change in private life was accompanied by change in the outside world. In foreign affairs Burghley had a momentary sense of the emergence of a new pattern of alliances in Europe, of a new distribution of power. At Court the death of Leicester had temporarily destroyed the balance of faction. When a new equilibrium would be achieved through the Queen's distribution of her favours was not yet clear. It was a sign of his wisdom that Burghley was not beguiled by the appearance of his supremacy. He knew that Elizabeth would live up to her motto, *Semper Eadem*. Amidst the tides of change his loyalty to her was his anchor. The old pilot knew his duties.

CHAPTER XIV

Old Leviathan and his Cub

IN 1590 Burghley was seventy years of age. Leicester and Mildmay had gone, Walsingham and Hatton were about to follow them to the grave. Old William had outlived his contemporaries and early friends in the government. The loss of his intimates and the death of mother, wife and daughter had not, however, destroyed the emotional basis of his life. His emotions found their greatest relaxation in the company of his grandchildren and their strongest purpose in forwarding the career of his son, Robert. The desire to pass to Robert his political power became one of the sustaining hopes of his life. The long-conditioned reflexes to the demands of his sovereign and the stimulus of national danger still responded. Yet it needed all Burghley's stamina and spirit to 'jog his body now being in that case he is'.[1] For many months each year he was in bad health. He was growing deaf and becoming irritable. Yet his mind remained clear. In 1595 he wrote of himself, 'in body not half a man, but in mind passable'.[2] It was a fair judgement.

On the death of Walsingham in April 1590 Burghley was saddled with the responsibilities of the Secretaryship. He took the opportunity to hold the office in unofficial trust for his son Robert whom he called in to aid him. Father and son worked closely together. 'Old Leviathan and his cub' became the effective Cecil partnership in public affairs.[3] Without his son Burghley's influence would have faded more rapidly, although the Queen still wanted to hear his advice on great matters. But as the nineties passed so the shift of power from father to son took place. Burghley was still 'companied with excess of suitors',[4] but the important men were beginning to write increasingly to Robert. The younger generation naturally turned to Burghley's son. Burghley for his part handed over more work to his able understudy. From early in 1593 he passed on the bulk of foreign correspondence to Robert with no more than a few comments.

Yet no one could ignore Burghley. When the ailing old man would suddenly show extraordinary resilience was unpredictable. Suitors, ambassadors and officials were careful to pay their respects to him and acknowledge his authority. They requested Robert to put their matters before his father. They excused themselves for dealing directly with Robert. One wrote to Robert in order to 'void his Lordship's trouble'; another, 'knowing that what I do write unto my Lord your Father comes quickly to your reading'; another to spare the old man news 'which doth not a little hinder his health'.[5] There were mixed motives in steering clear of 'old Leviathan'.

Things were being done behind Burghley's back. The understanding between Robert and his father's secretaries, Maynard and Hickes, was close.[6] It made it possible to arrange little matters of patronage and mutually advantageous deals without bothering the Lord Treasurer. Thomas Middleton warned Robert not to let his father know that he had sent Lord Buckhurst's letter lest it offend him. Nicholas Giffe suggested to Robert that they should use Burghley's authority without informing the Queen to settle a land deal. Essex asked Robert to add the Lord Admiral's name to a letter when he put it to his father. Gifts were offered more blatantly to the younger Cecil. Men thanked him for moving his father to favour them. The Lord Admiral thought it necessary in writing to Robert on naval affairs to add, 'I pray you acquaint your father with it.'[7] The line between tact and deception in handling the old man was not always clear.

As time went on Robert began to take over ecclesiastical patronage and deal in wardships. He developed his own intelligence system and borough patronage. Such actions were all justified by the performance of his task. There was no sign that his father resented the process by which Robert became his *alter ego*. Indeed Burghley was content to see his son step into his shoes. He gave Robert the benefit of his advice just as Elizabeth was revealing to James VI of Scotland the secrets of statecraft. Both were preparing their successors. Robert recognised 'the great wisdom and learning of his schoolmaster' and felt that his lessons put him well ahead of his contemporaries.[8]

The long process of handing over responsibility and obtaining official recognition from the Queen for the task which his son was performing kept Burghley in the struggle for power. The vacancy of the Secretaryship in 1590 came too early for Burghley to be able to put forward Robert with any confidence of success. Essex, with the laurels of the Portugal expedition still fresh, tried to fill his stepfather's role and, although a mere courtier, he importuned the Queen to appoint William Davison, the scapegoat for Mary's execution. Burghley had little to fear from such an ill-chosen candidate but able men like Edward Wotton, the diplomatist, Sir Thomas Wilkes, a clerk of the Council, and Edward Dyer were in the running. Burghley proposed that the principal councillors should share the responsibilities of the Secretaryship among themselves.[9] But since he, almost alone, was suited to such a task, it was clear that he was ready to act while he prepared the ground for his son. Fortunately Edward Dyer, whom the Queen seemed disposed to favour, had no powerful backer. Burghley submitted to the yoke. At seventy he had become the greatest pluralist in the State.

Although it seemed that, having secured a hold on the Secretaryship, Burghley might retain unofficial control 'as long as he shall live and be able to travel',[10] he was playing for time. By the end of 1590 there was talk of the appointment of Robert Cecil along with Wilkes or Wotton. But the Queen made no appointment. In May 1591 on her arrival at Theobalds, Burghley suggested to the Queen through the allegory of the show of welcome that he should retire in favour of his son. The theme of Robert's appointment as Secretary was followed up in an interlude played before her Majesty. The only consolation which Burghley got for his broad but oblique hints was a knighthood for Robert on the Queen's departure.[11]

Essex thought that Burghley might despair of his son's promotion. But the knighthood was a mark of considerable favour from a Queen who was sparing in giving honours. While Essex was away in France during the summer, Robert was made a councillor. Step by step, as the Queen allowed, Burghley was pushing his son forward. Those who expected a Secretary other than Robert Cecil to be named had forgotten that Burghley's plan for councillors to carry out the Secretary's tasks could now be made to work more effectively. Wilkes, a discouraged contender, believed that the placing of Robert Cecil in the Council could be 'a ban on the choice of any Secretary during the life of his father'.[12] The whole management of the Secretary's office was now in the hands of the two Cecils in Council. With the substance of power securely held, they could afford to wait patiently for formal recognition of the facts.

At this stage the struggle for control of the administration became more closely involved with rivalry over the recommendations of policy. Both in the treatment of puritans and the handling of foreign affairs, Burghley and Essex were beginning to come into opposition. Early in 1590 Burghley urged further restrictions on Catholic recusants in the light of the continuing threat from Spain. But he had also shown a marked reaction to the puritan attack upon episcopacy which reached a shocking virulence in the Marprelate Tracts.[13] His partiality to ministers of the Word had made him lenient in the past towards puritan extremists but now he grew suspicious of the sectaries and separatists whose activities threatened the established Church. Thus Burghley grew more unsympathetic towards those puritans who turned in hope of help to the heir of their great patron Leicester, the young Earl of Essex.

Abroad the danger lay in the continuing war with Spain. Early in 1591 the Emperor Rudolph's attempt to mediate between Spain and the United Provinces brought Burghley into action to discredit a move that would have isolated England. He wrote a powerful pamphlet, too strong for the Queen's approval, condemning Philip II's policy in the Netherlands.[14] His persistent attempts to have his pamphlet published and officially adopted by the Queen and by the government of the United Provinces failed, but so did the Emperor's efforts for peace.

More serious was the threat of Spanish control in Brittany and the Channel ports, the springboards for an invasion of England. Burghley was ready to support Henry IV of France in his struggle to establish his authority, if it meant preventing the Spaniards from gaining a foothold on the coastline opposite England. On a commission with Howard and Hunsdon, he came to terms with the French over financing and sending an English force to Brittany.[15] In July 1591 Essex opened another front by going to relieve the siege of Rouen, the key to the ports of Normandy. As the scale of English commitments grew, Burghley became worried over the increasing cost. He had the task of communicating to Essex not only the government's financial worries, but also the Queen's censures over the Earl's reckless behaviour and his lavish distribution of knighthoods.[16] Thus it was that, when Essex returned from an ineffectual campaign, he felt that Burghley had betrayed him in his absence.

The appointment of Robert Cecil to the Council did not sweeten Essex's regard for the Cecils. The Earl was becoming the focus for the discontent of those who felt frustrated by the Cecils' apparent monopoly of patronage. Burghley's able nephews, Francis and Anthony Bacon, were beginning to look to the new favourite in hopes of advancement. When Essex failed to obtain the Chancellorship of Oxford University and it went to a friend of the Cecils, Buckhurst, he felt that both at home and abroad he was being cheated of his deserts by Burghley and his son. Essex began to take politics at Court seriously and to aim at 'domestical greatness'.

Even when the Cecils and Essex were at one they did not find it easy to influence the mature Queen. In 1592 after a series of attacks upon the former Lord Deputy of Ireland, Sir John Perrott, Elizabeth brought him to trial. The combined efforts of the Cecils and Essex could not save him from the sentence of treason.[17] Sir John's claim to be a bastard of Henry VIII involved him in obscure family feeling with the Queen: feeling too venomous to be relieved with the ordinary political antidote. Perrott's fate ought to have been a warning to Essex that the Queen would not be disparaged or challenged.

In February 1593 Essex became a councillor and in that same month he demonstrated the value of his patronage by securing for his friends a large number of borough seats in the spring Parliament. But the business of the session was dominated by the Cecils. Burghley led the Lords; Robert Cecil, the Commons. In

the legislation on religious matters Burghley's determination to
press hard upon recusants of any persuasion showed itself in two
ultimately successful Bills which imposed a five-mile limit on the
movement of Catholics from their homes and threatened seditious
sectaries with imprisonment and, for persistent non-attendance at
Church, with banishment.[18] Burghley's attitude over the dangers
of puritan dissent was hardening.

Over finance, the main purpose of the Parliament, Burghley
waxed eloquent in the Lords. He warned of the Spanish design to
conquer France, England and Ireland and of the renewal of
attempts at invasion. He brought his gloomy prognostications
home by disclosing a Spanish plot in Scotland. The emergency,
which he laboured to stress, was intended to justify the call for a
triple subsidy. Burghley tried to crush opposition in the Commons
by a heavy-handed demand in a joint committee of Lords and
Commons for the triple subsidy, when the Commons had already
decided against granting more than a double subsidy. His attempt
to take the initiative for the Lords in a money matter was resented.
But after much show of indignation the Commons did agree to the
triple subsidy. Robert Cecil had the difficult task of softening the
blow which his father had inflicted on the pride and the pockets of
the Commons.[19]

Burghley's speech in the Lords on the need to prohibit the
further expansion of London was better argued and more popular
than his financial demand but in the end it was to prove less
effective.[20] The Act, attempting to restrict building and over-
crowding, was passed but there was little that legislation could do
to hold up the forces which were making London the mercantile
capital of England. As so often in the social legislation the
symptoms rather than the causes were treated. But it was the
symptoms which Burghley disliked. The causes he had usually
encouraged.

In the summer following the Parliament another clash between
the Cecils and Essex occurred. Essex was seeking to place in the
Attorney-Generalship the young Francis Bacon, who had dis-
graced himself by opposition in the Commons. Robert Cecil
wondered why the Earl should spend his influence 'in so unlikely

or impossible matter'.[21] The Earl was piqued and when the Queen chose Sir Edward Coke, the candidate most expected by the Cecils to succeed, he believed that the Cecils had once again triumphed over him.

Essex found some compensation in the fruits of his newly created intelligence system. Determined to show himself the watchdog of the Queen, he fastened upon what to his eager eyes appeared to be a plot to take the life of Elizabeth. Roderigo Lopez, a Jewish physician from Portugal in attendance on the Queen, was the victim of the Earl's suspicions. The case was weak. Robert Cecil gave his opinion on the evidence to the Queen before Essex made the revelation of his findings. When Essex came to make his disclosures, the Queen rounded on him 'calling him a rash and temerarious youth to enter into a matter which displeased her much and whose innocence she knew well enough'.[22] Robert's action forced Essex to vindicate himself. The Earl was not to be denied and he obtained the condemnation of Lopez and the acquiescence of the Cecils. Burghley, anxious not to push antagonism to extremes, made the gesture of writing a pamphlet on the 'horrible conspiracies of late detected' in which he took the opportunity to return to the charge which he had made, much to the Queen's distaste, in his attack on the Emperor's plan for mediation.[23] The charge was that Philip II was the chief instigator of attempts on Elizabeth's life. Yet, for all his political hatred of Philip II, Burghley could not forbear to write sympathetically on a report that his old antagonist had lost his teeth, 'The King must eat minced meat.'[24]

During the spring of 1594 Burghley, contending with ill-health, had plodded on, attending Council and the Courts of the Exchequer and of the Wards. In June the routine of his days was broken by a visit of the Queen to Theobalds. This royal favour was not the only event to cheer him. His attempts to reconcile Essex and his son Robert had had some success. Burghley recognised that Essex had established himself as a royal favourite and that the time had come to balance the factions and to contain the Earl's influence within those spheres allotted by the Queen. In foreign affairs Burghley and Essex were agreed on the need to keep troops in Brittany. During October, Burghley supported a grant of royal lands to the Earl.[25] Both in patronage and policy there was a truce. The final months of the year were lightened for Burghley by the prospect of his granddaughter's wedding with the Earl of Derby. He nursed himself for the great event. 'I will be a precise keeper of myself from all cold', he wrote.[26]

After the wedding in January 1595 Burghley seemed refreshed. He took up the problem of the debts, owed by the United Provinces to the Queen, in a legalistic memorandum and in negotiations. He went on to deal with family difficulties raised by Thomas Cecil's challenge to Lord Willoughby and by the attempts of his son-in-law, Oxford, to obtain from the Queen the right of pre-emption for tin.[27] In the summer he was busy with financial matters. The strain of war upon the royal resources forced Burghley in his last years to look closely at the collection of customs and purveyance. During the nineties his promotion of economy and efficiency in the financial system was at its most intensive.[28] He had hoped for gold from the alchemist Edward Kelly in 1591 and now he was ready to support a voyage by Drake and Hawkins to capture the Spanish treasure fleet in the Caribbean.[29]

The approach of autumn depressed Burghley. In September he wrote, 'I shall despair to continue the next winter alive or out of misery.'[30] But on his good days he was active, advising about Irish affairs, attending Star Chamber and preparing detailed plans for the defence of the realm against Spanish attack.[31] Up to the last, Burghley was regarded as the expert on defence measures. During the year he had allowed his mind to wander back over the Queen's reign and had produced his *Meditations on the State of England*. It was his sketch of the history 'to eternise the memory of that renowned Queen' which he had urged Camden to write.[32] His memory panned the turbulent stream of the past for the gold of success. Under the glorification of the Queen lay the apology for the life of her servant.

In December Burghley wrote to Robert a letter which reveals the frustration which the old man suffered in his last years. 'I bethink with myself of so many things meet to be considered by

Robert Devereux, Earl of Essex

LA COPIE D'VNE

LETTRE ENVOYEE D'AN-
GLETERRE A DOM BERNARDIN
de Mendoze Ambassadeur en France
pour le Roy d'Espagne.

LAQVELLE EST DECLARE
du Roiaume d'Angleterre, contre l'attente
Dom Bernardin & de tous ses par-
tizans Espagnols & aultres.

es que ceste lettre fust enuoiée à Dom Bernardin de
ze, toutesfois de bon heur, la Copie d'icelle, tant en
ois qu'en François, a esté trouuée en la chambre
RICHARD LEYGH *Seminaire*, lequel n'a-
gueres fut executé pour crime de leze-
Maiesté & trahison commise au
temps que l'armée d'E-
spagne estoit en
mer.

Nouuellement Imprimé.
1588.

Burghley's propaganda: Title-page of a French version of A Copy of a
Letter . . . to Don Bernardino de Mendoza

her Majesty and by her authority to her Council for her affairs in respect of the noise from Spain, as, though I cannot without conference with such councillors as her Majesty shall please to name, do or further such things to execution by myself, yet I am willing to come thither to be near her Majesty though I am not able to make access to her person, but of force, without more amendment of strength, must presume to keep my chamber; not as a potentate, but as an impotent aged man. . . .'[33]

During 1596 the ailing Burghley was still on occasion a formative influence in great affairs. In the spring he took an active interest in Sir Henry Unton's embassy to France, designed to prevent a Franco-Spanish peace. He supported and drew up instructions for a projected attack upon Spain under the command of Howard and Essex. But all plans were upset by the capture of Calais by the Spaniards early in April. 'The alarm of Calais,' wrote Burghley, 'hath kept me waking all night and hath stirred up in me many cogitations.'[34] There was nothing of the resignation of old age about the Lord Treasurer as he set to work to finance a relief expedition. When the Queen decided not to intervene at Calais, Burghley led the negotiations with the French embassy which Henry IV had sent to test English feeling before making a final decision on peace with Spain.[35] Despite Burghley's diplomatic skill there was nothing that he could do but to offer the French King, whom he distrusted, further aid.

With Calais in Spanish hands and Drake and Hawkins dead, Burghley considered again the proposed expedition by Howard and Essex to Cadiz. His reappraisal ended in support for the plan and he wrote a *Declaration of Causes moving the Queen's Majesty to prepare and send a navy to the seas for defence of her realm against the King of Spain's forces.*[36] For the success of the attack on Cadiz Burghley composed a thanksgiving prayer. But the joy of the victory was greatly enhanced for him by the Queen's appointment in July, while Essex was away, of Robert Cecil as Secretary. Anthony Bacon knew what it meant to the father to have passed on his power to his son. 'Now the old man', he wrote, 'may say with the rich man in the Gospel *requiescat mea anima.*'[37] But the old man did not relax. He fussed Robert with endless reminders of

N

business to be done and appeared regularly in Council until November.

The glory which Essex had won at Cadiz had been counterbalanced by Robert Cecil's Secretaryship. But tension between the factions increased. Burghley was determined to keep at least the appearance of amity with the Queen's favourite. Despite the mischief-makers he succeeded. In the autumn he was free to turn his attention to dealing with the Dutch over the debts which they owed to Elizabeth. The negotiations were indecisive.[38] Both the Dutch and the French knew that it was in the interest of England to pay others for its defence. Nevertheless, at the end of the year, the fear of a Spanish riposte for Cadiz brought the Queen's advisers around Burghley once again to consider his plans for defence.

In 1597 the flow of Burghley's memoranda, and his attendance at Council did not abate. To the haunting problems of French, Spanish and Irish affairs was added the threat of famine at home. The old councillor met them all with his practical understanding of what had to be done. There was nothing new in his remedies. He drew upon past experience. He had success in completing arrangements for purveyance to maintain the Household. He kept relations between Robert and Essex in repair while the Earl was preparing for the Islands Voyage. A surprised observer commented, 'Here all is love and kindness between Essex and Burghley with the rest of that tribe and furtherance given to his desires.'[39]

At the beginning of July his secretary, Michael Hickes, gave a rare glimpse of Burghley in repose. Late in the afternoon after dinner, when the business callers had left Theobalds, he wrote, 'and now we be alone, my lord under a tree in the walks with a book in his hand to keep him from sleeping and we ready to take bowls into our hands but that the weather is somewhat too warm yet.'[40] Even on that hot summer day, as he sat apart in the shade, Burghley did not choose to doze or would not have it thought that he nodded.

On the less tranquil occasion in July of the Queen's crushing reply in extempore Latin to the Polish ambassador's complaint about the seizure of Polish grain ships, Burghley was present and he won the Queen's praise for composing a further rejoinder.[41] In the same month, while Essex was absent on the Islands Voyage, old William saw another side of royal emotion. Elizabeth rewarded him by making Robert Chancellor of the Duchy of Lancaster. The appointment was a gesture of confidence since it put all the revenue courts of the realm in the hands of the Cecils.

The relationship between the Queen and Burghley in his last years was not always one of confidence and good humour. The Lord Treasurer was less easy to manage in his old age. Ambassadors found his asperity disconcerting. His ability to hide his emotions weakened. 'The Lord Treasurer thereupon began to start in his chair and to alter his voice and countenance from a kind of crossing and wayward manner, which he hath into a tune of choler', wrote one of Essex's men in 1594.[42] The Queen, who had never minced her words, called him 'a forward old fool' in 1596.[43] But her appointment of Robert Cecil to the Secretaryship was accompanied by one of her rare outbursts of gratitude to her old councillor. Lord Admiral Howard with tears in his eyes wrote to Burghley of the Queen's graciousness, 'Her Majesty giveth your son great thanks that he is the cause of your stay, for, she saith, wheresoever your Lordship is, your services to her giveth hourly thanks, and prayeth your Lordship to use all the rest possible you may that you may be able to serve her at the time that cometh.' Over twenty-five years before Walsingham had wondered how the ailing Cecil might be preserved to serve the Queen.[44]

Burghley rose to the Queen's hope of future service, not by resting, but by continuing to pursue his duties in the Council and the Courts. He took his seat in the Lords in the autumn Parliament and chided absent peers. Among the Bills which he supported was one intended to prevent officials, like Mr Goring of the Court of Wards, from defaulting with impunity on sums owed to the Crown. He was active against bureaucratic corruption to the end. Points of procedure were put to him as 'the most ancient parliament man of any that were at that time present either of the Upper House or House of Commons'.[45] But he was not called upon to deal with any of those difficult issues which brought the Queen and the Commons into collision. It was not an obstreperous Parliament.

During the autumn Burghley was nursing Essex, who was sulking over the Queen's cool reception of the failure of the Islands Voyage. He had no desire to fan the rivalry of the Earl and his son which smouldered again over the Chancellorship of the Duchy of Lancaster. But, while he was conciliating Essex, events were forcing him to consider policies which would meet with the belligerent favourite's opposition. The financial argument for peace with Spain had only been strengthened by the failure of the Islands Voyage to bring home the treasure. The diplomatic arguments too were leading to peace.

In December Burghley met another French mission which came to discover if Elizabeth wished to join in a settlement with Spain. The French ambassador was impressed by the venerable white-haired Lord Treasurer who was carried about in his chair and who was the dominant personality in the negotiations.[46] Burghley insisted that the Dutch should be included in any general pacification. But the French were too close to agreement with Spain to accept any delays or complications. Elizabeth procrastinated but promised to send commissioners to France. The talks ended in January 1598 without decision. Burghley was convinced that a peace on favourable terms must be concluded.

In February Robert Cecil went to France with the commissioners. Essex aided Burghley with the tasks of the Secretaryship. Both father and son felt the strain of being parted. Emotion and interest held old Leviathan and his cub together. When at last he returned at the end of April, Robert came dashing back to England, calling on his father before he reported to the Queen.[47] Although Robert's mission had not been a success in that it failed to prevent a separate peace between France and Spain in the treaty of Vervins, yet his return seemed to enliven his father.

With Robert safely back, Burghley resumed his seat in Council and his work in the Courts. Despite frequent relapses into illness he was busy pondering over the terms upon which peace with Spain could be concluded. Although he did not welcome Dutch intransigence, he insisted that recognition of the *de facto* independence of the United Provinces must be one of the necessary terms for a satisfactory settlement. In his determination to define and seek a treaty he clashed with Essex, who saw his way to power through a continuation of the war. In Council the Lord Treasurer said of Essex that 'he breathed forth nothing but war, slaughter and blood, and after a hot dispute about this matter, as if he presaged what would after be, he drew forth a psalm book saying nothing pointed him to this verse, Men of blood shall not live out half their days'.[48]

It was believed that dying men were gifted with prophecy. Burghley was dying. Elizabeth came to his bedside to feed him and console him as she had done for Hatton. He offered to resign all his offices but the Queen would not accept this gesture of his deeper resignation.[49] But he was nearing the death-bed scene where men of his time expected to see faith tested and the prospects of salvation indicated in the last words and actions of the dying man. Death was a great family and household occasion when the patriarch blessed and admonished his offspring and revealed his will and testament.

In his house in the Strand, Burghley began the last scene of all on 3 August, when, with his chaplain in attendance, he summoned the members of his family to his bedside.[50] Having blessed them and commanded them to fear God and love one another, he prayed for the Queen and put his will into the hands of his faithful steward Thomas Bellot. Burghley was ready to die. 'Oh what a heart have I that will not die' he complained. He rebuked his attendants for trying to revive him. His last recorded words assured all of his salvation. 'Lord receive my spirit' he murmured, 'Lord have mercy upon me.' Between seven and eight o'clock in the morning of the following day, without any of the struggles and convulsions of a guilty soul, he died. Those who had kept vigil throughout the night could scarcely perceive 'when the breath went out of his body'. It was a perfect example of holy dying.

The funeral was held in Westminster Abbey. There were over 500 mourners including many of the nobility, among whom was a downcast Essex. The fifteen-year old Godfrey Goodman, nephew of one of Burghley's executors, was much impressed and recalled over forty-five years later how the Queen herself had spoken in praise of her counsellor. When the ceremonies were over, the body was taken to be buried at St Martin's Church, Stamford.[51]

From Burghley's tomb two ghosts have been conjured up to haunt the popular memory. The one, celebrated by the earliest biographers and Camden, was of a wise statesman, the right hand of the protestant national heroine, Queen Elizabeth. The other, first delineated by the author of the *Treatise of Treasons*, was a foxy Machiavellian creature who deceived his Queen and was a traitor to his country by being the enemy of Rome. The ghosts have remained as lively as the religious divisions which evoked them. No biographer of William Cecil has been able to ignore these phantoms of emotion because, when they are laid, the memory of Lord Burghley himself will lose its significance and the spirit of his age will have vanished beyond recall.

Part Two

Part Two

CHAPTER XV

The Character of a Statesman

'Your Lordship must pardon my evil scribbling for I am called so often from it as at every x lines I am forced to break off', wrote Cecil. He was a busy man. 'I alone carry the burden', he asserted and on another occasion he complained, 'I am like a slave put to do the drudgery.' But his trials were the self-imposed mortifications of one of those lay ascetics in which the protestant world began to abound. He chastened his moral and physical weaknesses with hard labour. His puritan sense of vocation and of the virtue of work made him declare, 'Serve God by serving the Queen, for all other service is indeed bondage to the Devil.'[1]

Cecil believed that 'there is no such prevalent workman as sedulity and diligence'. The profusion of records in his own handwriting is testimony of his belief. Hard work gave him power over himself and over others. It was noted of Cecil and his rivals that 'he is more diligent than they and keeps his footing'. By his long hours of toil he obtained the reputation of being 'the Atlas of this commonwealth'.[2]

The weight of affairs was supported by a strong will but an increasingly frail body. By his early thirties Cecil was the victim of gout. It affected his feet, legs and on occasion his hands. It confirmed the sedentary habits of his scholarly youth and the pessimism and patience of his outlook. It reinforced his belief that argument rather than violence was the prime means of policy and that thought as much as action was the substance of politics. He had the Queen's assurance, 'My Lord, we make use of you not for your bad legs, but your good head.'[3] Gout kept him near the centre of power but on occasion it held him away from Court. His bouts of illness were never consciously diplomatic devices. But the strain of hard work and events acted upon his body in moments of crisis.

In his *Method of Phisicke*, dedicated to Burghley, Philip Barrow noted with professional integrity that the causes of gout were a sedentary life or over-indulgence in the pleasures of bed or board. Friends had no doubt that the first of these causes was the sole explanation of Burghley's affliction. His gout was also explained by 'the coldness of his nature', that predominance of the cold elements, which went with rheumatism, melancholy and a calm demeanour. In the current astrological terminology, the descriptive psychology of the time, Cecil was a saturnine character. It was the recognised type for politicians. Burghley was called 'old Saturnus'.[4] Self-discipline was the lesson of contemporary medicine and psychology as it was of humanist stoicism and protestant precept. The balance and moderation which Burghley achieved may in part have been the result of his innate character but it also came from an effort of will. In the psychological sense he was a self-made man.

Despite his gout and depression Burghley, for all his self-pity, was not a hypochondriac. Like many fundamentally pessimistic men, he had a cheerful manner in company. With painful hand he wrote to Walsingham, 'You see I can be merry with you even in the midst of grief.' Anxious friends pressed upon him remedies which ranged from a well-sprung coach to potent concoctions.[5] The waters of Buxton could not prevail. But if there was no cure the disease was not fatal.

Burghley had extraordinary stamina and he knew how to preserve it. His moderate eating and drinking nourished him but did not load his light frame with fat. In contrast to his porcine brother-in-law, Nicholas Bacon, whose soul, the Queen declared, 'lodged well', he remained spare and slight. His refusal to discuss business at meal-time preserved his digestion. He could throw off his responsibilities at bedtime, as is recorded in Fuller's tale of how Burghley, when he put off his gown at night, used to say, 'Lie there Lord Treasurer'. But, if sleep did not come, he claimed that he 'found out more resolutions in his bed, than when he was up'.[6] The regimen of his daily life matched the discipline of his emotions and mind.

Just as by careful living Burghley strove to lessen his bodily affliction, so by mental absorption in affairs and study he attempted to suppress his doubt and fears. The spiritual and social insecurity of a perceptive man who had attained greatness in this world challenged his peace of mind. 'No man can be counted happy in this world that is not wise. And he that is wisest, seeth most of his own unhappiness,' he used to say.[7] Always on guard, he seemed possessed by defensive forebodings of worse to come. His courage was a kind of fearful confidence that he could make the best of an inevitably bad job and somehow contrive to circumvent irreparable disaster. His belief that forewarned is forearmed prevented him from succumbing to his pessimism. The barriers of bland benignity and studied moderation which controlled the inner tides of feeling generally held. But he confessed to a friend, 'If I open this gate, I should lead you into a bottomless pit of my miseries.'[8]

By being all things to all men, Burghley presented a baffling mirror to those observers to whom he did not choose to reveal himself. He could discern 'what things are to be laid open, and what to be secreted and what to be showed at half lights and to whom and when.' To those foreign ambassadors who expected a cunning politician he was no disappointment. Yet to that honest and perspicacious Spaniard de Silva he appeared straightforward. Like Elizabeth, who knew that princes were set upon a stage for all the world to see, Burghley understood that public life was a play and he acted his part behind the appropriate masks. He was well aware of what Cranmer had once written to him, 'For the example of rulers and heads will the people follow.' His poses were calculated and dutiful responses to conventional expectations. He took the roles of wise counsellor, great lord, just judge in the morality play of the public imagination. If in the end he was taken for Polonius, it was the penalty of having held the stage so long.[9]

Although Burghley understood the uses of his official manner in society and politics, his control of countenance, voice and gesture served the deeper needs of his nature. His sense of vulnerability, his need for self-protection, made him loath to show his emotions. His self-contained air and latent force of personality gave him a certain affinity with the clever women of his time. In his youth Catherine Parr and the Duchess of Suffolk made him one of their young men. The formidable Mildred Cooke married him. Elizabeth chose him and called him her 'Spirit'. He was practical, patient, pertinacious, pious and non-violent. He was a good housekeeper and he cared deeply about his children. His reputation for emotional control was to be seen in the way in which ladies in distress turned to him and in the readiness with which nobles entrusted their wives to his care. The praise for having borne himself 'without blemish in his private course of life' was a recommendation to a Virgin Queen who had to deny her emotions.[10]

In public life the force of Burghley's character was not of an obvious kind. He was neither physically impressive nor did he possess a dominant presence — 'in countenance grave but without authority'. He was 'never noted for an imperious or overruling man'. A talent for compromise robbed him of the rigid strength of a man of principle. His practice of the politics of patience exasperated men of action. 'It is for omnipotence to do mighty things in a moment,' he remarked, 'but degreeingly to grow to greatness is the course he hath left for man.' He was dispiritingly cautious rather than inspiringly bold. 'Courses of perils' rather than final solutions were what he offered. He did not attempt to draw men to him 'by any popular or insinuative carriage of himself'. In the hour of decision he was self-effacing. Such was Burghley's ability to walk in the shadows that Francis Bacon found it necessary to declare that it was impossible for Burghley 'to walk invisible' at Court.[11] Yet the means by which Burghley made his influence invisible were many and subtle.

While Burghley was willing to see in the Queen the personification of royalty, he did not personalise his own power in politics. Experience of government under Edward VI and his legal training tended to make him see authority in office, in institutions and in the law. He did not neglect 'the reputation of his place'. To a bishop he confided that 'with the higher sort authority is a match'. He sought to dissociate the official actions of office from his personal behaviour. Even a friendly Cobham had to accept the verdict, not of Lord Burghley, but of the Lord Treasurer.[12] In his correspondence, whatever the *bonhomie* on private matters, the official command was supported by good legal backing. He was adept at letting the vizor of officialdom fall over his features and at speaking in the anonymous voice of the State.

Burghley used the mantle of the law to clothe his decisions. The processes of the law were his routine in the courts, but in politics, as in administration, he chose to act on legal issues. It was one way of considering the factors in a case and of limiting the risks. Even the maintenance of the appearances of legality imposed a cautious approach. In foreign affairs he was always anxious to argue the justice of any action upon which England embarked. In focusing attention upon the sanctions and obligations of the law, he relieved himself of personal responsibilities and appeared to be working in accordance with the dictates of an external impersonal authority. Burghley's most usual response to problems was to seek a legalistic solution.

Burghley's personal ambition was sublimated into loyalty to the throne and service to the State. If his loyalty grew from a mixture of feudal allegiance and protestant respect for the Godly Prince, his belief in service to the State was similarly derived from varied sources. In William Cecil's youth, Sir Thomas Elyot was urging those who would be 'governours' to cultivate a sense of duty as an individual moral quality, and Thomas Cromwell was reviving the ideas of Marsilio of Padua about the State. When William Cecil entered government, humanist moral teaching, protestant conviction and the Cromwellian notions of the sovereign State combined to make the conscientious bureaucrat aware of the obligations of his task. Against such a background Cecil could self-righteously claim, 'indeed for service I have forborne wife, children, kin, friends, house; yea all mine own to serve which I know not that any other hath done in this time'.[13] His sense of duty was his stay in times of depression. After the disappointment of the Queen's reception of the Treaty of Edinburgh, he wrote, 'Yet all this service seemeth duty and so it is indeed.'[14] If he was an opportunist, he took his opportunities with a sense of obligation. Those who praised him for his integrity recognised that, in suppressing personal motives, Burghley had achieved disinterested service.

As a statesman, Burghley did not parade the intuitions of a

wizard or pose as an oracle. He was not a 'transported man in matters of State'. His processes of persuasion appeared to be laboriously, even tediously, commonsense. Precedent and factual evidence, legal, historical and moral argument were used to justify the national interest. Personal convictions and assumptions did not obtrude. Recommendations were practical and within the compass of available resources. 'Each person that respects her Majesty's service and his own credit ought to look to the end of his action, that it be good, and that there be apparent good means to bring it to that', was advice which he admired. His foresight was preventative and precautionary. 'An ounce of advice is more worth to be executed aforehand than in sight of perils', he wrote. He believed that 'it is an office in Princes, wise and of staid condition, to foresee so much as they may the means to prevent the worst of their fortunes'.[15]

Burghley's method of political analysis derived in part from the dialogue form which came easily to humanists and in part from the lawyers' moot. It purported to present both sides of the question and it did not minimise the difficulties of political calculation. It is the necessity of those who must make decisions to simplify the issues so that the choice is clear. But in his caution and desire for 'calling into equal consideration all circumstances', Burghley did not always render the decision obvious. 'I see such extremities on both sides as I can make no choice', he wrote on policy towards France in 1572.[16] Some of his indecision was deliberate in order to leave the final word with the Queen, but some of it arose from his ability to see more than one side to a problem. He could, however, lay bare the grounds upon which a conclusion could be reached. Sometimes he needed the stimulus of discussion to precipitate him into decision. 'He would never deliver his opinion in matters of counsel, but he might debate it and give the reasons of his opinion.'[17]

Debate had advantages in Council. The hard-working William Cecil, like a good chairman, knew the gain in initiative in preparing the agenda. Conflict took place on ground of his choosing. In debate his opponents had the opportunity for graceful withdrawal in the name of royal or national interest over carefully contrived escape routes. When he won, it was meant to appear that the collective or royal wisdom had triumphed. Burghley remained invisible at the moment of decision.

The hold which Burghley had upon the Queen and his colleagues was due to the force of his well-prepared intellect, which he applied with an understanding of human nature. Intellectual as he was, Burghley was not an austere political thinker, guiding policy by principles and theoretical deductions. An acceptance of 'God's Providence' and experience gave him modest expectations of 'remedies such as by human judgement can be thought of'.[18] He had none of the arrogance of the rationalist or the idealist. His statecraft was tempered by the practical imagination of an administrator and a shrewd estimate of the possible. He let his mind play upon realities and he achieved a considerable degree of flexibility despite his prejudices. In politics, while sheer intellectual capacity is an asset, sound judgement is necessary for success. Burghley's judgement was recognised by his humanist contemporaries as that secular practical wisdom, based on a knowledge of things human as much as upon an understanding of things divine, which they admired in Cicero. It was to John Knox 'the carnal wisdom and worldly policy' of William Cecil.[19]

Burghley's wisdom gave him his eminence in the Elizabethan political scene. He exercised wisdom in a judicial manner. While he sought to play the advocate of the wiser, if not always of the greater, part of the Council before the Queen, he liked to act as referee among his fellow councillors. He exploited his strength as an arbiter, the moderate to whom men could turn for a judicious compromise. In his methods of argument and debate, in the positions he took up, Burghley wished to avoid the appearance of personal dominance. He did not enjoy power in a sensuous and obvious way. His satisfaction lay modestly hidden in his conscience behind an imperturbable countenance.

It suited Burghley's character to disguise his power. His pessimism, his sense of responsibility and his recognition of his limitations prompted him to play down his role. But there was a good political reason for cultivating invisibility. Just as the enemies of Leicester spoke of 'Leicester's Commonwealth' so

Burghley's enemies spoke of '*regnum Cecilianum*' and accused him of being 'the *primum mobile* in every action'.[20] Over-mighty subjects were not loved by the Commons or the monarch. Elizabeth had once told Leicester, 'I will have here but one mistress and no master.' From experience Burghley had learned how dangerous it was to appear too powerful in the Queen's eyes. On the two occasions when he had united the Council against the Queen, over the Scottish campaign in the early days and on the execution of Mary Queen of Scots, he had come nearest to resignation. It paid him to proclaim his 'bondage to her both by God's ordinance and by her royal and princely favour'.[21]

Under the cloak of invisibility, so necessary to Burghley's political strategy, lay his motives. Among them were his personal and dynastic ambitions, loyalty to the throne, religious conviction and patriotism. In the reign of Edward VI William Cecil had experimented in the light of experience with the problem of combining these forces. By the accession of Mary he had temporarily satisfied his self-interest with lands and a knighthood and he was ready to allow his religion a moderate sway by retiring from the Court. In the fallow years his political understanding, his patriotism and his religious thinking were enriched. In 1558 he was ready to emerge in his prime as a statesman in whom the motives of action were well blended. In Elizabeth's reign he became *pater patriae* and young men knew that they would not see his like again.

To reduce Burghley's motives to ambition, loyalty to the throne, religious conviction and patriotism is not only to simplify them, but also to suggest a harmony where there was often conflict. Yet it would be impossible to trace the fusion and admixture of motives in every move he made. There was, moreover, a complication in the texture of thought and feeling of the age. Burghley lived in a period when a fundamental cleavage was appearing in political thought. In every such time, when men act upon the new emergent diagnosis of events and yet turn to the old conventions for justification, hypocrisy appears to be rampant. Aware of the tensions and contradictions between the old and the new, Burghley tried to stretch the traditional arguments to justify

Thomas Cecil, Lord Burghley's eldest son

Robert Cecil, Lord Burghley's son by Mildred Cooke

his actions. He shared this dilemma with most of his contemporaries in Church and State and, like them, he tried to resolve paradoxes by unchallenged assumptions and to make contradictory ends meet. If the ice upon which they skated was thin, it was strong enough to support their self-respect and the respect of the majority for them. It was opaque enough to hide from view the depths of the great issues over which they glided.

Burghley was not a systematic thinker, but his humanist and legal training, along with his religious faith, enabled him to persuade himself and others. He was an eclectic and an advocate who drew upon whatever seemed appropriate to the task in hand. His grasp upon the stock arguments of his time was sure, but he added nothing original and did nothing to deepen them. Statesmen seldom are original, for it is their task to resolve the common mood and the accepted beliefs into the seemingly inevitable. Rather than probe the conflict of values, men of Cecil's generation turned to the ready-made self-contained wisdom of proverbs. It was an age of adages. Humanists drew them from the Ancients, reformers from the Bible. Men like Machiavelli and Bacon coined them. The less creative Barnaby Googe sought to please Burghley by dedicating to him a collection of translated Spanish proverbs. His biographers recorded Burghley's own apophthegms.[22] In looking at Burghley's motives it is as wrong to seek a coherent philosophy as to sense a fundamental hypocrisy.

Obedience and loyalty to the Crown were the greatest of the political virtues in which men of Cecil's generation were schooled. Burghley knew that his first duty was to give good advice to the monarch. He was a persuader of flexibility and tenacity. 'I am no opiniaster but an opiner,' he admitted.[23] Yet, if he sacrificed the satisfaction of having his own way, he preserved his integrity. 'I do hold and will always, this course in such matters as I differ from her Majesty,' he wrote, 'as long as I may be allowed to give advice, I will not change my opinion by affirming the contrary, for that were to offend God, to whom I am sworn first, but as a servant I will obey her Majesty's commandment, and no wise contrary the same, presuming that she being God's chief minister here, it shall be God's will to have her commandments obeyed,

o

after that I have performed my duty as a counsellor and shall in my
heart wish her commandments to have such good successes as I
am sure she intendeth.'[24] In such a way did Burghley recognise the
Godly Prince, fulfil his loyalty and behave in the practical
manner of one who knew that the object of government was to
govern.

In practice Burghley was encouraged to give advice to the
Queen, because she trusted him to accept her as the final arbiter
and because she cultivated variety of counsel. Persistence was
rewarded since the Queen frequently changed her mind and would
accept what she had at first rejected. Because Elizabeth expected
her ministers to execute royal policy, Burghley was often in the
position of carrying out policies with which he did not agree. This
was not a mark of his duplicity but of his duty as a loyal servant of
a Queen regnant. It laid him open, however, to the criticism of his
friends, who did not understand that his actions resulted from an
agreement to differ with the Queen only in private. Burghley used
the Council, the Parliament, the diplomatic reports and all his
resources, including obstruction and deception, to persuade the
Queen, but ultimately he was obedient. He was skilled at presenting
arguments to her in terms which would appeal to her secular
realism. Only rarely did he go against the Queen to the perilous
end and then it was upon issues where he believed the Queen's
judgement to be clouded by emotion, as in the early courtship of
Robert Dudley and over the execution of Mary Queen of Scots.

Yet under Elizabeth, Burghley was able to go far in identifying
his loyalty to the throne with the person of the ruler. From the
start he recognised her intellectual powers. He warned the dons at
Cambridge not to patronise the royal visitor 'who hath knowledge
to understand very well in all common sciences'. Despite all his
grumbles, he came to admire her political judgement. He was not
unaware of her faults but he admitted that 'she had so rare gifts, as
when her counsellors had said all they could say, she would frame
out a wise counsel beyond all theirs'. Ready to foster the cult of
the Queen, he was content to succumb to the adoration of the
Virgin Queen and to become 'Her Spirit'.[25] In Elizabeth, Burghley
found a monarch whom he could serve with intellectual respect,

political admiration and as much emotion as he cared to show. The convention of kneeling before her was for Burghley not a hollow gesture but a demonstration of his feelings for the Queen both as a person and as a representative of God.

The personal relationship of the Queen and Burghley grew deeper as they survived into later generations.[26] But neither liked to curdle politics with sentiment. Theirs was never a simple partnership in affairs of State. Burghley was a trusted member of the Elizabethan ensemble, but the Queen had no relish for simple duets with him nor for solos by a minister. Yet she found it easy to strike harmony with Burghley. His moderation suited the Queen's uncommitted opportunism; his caution, her defensiveness; his pessimism, her defiance. His sense of the possible and the practicable gave her a basis for the manipulation of the mechanisms of power politics. His patience allowed her to hesitate, to have second thoughts and to make eleventh-hour decisions. His sense of the long-term national interests provided a continuity through her day-to-day improvisations. His powers of conciliation secured her efforts to balance factions. They were both post-revolutionary conservatives in that they strove to preserve the changes of Henry VIII's and Edward VI's reigns. They were contemporary in that they were not bemused by visions of a bright future or a golden past. They were not eager to exchange known difficulties for unknown problems by deliberate innovation. Characteristic of their desire to slow the pace of change was their preference for diplomacy rather than force. Their adaptation to the existing environment gave them the fitness to survive.

In much the Queen and Burghley were complementary or alike. Yet on the main issues of ecclesiastical and foreign policy as well as upon the question of the succession there were significant differences between sovereign and minister. The Church of England would have yielded more to the puritans had Burghley's sympathies and political arguments prevailed. But it was the Queen's less obviously defensible determination to preserve the settlement of 1559 which succeeded. In foreign affairs Burghley saw clearly the strategic importance of Scotland, Ireland and the Netherlands, but his touch was less sure than the Queen's in dealing with France and Spain. The royal diagnosis of power politics triumphed over his tendency to ideological analysis. If his efforts to make the Queen marry had been successful, he would have sacrificed not only his own position, but also the flexibility of English diplomacy itself.

William Cecil's period of greatest influence was in the first months of Elizabeth's reign. He secured the new Queen on the throne and made firm the foundations of her rule by his achievements in foreign, religious and economic measures with the Treaty of Edinburgh, the Church Settlement and the recoinage. In all this he played a vital role. But Elizabeth soon caught him in the net of faction and dictated his sphere of duty. He acknowledged that the negotiations with the Netherlands in 1587 were 'not within my compass to deal in except her Majesty shall otherwise direct me'.[27] The royal power of final decision also meant that, when his advice was accepted, the timing of its execution usually depended on the Queen. Burghley appeared almighty to contemporaries because he put his energies into realising royal policy, which he was content for the most part to make his own. 'I will then only love my opinions when your Majesty liketh them,' he assured the Queen.[28] That Elizabeth continued to trust him showed that she took his assurance at its face value.

Burghley had learned to deal with the Queen as he advised Essex to handle her, 'Good my Lord, overcome her with yielding, without disparagement of your honour and plead your own cause with your presence.'[29] It took courage to face Elizabeth, admit her sovereignty and then argue the case. Burghley had that political courage and dared, on occasion, to threaten resignation. If with the Queen and his equals he was flexible and on occasion indecisive, he was not weak. To the subtle Robert he admitted, 'Thus you see how I begin to wander before I dare affirm anything.'[30] Thomas Cecil, however, thought of his father as 'that undivided spirit which never knew more ways than one'.[31] Firm and authoritative to those below, he was persistent, but not rigid, at his own and higher levels.

Respectful as he was of the royal prerogative, Burghley appreciated the powers and privileges of Parliament. 'He loved

always, they say, to wrap the prerogatives in the laws of the land.'
He knew that a King of England could not impose general direct
taxes or make statutes without the consent of Parliament. It was
reported that he once said that 'he knew not what an act of
parliament could not do in England'. Like most lawyers, he
accepted the sovereignty of statute, while arguing that the laws of
England were 'grounded upon truth and reason'.[32]

While he had no doubt of the sovereignty of the 'laws of the
parliament' he could advise the Queen that she was free to proceed
by the 'direct and ordinary course of your laws as also by virtue of
your Majesty's supreme power, from whom law proceedeth'.[33]
Although Cecil was well aware of the conflict of jurisdictions and
the clashes of the Commons with the prerogative, he did not accept
that the sovereignties of Crown and Parliament were mutually
exclusive. To a lawyer concerned with government they appeared
complementary. They provided a choice of weapons, necessary to
deal with changes of political circumstances. There was room for
contradictions in the idea of a mixed polity which was expounded
by Sir John Fortescue, the fifteenth-century eulogist of English
Law, whose works were still revered in the Inns of Court.
Burghley's humanist Cambridge friends, Sir Thomas Smith and
John Aylmer, drawing on classical sources which were familiar
to him, also put forward the adaptable doctrine of a mixed
constitution.[34]

The notion of a mixed polity offered Burghley an opportunity
for compromise and balance both in legal and social terms. If
statute and prerogative could be balanced so could the parliamentary mixture of monarchy, aristocracy and democracy.
Burghley had no doubt where the weight lay in a mixed polity.
After his experience of Somerset's disastrous courtship of the
Commons, he was no advocate of 'popularity'. He sensed 'an
inbred disaffection in the vulgar towards the Nobility'. With the
gentry in the House of Commons he had sympathy for they were
'possessioners', whom he regarded as 'the wiser sort of the people
of this land'.[35] They had to be carried and were worthy of his skill
as a parliamentary manager. Burghley acted as if the Lords were a
means to control the Commons rather than to check the monarch.

He saw Parliament from the viewpoint of the government and, as a member of the Council, he represented the collective aristocratic wisdom which was, for him, a more acceptable concept of a check upon the monarchy.

The interest of the Crown, hedged by divinity, was paramount for him, even if, on occasion, Burghley was prepared to try to influence the person of its holder. His efforts to foster parliamentary initiative on the succession were his most blatant. On ecclesiastical matters he stood by the existing statutes, although he was prepared to support the puritans on minor issues such as Sabbath observance. Burghley successfully resisted attempts to legislate on the prerogative right of purveyance by which the Household was maintained.[36] Both as Secretary and later as Lord Treasurer, he championed the royal demands for parliamentary grants.

William Cecil was not a 'parliamentary statesman' like Thomas Cromwell. Late in life he praised Elizabeth for holding fewer Parliaments than her father. There was no Parliament under Elizabeth to compare with the Reformation Parliament, either in length or in the magnitude of its legislative achievement. The Church Settlement of 1559 relied on a revival of Cromwell's measures. The Queen's determined defence of her prerogative stifled Burghley's efforts to deal with the succession in Parliament. His hopes of minor legal reforms, his suggestions for a regency council, supported by Parliament, to take over government in the event of the Queen's death and his desire for certain ecclesiastical measures did not materialise.[37] It is significant that Burghley's skill as a parliamentary manager rarely produced positive results unless he had the support of the Queen.

His awareness of the force of the Queen's character and of the prerogative persuaded Burghley not to press too far the potentialities of parliamentary initiative. In the Council it was equally difficult to find any leverage for persuading the Queen. The Council hardly ever acted as a body in shaping policy. Before great decisions the Queen questioned and examined her principal councillors individually. In moments of crisis Burghley tried to unite at least the principal councillors. At such times he urged that 'division in counsel was dangerous, if not a subversion of a State'.

But the Queen did not accept the collective responsibility of the Council. Burghley was nearer to the Queen's view, when he declared, 'A good Prince must hear all, but strive to follow the best counsel.'[38] In such circumstances it did not greatly matter that Burghley could not expect to control the Council. Only in rare actions, like the move to execute Mary Queen of Scots, did Burghley succeed in inducing the inner ring of the Council to take independent action on other than routine matters.

While Elizabeth was Queen, personal monarchy flourished. There was little opportunity and no encouragement for a statesman to organise constitutional sanctions behind his influence and play the role of Prime Minister. Moreover, principles and firm policies were a liability to a minister under a Queen who relied on expediency. The tasks of government both at home and abroad were defensive and preservative rather than creative and reformatory. In the long rearguard action to sustain the Tudor system which marked Elizabeth's reign, reliance on precedent and codification of previous experiment were the requirements of government. In this conservative atmosphere Burghley felt at home. He was not called upon to press new policies and urge dynamic reform. He rarely felt the need to be other than a servant of the Queen.

His approach to policy-making was influenced by the fact that there was no contemporary distinction between Burghley's role as a civil servant and as a minister. He was concerned not so much with forcing his own policy as with obtaining a viable policy. Like a good bureaucrat, he knew that 'counsel without resolution and execution was but wind'. He practised neither the doctrinaire planning of a partisan nor the assertion of the dominant will of an ambitious egoist. Mostly he was striving to define and formulate a policy which would have the consensus of opinion in the Council behind it and the vital assent of the Queen. The records of Council preserved its agreements not its conflicts, but Burghley knew from experience that 'no conclusions do last, being as variable as the weather'.[39] The means of maintaining a policy was normally something to be discovered: it was not a preconceived programme.

To bring policy within available resources was Burghley's constant endeavour. There were few stronger arguments for caution than the royal accounts. As Queen Elizabeth's Secretary he kept himself informed of the state of royal finances. From Gresham he learned about the perils of international credit. His friend Walter Mildmay versed him in the view of the Exchequer. His experience of the Henrician debasement taught him the importance of monetary policy and led him to press for the recoinage of 1561 as the remedy for rising prices. The management of his own wealth induced him to view the budget of the State as he did his own. When the State was run as a 'manor' the lure of increasing income made fiscalism a powerful motive in statecraft. For example, the Customs, which might have been used to manipulate the balance of trade, appear to have been regarded simply as a source of revenue. Likewise the encouragement of the mercantile oligarchy of the Merchant Adventurers served to make it easier for the government to apply blackmail to obtain loans.[40] He tended to view the economy in terms of fiscal opportunities. But there were other considerations of weight.

Defence and justice were the foundations of the welfare of the State. Even Thomas More's *Utopia* had to be defended. The preservation of national independence and self-sufficiency was also a motive of Burghley's statecraft. He disliked the situation when 'the realm is driven to be furnished with foreign corn'. He encouraged the Eastland Company in order to obtain naval supplies, and fisheries to provide experienced mariners. Trade with German ports was arranged to nullify the blackmail of closures of Antwerp rather than for its own sake.[41] He was suspicious of commerce which traded valuable commodities in return for wine and luxuries. 'No country robbeth England so much as France', he declared. 'When more merchandise is brought into the realm than is carried forth', he grudged paying the balance in 'fine gold'.[42] But by the 1580s Burghley came to recognise that the advantages of foreign trade outweighed its potential hazards.

The need for protection against foreign enemies was matched by concern for domestic peace and security. Burghley branded profiteers as *inimici patriae* and was suspicious of the usurer and merchant who traded on credit. In a slump Burghley tried to enforce employment because he feared that 'by lack of vent tumults will follow in clothing counties'. The increase of vagabondage was an incentive to prevent depopulation by enclosure. The judicious use of patronage among the aristocracy bought the loyalty of those who could maintain the Queen's peace. Royal service, which amounted to indirect taxation, alleviated the direct taxation which always bred resentment. Burghley kept the nobles sweet by allowing them nominal assessments for the subsidy, by offering them large credits and by not pressing for repayment of royal loans until after their deaths, when their unestablished heirs had to pay the debts of their more powerful fathers. Even the Court of Wards was handled with sufficient show of equitable restraint to make its vexatious exactions tolerable.[43]

Burghley's financial policy was intended to strike a balance between the claims of the throne and of the subject. 'He never liked (as he was wont to say) that the Treasury should grow too great like the spleen, whilst the rest of the members languished and pined away: and he made it his great endeavour, not without good success, that both Prince and people might grow rich: saying oftentimes, that nothing is truly for a Prince's profit which is not conjoined with honour.'[44] Preserving any sense of honour in government finance was a difficult task. The measure of its importance is to be seen in the contrast between the Elizabethan and Jacobean financial atmosphere. In terms of cash Burghley's provision was barely adequate for the Queen's requirements but its tone, the quality of its statesmanship, helped the Queen to rule with the love of her people.

Bacon's distinction between a 'consideration of power' and a 'consideration of plenty' was not a differentiation between a political and an economic policy.[45] The idea that politics and economics were separable was not a fallacy of the sixteenth century. Power was for defence from external enemies; plenty for security at home. Burghley pursued both power and plenty. They were the foreign and domestic aspects of his economic nationalism. His methods derived from a repertoire of devices which had been the stock in trade of late medieval government. They were measures justified by experience and morality rather than by theory. Implicit in his approach to economic affairs were a knowledge of international exchange and credit, the concept of a balance of trade and a belief that bullion was real wealth. He learned much from Gresham, William Lane, Peter Osborne and others who offered advice on economic problems. Behind the attempts to stabilise the domestic economy were notions about hierarchic society, the just price and wage, and the moral obligation to labour. Such ideas came to Burghley from the 'Commonwealth men' of Edward VI's day. But economic theory was not yet autonomous and systematic. Thomas Gresham's observation upon the effects of base coinage was not called Gresham's Law.

To abstract Burghley's economic measures from their setting and to suggest that they were motivated primarily by a coherent economic theory is an exercise in anachronism. Successful practitioners in business and in economic statesmanship have seldom in any age been renowned for their grasp of theory. The predicament of reality has its own logic and it was to this logic that Burghley responded, not as a theoretical economist, but as a Treasury man, a strategist, a lawyer, an aristocrat and a puritan. Over a slump in cloth exports he admitted, 'it is our duties that are counsellors to think of some remedies in time before the same become remediless'.[46] But, if Burghley was paternal over economic and social affairs, he was not, and could not conceive himself to be, the master planner of the Elizabethan economy. He lived in a world planned by God and not by men.

The responsibility of government was to provide remedies to restore the natural order, not to create a new order. Although there was scope for human devices and reason in economic activities there was little sense of human control over society and environment. Storm, plague and famine were the most obvious reminders that man was not the master of his economic destiny. It was this awareness of Providence that caused Burghley, whenever he surveyed the state of the realm, to consider means by which the godliness of the people might be increased. Prosperity was in God's gift. Hard work was a virtue to be rewarded only in those who practised true religion.

The dictates of Providence were also manifest in the law, founded on reason. Legal rights did much to determine economic relationships. The effect of his legal training was clear in Burghley's attitude to the copyholder and the monopolist. He was influenced by the common law tradition of protecting the copyholder. In his attitude to patents, he upheld the right of the subject to pursue his lawful calling against any prerogative grant of monopoly. He was reluctant to accept absolute monopoly, although in the interests of fiscal and commercial policy he became increasingly ready to accept patents with monopolistic tendencies. He shared in a patent for salt manufacture, which was not restrictive, but intended to encourage home manufacture. Burghley was remembered by Chief Justice Popham as the man who had limited the power of the merchants and had prevented them from exploiting their charters to the detriment of the State.[47]

The motives behind Burghley's economic nationalism were mixed. Equally complex was his attitude to the role of Providence in politics. On the relationship of religion and statecraft, the doctrines of Machiavelli could not be ignored. The Florentine's works were well known to Burghley and his circle. Men like Richard Morison, Thomas Smith and John Jewel all quoted from those books of his which were officially banned in England. Machiavelli both fascinated and repelled English intellectuals.[48] For a description of the way in which things actually happened in politics he was an attractive guide. His maxims were cogent and tallied with experience. Burghley indulged in amoral comment worthy of the Italian. When he wrote, 'I must distinguish between discontent and despair, for it is sufficient to weaken the discontented, but there is no way but to kill desparates,' he seemed to be the 'politic Machiavel' himself.[49]

But Burghley would not have been any more ready to admit the moral implications of such a comment than he would have been to have accepted the political philosophy which lay behind similar phrases in Machiavelli's own works. Machiavelli repelled Burghley and his friends, like Cheke and Ascham, by his 'atheism'. They

could not accept that the ends of political power were human and
that morality and divine providence were irrelevant in statecraft.
In the theoretical conception and justification of politics they
rejected the ultimate implications of Machiavellianism.

The contradiction between the theory and practice of politics
required some strained explanations. Burghley, like Machiavelli,
knew that success was a good practical criterion. It was common,
as he wrote, 'to judge the counsel of men and the condition of
things by the event'. But he felt the need of some higher sanction.
He was, therefore, ready to justify 'reason of state' on many planes.
Defending any move made by a threatened State, he wrote, 'all
forces and resistance begun upon urgent and necessary occasions
for the safety of any state whose ruin is greedily sought after is
allowed of God, conformable with nature and disposition of men
and by daily experience continued through the whole world'.[50] It
was simple enough for Burghley's enemies to say that his actions
belied his words, that he was trying to disguise his Machiavellian
conduct by cant.

It is, however, difficult to dismiss all the Biblical quotations,
references to Providence and pious allusions made by Burghley
and his contemporaries in politics as mere humbug. They are too
voluminous and persistent to be taken for a smoke-screen without
fire. The flames of emotion and faith were there. It was, indeed,
the very fact of the emotional involvement, of the spiritual
uneasiness, generating clouds of sanctimony, which distinguished
the outlook of Burghley and his friends from the secular clarity of
the untroubled amoral vision of Machiavelli. If the efforts of
Burghley and 'his brethren in Christ' to smother the conflict of
values in holiness seemed tedious, as they did on occasion to
Queen Elizabeth, they were nevertheless, indicative of the in-
escapable and genuine confusions of the time. Burghley himself
explained 'You see I am in a mixture of divinity and policy.
Preferring in policy her Majesty before all others on the earth and
in divinity, the King of Heaven above all betwixt alpha and
omega'.[51] The Puritans and Catholics who labelled Burghley as
Machiavellian were failing to do justice to the perplexities of his
position and to the dilemma of the age.

It was in the execution of ecclesiastical policy that Burghley was most frequently charged with being a 'Machiavel'.[52] But the accusation of subordinating the Church to the State and of putting political before religious considerations only made sense to the Calvinists and Catholics who regarded the spiritual Church and the secular State as separate institutions. Cecil's doctrine of the relations of Church and State did not recognise such a division. They constituted one body politic infused with divine right and ruled by a Queen who was also Supreme Governor. It was not a question of subordinating the spiritual to the secular, but of their mutual interaction and support in a realm where Church and State were one. He consequently believed that a 'state could never be in safety where there was toleration of two religions'.[53] Such thinking preserved the theological basis of politics and precluded the acceptance of religion as a device of secular statecraft. While Burghley agreed with Machiavelli that common piety and religious observance were the basis of stable government, Burghley's agreement rested on religious belief and that of Machiavelli on amoral calculation.

Later historians have called Burghley a 'politique' statesman. If by that term it is understood that Burghley put the interests of the State before those of religion, then it is as misleading as the epithet 'Machiavellian'. Burghley reconciled the interests of Church and State, of conscience and law, in a manner which preserved religious conviction and united the Church and the State. His theory was as open to abuse in practice as were the catholic and calvinist doctrines. Burghley was indeed as guilty of such abuse as were Philip II and William of Orange. But this doctrine was as firmly based on the foundations of theology and conscience as those of his opponents. He did not disregard the claims of religion.

The separation which Cecil made was not between Church and State, but between private conscience and public behaviour. The distinction, derived from Marsilio of Padua, was given currency in England by the intellectual entourage of Thomas Cromwell.[54] It was vital to the Elizabethan policy of demanding outward conformity in religious practice without probing personal faith.

To this policy Burghley devoted his most thoughtful pamphlet in which he argued the justice of treating catholic missionaries as traitors rather than as persecuted martyrs for the faith.[55] That the insistence on outward conformity, the minimum requirement for religious peace, was both practical and tolerant, was no proof that it was a mere expedient. It squared with the experience of Burghley and of the majority of Englishmen as the best means of avoiding religious strife but it also rested upon intellectual foundations which had been laid in the Middle Ages.

If Burghley used Marsilian doctrines to combat the catholic attack, he turned to Melanchthon for defence against the Puritans. Adiaphorism, the belief that, while divine ends were immutable, the means of realising them might differ and were a matter for human reason and positive law, was used to shatter the puritan objections to the religious practices authorised by statute. Burghley had no sympathy with the puritan attack upon vestments or the episcopate. In being an adiaphorist, he was in the growing Anglican tradition which was expressed with such mild magnificence by Hooker. Burghley regarded the law as the necessary shield of the religious heart of the one body politic.[56]

In foreign affairs, when he took the broad view, Burghley's outlook was often coloured by religion. The political structure of Europe could be seen in terms of power or as an ideological pattern. Burghley was capable of either vision. Fortunately for him the ideological design generally coincided with that of power. He was free to talk of the 'common cause' of Protestantism to religious sympathisers and of national and dynastic interests to less partisan politicians, like the Queen. Dilemma arose when, for example, Henry IV of France became Catholic or the need for peace with Spain was manifest. On such occasions Burghley continued to voice horror at apostasy and papal tyranny but followed the path of political safety.[57]

His political religion derived from his private convictions. In his household, free from the compulsion of outward conformity, Burghley could exercise his conscience. For Thomas he set out his ideal of private devotion with its prayers, Bible readings and conscience probing. 'In common usage', as he wrote, 'of my morning prayer', he discovered guidance in pertinent texts. He may have mistaken piety and the religious idiom in which his mind was steeped for faith, but of the strictness of his practices there was no doubt. He assured his son that in seeing suitors on a Sunday he had not profaned the Sabbath.[58] In middle life he had been ready to die in his faith and when his end came he had mastered the art of holy dying. Without fanaticism he bore himself 'reverently and without scandal in matters of religion'. Yet, for a layman, he gave religion more time and consideration than was required by social convention. Those who knew him were impressed 'above all by his singular piety towards God'.[59]

Burghley felt an official need of the Lord of Hosts. He once said, 'I hold it meet for us to ask God's grace to keep us sound of heart, who have so much in our power.' He dutifully gave precedence to religious considerations in his memoranda and instructions. In 'fond mood' also he found himself apt 'to fall thus low into divinity'. Under stress, he came to look more to the Psalms than to the Ancients. In public affairs his faith became his carapace. 'I am, I thank God,' he wrote, 'provided of an armour proof to defend my conscience from all attacks and I hope in God to make profit of any adversity.'[60] Burghley treated his armour of faith as something stronger than the painted cardboard of hypocrisy.

In international affairs Burghley understood the value of appearances in maintaining civilised intercourse. 'All princes', he wrote, 'and especially such as profess the sincerity of true religion ought so to regard their leagues and promises as, although through necessity they are urged in certain manner to violate the same, yet not in so open and so violent a sort as it shall manifestly appear to the whole world.'[61] He may have confused both private and public manners with morality but he discerned more clearly than the cynics that ritual and procedure were the basis of order and decency in politics and diplomacy, in law and religion.

When his religion was fused with his patriotism, he was convinced of the malignity of the papal Antichrist. 'The first and last Comforter for her Majesty to take hold on', he wrote, 'is the Lord of Hosts, for whose course only her enemies are risen with might and fury to overthrow the Gospel and the professors

thereof. . . .' Accommodation with foreign Catholicism was not
simply expediency but an attempt to secure a base for Protestantism
in England. He saw England as the chief bastion of Protestantism.
'It is . . . a principle', he wrote, 'that if England . . . may be
subdued and forced to return to the Romish Religion, all other
parts of Christendom that are opposite to Rome will fall themselves
without any great force or long war.'[62]

The defence of the Gospel did not make Burghley a crusader.
With Erasmian pacificism he had once, as a Christian, denounced
the relish for violence in Ireland. Yet his moral scruples were
reinforced by his doubts about war as an efficient instrument of
statecraft. Warfare was costly, uncertain and administratively
burdensome. His love of flexibility and compromise destroyed his
taste for 'a stratagem of war wherein a man can err but once'. While
he seldom sought peace for its own sake, he asserted, 'It may not
be denied but a peace assuredly obtained is better than any war.'[63]

In the conduct of war Burghley was as efficient and unscrupulous
as the Utopians. He encouraged civil wars among his enemies
rather than become directly involved in battle. He was a master of
logistics and military intelligence. His forecast of the Armada
campaign and his directions for action in the Netherlands
demonstrated his grasp of strategy at sea and on land. Most
important was his realisation that the navy was the decisive
weapon of an island fortress.[64] Although he thought that soldiers
in peace time were like chimneys in summer, he built up the
military potential of England. While he was defensive rather than
aggressive in outlook, he did not hesitate to advocate war when it
appeared advantageous. He was responsible for the campaign in
Scotland in 1559. Even at Le Havre in 1563 he wanted to be able
'to bid the enemy a good breakfast'. He supported Drake's
voyages in 1587 and 1595 and the Islands Voyage of Essex. But he
opposed projects, like that of Drake in 1577, which seemed to be
provocative and without predictable consequences. 'I think,' he
declared, 'no surety to enter into war without just cause.' 'I hate all
pirates mortally', he wrote.[65] He was no more of an imperialist
than the Queen and he mistrusted the vast claims to Arthurian
Empire which John Dee put forward.[66]

In war as in peace Burghley was a patriot with a shrewd sense of the practical limits of national interest. Yet behind his patriotism lay a rich mystique. Loyal to the House of Tudor, he was loyal to the myth of British History which linked the Tudors with King Arthur and Cadwaladr. Although the myth, created by Geoffrey of Monmouth, had been discredited by Polydore Vergil at the very time of its resurrection under Henry VII, patriotic and obscurantist scholarship had kept it alive by acrimonious controversy. The popular story of Brutus and King Arthur was repeated in the chronicles of Grafton and Holinshed, the dedications of which Burghley accepted without demur. When Burghley accepted the *Historiae Britannicae Defensio* of Sir John Price in 1573, he was lending his authority to the principal scholarly defence of the Tudor cult of British History. It might be suspected that Burghley's humanist tongue was in his cheek, were it not that he showed the same uncritical relish for history as for doubtful genealogy and wrote, 'in the British blood none is of more noble memory either by our own writers of histories or by strangers than the famous King Arthur'.[67]

Acceptance of the British History was one side of the medal of patriotism. On the other side, Protestantism had stamped its own picture of the past. While scholars, like Parker, were content to return to the history of the Anglo-Saxon Church for the origins of the Church of England, John Foxe, the martyrologist, gave new significance to the story of Joseph of Arimathea. Through Joseph, England had been chosen to receive Christianity in its pristine purity before contamination by popery. Burghley himself, like Elizabeth before him, asserted that it was 'at Glastonbury where Joseph of Arimathea first planted the Christian religion'.[68] Thus had God blessed England and chosen his people to revive the true religion in later days.

From history Burghley gained instruction as well as inspiration. He recalled the time 'when the title of the Crown was tossed in question between two royal houses of Lancaster and York', and he strove to settle the succession. 'The world is marvellously changed', he noted in 1589, 'when we true Englishmen have cause for our own quietness to wish good success to a French King and

P

a King of Scots'.[69] He drew up diaries of foreign affairs and studied the history behind current negotiations. But the sort of history which suggested a revival of Arthurian greatness and of true religion in the reign of Elizabeth, the climax of the ages, offered a patriotic inspiration to fulfil England's destiny. It stirred national rather than local loyalties. It made possible, by fusing the royal and religious history of England, Burghley's belief that it was his duty to serve God by serving the Queen.

To discount Burghley's religious faith, to depreciate his patriotism, to doubt his ideal of loyalty and duty and to reduce him to a self-seeking time server is to do less than justice to Burghley and to those who gave him their trust and respect for so long. If his faith and ideals were rationalisations of his secular, economic and social ambitions, it must be remembered that rationalisations, once made, have a power and efficacy as real as, and often stronger than, the sources from which they are fabricated. In satisfying his conscience Burghley released his own energies and those of like-minded men. The verities and illusions which enabled him to make sense of his life, his task and the world around him were an important part of his character as a statesman.

In foreign affairs Burghley's statesmanship, modified by the Queen's control, was justified by events. Aware of the precariousness of England's position, he saw the realm as a 'centre of happiness where the circumference is in open calamity'.[70] To preserve the internal peace, the independence and the Protestantism of the insular centre from which he viewed the world, he sought the amity of Scotland and the control of Ireland. On the encircling seas he built up naval defences against the surrounding calamity. On the Continent he realised that a strategic and political balance of Europe, favourable to England, depended on the virtual independence of the Netherlands. These objectives were the foundations of his success. They presented opportunities which England was able to exploit. Unable to dictate grand strategy, Burghley was content to make limited and opportunist responses to the moves of Spain and France. For all the shifts in his relations with the two great kingdoms, he realised that England's hope of survival lay in the acceptance and manipulation of existing tensions.

He cooled towards the protestant common cause and resisted any moves which might radically upset the balance of forces. Because England had the power to maintain but not to alter the European political pattern, Burghley's foreign policies were fundamentally as conservative as was his conduct of domestic affairs.

At home his aim was 'to content the people with justice and favourable government which is not to exact frequent payments nor molest them with innovations'.[71] It was a timely conservatism. In matters of religion 'he dissented from the papist and the puritan, disliking the superstition of the one and the singularity of the other, after holding midway between them'. He grew to realise the viability of the Church of England. 'To speak all in a word,' Camden wrote, 'the Queen was happy in so great a Counsellor, and the State of England forever indebted to him for his sage and prudent counsels.'[72]

CHAPTER XVI

Politician and Administrator

As a politician William Cecil was concerned with the struggle for power. He practised what Francis Bacon preached, 'All rising to great place is by a winding stair, and, if there be faction, it is good to side a man's self whilst he is rising and to balance himself when he is placed.'[1] Cecil had sided himself in Edward VI's reign but even then he had worked to reconcile Somerset and Northumberland. In 1566, deploring the quarrel between Leicester and Sussex, he wrote, 'I wish God would direct the hearts of these two Earls to behold the harm that ensueth of small sparks of dissension betwixt noble houses, especially such as have alliances and followers.' That he regarded faction strife as dangerous to the safety of the State can be seen from the way in which he tried to encourage it in foreign countries.[2] Cecil was by training and temperament a conciliator and he sought to 'balance himself' as a long line of Tudor administrators had done.

Cecil's desire to balance himself was supported by Elizabeth's wish to divide and rule. The way to power lay not in attempting obvious dominance over rivals which would be countered by the Queen or in forming open alliances between factions which would be resisted by the Queen. It lay in achieving that equipoise in which the Queen felt free from restraint and able to choose what Cecil sought to provide, the best advice. In 1565 Cecil wrote, 'I have no affection to be of a party, but for the Queen's Majesty.'[3] It was the only safe position for ultimately, as Cecil found in 1569, it was the Queen and not the faction leaders who determined survival.

The very differences in personality among the Queen's advisers led to the emergence of faction upon which the Queen played. The differences between the factions were those of personalities rather than of principles, of degree rather than of kind, of means rather than of ends. Factions were shifting affinities, based on personal, local, social and religious sympathies, not disciplined parties with rival legislative programmes. But Cecil could list Leicester's supporters.[4] The friction between them was as much over competition for the means to power, the Queen's favour, as over policies. They bickered more over the spoils of government than they did over the conduct of affairs. The factions which centred in the Court spread into the provinces. But, since the leaders were all in the government and the Queen knew how to share her favours, there was no clear distinction between government and opposition. The Queen made the final decisions and she demanded the loyal support of all her ministers.

While the greater men, except young Essex, learned to share the Queen's favour, the lesser men grew bitter with frustration. To those who had never experienced the predicament of power the illusion that those about the throne were all hypocrites and self-deceivers was strong. 'Oh! that Treasurer spoils all: he is a devil: were it not for him all would go well of our side' was a typical outburst. Scandalmongers spread rumours, like the story of the poisoning of Sir Nicholas Throckmorton at Burghley's table. There were threats to Burghley's life.[5] The sense of insecurity at the competitive Court bred revulsion and acrimony. Of all the sins of the Court, envy drew the most comment. Burghley was often enveloped in intrigue and he sometimes indulged his own relish for it but he was not overwhelmed or lost in the maze of machinations. He remained able to distinguish the national from the factional interest.

In such conditions there was scope for a man like Burghley, who was 'neither fierce nor furious, nor desirous of revenge'. He boasted that 'he had gotten more by his patience than ever he did by his wit'. His friendships cut across faction. He tried to keep personalities out of government business. Emphasis on loyalty to the Queen and a readiness to carry out the royal decision, even when it had been prompted by rivals, tended to detach Burghley from partisanship. His facility for moving to the centre in disputes and his reputation for moderation made it seem that, when factions clashed, 'then Cecil as Neuter served himself of them both'.[6] He was not a party leader by choice. It was his hold upon power that drew men to him.

The attractions of power drew men to Burghley: his qualities held them. Those who had a genuine liking and respect for Burghley were some of the ablest and most powerful of his contemporaries. There were the Archbishops, Cranmer, Parker, Grindal, Sandys, Hutton: the laymen, Sussex and Sir Henry Sidney, who, between them, had in their time represented the Queen in Ireland and in the Councils of the North and in the Marches of Wales. There were Cobham, Warden of the Cinque Ports, and Hunsdon, Warden of Berwick. There were Smith, Mildmay and Wilson. Those who thought well of Burghley form an impressive list of men of action and academically minded bureaucrats and churchmen. Even with less balanced characters, like Throckmorton, Walsingham, Norfolk, Leicester, Essex and Whitgift, he achieved periods of friendly understanding. There was some substance in his comment, 'I know I have some enemies who do malice me, but so do not I them. God forgive them. And I thank God I never went to bed out of charity with any man.'[7]

Cecil had what Francis Bacon described as 'the best composition and temperature' for a politician to have: 'openness in fame and opinion, secrecy in habit, dissimulation in seasonable use and power to feign if there be no remedy'. It enabled him to work without faction. In 1561 he wrote, 'I found my Lord Marquis, my Lord Keeper and my Lord of Pembroke in this matter my best pillars and yet I was forced to seek byways.' Yet whatever those byways were, Cecil did not encourage open violence. That Elizabeth's reign was celebrated for its domestic peace was in some measure due to Cecil's determined conciliation and emollient methods. The Queen recognised his role when at his funeral she gave him the title 'Pater pacis patriae'.[8]

Since the main factions up to 1588 formed about Leicester and Burghley, the men to whom the Queen gave most power, it is tempting to see the rivalry as being between the courtiers and the bureaucrats, the soldiers and the diplomats, the favourites and officials. But Leicester drew the bureaucrat, Walsingham, and Burghley the soldier, Hunsdon, to themselves. Each faction needed its share of men of action and sedentary advisers. Cecil worked to have on his side men to match his rivals: Norfolk to match Leicester and later Oxford and Raleigh to offset Essex. Yet the dominance of Leicester and then of Essex on one side and of the Cecils on the other did mean a continual contrast between militancy and caution, expenditure and economy, expansion and preservation.

Through the complexities of faction politics there did emerge, however, differences of policy too deep for conciliation, which could only be settled by royal decision. Up to 1588 the dividing issue was basically religious although it centred on the succession. In the first decade of the reign Cecil was the Protestant resisting the catholic implications of first Leicester's and then Norfolk's solution to the succession problem. The clash over policy led to the sharp struggle for power when in 1569 the alliance of Leicester and Norfolk against Cecil destroyed the balance of faction. In the seventies and eighties, the puritanism of Leicester and Walsingham, which threatened the established Church at home and tended to commit England to the 'common Cause' of Protestantism in Europe, was opposed by Burghley's Anglican nationalism. The Queen held the ring in this period. In the nineties the strain of war finance finally persuaded Burghley that England could not afford provocation and further commitments. Essex advocated war and struggled to upset the balance of faction to his advantage.

Cecil's success in faction politics was considerable. He accepted those 'many troubles amongst which others some worse than emulations, disdains, backbiting and such like'.[9] But he held the trust of the Queen through the crisis of 1569 and survived the execution of Mary Queen of Scots. Since the Queen decided her own policy it was not altogether the recommendation of particular lines of action which won her favour. Royal trust went to those who could handle the instruments of power which allowed the Queen to pursue the policy of her choice. Those instruments included intelligence, which provided a basis for decision, propaganda, which justified and gained acceptance for royal moves, patronage, which secured support, and administration, especially financial administration, which allowed for the realisation of policy. In the use of all these tools of statecraft Cecil was a master.

Without a standing army or a strong bureaucracy the government needed to know how best to apply its slender resources. As Secretary, responsible for the security of the realm, Cecil created an intelligence network at home and abroad. To Lord Willoughby in France he wrote, 'We might hear more frequently from Venice than we have done from your Lordship.' Always pressing for information, he adjured Sir Thomas Smith, 'For God's sake make some shifts to let us know somewhat.' Merchants, travellers, diplomats and agents abroad were pumped.[10] At home his informants were legion. Cecil weighed the mood and resources of his friends and adversaries. Everything from the state of the harvest, the whereabouts of refugees and the cargoes of ships, to the more obvious reports on the military, political, diplomatic, commercial and financial situation was considered. His reputation for omniscience made many of his correspondents end their recitals of news with apologies for repeating what they expected that he knew already.

More difficult was the problem of eliciting information about secret diplomacy and clandestine activities. Cecil matched his enemies in secrecy, ingenuity and ruthlessness. The interrogatories which he framed for prisoners showed his unerring sense of the significant. 'I went to lay some lime twigs for certain woodcock which I have taken,' he might lightly announce, but behind the sporting metaphor lay the work of the agent provocateur, the informer, the apostate, the traitor, the spy, the torturer and the jailer. The woodcocks squeaked and betrayed the presence of the big game. When Burghley declared, 'The glory shall be great to her majesty in many ways to have the old fox La Motte overreached in his own den. . . .' it was the prelude to inglorious excursions into the diplomatic warren.[11] Over the treatment of the Jesuits, Burghley found it necessary to counter the lawyers' dislike of torture which Sir Thomas Smith assumed to be natural to Englishmen. Burghley had it made clear that Campion 'was never so racked but that he was able to walk' and that those in charge of examining traitors had been ordered to apply the rack 'in as charitable manner, as such a thing might be'.[12] But Mr Norton, the rackmaster, rejoiced in having stretched a priest a foot longer than God had made him.

The methods which Burghley used to gain information were common practice in Europe. At home also every councillor loved to be in the know and had a few informants. Essex vied with the Cecils in creating an intelligence system. But only Walsingham surpassed Burghley in efficiency and in the organisation of foreign correspondents. It was significant that one of Burghley's disreputable agents was arrested by Walsingham's men and Burghley had to explain.[13] The sheer accumulation of information in his memory and papers, the variety of means by which he collected it, made Burghley's intelligence activities impressive, but it was the mind which sifted the results that guaranteed their effectiveness.

To keep before him the salient political facts Burghley used visual aids. His maps helped him to follow the campaigns in, and colonisation of, Ireland, the wars in Normandy and the hold of recusancy in Lancashire. From his book of maps he could check a claim to land in Ireland. He obtained the latest 'Charts of France' from Sir Henry Norris.[14] His maps and pictures supplied him with some of the knowledge of which his reluctance to travel deprived him. It was significant that at Theobalds the murals included a map of England and the family trees of the leading houses in each county as well as heraldic devices of the nobility. It was fine and fashionable decoration but for Burghley it was a directory of the ruling class. Other murals depicted the principal cities of Europe and in the gallery were portraits of 'the Chief in Europe'.[15] Burghley liked information in graphic form. His lists, abstracts, maps, murals and pictures were all part of his constant effort to comprehend the political scene.

Closely allied to intelligence was propaganda. Its negative side was censorship. Cecil became a censor in 1549 and under Elizabeth he resumed this role as a member of the Council. The suppression of dangerous literature had become a European problem since the invention of the printing press. Catholic and puritan tracts printed abroad or on secret presses in England were countered by proclamations banning the offending works and by pro-

ceedings against the authors and publishers. Diplomatic pressure
was used. In 1568 Cecil complained to de Silva about abuse of
Elizabeth in a Spanish work by Gonsalo de Ilescas.[16] At home
Cecil wielded the censorship with discretion and except in times
of crisis the full penalties were seldom applied. Spenser's attack
on Burghley in Mother Hubberd's Tale resulted in no more than
the recall of the edition.[17]

On the positive side Burghley was Elizabeth's director of
propaganda. To the defence of the Church he called Jewel and
Haddon and, without success, Aylmer. Like Parker he employed
John Day, the printer of Foxe's Book of Martyrs. His support of the
Bishop's Bible was well known and his engraved portrait and a
dedication appeared in the first three editions. He was presented
with sermons, catechisms, and translations from foreign divines.
Tracts of the eighties against the Jesuits and of the nineties against
the Separatists were dedicated to him and, ironically, so was the
reply of Henry Barrow, the Separatist leader.[18] The young editor
of the Lamentations of a Sinner became in his old age a considerable
patron of protestant literature.

The new protestant positions had to be established by indoctrination. Burghley believed in 'careful catechising and diligent
preaching'. In Edward's reign he had learned the value of preachers
at Court, where he had introduced Bernard Gilpin the future
Apostle of the North. When he had a point to make, he looked for
preachers at the popular open-air pulpit of St Paul's Cross
'prepared to say something on his behalf'. At St Clement Danes,
one of his advowsons, he installed 'silver-tongued' Smith and at
the Temple, another puritan, Walter Travers.[19] He wrote prayers
for special occasions. He told the suspicious Queen that she had
'especial cause to use and employ' preachers. Alexander Nowell
was commissioned by Burghley to compose his Catechism and he
told William Day, the Dean of Windsor, who, in deference to the
Queen's prohibition of all innovations, had forbidden catechising,
that he was obliged to do it by law. Becon dedicated a catechism to
young Thomas Cecil.[20]

Burghley used the bishops to collect information about the
religious sympathies of the Justices of the Peace and to disseminate

the contents of his tracts. In 1596 the Archbishop of York told him how he had caused 'three little books', sent by Burghley, to be 'published' before the Mayor and Alderman of the City and of how their public reading 'was received with great applause'. Copies were given by the Archbishop to the Bishops of Durham, Chester and Carlisle.[21] The Church was a powerful propaganda agency.

The City of London, 'a mighty arm and instrument to bring any great desire to effect, if it may be won to a man's devotion', was wooed by Elizabeth and her minister. While Burghley won the populace with charities and preachers, he held the mercantile community with policy. He made his firm control acceptable by such measures as favouring the great men, maintaining the old customs rates and championing English merchants against foreign competitors. The Levant merchants remembered him with gratitude. Through his friends, like Gresham, Billingsley, the customs official, Fleetwood, the Recorder, and Grindal, the Bishop of London, he acquainted himself with the mood of the City.[22]

The opinion of the gentry he moulded and tested by addresses to the Justices of the Peace in Star Chamber, his speeches in Parliament and by his drafts of Proclamations. It is notable that in the pamphlets which Burghley himself composed he was not attempting to stir the emotion of the masses, but that he was addressing himself to the educated ruling class, with argument, factual reporting, historical example and documentary evidence. Many of his works were translated into foreign languages to appeal to the men who made opinion in Europe. There was a tradition of political pamphleteering amongst the humanists. Cheke had written the *Hurt of Sedition*.

Burghley wrote and published propagandist works on the occasion of the theological debate in the Easter recess of 1559, of the invasion of Scotland in 1560, the expedition to France in 1563, the Jesuit mission in 1583, the war in the Netherlands in 1585, the Armada, the Lopez Plot in 1594 and the Cadiz expedition in 1596.[23] He composed but did not either finish or issue some ten other pieces.

His most successful tracts were *The Execution of Justice in*

England, justifying the treatment of catholic missionaries as traitors, and his *Copy of a Letter . . . to Don Bernardino Mendoza,* in which he wrote as a disillusioned supporter of the catholic cause on the failure of the Armada. In his propaganda Burghley showed a variety of method, an appreciation of the occasion and a conviction which enabled him to maintain the moral tone of outraged decency.

His full skill as a propagandist was not revealed in his own works but in his generalship of the battle of books. He forced the enemy on to the defensive. He chose able marksmen in Jewel, Haddon, Munday, Norton, Wilson, Whetstone, Wingfield, Walsingham, Whitaker, Beale, his own son Robert and the notorious Stubbs, who lost a hand for writing too well against the Queen's French marriage proposals. If they were not deep-thinking radical writers, like those whom Thomas Cromwell employed, they were men of intelligence and style. His control of a long and delicate campaign is demonstrated in the conduct of unofficial attacks upon the Queen's official royal sister, Mary Queen of Scots.[24] He used the work of the Scot, Buchanan, to denigrate her character until he could switch to an open attack on her treasonable activities at her execution. His attendance at her funeral and his son's role as pall-bearer anticipated the next shift in propaganda which was to cultivate regard for the mother of the most probable heir to England's throne. The manipulation of Mary's reputation was achieved by a repertoire of faking, forgery and bland disclaimers which matched the bizarre reality of Mary's career.

When Burghley announced, 'I never forbear to help any who I think worthy of virtue or for actual good service', he revealed another of his sources of power, patronage.[25] Because the government lacked the resources to finance an administrative machine to carry out its tasks, it fostered patronage as a means of securing the active support of the recipients of favour. The demand for favour was accentuated by the initiative of a growing class of wealthy and educated men, seeking opportunities for their capital and talents in an under-developed economy and for their social ambition in an aristocratic society. The limitations of the government and the economy focused pressure for a share of scarce resources upon whoever had political authority. In such conditions the standing of the ministers with the Queen and with the political nation depended very much upon their ability to handle patronage wisely.

The original source of patronage was the Queen, who divided the disposal of titles, offices, pensions, leases, commercial and industrial rights among her ministers, while retaining the power to intervene in the gift of any of her favours. It was a mark of her expectation that Burghley would use patronage to her royal, rather than to his selfish, advantage that the Queen entrusted him with a larger share than any other man. As other trusted courtiers died, Burghley became more and more the channel of royal favour. It was said that the Queen never resolved 'any private suit or grant from herself that was not first referred to his consideration'. He became 'the screen' between Elizabeth and importunate suitors.[26]

The scope of Burghley's patronage was great. As Secretary he had enjoyed a large undefined influence to make or mar suits. As Master of the Court of Wards, he had at his disposal not only the posts of that institution, but also the fate of great inheritances with all the patronage belonging to the wards such as advowsons, parliamentary seats and estate offices. As Lord Treasurer, he made appointments throughout the financial administration from officials in the Exchequer and the Mint to customs men in the ports and sheriffs and escheators in the counties. He advised on the leases and exchanges of royal lands and on pensions. His pluralism, which included the Chancellorship of Cambridge University and the High Stewardships of some half-dozen towns, extended the patronage which he wielded from the centre of government.[27]

The important offices of State and Household were fiercely contested by faction but Burghley did his best to ensure that his men were appointed to Council, to the officialdom in Ireland, to the staff of the Council of the North, of the Council in the Marches of Wales and of the Duchy of Lancaster, to embassies and to the lucrative posts in the Royal Household. In local government he made his voice heard in the selection of Lords Lieutenant, Judges and Justices of the Peace.[28]

To Spenser it seemed that Burghley,

And now broad spreading like an aged tree
lets none shoot up that nigh him planted be.

But those who believed that Burghley was omnipotent in securing
or excluding from office any man he chose were as misled as those
who believed the same of Leicester. When in a letter to Lady
Bacon, promising to help her sons, he protested, 'though I am of
less power to do my friends good than the world thinketh', he was
telling the truth.[29] Despite Burghley's mastery of Court intrigue,
the Queen settled great offices and by no means always to
Burghley's liking. He himself was suitor to the Queen. He told
Ralph Sadler, 'As fish are gotten with baits so are offices with
seeking.' His difficulty in obtaining the Secretaryship for his son
was evidence of the stubbornness of the royal will. From his
experience he wrote to Sir Henry Sidney 'to let them which do
well find their comfort by you; and in other causes in your choice
to prefer them whom you find the Prince most disposed to have
favoured.'[30]

The 'excess of suitors' which besieged Burghley and his family
was testimony to his reputation as a good lord. However much he
complained of the siege, Burghley was noted for his gracious
treatment of suitors. Dealing with a great variety of requests was a
large part of his work, and it kept his secretary, Michael Hickes
busy in Burghley's later years.[31] He won the thanks of the
aristocrats, academics, lawyers, and the gratitude of many humbler
men. He did not 'exclude inferior matters of access amongst the
care of great'. But the malice of the frustrated fell upon him.
Walsingham believed that Burghley obstructed his suit for a farm
of Customs.[32] Elizabeth always put the odious duty of refusing a
suit on her courtiers. It was a duty which often fell to Burghley.
Patronage was double-edged: it created friends and enemies. The
envies of the Court focused upon the gamble for office.

Burghley had to protect his position. He would tolerate no
poaching. In 1581 he berated Thomas Wilkes before Council for
venturing to put a suit to the Queen through Walsingham instead
of by his means. At Cambridge he resented an appointment to a

proctorship, made by Hatton, and he cancelled it. The Lord
Treasurer was apt to fall into 'high indignation' with lesser men
'for nourishing a dependency upon others besides his lordship'.[33]
The firm grip which he kept upon patronage tended to centralise
influence in the Court and weaken the sway of provincial magnates
whose power came to be judged by their ability to arrange things
at Court. Moreover the offices which great magnates held were
distributed upon their deaths to lesser men. Burghley did not
encourage pluralism in others. He placed the Queen's nominees,
who were strangers to the neighbourhood, in offices, such as the
Presidency of the Council of the North. Such acts tended to
divorce the authority of office from the local influence of the
holder and make it more dependent on the government.

Patronage was a lever which could shift power from the great
nobility to the gentry, from rural lords to Court aristocrats, from
provincial centres to London. It could contribute to changing the
balance of forces in society. Its judicious distribution attached the
ruling class to the throne. When Burghley used patronage to these
purposes, of which he was well aware, he could boast, 'I prefer the
Queen's Majesty and the Common wealth above all sorts.' There
was some justice in his claim. He made no effort to oust the
bureaucratic dynasties from the central government. He frowned
on the sale of offices when their disposal was solely for pecuniary
considerations. In 1584 Mary Queen of Scots admitted that he
'loves his country without passion or faction'. Not until Essex
began ruthless competition, did Burghley's patronage become
increasingly partisan and political. Yet, as late as 1591, even
Francis Bacon declared that Burghley 'was never a factious
commender of men to her Majesty'.[34] At this period the Queen's
determination to block the protégés of Essex made Burghley look
more of a party man than he was; while Burghley's dynastic
ambition gave the appearance of a more consistent political
motive in placing men than he usually had.

In Parliament Burghley did little to make political capital out of
the competition of the gentry for seats and Bills in their favour.
Those with Bills sought permission 'to creep for help under his
lordship's wing'. Lady Russell sent to my Lord Treasurer for his

furtherance in the Upper House. There was wide recognition of
Burghley's capacity to manage Parliament.[35] He had at his disposal
a number of seats in the Commons. But even at Grantham he did
not maintain his right of nomination. Since factions did not
formulate their differences in legislative programmes and the royal
means of parliamentary control were numerous, there was no urge
to pack Parliament. Burghley obtained seats for his friends and
relations. He put a twenty-three-year old grandson in the
Commons.[36] But while support was helpful it was not organised
with a view to securing a numerical majority. The right to nominate
men for seats was a matter of personal and local patronage rather
than of national politics. Only as late as 1593 did the results of the
borough patronage of Essex warn Burghley of its potential
political uses.

If Burghley was a great patron in the State he was also influential
in the Church. Like the humanists, he believed that the wealth of
the Church could be put to better uses, among which he suggested
the endowment of the Crown, the young nobility, schools, the
impotent poor and of the ministry itself. He had an anticlerical
hatred of ecclesiastical wealth as the buttress of papal tyranny and
he believed that the dissolution of the monasteries and chantries
had prevented the revival of popery in England. Such opinions
and his own share of church property made him eager to ascertain
before the appointment of bishops that 'there be sufficient
provision and assurance to her Majesty of such rents and annuities
as ought to be assured by them'. Besides gifts and leases of Church
land, he acquired ten advowsons and stewardships of lands of
three bishoprics.[37]

'I refer the standing or falling altogether to your own considerations whether Her Majesty and you will have any Archbishop or
Bishops or how you will have them ordered.' Parker's words to
Burghley expressed the dependence of the episcopate upon the
throne which had been accepted as *de jure* at the Reformation. It
was for Burghley to deal with the 'packing and purchasing' that
preceded high clerical appointments. Under Edward VI he had
had a large say in the disposal of sees; in Elizabeth's reign, in the
absence of clerics in the Council until 1586, he established himself

as a leading adviser on filling Church offices. To Burghley, Parker admitted that he 'sued by mediation of your Honour'.[38] The Earl of Bedford took it for granted that Burghley would appoint the Bishop of Exeter and expressed the hope that he would provide a preaching bishop. Burghley was the patron of many churchmen, among them Parker, Sandys, Cox, Barnes, Parkhurst, Aylmer, Overton, Howland and Grindal, for whom he secured Canterbury. When Burghley brought Whitgift into the Council in 1586, the Archbishop called on Burghley to continue his care in placing fit men in the Church but later ventured to challenge his patron's choice, as over the bishopric of Worcester, where Burghley succeeded in installing his man, Bilson.[39]

Burghley acted as mediator in the quarrels and bargains among the bishops, and between them and the Queen. He resisted the Queen's wish to ban clerical marriage. He was the confidant of the bishops in their troubles. He protected them in times of scandal. But he was no champion of episcopal power or wealth. He was alarmed at any suggestion of the divine right of the episcopate and he watched the limits of ecclesiastical jurisdiction with care. Whitgift's use of the *ex officio* oath and the Court of High Commission seemed to Burghley to be too like the Spanish Inquisition.[40]

Among the lower clergy Burghley was sympathetic to the 'preciser sort', whom he dared to defend to Elizabeth as the chief opponents of popery. His livings went to ministers of the Word, the puritan reformers. He was thanked for his protection of the notoriously puritan clergy of Essex and he made an exception to his insistence on vestments in allowing eight puritan preachers to dispense with them during their labours in converting the Catholics of Lancashire. One minister, Francis Merburn, appealed to Burghley as 'an Angel of God' to defend him. Like him, his wife was 'the staff of poor chaplains in her life time'. He wanted to raise the stipends of the lower clergy. But Burghley was not, like Leicester, ready to forward the presbyterian aims of those who attacked the polity of the Church. He had no sympathy for sectarians.[41]

Patronage in Church and State was a large part of administration.

Q

The government had to work through society. It was Burghley's understanding of how to utilise social forces to the advantage of the Crown that made him such an effective servant of the Queen. 'Forget not other men's vocations and degrees,' he wrote. He studied, in part through genealogies, the dynastic structure of the aristocracy. 'What nobleman or gentleman and their dwellings, matches and pedigrees did he not know?'[42] The feuds and alliances, the dynastic ambitions and traditions of these men were a powerful element in the social motivation which Cecil had to gear to the administrative mill. The lack of a bureaucracy meant that *ad hoc* commissions and personal agents were used to deal with particular problems. Burghley sat on many commissions and played a large part in nominating many more. His skill in choosing the right noble, gentleman, lawyer, merchant for a governmental task helped to increase the efficiency of the administration.

Burghley's first experience in government had been as a bureaucrat. Among his earliest friends were officials such as Mildmay and Nicholas Bacon. His very manner and attitude to administration had been absorbed from such perdurable office-holders as William Petre, who had served the father of English bureaucracy, Thomas Cromwell. When Sir Thomas Smith wrote, 'Now is the time when you may show yourself to be of that nature whereof I have heard you, and as I think worthily, glory, that is no seeker of extremity nor blood but of moderation in all things', he might have been addressing Burghley not his mentor, Petre. Burghley acquired, like Petre, the protective and distinctive characteristics both in manner and in dress of a functionary. With his skull-cap and flat hat and sombre clothes he fitted into the gallery which included the episcopal civil servants of the past and their lay successors, Paulet, Petre, Bacon, Wilson. When Hatton became Lord Chancellor, he laid aside his feathered hat and took to wearing a flat velvet cap like Burghley's.[43] Even on his tomb Burghley's effigy holds the staff of the Lord Treasurer's office. By experience, training and temperament William Cecil was a bureaucrat. It was his ability to administer that was a great, if not his greatest, recommendation in the eyes of the Queen.

Under Edward VI Cecil had witnessed a decline in the standards of administration and, like his colleagues, he had taken personal advantage of the laxity of the times. Under Elizabeth's more exacting supervision he had proved a more mature and responsible servant of the State. As an administrator he lacked the original constructive abilities of Thomas Cromwell but he shared his capacity for work, grasp of detail and urge for efficiency. His most obvious limitation was his resistance to delegating his heavy tasks. If Burghley brought no great reforms or radical reconstruction, it must be remembered that he reached his peak of authority at the end of a period of experiment and alteration, when the limits of mutation had been reached within the governmental and social environment. While on occasion Burghley reacted sharply to the weaknesses of the system, neither he nor his age could rise above them. It was an age of equipoise in the administration after the changes of earlier Tudor reigns. Burghley's strength lay in his capacity to consolidate, conserve and make the existing apparatus of government work.

The first royal office held by William Cecil was the Secretaryship. For three years he played second string to Petre under Edward VI. But the Secretary, 'an artificer of practices and counsels', as Cecil called him, had great opportunities. Thomas Cromwell had made the office the governmental centre of gravity in domestic as well as in foreign affairs.[44] Unbound by the routines of older offices of State, its elastic powers, as an agency of the royal prerogative, depended on the personality of the holder and the degree of trust which he inspired in the monarch. When, under Elizabeth, Cecil was sole Secretary for the first fourteen years of the reign, he raised the office up again to its Cromwellian capacity and managed single-handed an office in which it had become usual to employ two men. He dominated his successor Sir Thomas Smith until Walsingham took office in December 1573. He resumed the tasks of the Secretaryship in 1590 at Walsingham's death and unofficially supervised its functions with his son Robert and others until the Queen saw fit to give the official appointment to Robert Cecil in July 1596.

William Cecil left his mark on the office. Descriptions of the nineties, while based on Walsingham's practice, cite Cecil's methods with approval, in particular his economic clerical organisation.[45] All through his career he used the minimum of secretarial aid. Even when he held the great offices of State he never had more than four private secretaries. The accounts of the business methods, collection of records and classification of information retail Cecil's administrative tools down to the maps and pedigrees. Yet, despite all the routines, it was against the nature of an office dependent on personality to become an institution. The filing system remained rudimentary. The records of the Secretaryship were the working papers of an individual, arranged for personal convenience, rather than the formal departmental documents classified with archival efficiency for public reference. Camden, the historian, found difficulty in using the dusty bundles of records. Another mark of informality was Cecil's employment of personal secretaries and agents and private funds.[46] The diplomatic functions under the control of the Secretary provided the example of ambassadors paying heavily out of their own pockets and engaging staff as personal servants.

However ready great officials were to extend bureaucratic means of administration, they tried to avoid allowing their initiative to be institutionalised. When Burghley arranged for the elderly Sir Thomas Smith to become Secretary in 1572, it was clear that he was loath to leave his initiative in the Secretaryship. Walsingham was an able Secretary but for half his tenure he shared the office with others. He never enjoyed the measure of royal trust which was vouchsafed to William Cecil and the authority of the Secretary was challenged. Thus Cecil emerged as one of the two great sixteenth-century holders of an office which as he knew was 'adjudged a shop for cunning men'.[47]

After the Secretaryship Cecil's next important office was Master of the Court of Wards, which he held for the thirty-seven years between 1561 and his death.[48] The success with which he managed the Court did not show in any reform but in the discreet conservatism with which he struggled to keep its administration economical and efficient and its reputation as sweet as possible. Judged as a means of raising the feudal revenues of the Crown, the Court under Burghley was neither an important nor an expanding source of wealth. While he increased the number of wardships for sale by nearly a third, the average annual profits during his Mastership were only two-thirds of those raised by his predecessor. Evidently Burghley had in mind other purposes for the Court of Wards than the expansion of the royal income.

In the dynastic world of the aristocracy the delicate social purpose of the Court was to deal with the interests of minors and of the mentally deranged as well as with the marriage of widows. The wasting of inheritances, the contraction of inappropriate marriages, the neglect of a ward's education were all matters which struck at aristocratic interests. Burghley did not intend to alienate the strongest section of society. There was no official exploitation. He authorised a reasonable and steady price level for the sale of wardships. He curbed abuse in guardianship and was exemplary in the education and treatment of his own wards. His claim concerning Oxford's wardship, 'During his minority I preserved his title to his earldom the Lord Windsor attempting to have made him illegitimate', could be substantiated with other instances of his conscientious paternalism.[49] Burghley recognised the need to calm the dynastic fears of aristocratic society when the opportunities for abuse were so obvious.

But the most effective way of winning tolerance for the royal insistence upon its antiquated feudal rights was to create a vested interest in their continuance. While the sales of wards, which allowed 'a freeman and gentleman to be bought and sold like an horse or an ox', brought little to the royal coffers, they proved lucrative to those permitted to buy. Burghley took a substantial share from the unofficial profits of such deals but he saw to it that there was a sufficiently wide participation to make these transactions acceptable. He used the grant of wardships primarily to supplement the inadequate pay of government officials. He dropped windfalls in the way of ladies who persuaded society of the maternal benefits of wardship. Thus Burghley's apparently unenterprising and seemingly corrupt conduct of the Court of Wards served the necessary purposes of supplementing the pay of government officials, of enlarging royal patronage and of gaining a small income for the Crown. He put the Court to one further important use. The wards from catholic families were placed where they would be brought up in the protestant faith.[50] In the context of the time Burghley used his Mastership well and above all he avoided creating too great an odium for an institution which was inevitably obnoxious to the politically effective classes.

The third great office, that of Lord Treasurer, which came to Burghley in 1572, he held until his death twenty-six years later. He was fortunate in taking office at a time when the reforms of his predecessor, William Paulet, Marquis of Winchester, had been completed and tried in a revived Exchequer. It suited Burghley's conservative temper to inherit a going concern. If the machinery was antiquated, it ran reasonably smoothly and there was no obvious call for a technical overhaul. Attempts to tidy up the Lord Treasurer's records in the Exchequer failed. The changes in the routines of the Exchequer in Burghley's last years were the result of rivalry between officials rather than of a rational review of methods.[51] They re-established accounting methods abandoned before the sixteenth century.

Burghley was not only lucky in succeeding to the work of Paulet, who had made the Treasurership a major post in government, but also in having in the office of Chancellor of the Exchequer his friend, Sir Walter Mildmay. In the last years of the aged Paulet, Mildmay, who had long experience of financial affairs, had virtually run the Exchequer and had followed the example of Thomas Cromwell in raising the Chancellorship of the Exchequer to dominate that institution. It was Mildmay's ability to run the routine of financial business until his death in 1589, when he was followed by the able Sir John Fortescue, that gave Burghley the freedom to play the role of Finance Minister of the State and to apply the power of the purse to policy.[52]

The scope of the Lord Treasurership was extensive. Burghley authorised the payment of pensions, fees and allowances. He controlled the customs. He granted the leases of crown property and supervised the administration of royal lands. His warrants largely regulated revenue matters. In the Exchequer Court he sat as a judge whenever he chose. He advised the Council and the Queen on all financial problems. He was 'the great paymaster' of the realm. The importance of finance in a period of rising prices and growing governmental expenditure enabled Burghley to press his financial control into the military and naval organisation. He sat on many commissions dealing with prizes taken at sea. He continually investigated Household costs and sat on a commission from 1591 to supervise them. In 1575 he became Royal Exchanger. Thus Burghley spread the influence of the Lord Treasurer so that he was held to be the man 'who hath the purse and the wisdom of this land both in one hand'.[53]

In handling parliamentary revenues Burghley showed little originality. His proposals in 1579 for higher taxes and for appropriation as a means of encouraging the Commons to make grants for specific purposes were as fruitless as his complaints about under-assessment in 1593. He preserved his own derisory assessment of £200 for the subsidy. The old forms of taxes and assessment remained. As their nominal yield fell Parliament by Parliament, their real value dropped even more sharply. In order to avoid more frequent Parliaments, Burghley resorted to demanding triple grants in 1593 and 1597 instead of the normal double grant. Despite inflation and the irrelevant nature of the taxes, Burghley met about half the extraordinary expenditure of the war years after 1588 from parliamentary taxation.[54]

To later generations, inured to taxation, it might seem that Burghley's failure was in not devising some means of extracting for the Crown its proportionate share of the rising wealth at a time of inflation. But Burghley, like his Queen, had a keen appreciation of the immediate social and political effects of taxation. Knowing 'the nature of the common people of England, inclinable to sedition, if they be oppressed with extraordinary payments', Burghley preferred co-operation to resistance.[55] It was next to impossible to remove the limitations of parliamentary taxation without shifting the centre of authority further from the Crown and nearer Parliament. Moreover Burghley shared the common conviction that parliamentary taxation was an extraordinary device only justified by abnormal circumstances.

Foreign loans which had been a feature of Winchester's finance virtually ceased under Burghley. After the crisis of 1569–70,

Antwerp, Gresham's chief source, was dry. The scouring of the
German money markets in 1575 revealed that large-scale borrowing abroad was no longer feasible. Having cleared all foreign debts
by 1574, Burghley was forced on occasion to look for credit at
home. He used the traditional methods. Loans under the Privy
Seal which had the advantage of being without interest and
susceptible to the manipulation of their terms by the authority of
the prerogative were raised in 1575–6 and 1588–93. The Corporation
and merchants of London were tapped for loans in the same years.
But Burghley, like Gresham and Mildmay, regarded borrowing
as a risky expedient for Princes and tried to keep it to a minimum.[56]

Large sums to meet the deficit, caused by extraordinary
expenditure, were raised by the sale of crown lands. Such sales
diminished the capital assets of the Crown and the basis of its
credit, but by legal processes the Crown was always acquiring
land. Burghley inquired into 'concealment' of crown rights over
land. The revenues from crown lands held up well, despite the
disposals made by Burghley.[57] The exploitation of royal lands and
woods was, however, limited by the need to sustain the reputation
for good lordship. It was with reluctance that Burghley raised
rents and fines.

The revenue from crown lands was one of the main items of the
ordinary income of the Queen, which included customs, the profits
of justice and various feudal and ecclesiastical items. Under
Burghley the nominal yield from customs increased. The larger
revenue seems to have derived not from any increase in trade or
rates but rather from the more profitable incidence of the customs
on an extended range of goods. Burghley gave way before the
opposition of the merchants and his moves to revise rates in 1577
and 1594 came to nothing. He was, however, content, it seems, to
maintain the old rates since they had the fiscal advantage of
encouraging imports which provided revenue. His close watch
over the collection of customs led to greater control and centralisa-
tion but confirmed his preference for farming by private enterprise
as a more profitable and calculable method than direct royal
administration. He extended farming to other economic controls
such as alnage.[58]

Burghley did not gain the reputation of being a seller of justice. The profits of justice were not exploited except at times of rebellion, when fines and forfeitures were considerable. Similarly, feudal rights were not made a means of extortion. The wealth of the Church was a shrinking asset but clerical taxation and benevolences were increased and episcopal riches were diverted to royal use. Recusancy was heavily penalised. One of his successes was his application in the shires of the well-tried procedure of composition for the collection of purveyance. By this means he was successful in raising the yield and lowering the resistance to the prerogative right of pre-emption for the royal Household.[59]

The ordinary revenues of the Crown were carefully managed by Burghley. During a dozen years as Lord Treasurer he accumulated a surplus in the ordinary account of more than a year's revenue. With this surplus he hoped to be able to make good the deficiencies of extraordinary revenue and be able to choose when to call Parliament. After 1588, when the strain of war continued, he increased the nominal yield of ordinary revenue by a third. But the record surplus of 1584 dwindled until it was no longer a significant reserve by 1592.[60] War and inflation after 1588 destroyed the adequacy of the ordinary revenue.

All over Europe a new scale of State activity was straining the apparatus of government finance and challenging the mentality which operated it. Burghley did not change administration and found it hard to accept as normal the extraordinary finance of prolonged warfare. He had long participated in Winchester's financial policy and he continued it. The object was to retrench rather than to increase revenues. This led to a tightening of discipline in all branches of revenue collection and audit. It looked like efficiency. The attack on extravagance, especially in the Household, seemed like justice. However superficial, the policy of economy worked well within the limits of social and political tolerance.

Holding down expenditure on official pensions, salaries and fees increased the need for unofficial remuneration in local and central government. Unchanged allotments for the running costs of departments caused them to squeeze their clients. The Council in the Marches of Wales exacted higher fines. Warfare was commercialised by partial reliance on private backing.[61] But while as a result of retrenchment the bureaucracy became less popular, the Crown still escaped opprobrium and got more for its money as inflation continued. Whatever its effects and weaknesses, Burghley's financial policy had the immediate justification of keeping the government solvent. The increasing resentment and the undermining of the financial capacity and credit of the government affected the future. Burghley was successful in his lifetime. To hand on problems without being overwhelmed by them is no small part of making a political reputation.

Burghley expected to be in London during the law terms. Much of his work was performed in the courts for, in the absence of administrative agencies, judicial means were used to execute the law. The Lord Treasurer was a commanding figure amongst the judges when they met in the Exchequer Chamber. It was significant that during Burghley's Treasurership the Exchequer Chamber enlarged its jurisdiction over appeals and that the Barons of Exchequer became the equals of the judges of the Courts of Queen's Bench and Common Pleas. Apart from his supremacy in the widening jurisdiction of the Exchequer, he was influential in a judicial capacity in the Court of Wards, Star Chamber, Council and special commissions. He was a vigilant supervisor of proceedings in the Councils of the North and in the Marches of Wales.[62]

While Burghley was too much a realist and a product of the Inns to risk upsetting the legal profession by reducing fees or initiating radical reform, he did attempt minor technical improvements in the law. He was worried by the malpractices of informers and he advised 'counsellors to deal truly and plainly with their clients'. Lawyers seeking promotion were careful to avoid chicanery before such an influential patron who insisted upon the due process of law. Burghley had a reputation for being merciful and for not insisting on the full rigours of the law when there were mitigating circumstances. Those who deceived the Queen could look for little mercy but 'he was so careful in administration of justice, as many times, he favoured the subject in causes of the Prince'.[63]

Although he upheld the rule of law rather than of men, Burghley knew how large a part men played in the execution of justice. He himself had once pleaded ignorance of the law in a case which affected him. Of Oxford he wrote, 'I did my best to have the jury find the death of a poor man which he killed in my house to be *se defendendo*.' Political considerations and social deference made him especially lenient to the nobility. In conformity with common practice he discussed and prearranged the course of trials with Hatton, the Lord Chancellor. In Council enquiries he followed European methods in employing torture to obtain evidence for state trials. But in treason trials he was not a bully like Coke. His skilled examination rather than any rough handling of the defendant proved lethal. The lewd saucy letter of Sir John Hollis, which accused Burghley of knowingly accepting biased evidence and of insulting Hollis and his family in court, may be accepted only as the exception which proves the rule of Burghley's customary good conduct.[64]

Burghley was generally regarded as an impartial judge who strove to demonstrate that justice had been done. Within a system in which the criminal procedure, based on deterrence, was savage and in which civil actions depended on complex technicalities Burghley worked with all possible integrity. It was noted that he had not sought for himself or his children 'any pennyworth of land or goods that appertained to any person attainted for any treason, felony or otherwise'. It was his rule to accept no gift before a case was closed and even then to refuse the too large or too obvious gratuity. Burghley set a standard of judicial behaviour which his age admired.[65]

The tone of the administration over which Burghley presided was no doubt raised by his conduct and efforts. But to the conditions which determined its standards he applied only palliatives and attempted no cure. An administration the financing of which depended largely on private gratuities and the exploitation of perquisites, in which patronage was the means of selection for appointment and promotion, in which office was regarded as a property, yielding interest upon the capital invested in its purchase or performance and in which the means of checking transactions were almost wholly lacking was not an administration which was designed to exclude abuse. Its conventions and customs were not in themselves corrupt but they were peculiarly vulnerable to selfish interests. There was much venality in Elizabethan government.[66]

With much nodding of his head Burghley once admitted, 'It doth sometimes a man harm to be virtuous and honest'. But he could recognise corruption. 'Private gain is the perverting of justice and the pestilence of the Commonwealth,' he declared. Yet private gain there had to be. The problem lay in deciding when patronage became favouritism, when customary gratuities became bribes, when the sale of offices became a swindle, and fees, extortion. It was difficult to determine what was economic and just. Burghley knew that 'the rule in Christian philosophy consisteth in difference betwixt *utile* and *honestum*'. He was satisfied that he could make the distinction in his own conduct. 'I marvel,' he wrote, 'that any malicious discoverer can note me a councillor that do abuse my credit to private gain.'[67]

Yet many believed that Burghley was avaricious, if not corrupt. His biographer declared that Burghley had not taken as much as he might have done from the Court of Wards and that what he had taken touched neither his honesty nor his honour. Such an ambiguous defence may be explained by the fact that over official finance Burghley was scrupulously correct and that the money which he obtained came from what were conveniently regarded as private transactions. While the bearers of private purses might complain, the Queen did not. Burghley was a stickler for accounts and tried to check fraudulent practices in the receipt and expenditure of royal funds. He contracted no debts to the Crown, although he stood surety for royal borrowings. His own affairs were kept separate from those of the throne. His son Thomas thought his father wise to have 'so little meddled with money matters acceptable to her Majesty'. Integrity and efficiency marked Burghley's handling of royal monies. Sir John Fortescue, Chancellor of the Exchequer, wrote, 'I know him to be such a counsellor *qualis, ut arbitror, nemo nunquam erit, ut affirmare possum, apud nos nunquam fuit.*'[68]

Even in the quagmire of gratuities, annuities, fees and gifts Burghley walked delicately to avoid the deeper bogs of corruption. His honour, that compound of altruism and self-interest, warned him to refuse foreign gold. Such offers as those from Mendoza, one of the paymasters of the agents of Spain, and from Catherine de Medici, the regent of France, were rejected. At home he accepted what he regarded as moderate acknowledgements of his services and friendship. On Burghley's refusal of a gift of plate from Lord Audley, he was sent a horse. He avoided putting himself under any obligation to those whom he mistrusted or opposed. He did not take gifts from Drake.[69] That his scruples were unusual and unexpected can be seen from the crudity of the offers made to him and the popular belief that his riches could not have been honestly won.

Burghley's example of moderation and official honesty did not spread its influence far. His own secretaries, Henry Maynard and Michael Hickes, made fortunes acting as intermediaries for their lord. But their activities were part of those informal transactions which were not subject to the safeguards of officialdom, but regulated solely by the public morality which Burghley recognised as vital to good government. There were, however, scandals enough in the bureaucracy. In the Court of Wards there was the large scale embezzlement of royal funds by Mr Goring, Receiver of the Court, revealed by his death and followed by the impudent offer of Edward More to Robert Cecil to pay £1,000 to him and to his father for the office.[70] Compared with those around him, Burghley was not a great offender by any standards. His wealth grew from the sheer volume of work that he handled and because he held in the Mastership of the Court of Wards and the Lord Treasurership two of the most profitable posts in the Elizabethan government, which continued to yield even in the stringent days of the Spanish war.

If Burghley was not a great reconstructor of the administration, it must be remembered that from his time onwards the main framework was not radically altered until the nineteenth century. The corruption which to modern eyes appears inherent in the necessary customs and conventions which geared society to government must not be exaggerated. The period of Burghley's greatest influence upon the administration was notably less corrupt than the thirty years which preceded and succeeded it. He was humane rather than heroic. Northumberland found him 'too ceremonious'. Elizabeth complained of his 'too great lenity'.[71] Yet he maintained for the people of England one of the least oppressive, and for the Queen one of the most efficient administrations in Europe.

CHAPTER XVII

Lover of Learning and Patron of the Arts

'LEARNING will serve you in all ages and in all places and fortunes', wrote Burghley. Like most of his contemporaries he believed in the moral and utilitarian value of education. The humanists had persuaded the age that they could supply the best training and that the talents, so trained, should be put at the service of the State. That 'general counsels, and plots, and marshalling of affairs come best from learned men' was a widely held opinion.[1] Burghley, who had risen by the new secular ladder of success from grammar school to university, to Inns of Court, to royal office, naturally endorsed such views. The New Learning had created the 'new men'. Those who owed their success to their education were its advocates.

Like most parents, Burghley found the theory of bringing up children more easy to state than to practise. He delivered himself of sound precepts: 'Bring thy children up in learning and obedience yet without outward austerity. Praise them openly, reprehend them secretly. Give them good countenance and convenient maintenance according to thy ability. And I am persuaded that the foolish cockering of some parents and over-stern carriage of others causeth more men and women to take ill courses than their own vicious inclinations.' Clearly the psychology of teaching interested him. At dinner he would discuss the use of corporal punishment in schools.[2] Roger Ascham's widow acted both wisely and appropriately when she dedicated her husband's book, *The Scholemaster*, to Burghley.

Burghley's interest in education did not end with the consideration of the responsibilities of parent and teacher. As a statesman and a Protestant he was aware of the propagandist nature of indoctrination. In his efforts to train the young nobility to serve the Queen he told young Rutland that the object of his education was to make him 'an ornament hereafter to your country'. 'As for schoolmasters' he wrote to the Queen, when advising her on how to reduce the menace from papists, 'they may be a principal means of diminishing their number.' He arranged for the heirs of important catholic families to be converted to Protestantism by their schooling. In order to spread true religion he had a plan to make 'parents in every shire to send their children to be virtuously brought up at a certain place for that end appointed.'³ The clash of ideologies in the Reformation and Counter-Reformation was making plain the advantages of compulsory education on lines laid down by the government.

Like his wife, Cecil was a patron of schools. He aided his old schools at Grantham and Stamford. He gave an annuity to Westminster School.⁴ His circle of acquaintances and protégés included notable schoolmasters like Camden, Savile, Ashton, Nowell and Malim. He fostered the movement to endow and found grammar schools. Yet for all his interest in raising the standards and improving the practice of teachers, he did not memorialise himself by giving his name to a school. As Chancellor of Cambridge University and Master of the Court of Wards, he concentrated his efforts where his chief responsibilities for education lay.

Cecil was made Chancellor at Cambridge in 1559 and, although in 1562 he considered his resignation, 'having no learning', as he modestly said, 'to judge of learned men', he remained in office until his death.⁵ While he championed the royal right of patronage within the University, he used it, unlike Leicester at Oxford, to academic rather than to political advantage. He attempted no educational reforms. Sir Thomas Smith's scheme for colleges devoted to Law and Medicine did not have his support. He did not anticipate the action of his friend Sir Walter Mildmay by planting the acorn of a new college.

The new statutes of his Chancellorship affected the constitution, not the curriculum, of the University. That they confirmed the increasing power of the heads of colleges was the result of

Burghley's authoritarian sympathies rather than of his recognition of the new role which independent colleges and tutors were playing in providing a broader education for gentlemen. While Burghley did his best to assuage the bitterness of university politics, on strictly academic matters he preferred to let sleeping dons lie or chew their own bones of contention unmolested. It was a period of assimilation rather than of new thinking in the University, which was recovering from the depression of the mid-century.[6]

About the dress and manners of those ever-decadent beings, undergraduates, Cecil protested, but his most powerful interventions were on religious matters. He demanded order 'both for religion and evil behaviour'. In 1559 he was appointed to the Visitation for ensuring the protestant reliability of the University. In the event Puritanism rather than Catholicism proved the more insubordinate. He acted when students at his own college refused to wear surplices in Chapel at the time of the puritan attack on vestments. The vigilant Chancellor consulted the archbishops on religious controversies at Cambridge. While he allowed the puritan Professor of Divinity, Thomas Cartwright, to be driven from Cambridge, he later showed partiality for the foreign divine, Baro, in the controversy over predestination with the strictly Calvinist Archbishop Whitgift. His flair for mediation was shown in the troublesome affair of John Browning, who preached heresy and doubted the jurisdiction of the High Commission over members of the University in 1568 and again in 1573. Under Burghley, Cambridge did not lose its reputation as the chief nursery of Protestantism in England.[7]

Cecil's pride in his University was shown in the way in which he stage-managed the Queen's visit in 1564.[8] His preoccupation with affairs of State prevented him from meddling in University matters except when he deemed them to be of national importance. He did not encourage reference to himself over affairs which lay within the competence of the Vice-Chancellor. When he did intervene, his tact and modesty were effective. He was the most successful of the new lay Chancellors of the sixteenth century.

It was as Master of the Court of Wards that Burghley was

R

personally responsible for the education of the Queen's wards. Most wards were sold and placed in households to be brought up according to their station but the noblest were kept in Burghley's own care.[9] He set a new standard of academic discipline and attainment in the education of the aristocracy. The regime of the young Earl of Oxford's long day included religious instruction, cosmography, French, Latin, calligraphy, drawing, and dancing. To the young Rutland on vacation, Burghley expressed the hope that 'you will, when you are wearying of hunting, recontinue some exercise of hunting in your book.' Burghley did not discourage sporting pursuits. He looked for a competent instructor in horsemanship for his wards. He regarded travel as an educational exercise and a knowledge of history as a necessary preparation for going abroad. He gave young Rutland elaborate instructions on what to note during his trip to the Continent so that he might, he wrote to him, 'be able to make satisfaction what you have gained for the expense of your time and money that may make you more worth than you were before your departure'.[10]

Burghley took his task as guardian seriously. He obtained notes on the method of educating the Earl of Surrey from the Earl's tutor. In his own household at one time or another he gathered an impressive array of teachers: Thomas Windebank, Walter Travers, Laurence Nowell, Arthur Golding, Richard Howland, Robert Ramsden, John Harte, Sylvius Frisius. With such talent available it was no wonder that Cecil House gained a reputation as an educational establishment. Although it was famed for its academic rather than its military education, there was competition to secure a place in it for wards and sons.[11] Lady Stanhope, the Countess of Lennox, Lady Russell, the Earl of Essex, the Duke of Norfolk, the Bishop of Ely and Sir Henry Sidney were among those who sought to put children in Burghley's care. There were often as many as twenty young gentlemen, learning their manners at his table, their religion at his prayers and their lessons from Burghley himself or their tutors.[12] The Cecil household maintained the tradition for training youth of the old ecclesiastical establishments, like those of Cardinals Morton and Wolsey, and stressed the new intellectual concerns which had been fostered in the houses of the recent lay leaders, Thomas Cromwell, Somerset and Northumberland. Burghley fused the medieval traditions of the episcopal household and castle with the influences of the Renaissance study and the pious family of the Reformation.

The households of Somerset and Northumberland had played an important part in Cecil's own intellectual development. After the classicism of Cambridge and the legalism of the Inns of Court they provided a broader vision of how the arts and sciences were applied to life. The Court was a centre of authority and wealth which attracted intellectuals for whom it appeared to offer the most desirable opportunity for fulfilment. It gave that setting of practical power in which academic concerns seemed relevant to the problems of the day. Learning could be put to 'the marshalling of affairs', art to enhancing the glory of the realm, science to the strengthening of the State and religion to put 'forward into life and performance what she understands to have the divine approbation'.[13]

While Burghley tended to subordinate all his knowledge and his patronage to the furtherance of his statecraft, he had other motives for being 'learned and a lover of learning'. His aesthetic sense mingled with his beliefs of what was socially decorous to produce an aristocratic taste which his wealth could largely satisfy. His religious convictions, his humanist respect for Antiquity and his curiosity in matters of science or natural philosophy constituted a wide range of interests to which he gave practical application in his private and public life. His acquaintance at Court, in the City, in the universities and noble households with the close-knit intellectual caste of Tudor England had its effect upon his mind and patronage. But, while he was ready to pick the brains of those he knew and was quick to learn from debate and discussion, he had a habit of serious study. He was an omnivorous reader.

Although, like his Queen, he read to divert his mind from affairs of State, Burghley usually read either to improve the minds of others by his duty of censorship or to improve his own mind. He was reputed to have carried Cicero's *Offices* in his pocket. He thought that the New Testament should be read four times a year and the Old Testament once. He preferred his books to cards, chess, bowls or any game. From his early manhood he obtained books and maps from abroad through diplomats and travellers.[14] In 1553 he purchased some seventy books. His love of books was known on the Continent. Foreign scholars presented their works to him and he was asked by an English scholar for letters of introduction to libraries in Europe. He created a library of his own 'in the riches whereof,' wrote the learned Matthew Parker in 1566, 'I rejoice as much as they were in mine own.'[15]

Burghley's 'bibliotheca instructissima', as Camden called it, has been dispersed. He left his working library, to which he devoted a room in his Strand house, to Thomas but his state papers he left to Robert Cecil. There is some evidence to show the range of his library but its size, perhaps some few thousand printed books and manuscripts, cannot be accurately known.[16] Burghley appears to have possessed books on many subjects. He had legal, medical, mathematical and architectural works. His collection of Greek and Latin authors contained purchases from the library of John Cheke, just as his theological collection contained works from Cranmer's library. The historical works included not only the classical historians, but also the Anglo-Saxon Chronicle, Bede's *Ecclesiastical History* and collections of medieval charters and chronicles as well as more modern documents and writings by such men as Guicciardini and Comines. Among the lighter works were the popular French romances, *Amadis de Gaul*, and the Spanish picaresque piece, *Celestina*. Burghley could range over the learning and literature of the Ancient world and of contemporary Europe.[17]

Although Burghley was modest about his conversational fluency in modern languages and once wrote of his being 'only meet to speak as my mother taught me', he rarely read in English. His preference was for works in Latin, Greek, French, Spanish and Italian. He was accustomed to read his Bible and to pray as well as to draft diplomatic correspondence and treaties in Latin. The Queen once complimented him on his Latin style. In his later years he conducted long negotiations in French and as a lawyer he knew the extraordinary jargon of law French. He learned from the translators whom he employed to deal with foreign dispatches and intelligence. John Baret and Thomas Thomas recognised his linguistic skill by dedicating to him their French and Latin dictionaries.[18] In a Court where every courtier was expected to be a linguist Burghley was outstandingly well equipped.

Amongst subjects for study Burghley always commended the common law and used to say that 'if he should begin again, he would follow that study'. He had spent his years well at the Inns of Court for, despite his modest disclaimers, his knowledge of the law was held in high respect by the professional lawyers. He knew much of the civil law, although it was typical of him that, having set out the bones of a case in civil law, he should add that good civilians might be able to support it with many more texts and examples of decrees. The quarrel over the *ex officio* oath between the common law lawyers and the canon law lawyers drew Burghley into the study of ecclesiastical law.[19] Diplomacy made Burghley think about *jus gentium* and argue for the freedom of the seas. About the usages and rights of embassies he instructed ambassadors. He had administered martial law and became Earl Marshal. In the intricacies of rights to arms, the rules governing heraldry, he was an expert. He knew something of the laws of the Border but when Lord Eure asked him to pronounce upon them it was too much for the aged Burghley, who refused.[20]

Clio was Burghley's favourite muse. History recommended itself to him and to his age as a storehouse of examples for political and personal conduct. It satisfied his legal taste for precedent and provided the foundations for his thinking about the constitution and the law. His friends among the antiquarians who anticipated the later Society of Antiquaries discussed the history of Parliament. Protestantism and, in particular, the Church of England found a powerful justification in a reinterpretation of the ecclesiastical past, as Burghley recognised, when he came to defend English religion. His historical approach to society was furthered by his study of genealogy. He himself wrote out the genealogies of many of the noble and royal families of Europe and the British Isles. 'If any books be newly set out, of genealogies or of armories, remember me,' he wrote to Smith in Paris. The College of Arms, with which he was closely associated, was a nursery of historical research.[21]

The study of history was well served by Burghley. He played a part in that movement begun by Leland to collect and preserve the sources of historical scholarship which had been scattered by the Reformation attack on the libraries of the monasteries, colleges and universities. With the support of men like Matthew Parker he did his best to rescue valuable books and documents from destruction or export. Besides helping to preserve the medieval heritage of historical material, he recognised the importance of the current records and papers of government. From them he desired his most outstanding protégé among historians, William Camden, to 'eternize the memory of that renowned Queen Elizabeth'. In his diaries of foreign affairs and in his briefing of ambassadors, he revealed his historical approach to the problems of contemporary politics.[22]

Burghley was a patron of historians. Working in his household were Laurence Nowell, a student of Anglo-Saxon history, and John Clapham, who wrote on the Tudors. Matthew Parker sent Burghley the manuscript of his *De Antiquitate Ecclesiae*. Grafton dedicated to him his popular history of England.[23] Holinshed, the chronicler, in his dedication to Burghley mentions that his patron had been 'an especial good lord to Master Wolfe'. Wolfe, the printer, died in 1572 but he had been the projector of a Universal Cosmography to which such men as Holinshed, William Harrison, Saxton and Thomas Seckford, a lawyer and official in the Court of Wards, were to have contributed. Burghley protected John Stow, the historian of London, from suffering for catholic sympathies. When Giles Fletcher, whose description of Russia Burghley had to suppress for the sake of amity with the Czar, considered writing a history of England, it was to Burghley that he turned for consultation.[24]

Those who sought patronage rightly judged him to be omnivorous in history. Arthur Golding presented him with translations from Leonardo Bruni and Julius Caesar. Thomas Danett, who compared Burghley to Comines, dedicated to the Lord Treasurer his revised translation of that French author along with translations from Guicciardini's works. For his history of the Roman Emperors, Richard Reynolds took Burghley as his patron as did the editors of the chronicle of Florentius Bravonius. Sir John Price's son dedicated to Burghley his father's defence of the historicity of King Arthur. Camden and Norden honoured Cecil's name with the *Britannia* of 1586 and the first part of the *Speculum Britanniae*. It is significant of Burghley's interest in historians that Aubrey's story about him is of his efforts to trace the writer of an account of the Battle of Lepanto who ended his life on the scaffold before his would-be patron could find him.[25]

While Burghley was an undoubted patron of historians, his reputation for the appreciation of the creative writers of vernacular literature of Elizabeth's reign has been that of a parsimonious Philistine. He suffered to some extent from the Queen's reluctance to reward the poets, as the following verse addressed to Elizabeth shows:

> *Madam,*
> *You bid your treasurer, on a time,*
> *To give me reason for my rhime,*
> *But since that time and that season*
> *He gave me neither rhime nor reason.*

Spenser felt that Burghley blamed his 'looser rhymes . . . for praising love' and branded him as a loveless moralist. The disappointed poet struck at the statesman in spiteful verse. Burghley did belong to that group of Protestants and humanists who rejected the chivalric and romantic strain in literature as 'open manslaughter and bold bawdry'. He was apt to see with a censor's eye.[26] But at the age of fifty, a statesman who had been brought up in 'the Drab Age' of English writing could hardly be expected to have much confidence in the vernacular and to be enthusiastic about new movements among young poets. Burghley was not alone in his indifference to the new poetry for as late as 1595 Philip Sidney's *Apologie for Poetrie* was first published. The patronage of creative writers was not sustained or lavish in Elizabeth's reign. They did less well than the utilitarian authors and translators.

Patriotic as Burghley was, he did not endorse the linguistic jingoism which vaunted the supremacy of the native tongue. Yet he appreciated the use of the vernacular in propaganda and education. He encouraged a number of translators, among whom Golding and Googe were pre-eminent. He was a friend of John Florio's father and, no doubt, helped the son. His school-mate Ralph Robinson dedicated to him the first English version of More's *Utopia* in 1551. While Burghley's taste in reading indicates that he doubted whether the vernacular could vie with 'subtle Greek and stately Latin', it must be remembered that the creator of euphuism, John Lyly, was loud in his praise of Burghley.[27] Yet it was to the English classical scholarly Renaissance of Cheke and Ascham, rather than to the European literary Renaissance of Sidney and Spenser that Burghley belonged.

The fact that the young nobility, like Oxford and Southampton, to whom Burghley was antipathetic, were the patrons of poets and dramatists served to stress the different taste of succeeding generations. Burghley wrote a Latin introductory verse to the Latin poem of his friend, Sir Thomas Chaloner. He helped the old exile John Heywood. His patronage of younger creative writers, like Lyly, was not in their literary careers. He did give Peele small commissions and accepted his versified history of Troy. But there was little to justify Richard Field, the stationer, in his dedication to Burghley of Puttenham's *Arte of English Poesie* for stating, 'I could not devise to have presented to your lordship any gift more agreeable to your appetite.' He was nearer the mark when he wrote, 'Perceiving besides the title to purport so slender a subject as nothing almost could be more discrepant from the gravity of your years and honourable function whose contemplations are every hour more seriously employed upon public administration and service.'[28] Age and occupation, no doubt, dulled Burghley's taste for the novelties of vernacular literature.

While classical plays stood on his shelves, Burghley had little encouragement to give to the contemporary drama. He accepted plays and interludes for purposes of propaganda or for entertaining distinguished guests. His acquaintance with such authors as Norton, Sackville and Lyly did not fire his enthusiasm. If he saw some of Shakespeare's plays, they did not inspire him to maintain, as did Leicester, Warwick and other nobles, a company of players.

His most influential connections with the theatre lay in his reorganisation of the Office of Revels and in the drawing up with the Recorder of London the rules for the performance of plays in the City. His puritan friend Edmund Grindal hoped to have Burghley's support in closing the London playhouses.[29]

Both Spenser and Grindal seem to have thought that Burghley would make moral rather than aesthetic judgements upon poetry and drama. Certainly William Cecil was not a literary man. He could make an English verse for a family occasion and a Latin verse for a dedication, he could write controversial pamphlets, compose prayers and coin epigrams but he was not a courtier poet, like Raleigh, or an essayist, like Francis Bacon. No learned or authoritative works came from his pen as they did from the hand of Sir Thomas Smith. Even in retirement under Mary, he did not carry out the proposals to which Cheke pressed him for translating Bracton's legal works and setting out *An Order of the Policy and Officers of the Realm*. He did not find time, as Parker hoped he would, to revise one of the *Epistles* in the Bishop's Bible.[30] In his long official life the pressure of work had tended to make him a man of 'notes and piecemeals' with an interest in schemes for shorthand like that set out by Trithemius's *Steganographia* about which John Dee wrote to him. Roger Ascham had been lavish in his praise of the English style of the young Cecil and much later Sir Edward Coke acknowledged the effectiveness of Burghley's pamphleteering technique. At its best Burghley's manner of writing was justly described by Clapham as 'short and plain without curiosity, but not altogether without ornament, for he especially regarded substance of matter and not artificial composition of words'.[31]

But if Burghley did not write like an angel neither did he speak like poor Poll. His protégé Thomas Wilson, author of *The Art of Rhetoric*, in dedicating to him some orations of Demosthenes, wrote to Burghley, 'he is your glass, I am well assured, whereupon you do often look and compare his time with this time'. He also reminded him of the rhetorical training which Cheke gave to Cecil at Cambridge and to Wilson at Padua. Oratory was held to be a useful art for counsellors and Burghley was regarded as a good speaker. Puttenham remarked upon his 'grave and natural eloquence' in Parliament, where he was ready to mix 'a merry tale' with sounding exhortations. Burghley outlined speeches for others, like Puckering and Hatton, and produced many official papers for public declamation. His loyal biographer recorded that 'his eloquence was so excellent as that what he spake was impossible to be delivered more rhetorically, clearly and significantly'.[32]

Ascham was one of those who regarded singing and music as aids to oratory but there is no sign that Burghley ever employed such training himself. No doubt he sang his beloved Psalms, for musical settings to them were dedicated to him at the end of his life. While it was later claimed that he took an interest in the choir at Westminster Abbey, he was not, like Parker, a patron of ecclesiastical music. Cecil, it seems, was neither a patron of musicians nor a lover of secular music. Unlike Sir Thomas Kytson, he did not keep musicians in his household. There must have been music in his houses on festive occasions. His son, Thomas, was taught to play the virginals and the lute. He would have found it difficult to avoid music at Court. But, apart from keeping a strict watch upon the pay of the Queen's musicians, he does not appear to have greatly encouraged what was recognised in Europe as the most flourishing art of Elizabethan England.[33]

It is significant that in the scheme for the education of wards which Nicholas Bacon presented to Burghley there is constant reference to the music master, but in the curriculum drawn up by Burghley and in the timetable of the Earl of Oxford there is no allowance for musical instruction, although music did, presumably, accompany the dancing which Burghley permitted.[34] Philip Sidney, who spent some time in Cecil House, regretted that he had not had a good musical education, a lack which his attendance at Shrewsbury did not remedy.

Burghley did not have music or reading aloud at his meals as was the custom in many noble households. He took the opportunity to relax and talk about everything except current politics. With old acquaintances he indulged in reminiscences and blossomed as a raconteur. Conversation was an art in the Renaissance court and Burghley knew how to season his remarks from his vast repertoire of texts, proverbs and adages, which were so much to the taste of the eclectic intellectuals of the day. He knew how to adjust his tone to the company. 'Be not scurrilous in conversation nor satirical in thy jests', he warned his son, 'for suspitious jests (when any of them savour of truth) leave a bitterness in the minds of those which are touched'. 'Nimble fancies' he condemned as 'the froth of wit' but he could not abide a tedious tale. In his old age he was on occasion sharp-tongued but in his prime the most notable features of his conversation were its good humour and varied range.[35]

In the course of his polymathic talk Burghley discussed matters of 'the learned professions'. His ill health gave him more than an academic interest in medicine, of which writers like Henry Wingfield, Timothy Bright and Philip Barrow took advantage in dedicating medical works to him. In his library was Nicolas Monardes' Spanish work on medicine in the West Indies. On law he spoke with authority. Matthew Hutton, a Regius Professor of Divinity, praised his learning in religion. His biblical knowledge enabled him to vie with such a textmonger as Edward Dering. His ability to 'call to mind anything he had done, seen or read' made him a stimulating talker.[36] Although academic topics of discussion were his delight, he discoursed on such practical matters as the 'science of artisans and men of mechanical trades'.[37]

Burghley was interested in what would now be called science and technology. As Secretary, he was expected to know 'of discoveries and new inventions'. His help was sought for legal aid in patents and for financial support. He was thus conversant with all the inventions and proposals of the growing host of projectors. He had to weigh their utility to the commonwealth. They caught his interest. 'The practick part of wisdom is the best', he once remarked. He knew what went on in the workshops, the laboratories of the period, and he read the learned treatises. He could agree with John Dee that 'there is nothing (the word of God only set apart) which so much beautifieth and adorneth the soul and mind of man as doth the knowledge of good arts and sciences: as the knowledge of natural and moral philosophy'. When Dee went on to show how mathematics could be applied by merchants, lawyers, soldiers, goldsmiths, doctors, navigators, geographers, surveyors, architects and others in their practical work, he was preaching what Burghley encouraged in practice. Burghley was well acquainted with Henry Billingsley, the London merchant and customs man, and with Dee, who had written the eloquent plea for applied science to introduce Billingsley's English translation of Euclid's *Elements of Geometry*.[38]

Both at Court and in the City there was a movement to use science to the benefit of man and the State. It was to be publicised by Francis Bacon and institutionalised by Gresham College. Edward Worsop, 'a simple man among the common people', dedicated to Burghley a popular exposition of surveying in which he wrote of 'his especial good lord . . . it is universally known that the continual application of your noble heart and mind is to the furtherance of learned knowledges, of equity in causes, suppressing of ignorance and to the commodity of the weal public (whereof your Honour is a principal pillar) . . .'. Burghley was obviously well known among the 'rude mechanicals' of London for his interest in the application of science. He found work in the Mint for Humphrey Cole, the goldsmith and 'mathematical mechanician' who had a shop for surveying instruments near the north door of St Paul's. While Cole dared to write to Burghley, he 'durst not presume to come to Court'.[39]

From his undergraduate days William Cecil had been subject to the influence of John Cheke's scientific interests. Cheke was a Professor of Greek but he loved chemical experiments and he was mathematician enough to construct an astronomical quadrant for a student. Cecil's 'divine spark' of scientific knowledge was 'partly received of him'. In the households of Somerset and Northumberland, in his membership of various companies, in his roles as statesman, Treasury official, landlord and investor, Cecil came into contact with a variety of scientific interests from surveying, cartography, astronomy, navigation, gunnery and ship-building to mining, metallurgy, botany, architecture, horse-breeding and alchemy. There was profit and power for the man who could find his way through what was for the men of the time a single territory of interrelated knowledge. 'The mathematical mind', wrote Dee, 'can by order descend to frame natural things to wonderful uses, and when he list, retire home into his own centre: and there prepare more means to ascend or descend by: and all to the glory of God and our honest delectation in earth.' These were the sort of mathematics in which Burghley was 'so well-seen' and by which he ascended to the theoretical and descended to the practical.[40]

In Burghley's own household Laurence Nowell spoke of his master's exacting standards in surveying and cartography but he was unable to induce his good lord to pay for the making of a series of county maps of England. Later Burghley did help John Norden, the topographer, by instructing the Justices of the Peace to aid him. Both Norden and Camden acknowledged Burghley's encouragement by dedications of their work. William Lambarde submitted the manuscript of his book on Kent, and Norden the manuscript of his work on Essex to Burghley's expert scrutiny. Like his colleague Thomas Seckford, the patron of Saxton, Burghley was one of the promoters of the remarkable cartographic and topographical activity of Elizabeth's reign. He annotated his 1579 edition of Saxton's maps. He was interested in the topography of the Border. In Ireland, where the political need to know the country was obvious, Burghley used such men as Robert Lythe and John Browne to make surveys and maps. His protégé, Humphrey Cole, made the first known English copper engraving of a map when he produced a map of Palestine for the Bishops' Bible.[41]

The geographical knowledge which Burghley acquired from his maps and books was detailed. 'What province, county, city or notable place in England could he not describe?' His interest extended to Europe and beyond. To Frobisher's sailing instructions he added the comment, 'not for the Isle of Friezland in the way'. In 1553 he purchased a History of the Indies. He was associated with travellers, navigators and geographers. Richard Eden, the publicist of the new discoveries, was Cecil's secretary under Northumberland and introduced him to John Dee. Governmental authorisation made Burghley conversant with every project. In the discovery of the North-East passage to Asia he backed the Muscovy Company, through which he came into contact with men like Anthony Jenkinson, who went to Persia via Russia and Robert Recorde, the algebraist. Later he supported Humphrey Gilbert and Martin Frobisher in their efforts to find the North-West passage.[42] No great traveller himself, Burghley roamed the world through his books, maps and acquaintances.

The wider universe intrigued Burghley. Thomas Digges' *Alae* on the mathematics of astronomy and John Blagrave's more practical *Mathematical Jewel*, dealing with the astrolabe, were dedicated to Burghley. He studied John Dee's plan to reform the calendar and suggested that Digges and scholars from the universities should be called to comment on it. The conventional ceiling decoration of a representation of the heavens was turned at Theobalds into something like a planetarium, with a mechanically propelled sun moving on its course, which suggests that it did not portray a Copernican universe. But Thomas Digges, a convinced Copernican, constructed a novel astronomical device for daytime use in Burghley's garden. If Burghley tended, like Cheke and Camden, to confuse astronomy and astrology, he was, nevertheless, well informed on the scientific side. The puritan William Fulke offered an astrological game for Burghley's approbation.[43]

Military science, like navigation, contributed to the greatness of the State and caught the humanist statesman's attention. Cheke had translated into Latin a Byzantine work on warfare. Besides the classical military histories, Burghley had a French work on the art of war and such manuscripts as *The Art of Shooting Great Ordonance* as well as notes by Thomas Hood, mathematical lecturer to the captains of the trained bands. Henry Marshall wrote to him about military inventions. Burghley himself collected data about muskets and their performance. He corresponded with such writers on military affairs as Thomas Digges and Sir John Smythe. He asked William Bourne, the Gravesend shipwright, about the buoyancy of vessels and commissioned him to write a tract on optics, but he does not seem to have given any encouragement to a book on sea warfare by the same author.[44]

The economic advantage to himself and to his country drew Burghley into metallurgical enterprises and an interest in industrial processes. He was a shareholder in the Mines Royal, the Mineral and Battery Works and in Sir Thomas Smith's Society of the New Art, all of them companies concerned with new techniques in mining and metallurgy. He watched work at the Mint and considered the details of lead-smelting processes. He sent Humphrey Cole on a prospecting trip to the North and was interested in prospecting in Ireland. His hopes that Dee or his pupil Edward Kelly might make gold were no more sanguine than those of the leading alchemists of the day. The charlatanism of Cornelius de Lannoy, who promised Elizabeth an elixir, Burghley did detect and he put the impostor in the Tower.[45] The importance of metal alloys in the making of weapons and in coining was not lost upon Burghley.

Burghley was numerically and mechanically minded. Although he had a Treasury man's preference for Roman numerals, he liked statistics and quantitative assessment, for which his financial preoccupations were good training. From the mathematical abstraction of accountancy Cecil and his circle were groping towards the application of scientific measurement in other spheres of statecraft. It was from Burghley that Francis Bacon, a student of his uncle's methods, learned that 'The greatness of an estate in bulk and territory doth fall under measure and the greatness of finances doth fall under computation. The population may appear by musters and the number and greatness of cities and towns by maps and cards.'[46]

While Burghley did not, as his biographer somewhat defensively noted, spend his leisure like Charles V taking 'asunder his clocks', he had an interest in mechanical devices. One of Burghley's clocks had belonged to Cheke. From Stade near Hamburg he was sent by Edward Kelly, the alchemist, a 'rock or mountain' which was most likely one of the popular German *Handsteine*, models of mountains made up of assays of ores, stone and crystals, showing the layout in section of mine workings with figures of miners at their different tasks. Burghley told Kelly, 'I will place it in my house where I bestow other things of workmanship'. Evidently Burghley had a *Wunderkammer*. The optimistic Edmund Jentill rated Burghley's interest in mechanisms so high that, having confessed to the treason of false coining, he hoped to buy the Lord Treasurer's favour by promising him an array of mechanical inventions. Burghley could think in mechanistic terms. It is recorded that he said, 'The world is a shop of instruments, whereof the wise man is master and a kingdom but a frame of engines whereunto he is a wheel.' He once likened the course of events to a wound-up clock.[47] Behind the divine creation Burghley, like many of his intellectual contemporaries, was becoming vaguely aware of a great machine.

Around his houses, where the great clocks ticked away the hours, were his gardens and estates. There was business to be done in exploiting his estates. By good marketing and careful survey, rather than by rack-renting, he made the best of his lands. The lord who employed a skilled surveyor, like Israel Amyce, scarcely needed the advice of the worthy Edward Worsop on how to obtain by survey a fair deal for landlord and tenant. Horse-breeding and sheep-rearing attracted him. He patronised Thomas Blundeville, who wrote on horse-management. Burghley knew the market and his agricultural methods were up-to-date. Above all he was, in accordance with the advice of the growing race of writers on estate management, the '*auditor auditorum*' in all his own business.[48]

The Elizabethan preoccupation with gardens, which shows itself in Shakespeare's imagery, had its hold upon Burghley's mind. The attraction of exotic plants from overseas, of the illustrated books on plants and garden design, of medicinal herbs and of the newly-acquired taste for salads, fruits and flowers drew wealthy men to the study of botany and horticulture. The garden had become both a work of art and of science.

At Burghley House there were formal gardens in front of the main entrance and in all some thirty acres, which Bacon considered the ideal area for a royal garden, were devoted to flower plots, bowling green, game bird enclosure, a mount, fishponds, canals, vineyard and bleaching grounds. In the fashionable Strand, Burghley's town house had gardens which he extended by purchases in Covent Garden. The garden at Theobalds, over the layout of which Burghley took great care, was described as 'of

Burghley House

THE
HERBALL
OR GENERALL
Historie of
Plantes.

Gathered by John Gerarde
of London Master in
CHIRVRGERIE.

Imprinted at London by
Iohn Norton.
1597

Title-page of John Gerard's Herbal, *which was dedicated to Lord Burghley*

immense extent and, as the palace is really most magnificent, so likewise in proportion is no expense spared on the garden: in a summer house there is a table made of a solid piece of black touchstone, fourteen spans long, seven wide and one span thick.' 'For state and magnificence' Burghley set up the busts of twelve Roman Emperors, purchased for him in Venice. Topiary art, statuary and summer houses made the fashionable formality 'beautiful' to foreign visitors. Norden praised 'the delightful walks and pleasant conceits'. Harrison regarded the gardens at Theobalds as fit to rank with those of Hampton Court, Nonsuch and Cobham as the finest in England, while others compared them to the most delicate in Italy.[49]

Behind the art lay the science. Burghley cultivated exotic plants. He obtained fifty sorts of seeds from Florence. Amongst the trees for which he sent abroad were lemon and myrtle, obtained from Paris along with instructions on their care. He received reports on grafting in his orchards. In Somerset's household he had met the Northumbrian puritan, classicist and naturalist, William Turner, of whose pioneering botanical pursuits he knew. John Gerard, herbalist and surgeon, who drew upon the knowledge of the discoverers and was the keeper of the physic garden at the Hall of the Royal College of Physicians, advised Burghley on his gardens at Cecil House and Theobalds and chose him as patron for his two learned botanical works. An edition of the popular *Gardener's Labyrinth* by Thomas Hill was also dedicated to Burghley. Horticulture was an applied science much to Burghley's taste.[50]

Gardens were the carefully designed settings to the great houses. The characteristic contemporary expression of artistic patronage was the house with all its rich and varied contents. The Tudor domestic peace permitted the building of what Burghley called 'castles of pleasure' and removed the limitations of defensive works. The prosperity of the ruling class provided the material foundations and the humanist concern with earthly life the mood for a building boom which reshaped the houses of the yeoman, gentleman and noble and framed new standards of living.[51]

Burghley was amongst the greatest builders of his time. He developed three impressive mansions. Cecil House in the Strand,

s

required by the great official in the governmental capital, was
nearly finished in 1561. It was of brick, 'proportionally adorned
with four turrets' and 'within curiously beautified with rare
devices'. The 'Mansion of his barony', Burghley House near
Stamford, was stone-built. Theobalds in Hertfordshire was of
brick and stone with '24 toweretts'. Its proximity to London, in a
neighbourhood favoured by government men, made it Burghley's
favourite home and he enlarged it to accommodate the Queen on
her visits.[52]

It was incumbent upon Burghley as a courtier, an official and a
noble to build and to build big. Wolsey, Somerset, Northumberland, Hatton and Nicholas Bacon had all felt the compulsion to
create vast establishments that were more than private abodes.
The Tudor courtiers needed houses which would establish their
social rank, provide offices for their own and state business, act as
a temporary residence for the Court and, like the royal palaces,
demonstrate dynastic and national prosperity and glory. They
planned monuments of fame not for domestic but for state
occasions. Their architectural response to the demands of public
life they liked to represent as voluntary acts of loyalty to the
glorification of the Queen. Theobalds had a council chamber, a
suitor's gallery and a suitor's walk in the garden. At all his houses
Cecil played host to the Queen and her entourage. He once wrote
to Hatton that they had 'both meant to exceed their purses' in
making their houses worthy of the Queen.[53]

Burghley's building activities spread over some thirty-five years.
He began work on Burghley House in 1553 and finished in 1589.
The site for Theobalds was purchased in 1563 and the house was
completed by 1585. During all this time he exercised a close
supervision of the works, making drawings, approving an 'upright
of the face', accepting a sketch of a window, considering what
sort of ceilings to erect. He employed able builders like Roger
Warde, Henry Hawthorne, John Symons and Thomas Fowler.
He took advice, but the credit for the final composition and choice
of detail rests with Burghley. 'The house itself doth show the
owner's wit', was Vallans's just line on Theobalds, which applied
also to Burghley House.[54]

With Sir Thomas Smith and many others Cecil shared the new learned interest in architecture. Both Somerset and Northumberland had encouraged the study of the latest continental designs. Cecil knew the works of his patrons and the men who advised them, Thynne, Sharington and Shute. Among his books on architecture were such modern treatises as Philibert de L'Orme's *Novels Inventions pour bien bastir*. He possessed numerous plans, including one of Longleat, and in 1595 he was still eager to see plans for Chelsea House by Torrington. His academic eclecticism showed itself in choice of design and detail, in the employment of foreign craftsmen, like Henryck and Caspar Vosbergh, and in the importation from abroad of materials and completed works such as balustrades and chimney-pieces. The vaulted stone staircase at Burghley House was in the French style. The Conduit Court at Theobalds bears all the marks of having been based on a plan in Sebastiano Serlio's *Architettura*.[55]

His houses were Burghley's most lavish and successful acts of artistic patronage and they were the products of his own taste. Theobalds was admired and visited by foreigners and natives as one of the remarkable sights of England. It exercised an important influence on the style of Holdenby and Audley End. He proudly presented the Queen with a picture of Theobalds. Burghley's opinion on architectural matters, which Hatton, Mildmay and many others held in high esteem, was both sound and enlightened by the standards of the day. If he still used the old court-yard plan which was later approved by Bacon, he thought in terms of 'largeness and lightsomeness', of coherence of 'pattern' or plan, of balanced elevation and 'grace'. Evolved over the years as their creator enlarged them, Theobalds and Burghley House became remarkably harmonious and impressive structures, in which the native and foreign elements, Flemish, French and Italian, were successfully fused. Few have builded better than Burghley in his day.[56]

The building and furnishing of great houses 'set on work' the poor and a host of artists and craftsmen. They were, in a sense, public works providing employment and stimulating industry. In them it was not 'rare to see abundance of arras, rich hangings of tapestry, silver vessels, and so much other plate as may furnish sundry cupboards to the sum of a thousand or two thousand pounds at the least, whereby the value of this and the rest of their stuff doth grow inestimable'. Apart from the purchase of furnishings, the largest sum which Burghley spent on building in a single year was £2,700 in 1571–2 on Theobalds. From 1567 to 1578 he spent on an average something over a £1,000 a year on his building activities. The interior decoration of his houses was elaborate. Visitors to Theobalds remarked on the murals, the use of the fashionable heraldic embellishments and on such conceits as the woodland room which contained trees so realistic that the birds flew in and sang upon the branches.[57]

In his collection of plate and jewellery Burghley combined sound investment with connoisseurship. He had a discriminating taste in silver and gold ware and made gifts of choice pieces to the Queen. He was reputed to have left between fourteen and fifteen thousand pounds worth of plate, which he had acquired by gift or purchase. He himself wore discreet jewellery like the cross-shaped piece on his flat black cap. His wife displayed in her portraits many gems in fine settings. They were not merely the flattering fancies of a court painter for she presented elaborate jewellery to the Queen.[58] Burghley could afford the valuable and fashionable adornments of the Renaissance Court.

His collector's instinct had, perhaps, no more fitting expression for a Lord Treasurer than his interest in numismatics. As early as 1553 Ascham gave him medals of Augustus and a gold coin of Nero. At the time of the recoinage William Cecil had asked Sir Thomas Smith to write a treatise on Roman coinage. The cult of Antiquity had produced a revival of the medal-maker's art and a fashion for acquiring classical and modern examples of that skill. William Harrison, who wrote the *Description of England*, was one of a number of Tudor numismatists. Part of the interest in such a study derived from the new regard for portraiture which was reflected in the current Tudor coinage. The self-awareness which came with the Renaissance gave portraiture in all its forms a fascination for Elizabethan gentlemen.[59]

Burghley, like Leicester, Lumley and the gentry at large, followed the royal lead in forming portrait galleries. He sent abroad for pictures and employed foreign and native artists. Portraiture, while it expressed the humanist desire for individual fame, also suited the taste of secular protestant patrons, for it savoured neither of Romish superstition nor of pagan impropriety. It had a moral value. Deloney's Jack of Newbury, when he showed his portraits of men who had been 'advanced to high estate' to his servants, urged them 'to imitate the like virtues that you might attain like honours'.[60]

At Theobalds on one side of the long gallery hung 'all the emperors beginning with Caesar: the other the pictures of the Chief in Europe'. There was also a 'lesser gallery with other common pictures'. Burghley had portraits of his family, of his blind mother, of his sons, of his second wife and of a grand-daughter in all the finery of a much spoiled five-year-old. In one picture he appeared with his favourite son, Robert. Family pride and a desire to memorialise those whom he loved mingled with the inspiration to imitate self-made Caesars, princes and notables. But for Burghley the political purpose could not be suppressed. A statesman who was dealing with the 'Chief in Europe' liked to know how they looked and ponder their characteristics.

In domestic politics the propaganda value of portraits was clear to Burghley, who pressed the Queen to have a good official likeness made which might be copied for distribution to her subjects. He took good care to ensure that his own portraits would do him credit in the copies which his clients proudly hung in their houses as a sign of his patronage or of their desire for it. His poor relatives at Alltyrynys wanted his portrait. It is significant of Burghley's regard for the symbols of patronage that more portraits of him survive than of any other Elizabethan except the Queen herself.[61]

Portraits in the sixteenth century were multiplied by copying authorised models rather than by frequent sittings. It appears that William Cecil had three such models from which his portraits were derived. The face or mask was the important part of the model and around it variations of pose, dress and background could be made. One group of paintings centres upon a portrait of himself which he had painted in the early 1560s. The standard version was a three-quarter-length study of the mature Secretary to the Queen. Another model, made in the 1580s showed him full-length as the impressive Lord Treasurer in his Garter robes. The third model, painted very late in his life, pictured the elder statesman full-length but seated and wearing over his customary skull-cap, not the characteristic flat cap, but a tall hat.[62]

The various versions did not fail in their purpose of asserting the authoritative mien and sober dignity of a great official. In each the clothing is rich but not obtrusively gorgeous or flamboyant. They often include the staff of office in his hand and the heraldic devices of his family. The later ones show him as a Knight of the Garter. They are consciously official representations and memorials of an important officer of the State.

Outside the three main series of conventional poses there survive two other paintings of Burghley. One is of the Court of Wards in session with Burghley in his place as Master.[63] Like the pictures of Kings and magnates presiding over some assembly, this one portrays Burghley in the seat of authority. It shows him in action as a judge. The other painting is of Burghley on his mule. It looks like a bureaucrat's parody of the militant equestrian figure of the soldier or of the representation of the sovereign on horseback, stamped on the reverse of the Great Seal. But it shows Burghley as he was to be seen, perambulating through his gardens on his little mule.[64] Perhaps Burghley had read in his Comines of how it was said of Louis XI that his council rode on his mule.

Of other forms of portraiture of Burghley there survive the engravings by Rogers and others for the Bishops' Bible and a miniature on a map. No bust like that of his brother-in-law, Nicholas Bacon, exists. The extant sculpted representations of Burghley are funerary effigies, a kneeling statuette on his wife's and daughter's joint tomb in Westminster Abbey and the recumbent life-size figure, probably by Cornelius Cure, upon his tomb in St Martin's Church at Stamford. On his great six-poster monument the effigy is of Burghley lying bare-headed, clad in armour with his Garter robe about him.[65]

In his lifetime Burghley secured his reputation as 'learned and a lover of learning' among the theologian bishops and the classicist courtiers, the dons of the universities, including a professor at remote St Andrews,[66] the scientific intellectuals, the historians, the topographers, and the mechanicians and stationers of London. While Leicester and Hatton were called lovers of learning they could not pretend to Burghley's scholarship. If Burghley did not match the versatility of Leicester as a Maecenas, he excelled all other Elizabethan councillors except, perhaps, Sir Thomas Smith, in the range and depth of his knowledge.[67] In assessing Burghley's erudition and artistic patronage, it must always be remembered that he was, as Richard Eden wrote, 'otherwise occupied in great affairs both in Court and Commonwealth'. He enjoyed a 'marvellous scantness of leisure from very weighty matters' in which to cultivate his intellectual concerns and play patron. 'All my time', Cecil wrote, 'is at the command of others'.[68]

What is remarkable is the scope of Burghley's interests and patronage rather than its limitations. In his intellectual concerns he was a product of the Cambridge circle around John Cheke. He was familiar with many aspects of Renaissance learning. He was the sort of amateur who could often confound the self-styled experts. Looking back at his Cambridge career, he saw himself not as the brilliant student whom Ascham knew but as 'a simple, small, unlearned, low member' of his college.[69] His modesty and the attack of a few vocal suppliants whose cupidity he disappointed have dimmed his historical reputation as a patron. His failure to appreciate the musical and creative vernacular literary movements of a later generation has tended to diminish the part which he played in the encouragement of the arts, the sciences and learning during Elizabeth's reign. In the art on which he lavished his taste and wealth, architecture, he achieved an acknowledged preeminence among his contemporaries. Standing before the last surviving monument of that achievement, Burghley House, a spectator may still today gain some appreciation of the magnanimity of William Cecil.

CHAPTER XVIII

Lord and Dynast

QUEEN Elizabeth was a strict guardian of the fount of honour. William Cecil did well to secure one of the ten new peerages created in her long reign by a Queen who preferred to ennoble 'old blood'. His was the only noble title to be given exclusively on the grounds of political and administrative services to the Crown. He was one of two among the new peers who did not already possess ancestral claims or blood relationship to the Queen.[1] His predecessor as Lord Treasurer, William Paulet, had received a marquisate and an earldom in Edward's reign. But Burghley could flatter himself that his was a rare honour which had not fallen to any of his contemporaries in Elizabethan officialdom. Admission to an *élite* of some sixty peers was a reward for a family which had given loyal service to the Tudors for nearly a century.

The origins of William Cecil were more respectable than those of such 'new men' as Thomas Wolsey, the Cardinal, or Thomas Cromwell, who became Earl of Essex. He belonged to the lower fringe of the untitled aristocracy, the lesser gentry, from which the Tudors had drawn many of their officials. He claimed to be sprung from 'no ignoble race', but his enemies among the Catholics and the nobility chose to regard him as a 'new man' and to suggest that his father was a Stamford innkeeper.[2] Cecil was a man of the New Learning and of the new religion and he became a new knight and a new noble, but he was scarcely a 'new man' in the contemporary sense of having been base born. Like any man who rises in society, he was subjected to the contempt of his superiors for a parvenu and the envy of his inferiors for a successful man. Of these social prejudices Cecil was always aware and he did his best to allay them.

Contemporaries disagreed about Cecil's attitude towards the nobility. The papists accused Cecil, as they accused Leicester, of aiming at the ruin of the old nobility. Camden and Clapham agreed that at the time of the rebellion of the Northern Earls there was envy and dislike among certain of the lords for Cecil.[3] The rebellion, often represented as arising from Cecil's hostility to the old nobility, was in fact caused by the hostility of some of them towards Cecil. The charge that Cecil was no friend of the nobility also rested upon his part in bringing Norfolk to the block, the blame for which the Queen laid upon him. But the charge ignored the fact that the Duke's treason forced Cecil's hand against a noble with whom he had long been friendly. Ever since the Scottish campaign of 1559–60, Cecil had sided with the Duke against Leicester, a new noble. He had saved Norfolk after the rebellion of 1569 and had offered him a marriage alliance with his widowed sister-in-law, Lady Hoby. At his end, Norfolk had left his 'brats' in Cecil's care.[4]

Cecil had amicable relations with a large number of the old nobility. He was the confidant of many nobles and their ladies, who corresponded with him about their family difficulties. He was frequently chosen as an executor by aristocrats. The seventh Lord Cobham became his dearest friend. The third Earl of Sussex was ready to 'stick like a shirt' to Cecil.[5] The Cecil family married into some of the oldest houses. Anne Cecil married a de Vere. There was no social hatred of the nobility in Cecil, who did all he could to uphold their social eminence. He was partial to the aristocracy and he flattered them by imitation. The distinction between the old and new nobility, based upon antiquity of lineage, did not determine Cecil's hostility or friendship.

The nobility were judged by Cecil according to their loyalty to the throne. If he worked against certain of the nobility, it was because of a political, not a social, antagonism. The rebellious Northumberland and Westmorland he called vermin because they were traitors.[6] In sacrificing Norfolk he was giving up the valuable support of a great and friendly East Anglian magnate whose sphere of influence kept the peace on the borders of his own territory. Cecil was undoubtedly an agent of the Crown, committed against any noble who sought to maintain a quasi-feudal independence of the central government.

But if Cecil was helping to destroy the old independent role of the provincial magnates, he was the champion of the new functions of the court aristocracy. It was this championship which made it possible for his biographer and for Francis Bacon to argue that Cecil was the defender and preserver of the nobility. By educating their heirs in the New Learning and right religion, by urging an increase in their numbers, by sparing their wealth from heavy taxation, by upholding their social pre-eminence and privilege, Cecil did all he could to make a loyal aristocracy into a strong prop for the throne. 'Gratify your nobility, and principal persons of the realm, to bind them fast to you,' was his advice to the Queen.[7]

The contribution which a well-educated, wealthy and respected nobility could make to government in military affairs, in diplomacy, in local matters, at Court, in Council and Parliament, was regarded as indispensable by Burghley. The first decade of Elizabeth's reign was a period when the monarchy was still balanced between dependence on and dominance over the nobility. Cecil's attitude reflected this uncertain poise. His aim was to exploit to the profit of the Crown the remaining independent power of the magnates and to persuade factious nobles that, if they could not coerce the government, they had better join it. He never doubted that there must be a nobility in the scheme of things. The only ambiguity was over the kind of nobility that could best serve the Queen.

The nature of nobility was a matter for debate throughout Europe. The adaptation of the aristocracy to changing economic and political conditions called for new ideals and social self-justification. Cecil had good reason to ponder the qualities of a nobleman. Stating the self-made man's best claim to nobility, he declared 'it is most precious, as the reward of virtue'. With Tully's *Offices* in his pocket and 'a breast stuffed with all godly virtues' he satisfied the humanist champions of virtue, like Ascham, and its protestant upholders, like Thomas Becon. 'Honour', he noted, 'is the reward of virtue but it is gotten with labour and held with danger.'[8]

Ascham, in words dedicated to Burghley, wrote, 'Nobility without virtue and wisdom is blood indeed, but blood truly without bones and sinews; and so of itself without other very weak to bear the burden of weighty affairs. But nobility, governed by learning and wisdom, is indeed most like a fair ship having wind and tide at will. . . .' William Cecil, deficient neither in learning nor in wisdom, could afford to agree. But Richard Pace's assertion that 'A true nobility is that made by virtue rather than by a famous and long pedigree', Burghley found less easy to endorse. The odour of virtue was vapid without 'the old smell of ancient race'.[9]

Castiglione, whose book, *The Courtier*, was translated into English by Cecil's relation Thomas Hoby in 1561 found strong arguments for the ennobling effect of a lofty lineage. In England, the prevalent dynastic pride, the laws of inheritance and an aristocratic Court made those in search of nobility consider their progenitors. The College of Arms, over which Burghley presided for a while, in commission and as Earl Marshal, was the institutional expression of this preoccupation with pedigree. Just as the nation was finding its distinctive identity in the history of its origins, so individuals looked to their family beginnings. While popular nationalism conjured up King Arthur, the would-be aristocracy invented equally ancient and fictitious ancestors.

William Cecil was addicted to the social and psychological satisfactions which the study of genealogy provided for his generation. His expertise as a genealogist was recognised long before he became a noble himself. Like his brother-in-law, Nicholas Bacon, and scores of other successful men, he cultivated his family tree. The historian of Wales, David Powell, traced the roots of the Sitsilts back to the eleventh century through fifteen generations. John Bossewell in *Workes of Armorie*, published in 1575 and dedicated to Lord Burghley, accepted the new peer's pedigree. When most family trees grew in glass-houses of pretence there were few who cared to throw stones. Indeed the latinised version of the Welsh family name which Burghley adopted suggested to some a descent from the Roman *Caecilli*. Only an exile, outside the charmed circle of aristocratic society, like Richard Verstegan, would dare to mock Burghley's pretensions.[10]

It was generally agreed with Aristotle that wealth was a necessity of noble status. 'For gentility is nothing else but ancient riches', was Burghley's version of a proverbial comment. Each rank had its appropriate scale of resources to support a befitting standard of living. Burghley himself refused an earldom because he claimed that he could not afford the expenses that it would entail. Sir Henry Sidney's wife begged Burghley to prevent her husband's elevation to the peerage because he was too poor and extravagant. Even knights were expected to have 'sufficient ability of inheritance'.[11] The overheads of social and political eminence were high. What was gained from royal favour could be dispersed in patronage, service, hospitality and suitable ostentation.

Acceptance of a barony was some indication of Burghley's wealth. His affluence was undeniable but neither his inheritance from his grandfather and father nor his own acquisitions in Edward's reign constituted ancient riches. Under Elizabeth he soon complained of the cost of royal service and sold land and office. But he reaped his rewards. He began with gains in Middlesex in 1559 and during 1561 and 1562 he was able to buy land and leases in the town of Stamford, in Rutlandshire, Northamptonshire and Lincolnshire. In the middle sixties a more speculative policy brought properties in Suffolk, Yorkshire, Middlesex and Hampshire. Towards the end of the decade he disposed of some of his outlying purchases and bought land in Northamptonshire and Hertfordshire, where he secured Cheshunt Park in 1570. In 1573–4 he paid Sir Henry Sidney about £3,000 for land in Lincolnshire and for extensive woodlands. In 1564 he bought Theobalds and by 1583 his holdings in Hertfordshire had cost him nearly £12,300. At his death 187 properties were listed. From them it was estimated that, after generous provision for his three Vere granddaughters, he drew some £4,000 per annum. Land provided his most reliable income which alone placed him among the wealthiest landed aristocrats.[12]

More speculative were his investments in companies like the Muscovy Company, the Mines Royal, the Mineral and Battery Works and his share in the profits of alum manufacture. It was estimated that he might double his capital in the Muscovy Company in 3 or 4 years. His investments in voyages like those of

Hawkins, Gilbert, Frobisher, Fenton and Raleigh were at great risk. One of his dreams was to re-establish Stamford, of which he was lord of the town and market, as a flourishing cloth town. He introduced foreign weavers and set up a dye works.[13] These industrial and commercial ventures were trifles. Cautiously limiting his investments, Burghley was not an aristocratic gambler rushing in where merchants feared to tread. He put small sums into those undertakings which he believed were sound and to the national good. Like most prudent men of his time he regarded commerce and industry as a means of acquiring capital with which to buy and improve land.

Another way of obtaining capital was from the windfalls of office. Official remuneration was not what made office profitable. Burghley dismissed his pay as Lord Treasurer as being not enough to defray the costs of his stable. The real rewards of office were to be found in the opportunities to make wealth that it provided. As the holder of many influential posts Cecil could expect to be showered with gifts. The City of Exeter insisted on paying him an annuity of £30 a year. In the later years of his Mastership of the Court of Wards he took for himself from the spoils of that institution some £2,500 a year, a sum five times greater than his official fees.[14] Such pickings were permitted up to the point where they stopped short of damaging the royal interest. Burghley took his share but he did not succumb to the Midas touch of corruption. For all the money which passed through his hands, he was at his death not as wealthy as many expected. Chamberlain wrote, 'Of his private wealth there is but £11,000 with £800 or £900 land bequeathed to his two nieces of Oxford. His lands seem not so great as was thought for Mr Secretary says his own part will not rise to £1,600 a year upon the rack.'[15]

Virtue, pedigree and wealth did much to make a noble but in martial prowess lay his traditional justification. Sir William Cecil had been a punctilious Chancellor of the Order of the Garter and Lord Burghley became one of its proudest members, having himself portrayed in his Garter robes. He left his insignia to Robert that 'his son's sons' should remember his honour.[16] But a taste for ceremonial was the limit of Burghley's participation in

the chivalric tradition. He did not share Spenser's delight in
reviving chivalry in verse or Sir Henry Lee's enthusiasm for
tiltings on Accession Day. The lesson of the civil wars of the
fifteenth century and of the Erasmian humanists inclined Burghley
to agree with Ascham that knightly deeds were 'open manslaughter'. But, when he declared that a soldier 'can hardly be an
honest man or a good Christian', he was reassuring Robert, his
crippled son.[17] He was happy enough to see Thomas Cecil crown
the tournaments at Kenilworth with a knighthood and joust
before Alençon. Burghley knew the value of martial men to the
realm.

It was recognised that Burghley was 'amongst the Togati, for he
had not to do with the sword'. But as a knight and a lord he had
military obligations. In 1558 Sir William was expected to provide
10 horse and 50 footmen. Thirty years later, under the threat of
the Armada, Lord Burghley offered 50 lances, 50 light horse and
300 footmen and visited the camp at Tilbury, after the famous
review by the Queen.[18] As Lord Lieutenant for three shires he was
responsible for the county musters and levies. He raised the
standard of recruits and in 1590 he could be proud of the 'whole
Essex regiment'. The City of London was advised to consult him
on the problems of mobilisation. But Burghley did not, like
Leicester at Kenilworth, munition and create a strong personal
fortress. His modest armoury was a threat to no one.[19] He did not,
like Essex, seek to organise an armed following in the manner of
bastard feudalism. But he did keep on good terms with the most
powerful garrison in the country at Berwick. There was no place
for soldiers of fortune or 'any contentious, vicious, or evil
disposed persons' in Burghley's personal following. His retinue
with its liveries and badges was never deployed in faction strife.
In 1595 he prohibited the appointment of retainers as Justices of
the Peace. He tried to ensure that the military and political uses of
retainers were dedicated wholly to 'the liking of the Queen',
Elizabeth.[20]

The traditions of a military aristocracy included a necessary
devotion to the chase. Burghley hunted, but not so often as to
incur the strictures of bookish moralists that he was wasting his

time on idle sport. In his youth he took the field with Catherine, Duchess of Suffolk and in his old age with Cobham. His parks were well stocked with game and his friends took full advantage of his invitations to hunt. He was a practised bowman and a good horseman although his greatest feats of riding seem to have been in pursuit of his business rather than of his pleasure. He was fond of horses. In 1594 he declared that he would die if his 'old jade' died. To Leicester, Burghley wrote enthusiastically of his hounds and hunting dogs and thanked him for the gift of a hound that 'hath never failed me almost for every day this week but brought me the right way to a deer'.[21] He knew enough of hounds, hawks and game to be at ease with sporting aristocrats.

Among the obligations of nobility was the need to be a good lord to the tenantry. The theory of degree society with its stress upon harmony emphasised the vertical relationships of the class structure as much as its horizontal divisions. In Edward's reign the 'Commonwealth men' condemned the 'step lords'. At this time Cecil was too busy amassing land to cultivate a reputation as a good lord. Sir Thomas Smith, accused of being an 'oppressor' and a 'great purchaser', claimed that he was no worse than William Cecil. He was in a position to know. The agrarian revolts of 1549 brought condemnation for the rebels rather than sympathy for their complaints from Cecil's friends, Cranmer and Cheke. The growing land hunger and rising prices made for tension between landlord and tenant. In 1559 there was a sale at the George Inn at Stamford of goods seized under distraint for rent. As late as 1596 there were complaints against eviction and against the farmers of Burghley's woods. The inhabitants of Wildmore protested when Burghley, as Lord of the soke of Burrow, began to drain the fen.[22] But, considering the scale of his operations as a landlord, Burghley's reputation remained remarkably sweet.

In his later years it was reputed that Burghley did not raise rents, evict, or harry his own tenants or those of crown lands through the courts. Tenants may be found giving evidence in his favour. His advice was, 'Undertake no suit against a poor man without receiving much wrong.' Certainly, Burghley had to put up with extraordinary annoyances from a tenant, Shute, who defamed him and robbed him. Yet the number of suits over land squabbles brought before him testifies to his reputation for justice in these matters. His aid was sought for a Bill to protect copyholders. Burghley's good lordship may well have been enhanced by his policy of dealing favourably with holders of royal lands in order to win their loyalty for the Queen, and by his readiness to favour tenants in quarrels with popish landlords as part of his scheme to discourage recusancy. He dealt well with the lands of his wards. Burghley was, no doubt, a good landlord. On one suit for a lease he qualified his assent with the note, 'So as it be not to expel any ancient tenants.'[23]

Charity was a social obligation of the wealthy which was hallowed by a long tradition of religious piety. Lady Burghley made her extensive benefactions discreetly without her husband's knowledge but Lord Burghley believed that 'if thou hast cause to bestow any great gratuity let it be daily in sight'. His charities were judiciously shared between the neighbourhoods in which he resided. Food, alms and casual employment were provided at his gates. His benevolences were said to cost him £500 a year in his later life. Apart from a small endowment to his old college at Cambridge and an alms-house for thirteen men at Stamford, he left no lasting monuments to his generosity.[24] His charity showed neither the sympathy of his wife's benevolence nor the social constructiveness of many of his contemporaries. But of its large scale while he lived, there can be no doubt.

If charity was expected by the poor, the prosperous demanded hospitality. Burghley was not a feudal lord committed by custom to keep open house. His retainers were servants, not gentry or tenantry who owed service and claimed hospitality and good lordship. 'For his number of attendants, he was as honourably and orderly served, as sorted with a man of his Lordship's place and degree.' The men who sat at Burghley's table were 'friends and followers', 'men of quality and ability', drawn by the reflected glory of royal favour rather than by the warmth of loyalty to an ancient house. 'The principal gentlemen in England sought to prefer their sons and heirs to his service.' Indeed Burghley complained that it was his 'disease' to have too many servants. But

Pater Patriae, Lord Burghley in old age

Lord Burghley's Tomb

new wealth and the tie of rents and leases did not create a feudal community. Theobalds it was said 'had neither lordship nor tenants'.[25] Wealthy young aristocrats came to the board of the Master of the Court of Wards, suitors thronged around Mr Secretary or My Lord Treasurer, country gentry attended the Lord Lieutenant. To them Lord Burghley gave hospitality.

Burghley's patronage in the countryside was political and official rather than feudal or tenurial. His territory was not a feudal complex but a county where, as he wrote, 'my principal house is and my name and posterity are living'. He liked to think of Northamptonshire as his county, where he was 'no new planted or new feathered gentleman', but he was ready to admit that it might be said that he was *homo novus* in Hertfordshire. A Lord Lieutenancy, the recognition of social supremacy in an area, was his substitute for feudal dominion. As Bacon saw, 'new nobility is an act of power but ancient nobility is an act of time'.[26]

It was characteristic of the new hospitality that it should reach its zenith when the Queen and her entourage visited on progress. Of the Queen's visit in 1566 Cecil wrote, 'God send me my heart's desire which is without regard of cost to have her Majesty see my good will in my service and all others to find no lack of good cheer'.[27] Leicester at Kenilworth, Petre at Ingatestone, Bacon at Gorhambury and numerous lesser men in humbler houses strained their patience and their purses to entertain the Queen. The fuss of feeding and festivities was enormous. Elizabeth visited all three of Burghley's great houses and called upon him some dozen times. Her fortnight's stay at Theobalds in 1575 cost Burghley £341, a three day call in 1577 cost only four pounds less. Ten days of entertaining in 1591 meant an outlay of £900. Burghley had to provide 'rich shows, pleasant devices and all manner of sports'.[28]

Burghley studied to behave like an aristocrat. In a fluid society, seeking stability in the fictitious rigidities of divinely ordained degree, appearances counted for much. Manners and dress were an obsession of the time. The Court tried to hide change in a framework of etiquette and ceremonial. Burghley was a stickler for the niceties of behaviour. For him manners were a kind of social morality. 'Towards thy superiors be humble yet generous. With

T

thine equals familiar yet respective. Towards thine inferiors shew much humanity and some familiarity,' he wrote in an advice to his son which took its place along with many other paternal counsels among the manuals on behaviour which abounded.[29] Burghley was an advocate of sumptuary laws which defined the apparel appropriate to each rank. He devised a distinctive dress for noble undergraduates to wear at Cambridge. Yet what appeared as snobbery to later ages was in Burghley a profound sense of the hierarchical nature of the universe as it manifested itself among mankind.

On his elevation to the peerage, Burghley showed that he understood the need to keep up noble appearances. He increased his household expenditure over the first five years of his nobility by about half.[30] In his three fine houses with their splendid gardens, in his household and retinue, he possessed all the apparatus of aristocratic splendour to satisfy both his peers and the populace that he was living like a lord. If his own rich dress was sombre in comparison with the finery of the peacock courtiers, his wife's garments and jewels were of the finest. Amidst all the magnificence and ostentation Burghley preserved his reputation for moderation by his frugal personal habits. He was no Sir Epicure Mammon. He strove to play the role, so much admired by the humanists, of the man who could remain virtuous amidst all the temptations of wealth. His restraint lay in keeping his expenses within the limits which he could afford.

Conspicuous consumption, the ostentation of wealth, made Burghley's conscience uneasy. He could not forget that 'when all the wealth and delight of this world is passed, we must come before that Judge . . .'. A puritan suspicion of worldly goods, anxiety about rousing envy, a desire to avoid higher tax assessments and the charge of corruption made him sensitive about his most extravagant display of his riches. While it was a common affectation for a rich man, like Leicester, to speak of 'his poor cottage', few tried so hard as Burghley to explain away their lavish building activities. He dismissed his extensive work at Burghley House as a few improvements made on his mother's behalf, and claimed that there were a dozen greater houses of lesser men in

Northamptonshire. He was 'enforced to enlarge' Theobalds 'rather for the Queen and her great train and to set the poor on work than for pomp or glory'. He thought that his house in the Strand was too old to arouse envy. On his elevation to the peerage he hastened to assure a friend that he was 'the poorest lord' in England.[31]

If Burghley is measured against that invention of sociology, the aristocratic ethic, there emerges something more than the individual variations from type which might be expected. He ran true to type in his belief that social harmony depended on a clearly defined hierarchy, that the poor would always be with society, and that service to the State was an obligation. But he was embarrassed by extravagance. His charity and hospitality flowed from a sense of duty rather than from open-handed liberality. He did not possess the self-confidence to indulge in arrogance. Instead he practised a studied humility and politeness. 'Humility shuns honour, and is the way to it,' he is reputed to have said.[32] Although he had the paternalist and patronising attitude of the great towards inferiors, he was sensitive to their feelings, especially their envy. He was neither indifferent to the sins of the flesh nor tolerant of emotional outbursts. Birth and inheritance he accepted as the props of nobility but he allowed for competition and equality of opportunity in his admiration for virtue and learning. His sense of values was as much quantitative as qualitative.

Indeed, Burghley possessed many of the characteristics which are comprehended in the opposite of the aristocratic ethic, the bourgeois or capitalist-protestant ethic. He practised self-improvement, hard work, sobriety and a relative thrift. He kept account of his money and his sins. Restraint marked his behaviour; asceticism his habits. Poverty and failure he regarded as signs of moral weakness. 'Riches', he wrote, 'were God's blessing to such as used them well; and his curse to such as did not.'[33]

That the norms of the aristocratic and bourgeois types mingled and conflicted in Burghley might be expected in an age when men sought to fuse Greek, Roman, Christian and traditional medieval social ideals and when experience was of the alliance between mercantile and aristocratic families and wealth. The domestic

Cecil, the product of his early home, and later married life, seemed to conform to the capitalist-protestant ethic, while the public Cecil approximated more closely to the aristocratic ethic. The contradictions of his private and public self can be seen as a reflection of the divergent trends in the Reformation household and the Renaissance court. The individual virtue of the puritan soul modified the social virtues of a class. Cecil responded to the aristocratic conventions of the Court and of the position that he won in society. But often his domestic behaviour was at odds with the values of the world in which he had found success. It is not an unusual predicament for the man who wants to make the best of both worlds.

Burghley exemplified a change which was overtaking the ideals of the English nobility and gentry. While there remained with Burghley the accidents of the feudal lord and the Renaissance courtier, his substance was that of a new type of accomplished protestant gentleman, whose virtues were less those of a social class than of a worthy individual.[34] Burghley coupled his conscience with his honour. Camden's description of Burghley reveals the new norms of gentility. 'Certainly he was a most excellent man, who (to say nothing of his reverend presence, his calm and undisturbed countenance) was so framed by Nature, so polished and adorned with learning and education that every way for honesty, gravity, temperance, industry and justice, he was the most accomplished person. Hereunto add his fluent and elegant speech (and that not affected, but plain, natural and easy), wisdom confirmed by experience and seasoned with great moderation; his approved fidelity; and above all his singular piety towards God.'[35]

As a lord, Burghley was perforce a dynast. Degree and dynasty were the moulds of the individualism of the Renaissance. Wealth and office usually followed family ties. The family was a frame of wide reference, from God, the Father, and Queen Elizabeth, the mother and wife of her people, to the humble husbandman who was lord in his house. Supported by the example of the patriarchs and the fifth commandment, Protestants made the father the religious leader of the household. The humanists made him the teacher in the home. Patriarchal sway was the model of govern-

mental authority. Politics and history were seen in terms of
dynasty. The Tudor age itself was known to have arisen from the
union of the houses of Lancaster and York.

In a commonwealth, conceived as a union of families, William
Cecil was a father and dynast. But he was cautious of being bound
by the ties of blood. Affable and hospitable to his kindred, he was
not lavish with gifts or preferment for them. His benevolent
regard for the Cecils of Alltyrynys brought them no great rewards.
He was a helpful uncle to Cheke's three sons. Distant relatives like
Barnaby Googe and Sir Geoffrey Fenton obtained no greater
patronage than those to which their talents entitled them. Often he
allowed a political affiliation with rivals to cancel the claims of
relatives upon him. His bumptious Bacon nephews who served
Essex complained that he did nothing for their advancement.
Cecil opposed the marriage to his sister-in-law of the promising
Henry Killigrew, a follower of Leicester. Yet he contemplated
marrying his daughter to Philip Sidney, the son of another of
Leicester's men. Cecil helped his kinsmen in trouble. He spoke on
behalf of his son-in-law, Oxford, when he was out of favour with
the Queen and rescued his remote relative the Separatist, Browne,
from prison.[36] Cecil judged his relatives on their merits, did what
he deemed best, but was never bound by the bonds of kinship.

Although Cecil had profited by his relationship with Cheke and
Cooke and from the marriages of his sisters-in-law, which brought
him the support of Nicholas Bacon and Thomas Hoby, he was
eager 'that the world might know that in bestowing benefits he
respected more the merit of the receiver than proximity of blood
or private inducement'. He did not like employing relatives in his
household because 'they expect much and do little'.[37] The
marriages of his own children were made by him perhaps more
for dynastic and social prestige than for political advantage. Even
in the treatment of his sons he kept his head. The able Robert was
groomed to follow his father, but the claims of Thomas for high
office were never pressed. Not until after his father's death did
Thomas acquire important posts at home. Burghley did well for
his family but his strong sense of kin did not blind him to their
deserts.

His family life with Mildred, for all its sorrows, proved a good partnership of mutual esteem and devotion such as might have exemplified the growing protestant ideal of marriage. Unlike her younger sisters, Mildred was a patient, quiet woman. Under her husband's watchful eye she managed his great household. She could act independently of him, as she did in her well-chosen charities, which revealed her sympathetic imagination and her ideals. Her recreations ranged from archery to translating a Greek sermon. She was 'a woman of a great wit and as some persons may suppose of more learning than is necessary for her sex'. Men not prepared to accept her as an intellectual equal found her an intolerable blue-stocking. Women hoped she would lay aside her learning and see with the eyes of love. But the character and intellect which were apparent in her long, severe countenance won the respect and liking of men as various as Sir Richard Morison, Sir Christopher Hatton and Sir Walter Raleigh.[38]

While she played her part as hostess to her husband's intellectual and political friends and acquaintances, she did not intrude upon his public life. She could write to diplomats and officials with discretion and an understanding of affairs. In dispensing patronage she took a hand, especially in the selection of guardians for wards. Suitors made gifts to her. At Court she did not hesitate to tackle the Queen in order to prevent her husband from being sent abroad. With less prudence she expressed her disapproval of the Queen's philandering with the Earl of Oxford. After that mistake she did not often go to Court but she had never been enamoured of court life.[39]

Mildred's life was one of emotional strain. The compression of her thin lips told of the self-discipline which expressed itself in puritan piety. The years of childless marriage, the frailty of her deformed son, the unhappiness and death of Anne and the early death of Elizabeth must have taxed the 'peerless mother'. The ill-health and bouts of depression which afflicted her husband weighed upon her. She died at the age of sixty-three years, comparatively young in her long-lived family. Burghley's grief at her death was deep. His reactions showed that she was, above all, a spiritual prop to him. He had drawn strength from her.[40] If he had not found the warmth and release of passion, he had received the intellectual approbation and emotional sanction of her piety which were so necessary to his controlled nature.

It was ironical that Mildred's death should have been a piece of dynastic good fortune. About the time of her death it had become clear to Burghley that he would have to found not one house but two. His wife's death freed him from the need to provide for her widowhood and enabled him to set up Robert, who had just married. Within a few months of her end, Theobalds and lands in Hertfordshire and London were settled upon Robert. Theobalds he feared 'would be too big for the small living he could leave his son'. The disposal of his wealth haunted the ageing Burghley. He tinkered constantly with his will and kept it close by him. By choosing impartial executors, leaving no great debts or over-generous charities at the expense of his heirs and limiting his own funeral expenses to a modest £1,000, Burghley did what he could to prevent a quarrel between his sons. On his marriage, Robert was given Essendine in his brother's country in order 'to continue familiarity and acquaintance between them'. Burghley was a successful father in promoting and maintaining good will between half-brothers with an age difference of twenty-one years between them.

In leaving the bulk of his landed wealth to Thomas, Burghley recognised the role of primogeniture in dynasticism. Thomas inherited the 'mansion of his barony', Burghley House, and the neighbouring estates, the accumulation of which had been begun by his great-grandfather. To him also was left his father's house in the Strand. Robert was given the inheritance newly created for him around Theobalds. In order to endow Robert, Burghley refused the costly honour of an Earldom. The endowment of two filial dynasties was a considerable feat of planning and thrift. It had meant cutting down Burghley's own household expenses in his last years and some grumbling about the meagre rewards for his service to the Queen.[41] If Thomas had been left with a title and the greater wealth, Robert was a knight with political influence and high office, the opportunity for greatness.

The nice judgement which Burghley showed in his will of his

sons' needs and capacities revealed itself also in their education, another preservative of family fortune. He did not send his sons to a grammar school or to Eton, Shrewsbury or Sherborne, but like the greater aristocrats he provided for their education at home. His care for their upbringing would have satisfied the most enlightened of the authors of the many manuals on the duties of parenthood which appeared at the time. His advice to the wayward Thomas was all stern moral precept and religious discipline. To the studious Robert he thought it necessary to impart such lessons as 'are rather gained by experience than by much reading' and he set out for him the ten commandments of worldly wisdom. In a household famous for its learning Burghley's sons had a good education. Mildred took a hand in bringing up the boys 'in the knowledge of God's will and good letters' and the girls to be eligible brides.[42] Thomas went on to travel with his tutor. Robert went to Gray's Inn and then in 1581 to his father's old college at Cambridge under the care of a former tutor, whom Burghley made Master of St John's.

All through their lives Burghley sought to give his sons the experience to suit them for advancement. Despite his dislike of the corrupting effect of Italy, he clung to the current belief in the educative value of travel as a kind of reconnaissance for the future diplomat or soldier. Even after Thomas's disastrous example, he sent Robert to Paris in 1584 and reluctantly allowed him to go on a diplomatic mission to the Netherlands in 1588. Burghley knew that, besides travel, military experience was a powerful recommendation to royal favour. Thomas went to the Border in the rebellion of 1569, to the siege of Edinburgh in 1573 and was picked by Leicester to accompany him to the Netherlands, where he became governor of Brill in 1585. During the Armada campaign Thomas went to sea and Robert was appointed Master of Ordnance at Tilbury camp. Burghley did his best to bring up his sons to their own commendation and the profit of the commonwealth.

At the great dynastic rites surrounding birth, marriage and death, Burghley maintained the repute of his family with lavish display. The birth of his daughter Elizabeth was attended by the Queen who stood as godmother to the child named after her.

Robert's son William, like his aunt, was honoured by the same royal godmother. The Queen was present at Anne Cecil's wedding in Westminster Abbey in December 1571 and at the great feast afterwards in Cecil House, at which many court notables were present. The spring nuptials of Elizabeth Cecil in 1582 were less of a court affair but the three days of festivities which followed them cost Burghley nearly £630. To Burghley's granddaughter, Elizabeth Vere, a Maid of Honour to the Queen, the royal palace of Greenwich was thrown open after her wedding in Westminster Abbey.[43]

With different emotions, Burghley planned the obsequies to his mother, his wife and his two grown daughters besides the three infant burials of his early married life with Mildred. The carefully planned funeral of his second wife with its procession of 315 mourners was amongst the most magnificent of those heraldic pageants of death which Burghley, as Earl Marshal, insisted that it was the duty of the nobility to stage for their family honour. It was a testimony of God's favour to Mildred's family, 'as manifestly may be seen about her hearse, by sundry coats of noble houses joined by blood with her . . .'.[44] To his daughter Anne and to his wife Mildred, 'dear to him beyond the whole race of womankind', he raised the magnificent, pinnacled and tiered tomb, twenty-four feet high, in St Nicholas' Chapel in Westminster Abbey. The festive and solemn rituals of life and death in a family gave expression to particular and personal emotions but to the gazing crowd of Elizabethan London they were a measure of dynastic worth.

Behind the splendour and emotion of family honour lay the calculations of the marriage market. As a statesman, dealing with the dynastic politics between royal houses, as Master of the Court of Wards, supervising the matches of wards, and as the confidant of many of the nobility on family matters, Burghley knew as much as anyone of matrimonial bargains and their legal niceties. He supported the Queen in efforts to patch up the bitter quarrel between the Earl of Shrewsbury and the forceful Countess, Bess of Hardwick. Lady Russell solicited his help in the persistent suit of Thomas Posthumus Hoby. Lord Paget thanked him for arranging his niece's marriage.[45] Burghley had a political interest in alliances which brought together great families and inheritances.

Yet Burghley preserved some sense of the involvement of personal emotions when it came to match-making in his own family. 'Use great prudence and circumspection in choosing thy wife,' he warned Robert, 'for from thence will spring all thy future good or evil.' Burghley recommended a bride 'not poor' but of good parents, disposition, physique and looks. It was sound advice for any young man entering the unromantic marriage market in which the business recommendations of a bride seldom seemed to tally with her personal attractions. At a time when parents arranged marriages over their childrens' infant heads, Burghley accepted that his son had a choice of spouse, although to parents of girls he recommended, 'Marry thy daughters in time, lest they marry themselves.'[46]

In his own first marriage Cecil had allowed emotion to triumph over calculation. His second marriage taught him that marital success could rest on other grounds than passion. But for all his political sense and legal skill in drafting marriage agreements, Burghley never forgot that wedded life might be a pleasure and a consolation as well as good business. His most callous attempt at political match-making within his family circle was made at the expense of his domineering sister-in-law, the widowed Lady Hoby, when he proposed her marriage to the Duke of Norfolk.[47] It failed.

With a commendable regard for social decorum and for the status of his family, Cecil achieved for three of his children honourable, but not socially over-ambitious or financially grasping matches in which there was regard for the feelings of the partners. As Sir William Cecil, he was content to see his son Thomas allied in 1564 to the well-connected Lord Latimer's daughter whose elder sister was married to Sir Henry Percy. Some nine years later Burghley turned down offers from the Earl of Essex and Lord Buckhurst for their sons to marry Elizabeth Cecil.[48] Two years later he protected his daughter from the Earl of Shrewsbury's proposal that she should marry a Talbot. The Earl's

connection with two such stormy petrels as Bess of Hardwick and
Mary Queen of Scots made it an unwelcome proposal. Contrary to
the current practice of infant betrothal, Burghley pleaded that his
daughter was too young to be committed. Later he accepted the
protestations of love for Elizabeth, made by the less distinguished
William Wentworth, even though it meant providing the young
couple with a home and offering £100 a year.[49] But it was not all
romantic altruism. The Wentworth influence in Norfolk and
Suffolk helped to consolidate the Cecils in eastern England. For
Robert it was a love match.[50] In 1589 he secured the charming
Elizabeth Brooke, daughter of his father's old friend, the seventh
Lord Cobham. With her came a dowry of £2,000 and the Cobham
influence over the numerous parliamentary seats nominated by the
Warden of the Cinque Ports.

To have arranged three successful marriages for his children
was a tribute to Burghley's parental wisdom. But over the
marriage of his favourite, Anne, he blundered. It was not a
dynastic mistake that he made for the children of the marriage
climbed the social peaks. The tragedy lay in the subsequent
unhappiness of his daughter and the misery it caused Burghley
himself. Originally he planned to marry Anne to his 'darling'
Philip Sidney, the son of his ever-impecunious friend Sir Henry.
But no sooner was Cecil made Lord Burghley than his former
ward, the Earl of Oxford, requested the hand of Anne. Of this
ambitious match the new Lord Treasurer wrote, 'I never meant to
seek it, nor hoped of it.' It would not have suited his sense of
propriety to have approached an earl of an ancient house any more
than it suited him to see Stafford angling for a rich citizen's
daughter.[51] If the initiative did not come from Edward de Vere, it
may have come from the spoiled Anne who was accused of having
'caught' a husband. The proposal was too good to refuse. Oxford
looked as if he might become a favourite of the Queen. Burghley
put down £3,000 as a marriage portion and with the Queen's
blessing the gay couple wed. For his 'poor daughter's affliction'
Burghley's deference for the old nobility rather than any cynical
auction of his daughter was to blame. If Burghley was culpable, it
was for hiding from himself what he knew of his ward's character

and for accepting the young man who was charming the Court with his graces. Repentance at leisure drew from Burghley the bitter words, 'No enemy I have can envy me this match.'[52]

In his old age Burghley became an amiable patriarch in his family circle. His sons with their families lived for the most part in or near his houses. Thomas had built his own house, Wimbledon Hall, by 1588. Robert and his bride lived at Pymmes close to Theobalds. The old widower sat lonely 'as an owl' in the absence of his grandchildren. But 'if he could get his table set around with his young little children, he was in his kingdom'. He played a paternal role to Lady Oxford's girls. Philip Sidney advised a friend that the best way to win Burghley's favour was to praise his children. The grandchildren were numerous. At the end of Burghley's life there were Thomas' five boys and six girls, Robert's son and two daughters, and the three Vere girls. Great-grandchildren were appearing. Burghley wished that his mother could have lived to see the family which had sprung from her only son.[53] The dynasty flourished.

As his grandchildren grew up another round of matchmaking began. Two of Thomas' girls married into the families of Hatton and Paulet and Thomas' eldest son married Baroness de Roos, a daughter of the Earl of Rutland, a neighbouring magnate. But it was in the fortunes of the Vere girls that Burghley was most active. It was rumoured that he had exercised his right as guardian of the young Earl of Southampton to arrange for the Earl's marriage to Elizabeth Vere and that it had cost the Earl £5,000 to get a release.[54] In 1592 there were negotiations with Northumberland which fell through. In 1594, however, Elizabeth Vere married William Stanley, Earl of Derby, in whose veins ran Tudor blood from his mother. Thus was achieved, if somewhat indirectly, that connection with a royal house at which Burghley's enemies accused him of aiming.[55] Three years later Burghley, hoping to bring Pembroke on to his side against Essex, arranged for a marriage between Bridget Vere and the Earl's son, William. Burghley offered £3,000 down and an annuity to begin at his death but when Pembroke demanded immediate payment of the annuity, negotiations ceased. In his will Burghley arranged that

Bridget and Susan Vere should receive £4,000 for marrying an
Earl; £3,000, a Baron; £2,000, a husband of lesser rank.[56] Both
granddaughters married nobles who became Earls.

Old William had done well as a dynast. He had established his
two sons according to their capabilities and provided each with a
fine house and supporting estates. They and their children, among
whom were the vital male heirs, allied with the higher aristocracy.
When the Queen teasingly hinted that she would expect Burghley
to dance at Elizabeth Vere's wedding feast at Greenwich, it was
no wonder that he had declared himself 'ready in mind to dance
with my heart'.[57] The advancement of his family had not led him
to ruin. He did not die in debt as Leicester and Hatton had done,
and Essex was to do. Refusal of an earldom had shown that he
knew how to control ambition. His social success in the linking of
titles and lands had been great but so also was his political
dynasticism.

Without the aid of his son Robert it is doubtful if Burghley
could have retained so much influence during the last eight years
of his life. His dynasticism not only prolonged his own political
life to the end of his days but projected his policies into the future.
Robert Cecil's two major achievements, the uncontested succession
of James I and the peace with Spain, were extensions of his father's
latest policies.

The settling of a second son in lucrative office was the dream of
every father. Burghley helped his old friend Ralph Sadler to place
his younger son. But for Burghley there was something more than
merely securing a livelihood for Robert in obtaining for him such
positions as the Secretaryship and the Chancellorship of the Duchy
of Lancaster. It meant that he could die in the knowledge that his
power was in the hands of his son and pupil, who would carry on
the family tradition of service to the State. 'A rare blessing and
seldom befalling great councillors, to live and die in peace with
honour, leaving their posterity to succeed them in like estate.'
Burghley was not enough of the humanist individual to be
content with his own fame. His hopes for the future greatness of
his house broke forth when as the oldest William amongst the
Cecils he greeted the youngest William, Thomas's son. 'God bless

him', wrote Burghley, 'to follow my purpose but not my pains nor dangers.'[58]

At Burghley's death the ties of dynasty triumphed. He did not choose to lie near Mildred in Westminster Abbey, close to the scenes of his life at Court. The memories of the splendour of Theobalds and its gardens in summer did not tempt him to lie at nearby Cheshunt. It was to the little grey stone town on the Welland that his body was taken. The State had claimed his life: his ancestors claimed his bones. 'I have already caused a place in St Martin's Church in Stamford Baron in the county of Northampton wherein my house of Burghley is situated to be made fit for a burial place for the bodies of my grandfather, father and mother and myself', he wrote in his will. It was his son Thomas, the second Lord Burghley, who responded to this last gesture of a great dynast, when he wrote of his father 'with whom love and duty, beyond wit to utter, do lie entombed'.[59]

Notes

Abbreviations in the Notes

Add. MS.	Additional Manuscript
B.M.	British Museum
C.P.R.	*Calendar of Patent Rolls*
C.S.P.	*Calendar of State Papers*
Ec. Hist. Rev.	*Economic History Review*
E.H.R.	*English Historical Review*
H.M.C.	Historical Manuscripts Commission
P.R.O.	Public Record Office
S.P.	State Papers
S.T.C.	Short-Title Catalogue
V.C.H.	*Victoria County Histories of the Counties of England*

Place of publication London unless otherwise stated.

Chapter One: Origins

1. H.M.C., *Salisbury MSS.* viii. 287; G. R. Dennis, *The House of Cecil* (1914), 7–8.

2. Hatfield MSS. cxliii. 8; A. L. Rowse, 'The Cecils of Alltyrynys', *E.H.R.* (1960), lxxv. 54–76.

3. O. Barron, 'Northamptonshire Families', *V.C.H.*, *Northamptonshire* (1906), 25–26.

4. A. Rogers, *The Making of Stamford* (Leicester U.P., 1965), 58–59.

5. *C.P.R. 1494–1509*, 358, 410, 498; *Letters and Papers, Foreign and Domestic, of the reign of Henry VIII*, ed. J. S. Brewer, J. Gairdner and R. H. Brodie, ii, pt. 2, 967 (hereafter cited as *L. & P.*).

6. *C.P.R. 1494–1509*, 514, 467.

7. *L. & P.* i. 40; ii, pt. 2, 1128; i. 708.

8. Barron, art. cit. 26–27.

9. *L. & P.* ii, pt. 2, 967.

10. Ibid. iii, pt. 1, 244.

11. H.M.C., *Salisbury MSS.* v. 69.

12. *V.C.H.*, *Northamptonshire* (1906), ii. 524.

13. *Narratives of the Days of the Reformation*, ed. J. G. Nichols (Camden Soc., 1859), lxxvii. 239.

14. R. Ascham, *English Works*, ed. W. A. Wright (Cambridge, 1904), 175–6.

15. Ibid. 184.

16. *L. & P.* iv, pt. 1, 692.

17. Ibid. v. 504, 640; x. 499.

18. N. H. Nicolas, *Testamenta Vetusta* (1826), ii. 690–1, 728–9.

19. *L. & P.* xiv, pt. 2, 221; xiii, pt. 1, 520; xv. 471; xvii. 700; xviii, pt. 1, 552; *C.P.R. 1547–8,* 220, 241.

20. *L. & P.* v. 59; iii, pt. 2, 594, 889; xvii. 567.

21. Ibid. x. 158.

22. Ibid. xix, pt. 1, 164.

23. Ibid. xxi, pt. 2, 322; *Acts of the Privy Council of England, 1542–7,* N.S., ed. J. R. Dasent, ii. 226 (hereafter cited as *A.P.C.*).

24. Ibid. v. 307, 747.

25. *C.P.R. 1553,* 39.

26. H.M.C., *Salisbury MSS.* ii. 52–53.

27. *C.P.R. 1494–1509,* 515.

28. *L. & P.* ix. 206–7.

29. J. Bradford, *Works* (Parker Soc., 1853), 397.

30. W. Camden, *The Historie of the most renowned and victorious princesse Elizabeth, late Queene of England . . . Composed by way of Annals* (1675), 154.

Chapter Two: University and Inns of Court

1. H. C. Porter, *Reformation and Reaction in Tudor Cambridge* (Cambridge, 1958), chs. 1–3.

2. Ascham, op. cit. 279–80.

3. H.M.C., *Salisbury MSS.* v. 69.

4. J. Strype, *Life of Sir John Cheke* (Oxford, 1821), 5–12.

5. A. Fairbank and B. Wolpe, *Renaissance Handwriting* (1960), 31–33.

6. F. Peck, *Desiderata Curiosa* (1779), 4.

7. Ascham, op. cit. 282; L. V. Ryan, *Roger Ascham* (Stanford U.P. and Oxford, 1963), 16.

8. M. H. Curtis, *Oxford and Cambridge in Transition 1558–1642* (Oxford, 1959), 17–53.

9. Strype, *Cheke,* 170.

10. In his will Burghley wrote of being 'by order of my good parents brought up and instructed in my young years; after that I did come to the years of discretion to have knowledge of the Gospel of our Saviour Jesus Christ, the knowledge whereof began about that time to be more clearly revealed here in England than it had been many years before'. A. Collins, *Life of . . . , Lord Burghley* (1732), 81.

11. P.R.O., S.P. 70–77–918; M. Dewar, *Sir Thomas Smith* (1964), 135 n.; M. A. S. Hume, *The Great Lord Burghley* (1906), 10; M. A. S. Hume, *The Courtships of Queen Elizabeth* (1896), 85.

12. Barron, art. cit. 28.

13. H.M.C., *Salisbury MSS*. i. 116.

14. Cecil was made an honorary M.A. of Cambridge University in 1564, J. Nichols, *The Progresses and public processions of Queen Elizabeth* (1823), i. 189.

15. B.M., Lansdowne MSS. cxviii. 82; H.M.C., *Salisbury MSS*. v. 69.

16. Ibid.

17. Ibid.

18. Ibid.

19. Peck, op. cit. 5.

20. B.M., Lansdowne MSS. ciii. 94.

21. Peck, op. cit. 5.

22. H.M.C., *Salisbury MSS*. v. 69.

23. R. Holinshed, *Chronicles*, ed. J. Johnson *et al.* (1808), iii. 826.

24. B.M., Lansdowne MSS. cxviii. 82.

25. M. St C. Byrne, 'The First Lady Burghley', *National Review* (1934), ciii. 356–63.

26. *C.P.R. 1547–8*, 85; *1548–9*, 3; *L. & P.* xx, pt. 2, 455.

Chapter Three: The King's Path

1. A. F. Pollard, *England under Protector Somerset* (1900), *passim*.

2. Peck, op. cit. 6.

3. W. Patten, 'The Late Expedition into Scotland, 1544', *Tudor Tracts 1532–1588*, ed. A. F. Pollard (1903), 155.

4. Ibid.

5. *Harleian Miscellany* (1808), i. 268–313.

6. J. Foxe, *Acts and Monuments*, ed. J. Pratt (1870), vi. 86, 107–9, 231, 260; Strype, *Cheke*, 15–19.

7. Foxe, op. cit. v. 723, 777, 781.

8. M. Parker, *Correspondence* (Parker Soc., 1853), 234.

9. *C.P.R. 1548–9*, 406.

10. *A.P.C.* ii. 312.

11. *C.P.R. 1548–9*, 354.

12. J. Strype, *Memorials of Archbishop Cranmer* (1812; 3 vols., Oxford, 1848–54), ii. 792–4.

13. H.M.C., *Salisbury MSS*. v. 69.

14. C. Goff, *A Woman of the Tudor Age* (1930), 236–67.

15. P.R.O., S.P. 10–8–124; Camden, op. cit. 557.

16. B.M., Lansdowne MSS. cviii. 81.

17. Foxe, op. cit. vi. 144.

18. P. F. Tytler, *England under the Reigns of Edward VI and Mary* (1839), i. 194.

19. Ibid. 115–16.

u

20. P.R.O., S.P. 10–9–48.

21. *A.P.C.* ii. 372.

22. *C.S.P. Spanish, 1547–9,* 478.

23. *A.P.C.* ii. 343.

24. E. Read, *Catherine, Duchess of Suffolk, 1520–80* (1962), 75.

25. *Rogeri Aschami Epistolorum Libri Quattuor* (Oxford, 1703), 201.

26. *A.P.C.* iii. 118; F. G. Emmison, *Tudor Secretary* (1961), 89–90.

27. P.R.O., S.P. 10–10–36, 44.

28. C. S. S. Higham, *Wimbledon Manor House under the Cecils* (1962), 3–17.

29. Tytler, op. cit. i. 338–9, 323.

30. *C.S.P. Domestic, 1547–80,* 47, 32, 28; Tytler, op. cit. i. 425.

31. J. G. Nichols, *Literary Remains of Edward VI* (1857), ii. 539–43.

32. *C.S.P. Foreign, 1547–53,* 56–226.

33. Tytler, op. cit. i. 333–7, 364–7, 430–2; Strype, *Cranmer,* 279, 280, 336–9, 346, 349, 573, 1017.

34. Tytler, op. cit. i. 356, 341; R. H. Tawney and E. Power, *Tudor Economic Documents* (1937), ii. 182–6.

35. Tytler, op. cit. ii. 21–23.

36. J. G. Nichols, *Literary Remains of Edward VI,* ii. 356.

37. Ibid. 352.

38. Peck, op. cit. 7.

39. J. G. Nichols, *Literary Remains of Edward VI,* ii. 354.

40. Tytler, op. cit. ii. 67.

41. *C.P.R. 1550–3,* 197.

42. Holinshed, *Chronicles* (1587), 1550.

Chapter Four: The Problem of Obedience

1. Tytler, op. cit. i. 427.

2. *A.P.C.* iii. 382.

3. Strype, *Cheke,* 71; Strype, *Memorials of the English Reformation* (Oxford, 1822), i. 534–5.

4. Foxe, op. cit. vi. 97; *A.P.C.* iii. 336–52; *C.S.P. Spanish, 1550–2,* 356–64.

5. *Journals of the House of Commons* (1803), i. 18, 19.

6. *C.S.P. Domestic, 1547–80,* 39; P.R.O., S.P. 10–14–121.

7. J. G. Nichols, *Literary Remains of Edward VI,* ii. 539, 504–10; P.R.O., S.P. 10–15–88; 10–15–92; 10–15–148.

8. Strype, *Cranmer,* ii. 627; S. Haynes, *State Papers* (1740), 125.

9. Strype, *Cranmer,* ii. 383, 672; Tytler, op. cit. ii. 142.

10. J. G. Nichols, *Literary Remains of Edward VI,* ii. 458–9.

11. Tytler, op. cit. ii. 160; Haynes, op. cit. 201–2; B.M., Lansdowne MSS. iii. 75.

12. *C.P.R. 1553*, 39; Haynes, op. cit. 150, 201.

13. B.M., Lansdowne MSS. cxviii. 84; Haynes, op. cit. 148; Strype, *Memorials*, ii, pt. 2, 505; Tytler, op. cit. ii. 170.

14. Strype, *Annals of the Reformation in England* (Oxford, 1824), iv. 485–6; Tytler, op. cit. ii. 194–5.

15. T. Fuller, *Church History* (ed. J. Nichols, 1842), ii. 369; Strype, *Annals*, iv. 486.

16. Ibid.; Fuller, op. cit. ii. 372.

17. B.M., Lansdowne MSS. civ. 2.

18. Strype, *Annals*, iv. 487; Tytler, op. cit. ii. 192.

19. H.M.C., *Salisbury MSS*. i. 139; Strype, *Annals*, iv. 487; Tytler, op. cit. ii. 192.

20. *C.S.P. Spanish, 1553*, 78.

21. Tytler, op. cit. ii. 193.

22. Strype, *Annals*, iv. 487–8.

23. Tytler, op. cit. ii. 193–4.

24. Strype, *Annals*, iv. 489.

25. Ibid.

Chapter Five: In the Wilderness

1. Peck, op. cit. 8.

2. Ibid.

3. *A.P.C.* iii. 348.

4. P.R.O., S.P. 69–5–122; Emmison, op. cit. 182.

5. Strype, *Annals*, iv. 489.

6. Haynes, op. cit. 172, 201; *C.P.R. 1553*, 185; ibid. *1553–4*, 54, 77, 603; E. Lodge, *Illustrations of British History* (1838), i. 229.

7. *C.P.R. 1553–4*, 453, 21, 36; ibid. *1554–5*, 109.

8. B.M., Lansdowne MSS. cxviii. 7–11, 26, 39, 40.

9. *C.P.R. 1553*, 6; ibid. *1548–9*, 354–62; ibid. *1549–51*, 236; ibid. *1550–3*, 197–9, 427; ibid. *1553*, 49, 182–4.

10. Ibid. 136–7.

11. B.M., Lansdowne MSS. cxviii. 7–9, 57–58, 32, 35; Peck, op. cit. 48.

12. B.M., Lansdowne MSS. cxviii. 27, 77; T. S. Willan, *The Early History of the Russia Company 1553–1603* (Manchester, 1956), 41–42; *C.P.R. 1554–5*, 55; H.M.C., *Salisbury MSS*. v. 462.

13. B.M., Lansdowne MSS. cxviii. 59.

14. Peck, op. cit. 47, 48.

15. B.M. Lansdowne MSS. cxviii. 36, 54, 78, 50–51; H.M.C., *Salisbury MSS*. i. 127, 142; *C.S.P. Domestic, 1547–80*, 86; Hatfield MSS. cxliii. 91; *C.S.P. Domestic, 1547–80*, 85; W. Murdin, *State Papers* (1759), 747.

16. H.M.C., *Salisbury MSS*. v. 69; Tytler, op. cit. ii. 494–5.

17. Peck, op. cit. 47, 48.

18. H.M.C., *Salisbury MSS.* i. 140–6, 139; Haynes, op. cit. 204; *C.S.P. Domestic, 1547–80*, 116.

19. Strype, *Cheke*, 99 n. a.; Haynes, op. cit. 203.

20. Murdin, op. cit. 746.

21. Tytler, op. cit. ii. 443; Strype, *Cheke*, 100 n. a. His enemies twitted Cecil with having 'laboured a paire of great beads' in Mary's reign. Anon., *An Advertisement written to a Secretary of my Lord Treasurer* (1592), 16.

22. B.M., Lansdowne MSS. cxviii. 82.

23. Ibid. 83; H.M.C., *Salisbury MSS.* v. 69.

24. E. H. Harbison, *Rival Ambassadors at the Court of Queen Mary* [Tudor] (Princeton U.P. and Oxford, 1940), 273–80.

25. *Journals of the House of Commons*, i. 43, 44, 45.

26. Ibid. 46.

27. Peck, op. cit. 9; Murdin, op. cit. 746.

28. Peck, op. cit. 9 n. 1; Strype, *Cheke*, 99 n. a.

29. *A.P.C.* v. 232; ibid. 282; B.M., Lansdowne MSS. iii. 159.

30. Murdin, op. cit. 746.

Chapter Six: Return to Power

1. Tytler, op. cit. i. 425–6.

2. F. A. Mumby, *The Girlhood of Queen Elizabeth* (1909), 62.

3. Tytler, op. cit. i. 323.

4. Peck, op. cit. 47.

5. *C.S.P. Spanish, 1558–67*, 38, 191.

6. B.M., Cotton MSS., Vespasian F, xiii. 287.

7. Tytler, op. cit. ii. 499.

8. J. Harington, *Nugae Antiquae* (1779), ii. 311.

9. A. Simpson, *The Wealth of the Gentry 1500-1660* (Cambridge, 1961), ch. 2.

10. Strype, *Annals*, i. 6–7.

11. *C.S.P. Spanish, 1558–67*, 7.

12. *C.S.P. Foreign, 1558–9*, 6.

13. P. Forbes, *Full View of the Public Transactions in the Reign of Queen Elizabeth* (1740), i. 4, 6.

14. A. L. Rowse, 'The Coronation of Elizabeth I', *An Elizabethan Garland* (1953), 11–28; N. J. Williams, 'The Coronation of Queen Elizabeth I', *Quarterly Review* (1953), ccxci. 397–410.

15. J. E. Neale, *Elizabeth I and her Parliaments, 1559–81* (1953), 33–84.

16. *Members of Parliament 1213–1874* (1878), i. 401.

17. *C.S.P. Spanish, 1558–67*, 33, 36, 52.

18. H. Gee, *The Elizabethan Prayer Book and Ornaments* (1922), 68–74 n.; C. H. Garrett, *The Marian Exiles* (Cambridge, 1938).

19. Peck, op. cit. 10; S.T.C., 25286.

20. Forbes, op. cit. i. 1–84.

21. H. Machyn, *Diary* (Camden Soc., 1848), xlii. 189; *C.S.P. Spanish, 1558–67*, 36.

22. Neale, op. cit. 76–77; Gee, op. cit. 215–24.

23. Goff, op. cit. 236–8.

24. Gee, op. cit. 197.

25. Parker, op. cit. 66.

26. *C.S.P. Spanish, 1558–67*, 62.

27. Parker, op. cit. 479.

28. J. K. McConica, *English Humanists and Reformation Politics* (Oxford, 1965), 278–81; A. G. Dickens, *The English Reformation* (1964), 181–2.

29. V. J. K. Brook, *Life of Archbishop Parker* (Oxford, 1962).

30. Strype, *Life of Sir Thomas Smith* (Oxford, 1820), 250.

31. *C.P.R. 1558–60*, 66; Haynes, op. cit. 207–9.

Chapter Seven: Laying Foundations

1. *C.S.P. Scottish, 1547–63*, 140–41, 152–3, 178–80; *C.S.P. Domestic, 1547–90*, 8, 44, 48.

2. *C.S.P. Foreign, 1558–9*, 120.

3. *The Works of John Knox*, ed. D. Laing (Edinburgh, 1864), vi. 15–21.

4. *C.S.P. Scottish, 1547–63*, 235.

5. *C.S.P. Foreign, 1558–9*, 339.

6. *C.S.P. Scottish, 1547–63*, 223.

7. Ibid.; Forbes, op. cit. i. 137, 148.

8. *C.S.P. Foreign, 1558–9*, 508.

9. H. Ellis, *Original Letters illustrative of English History*, 2nd ser. (1827), ii. 301–2.

10. *C.S.P. Foreign, 1558–9*, 453.

11. *Sadler Papers* (Edinburgh, 1809), i. 377–83.

12. Ibid. 426.

13. Forbes, op. cit. i. 216.

14. *Sadler Papers*, i. 526.

15. Ibid. 534–5, 578.

16. Ibid. 566–73.

17. *C.S.P. Foreign, 1559–60*, 220.

18. P.R.O., S.P. 12–7–73.

19. Haynes, op. cit. 267; Forbes, op. cit. i. 390.

20. Haynes, op. cit. 268.

21. *C.S.P. Spanish, 1558–67*, 142–68.

22. Forbes, op. cit. i. 454–5.

23. Ibid. 460.

24. Ibid.

25. Haynes, op. cit. 320; Forbes, op. cit. i. 500; Haynes, op. cit. 327.

26. Haynes, op. cit. 352–3.

27. T. Wright, *Queen Elizabeth and Her Times* (1838), i. 38.

28. Cecil wrote: 'I shall be worse this 7 years for this northern service.' P.R.O., S.P. 70–17–130.

29. Ibid.

30. *C.S.P. Foreign, 1567*, 619; Haynes, op. cit. 361.

31. *C.S.P. Spanish, 1558–67*, 174–5.

32. Haynes, op. cit. 361.

33. C. Read, 'Profits of the Recoinage of 1560–61', *Ec. Hist. Rev.* (1956), vi. 186–93; R. Ruding, *Annals of the Coinage of Great Britain and its Dependencies* (1840), i. 334–6.

34. J. W. Burgon, *The Life and Times of Sir Thomas Gresham* (1839); S. E. Lehmberg, *Sir Walter Mildmay and Tudor Government* (Texas U.P., 1964).

35. *C.S.P. Scottish, 1547–63*, 426.

36. *C.P.R. 1558–60*, 44, 165.

37. *C.S.P. Foreign, 1560–1*, 478.

Chapter Eight: In the Political Thicket

1. Wright, op. cit. i. 64.

2. *C.S.P. Spanish, 1558–67*, 199–201.

3. J. H. Pollen, *English Catholics under Elizabeth* (1920), 69; P.R.O., S.P. 70–26–59; *C.S.P. Spanish, 1558–67*, 200.

4. P.R.O., S.P. 70–26–60; *Advice to a Son*, ed. L. B. Wright (Cornell U.P., 1962), 3–6.

5. *C.S.P. Foreign, 1561–2*, 579.

6. Haynes, op. cit. 366–8.

7. Hardwicke State Papers (1778), i. 174.

8. *C.S.P. Scottish, 1547–63*, 595.

9. Hardwicke State Papers, i. 177–8.

10. Haynes, op. cit. 388, 390; B.M., Cotton MSS., Caligula B, x. 209; *C.S.P. Scottish, 1547–63*, 641.

11. Wright, op. cit. i. 30–31.

12. *C.S.P. Foreign, 1562*, 83; *C.S.P. Spanish, 1558–67*, 241.

13. *C.S.P. Foreign, 1561–2*, 636.

14. Ibid., *1562*, 52, 97–98, 100, 119.

15. Forbes, op. cit. ii. 2.

16. Ibid. 5–6.

17. *C.S.P. Foreign, 1562*, 141.

18. *C.S.P. Scottish, 1547–63*, 445.

19. Wright, op. cit. i. 96.

20. *C.S.P. Spanish, 1558–67*, 262.

21. N. J. Williams, *Thomas Howard, Fourth Duke of Norfolk* (1964), ch. 6.

22. *C.S.P. Foreign, 1563*, 25; *C.S.P. Spanish, 1558–67*, 329–31.

23. Ibid. 265; Wright, op. cit. i. 117, 118, 312.

24. Ibid.

25. Ibid. 121, 124; *C.S.P. Spanish, 1558–67*, 315, 317.

26. Wright, op. cit. i. 126; P.R.O., S.P. 12–28–4.

27. P.R.O., S.P. 70–26–59; Forbes, op. cit. i. 460; Parker, op. cit. 145, 156–60.

28. S. D'Ewes, *Journals of all the Parliaments during the Reign of Queen Elizabeth* (1682), 79; Wright, op. cit. i. 126.

29. Ibid.; S. T. Bindoff, 'The Making of the Statute of Artificers', *Elizabethan Government and Society*, ed. S. T. Bindoff *et al.* (1961), 56–94; P.R.O., S.P. 12–27–72; D'Ewes, op. cit. 87.

30. Wright, op. cit. i. 126.

31. H.M.C. *Salisbury MSS.* v. 69.

32. *C.S.P. Foreign, 1563*, 574; Wright, op. cit. i. 171–2.

33. Ibid. 173.

34. Ibid. 172–4.

35. *C.S.P. Foreign, 1564–5*, 52–53, 58, 85; *C.S.P. Spanish, 1558–67*, 401–2.

36. Wright, op. cit. i. 175; Tawney and Power, op. cit. ii. 45.

37. B.M., Add. MS. 32091, f. 100. In August 1559 Cecil had expressed his aim, 'I covet to have this isle well united in concord', *Sadler Papers*, i. 404–5.

38. Wright, op. cit. i. 187.

39. *C.S.P. Spanish, 1558–67*, 382.

40. A. C. Miller, *Sir Henry Killigrew* (Leicester U.P., 1963), 99–100; H.M.C., *Salisbury MSS.* v. 70.

Chapter Nine: The Succession Predicament

1. H.M.C., *Salisbury MSS.* clxiv. 120.

2. B.M., Cotton MSS. Caligula B, x. 297–8.

3. *C.S.P. Scottish, 1562–9*, 145–50.

4. B.M., Cotton MSS., Caligula B, x. 297–306.

5. Wright, op. cit. 208–9; P.R.O., S.P. 63–18–62.

6. Murdin, op. cit. 762.

7. *C.S.P. Spanish, 1558–67*, 377, 443; *A.P.C.* vii. 312.

8. Haynes, op. cit. 444.

9. P.R.O., S.P. 12–40–225; B.M., Cotton Caligula B, x. 351–60; *C.S.P. Spanish, 1558–67*, 484; Wright, op. cit. i. 208.

10. *C.S.P. Scottish, 1563–9*, 227.

11. Ibid. 255, 298; Murdin, op. cit. 762.

12. P.R.O., S.P. 12–40–119. 195.

13. Murdin, op. cit. 762.

14. *C.S.P. Spanish, 1558–67*, 588; *Journals of the House of Commons*, i. 74–75.

15. *C.S.P. Spanish, 1558–67*, 591–4.

16. J. E. Neale, *Elizabeth I and her Parliaments 1559–81* (1953), 149–150.

17. P.R.O., S.P. 12–41–61; Neale, op. cit. 151–61.

18. P.R.O., S.P. 12–41–151.

19. Ibid. 12–40–149; *C.S.P. Spanish, 1558–67*, 406.

20. *C.S.P. Spanish, 1558–67*, 609; P.R.O., S.P. 12–41–75.

21. Miller, op. cit. 55–67; P.R.O., S.P. 63–20–67; *C.S.P. Scottish, 1566–8*, 202.

22. P.R.O., S.P. 63–21–59.

23. *Cabala, sive scrinia sacra . . .* (1691), 126, 129.

24. *C.S.P. Scottish, 1563–9*, 378–9.

25. *C.S.P. Foreign, 1566–8*, 324.

26. *C.S.P. Spanish, 1558–67*, 625; *C.S.P. Foreign, 1566–8*, 197, 210, 154; La Mothe-Fénelon, *Correspondence diplomatique, Paris et London* (1840), i. 46; Murdin, op. cit. 766; Haynes, op. cit. 462; *Cabala*, 144.

27. Cecil wrote: 'The event and success of these matters in the Low Countries, which as they shall fall out, so are like to produce consequences to the greater part of Christendom.' *Cabala*, 140.

28. *C.S.P. Spanish, 1558–67*, 558, 651, 667; J. A. Williamson, *Sir John Hawkins* (Oxford, 1927), 137–8.

29. *C.S.P. Spanish, 1568–79*, 37.

30. J. Anderson, *Collections relating to the History of Mary Queen of Scots* (Edinburgh, 1727), iv. 34–44.

31. *C.S.P. Scottish, 1563–9*, 441–2, 448.

32. Ibid. 510.

33. P.R.O., S.P. 63–26–8.

Chapter Ten: Challenge and Vindication

1. C. Read, 'Queen Elizabeth's Seizure of the Duke of Alva's Pay-ships', *Jour. Mod. Hist.* (1933), 443–64.

2. P.R.O., S.P. 63–27–3.

3. Haynes, op. cit. 579–88.

4. Fénelon, op. cit. i. 233.

5. Haynes, op. cit. 444.

6. Williams, *Thomas Howard, Fourth Duke of Norfolk* (1964), 16, 145.

7. Lodge, op. cit. i. 478.

8. P.R.O., S.P. 63–27–4.

9. *Collectanea Topographica et Geneologica*, ed. F. Madden *et al.* (1838), v. 322–8.

10. *C.S.P. Scottish, 1571–4*, 32–40; *Cabala*, 167.

11. E. E. Rich, 'The Population of Elizabethan England', *Ec. Hist. Rev.* (1950), ii. 248; P.R.O., S.P. 12–51–6.

12. Haynes, op. cit. 522.

13. Ibid. 534.

14. Fénelon, op. cit. ii. 272; *C.S.P. Spanish, 1568–79*, 198.

15. Fénelon, op. cit. ii. 304; *C.S.P. Scottish, 1563–9*, 684.

16. Haynes, op. cit. 560–3, 578–9; *Cabala*, 169; *Sadler Papers*, ii. 73, 166, 304.

17. Ibid. 340.

18. *C.S.P. Scottish, 1569–71*, 371, 374, 386; Haynes, op. cit. 608–21; *Cabala*, 165.

19. B.M., Cotton MSS., Caligula B, iv. 235; D. Digges, *The Compleat Ambassador* (1655), 3–4.

20. Camden, op. cit. 154.

21. Digges, op. cit. 45, 33.

22. B. M. Ward, *The Seventeenth Earl of Oxford* (1928), 61–66.

23. Digges, op. cit. 44, 53, 78; Fénelon, op. cit. iii. 275; Digges, op. cit. 53, 88; *C.S.P. Foreign, 1569–71*, 383; Digges, op. cit. 115.

24. Neale, op. cit. 216.

25. Murdin, op. cit. 1–147.

26. Ibid. 148–94; *State Trials*, ed. Howell (1730), i. 82–117; Lodge, op. cit. 526.

27. Ibid. 194–210.

28. *C.S.P. Scottish, 1571–4*, 61, 100, 103.

29. *C.S.P. Foreign, 1572–4*, 225, 248; *C.S.P. Spanish, 1568–79*, 451.

30. Ibid. 383, 379–80.

31. Digges, op. cit. 189.

32. Ibid. 203.

33. Murdin, op. cit. 745; B.M., Cotton MSS., Vespasian F, vi. 131.

34. Digges, op. cit. 212.

35. B.M., Cotton MSS., Vespasian F, vi. 131.

36. Lodge, op. cit. i. 547.

37. Murdin, op. cit. 225; Miller, op. cit. 133–46.
38. *C.S.P. Spanish, 1568–79*, 435, 451–2.

Chapter Eleven: Principal Councillor

1. Wright, op. cit. i. 456; *C.S.P. Scottish, 1571–4*, 562, 565, 569.
2. Fénelon, op. cit. v. 351, 360, 382, 396, 403, 407, 422.
3. W. H. Frere and C. E. Douglas, *Puritan Manifestoes* (1954), 1–39; Parker, op. cit. 437.
4. Strype, *Annals*, iii. 305; Parker, op. cit. 205.
5. Ibid. 479.
6. Strype, *Life and Acts of Matthew Parker* (Oxford, 1821), ii. 350–5.
7. T. H. Clancy, *Papist Pamphleteers* (Chicago, 1964), 15–16.
8. *Treatise of Treasons* (1572).
9. *Leycester's Commonwealth* (1641).
10. Fénelon, op. cit. v. 469.
11. Ibid. vi. 217, 206.
12. B.M., Harleian MSS. 6991, 216, 110.
13. *A.P.C.* viii. 332.
14. Lodge, op. cit. ii. 52.
15. *C.S.P. Foreign, 1575–7*, 158.
16. B.M., Cotton MSS., Galba C, v. 88; K. de Lettenhove and L. G. van Severen, *Relations politiques des Pays Bas et de L'Angleterre sous le règne de Philippe II* (Brussels, 1882–1900), viii. 127.
17. Neale, op. cit. *1559–81*, 349, 352, 354, 357–8.
18. Ward, op. cit. 118.
19. B.M., Cotton MSS., Galba C, v. 100; Lettenhove and Severen, op. cit. viii. 316.
20. Ward, op. cit. 113–29.
21. Lodge, op. cit. ii. 83.
22. H.M.C., *Rutland MSS.* i. 317.
23. J. Strype, *Life of Edmund Grindal* (Oxford, 1821), 348.
24. B.M., Cotton MSS., Galba C, vi. 119–20, 122–3; Lettenhove and Severen, op. cit. x. 125, 127, 152.
25. Ibid. 340.
26. B.M., Cotton MSS., Galba C, vii. 34; Lettenhove and Severen, op. cit. x. 465, 513.
27. Ibid. 593; *C.S.P. Foreign, 1578–9*, 86.
28. Lettenhove and Severen, op. cit. x. 702.
29. J. Nichols, op. cit. ii. 92, 113–14.
30. *C.S.P. Ireland, 1574–85*, 143–4; P.R.O., S.P. 12–126–5.
31. Hatfield MSS. cxlviii. 23, 25.
32. H.M.C., *Salisbury MSS.* ii. 249, 288.

33. N. H. Nicolas, *Memoirs of the Life and Times of Sir Christopher Hatton* (1847), 121–2; *A.P.C.* xi. 218.

34. Murdin, op. cit. 322–31.

35. H.M.C., *Salisbury MSS.* ii. 308; Murdin, op. cit. 339.

Chapter Twelve: Closing the Ranks

1. H.M.C., *Salisbury MSS.* ii. 339.

2. Murdin, op. cit. 339; B.M., Cotton MSS. Galba E, vi. 6; ibid., Titus B, ii. 438.

3. J. S. Corbett, *Drake and the Tudor Navy* (1898), i. 220–2, 254.

4. *C.S.P. Foreign, 1579–80,* 360.

5. R. Steele, *Tudor and Stuart Proclamations, 1485–1714* (Oxford, 1910), i. 80; Nicolas, op. cit. 121; *A.P.C.* xiii. 53.

6. Murdin, op. cit. 325, 236, 331, 340; *Harleian Miscellany* (1808), i. 493.

7. D'Ewes, *Journals of all the Parliaments during the Reign of Queen Elizabeth,* 287.

8. *Harleian Miscellany,* i. 489–513, 515–17.

9. *C.S.P. Spanish, 1580–6,* 120, 131–3; H.M.C., *Salisbury MSS.* ii. 394.

10. Strype, *Annals,* iii. pt. 2, 168–72.

11. Digges, op. cit. 374, 377, 390, 397; *C.S.P. Foreign, 1581–2,* 307.

12. *C.S.P. Scottish, 1581–3,* 178, 183.

13. Nicolas, op. cit. 280.

14. Ibid. 316; Strype, *Annals,* iii, pt. 1, 148.

15. *C.S.P. Scottish, 1581–3,* 316–17.

16. Strype, *Annals,* iii. pt. 1, 241.

17. *C.S.P. Scottish, 1581–3,* 581.

18. *Harleian Miscellany,* i. 489–513.

19. H.M.C., *Salisbury MSS.* ii. 521.

20. *C.S.P. Scottish, 1583–4,* 390; B.M., Cotton MSS. Caligula C, viii. 73; *C.S.P. Scottish, 1584–5,* 192.

21. B.M., Cotton MSS. Caligula C, ix. 64.

22. Camden, op. cit. 320.

23. Strype, *Life of John Whitgift* (Oxford, 1822), iii. 104; i. 317; H.M.C. *Salisbury MSS.* iii. 35, 90.

24. *Harleian Miscellany,* ii. 3–9.

25. P. M. Handover, *The Second Cecil* (1959), 38–43.

26. J. E. Neale, *Elizabeth I and her Parliaments, 1584–1601* (1957), 56–60, 84–85, 88–90, 91–94; D'Ewes, op. cit. 338, 350, 371–2, 373; Strype, *Annals,* iii. 136–42; Strype, *Whitgift,* i. 200–12; B.M., Lansdowne MSS. civ. 150.

27. *State Trials*, ed. T. B. Howell (1816), i. 1095–112.

28. C. Read, *Mr Secretary Walsingham and the Policy of Queen Elizabeth* (1925), iii. 384.

29. B.M., Harleian MSS. clxviii. 102, 122.

30. *C.S.P. Foreign, 1584–5*, 701–10.

31. Ellis, op. cit. 1st ser. ii. 304.

32. Strype, *Annals*, iii, pt. 2, 379, 384, 386; B.M., Lansdowne MSS. cii. 122; ibid. xlv. 34.

33. *Leycester Correspondence*, ed. J. Bruce (Camden Soc., 1844), xxvii. 24.

34. P.R.O., S.P. 12–184–133.

35. *Leycester Correspondence*, 45.

Chapter Thirteen: Adversary of the Queen's Adversaries

1. *Leycester Correspondence*, 104.

2. Ibid. 96.

3. Ibid. 200; Hardwicke State Papers, i. 334–40.

4. *The Bardon Papers*, ed. C. Read (Camden Soc., 1909), xvii. 43.

5. Ellis, op. cit., 1st ser., iii. 12.

6. *State Trials*, ed. Howell (1816), i. 1186.

7. *Leycester Correspondence*, 450.

8. Murdin, op. cit. 579–83.

9. Hatfield MSS. clxv. 10; Murdin, op. cit. 584–6; Hatfield MSS. clxiv. 18.

10. Wright, op. cit. ii. 332; Strype, *Annals*, iii, pt. 1, 540.

11. Hatfield MSS. clxv. 20–21; J. E. Phillips, *Images of a Queen* (O.U.P., 1964), 117–42.

12. B.M., Lansdowne MSS. cxv. 20.

13. Hatfield MSS. clxv. 20–21.

14. Ibid. clxiv. 17.

15. P.R.O., S.P. 12–203–137.

16. P.R.O., S.P. 12–201–92; *Leycester Correspondence*, 41, 157, 294, 308, 357, 398.

17. J. E. Neale, 'The Fame of Sir Edward Stafford', *E.H.R.* (1929), xliv. 203–20.

18. B.M., Cotton MSS., Galba C, xi. 79.

19. P.R.O., S.P. 10–15–17.

20. *C.S.P. Foreign, 1586–7*, 396.

21. B.M., Lansdowne MSS. lv. 75.

22. B.M., Cotton MSS., Vespasian, viii. 12.

23. P.R.O., S.P. 10–15–17; B.M., Cotton MSS., Vespasian, viii. 12.

24. Williamson, op. cit. 347; R. B. Wernham, *Before the Armada* (1966), ch. 21; P.R.O., S.P. 12–168–3.

25. P.R.O., S.P. 12–198–30; Strype, *Annals*, iv. 355; Anderson, op. cit. iv. 41.

26. B.M., Cotton MSS., Vespasian, viii. 14.

27. Ibid. 16.

28. P.R.O., S.P. 12–98–29; Wright, op. cit. ii. 358; W. R. Trimble, *The Catholic Laity in Elizabethan England, 1558–1603* (Harvard U.P., 1964), 127–8.

29. H.M.C., *Salisbury MSS.* iii. 319.

30. R. Flower, 'Laurence Nowell and the Discovery of England in Tudor Times', *Proc. Brit. Acad.* (1935), xxi. 65–66; H.M.C., *Salisbury MSS.* iv. 278; B.M., Lansdowne MSS. ciii. 68; *C.S.P. Ireland, 1509–73*, 188, 297; A. Collins, *Letters and Memorials of State* (1745), i. 362.

31. *C.S.P. Ireland, 1509–73*, 325; R. Bagwell, *Ireland under the Tudors* (1885–90).

32. W. R. Scott, *The Constitution and Finance of English, Scottish and Irish Joint Stock Companies to 1720* (Cambridge, 1910–12), iii. 516.

33. Strype, *Annals*, iii, pt. 2, 551.

34. *Harleian Miscellany*, ii. 47–59, 60–85, 117–29; Williamson, op. cit. 441; C. Read, *Lord Burghley and Queen Elizabeth* (1960), 437.

35. *Letters of Queen Elizabeth and James VI*, ed. J. Bruce (Camden Soc., 1849), xlvi. 53.

36. T. Fuller, *The Worthies of England* (1811), i. 159; P.R.O., S.P. 12–219–37; R. B. Wernham, 'Queen Elizabeth and the Portugal Expedition of 1589', *E.H.R.* (1951), xlvi. 1–26, 194–218.

37. B.M., Lansdowne MSS. ciii. 48.

38. D'Ewes, op. cit. 440, 442, 439.

39. B.M., Lansdowne MSS. cccxcvi. 59.

40. Strype, *Annals*, iii, pt. 2, 125; B.M., Harleian MSS. 6994, f. 168.

41. B.M., Lansdowne MSS. civ. 59.

42. *C.S.P. Scottish, 1589–93*, 125, 137, 144, 206, 209.

43. B.M., Lansdowne MSS. civ. 59.

44. *Unton Correspondence*, ed. J. Stevenson (Roxburghe Club, 1847), *passim*; J. B. Black, *Henry IV and Elizabeth* (Oxford, 1914), *passim*.

45. *A.P.C.* xxii. 7–11.

Chapter Fourteen: Old Leviathan and his Cub

1. H.M.C., *Salisbury MSS.* vi. 463.

2. Peck, op. cit. 170.

3. T. Birch, *Memoirs of the Reign of Queen Elizabeth* (1754), ii. 364.

4. H.M.C., *Salisbury MSS.* iv. 319.

5. Ibid. iv. 604, 486; v. 40.

6. A. R. G. Smith, 'Sir Michael Hickes and the Secretariat of the

Cecils, *c.* 1580–1612' (unpublished Ph.D. thesis, University of London, 1962); A. R. G. Smith, 'Portrait of an Elizabethan', *History Today* (1964), xiv. 716–25.

7. H.M.C., *Salisbury MSS.* iv. 244; v. 84; iv. 324; v. 219, 237, 173.
8. Birch, op. cit. i. 153.
9. P.R.O., S.P. 12–231–70.
10. Collins, op. cit. i. 312.
11. J. Nichols, *The Progresses and public processions of Queen Elizabeth* (1823), iii. 74–78.
12. Collins, op. cit. i. 329.
13. P.R.O., S.P. 12–231–225.
14. B.M., Lansdowne MSS. ciii. 63; B.M., Cotton MSS., Galba D, viii. 92, 95.
15. *Unton Correspondence*, 8.
16. Ibid. *passim.*
17. *C.S.P. Domestic, 1591–4*, 166–7, 218.
18. Neale, op. cit. *1584–1601*, 280–97.
19. Strype, *Annals*, iv. 149–56; D'Ewes, op. cit. 483.
20. B.M., Lansdowne MSS. ciii. 10.
21. Birch, op. cit. i. 152.
22. Ibid. 150.
23. P.R.O., S.P. 12–250–10; H.M.C., *Salisbury MSS.* v. 2.
24. Ibid. iv. 387. Burghley had loose teeth, *C.S.P. Domestic, 1547–80*, 672.
25. Wright, op. cit. 437.
26. Ibid. 441.
27. H.M.C., *Salisbury MSS.* v. 99; H.M.C., *Ancaster MSS.* 317–28; H.M.C., *Salisbury MSS.* v. 149; *C.S.P. Domestic, 1595–7*, 48–50, 56, 58.
28. A. Woodworth, 'Purveyance. . . in the Reign of Queen Elizabeth' (*Trans. Amer. Phil. Soc.*, 1945), xxxv, pt. 1; F. C. Dietz, 'Elizabethan Customs Administration', *E.H.R.* (1930), xlv. 35–58.
29. Strype, *Annals*, iv. 3–6; B.M., Harleian MSS. 6997, f. 84.
30. Wright, op. cit. ii. 448.
31. Collins, op. cit. i. 347; *C.S.P. Domestic, 1595–7*, 102–17, 127; Strype, *Annals*, iv. 309–14.
32. P.R.O., S.P. 12–255–84.
33. Peck, op. cit. 170.
34. Wright, op. cit. ii. 456; *C.S.P. Domestic, 1595–7*, 189; Wright, op. cit. ii. 459.
35. E. P. Cheyney, *A History of England* (New York, 1914–26), ii. 143–68.
36. Strype, *Annals*, iv. 361–4.

37. Ibid. 364; Birch, op. cit. ii. 61.

38. Ibid. 121, 131, 146–68; De Maisse, *Journal*, trans. G. B. Harrison *et al.* (1931), 114; H.M.C., *De L'Isle and Dudley MSS*. ii. 217; *C.S.P. Domestic, 1595–7,* 294.

39. H.M.C., *De L'Isle and Dudley MSS*. ii. 284.

40. H.M.C., *Salisbury MSS*. vii. 294.

41. Wright, op. cit. ii. 479; B.M., Lansdowne MSS. lxxxv. 23.

42. De Maisse, op. cit. 4; Birch, op. cit. ii. 329; i. 166.

43. Ibid. 448.

44. Ellis, op. cit. 3rd ser. iv. 148.

45. *Lords' Journals*, ii. 194–9; D'Ewes, op. cit. 538; R. Wilbraham, *Journal*, ed. H. S. Scott (Camden Soc., Misc. x, 1902), 13.

46. De Maisse, op. cit. 27, 29.

47. J. Chamberlain, *Letters*, ed. S. Williams (Camden Soc., 1861), 6.

48. Camden, op. cit. 555; Strype, *Annals*, iv. 451–64.

49. Wright, op. cit. ii. 488.

50. Peck, op. cit. 40–42.

51. Chamberlain, op. cit. 15; G. Goodman, *The Court of James I*, ed. J. S. Brewer (1839), i. 30–31; A. Collins, *The Life of . . . Lord Burghley* (1732), 85.

Chapter Fifteen: The Character of a Statesman

1. P.R.O., S.P. 63–27–4, 63–18–188, 63–27–41.

2. D. Lloyd, *State Worthies* (1766), i. 369; *C.S.P. Spanish, 1558–69,* 669; F. Bacon, *The Letters and Life of Francis Bacon*, ed. J. Spedding (1862), i. 56.

3. Lloyd, op. cit. i. 360.

4. W. S. C. Copeman, *A Short History of Gout* (California U.P., 1964), 63–64; Bacon, *Letters and Life*, ed. J. Spedding, i. 199; A. Collins, *Letters and Memorials of State*, i. 331. Cecil believed himself to be subject 'by study to sickness', P.R.O., S.P. 70–26–60.

5. P.R.O., S.P. 12–203–119; B.M., Harleian MSS. 6994, f. 98; H.M.C., *Salisbury MSS*. iii. 204.

6. T. Fuller, *Works*, ed. J. Nichols (1841), iv. 253; Peck, op. cit. 16.

7. Ibid. 45.

8. P.R.O., S.P. 63–27–41.

9. F. Bacon, 'Of Simulation and Dissimulation', *Essays* (Everyman ed., 1925), introd. O. Smeaton, 17; *C.S.P. Spanish, 1558–67,* 401; Strype, *Cranmer*, ii. 1037; G. W. Phillips, *Lord Burghley in Shakespeare* (1936), 125–52.

10. Bacon, *Letters and Life*, ed. J. Spedding, i. 201.

11. B.M., Add. MS. 22925, f. 31b; Bacon, *Letters and Life*, ed.

J. Spedding, i. 152; Lloyd, op. cit. i. 369; B.M., Cotton MSS. Caligula cii. 80; Bacon, *Letters and Life*, ed. J. Spedding, i. 153, 152.

12. B.M., Add. MS. 22925, f. 31b; Peck, op. cit. 91; H.M.C., *Salisbury MSS.* ii. 377.

13. B.M., Lansdowne MSS. cii. 37.

14. P.R.O., S.P. 70–17–130.

15. Bacon, *Letters and Life*, ed. J. Spedding, i. 200; H.M.C., *Salisbury MSS.* iii. 286; P.R.O., S.P. 63–25–137, 12–203–150.

16. P.R.O., S.P. 12–203–152; B.M., Cotton MSS., Vespasian F, vi. 131.

17. Peck, op. cit. 44.

18. Hatfield MSS. cxlviii. 27.

19. E. F. Rice, *The Renaissance Idea of Wisdom* (Harvard U.P., 1958); *C.S.P. Foreign, 1558–9*, 208.

20. Strype, *Annals*, iii, pt. 2, 380; Clancy, op. cit. 206 n. 39; B.M., Add. MS. 22925, f. 30; Bacon, *Letters and Life*, ed. J. Spedding, i. 198.

21. R. Naunton, *Fragmenta Regalia (Somers' Tracts*, 1809–15), i. 253; Peck, op. cit. 168.

22. *The Proverbs . . . of J. Lopez de Mendoza* (1579); Peck, op. cit. 45–46; Lloyd, op. cit. i. 364–9.

23. Peck, op. cit. 166.

24. Wright, op. cit. ii. 452.

25. Peck, op. cit. 259, 46, 168.

26. Harington, op. cit. ii. 311; Ellis, op. cit. 3rd ser. iv. 148.

27. P.R.O., S.P. 12–200–51.

28. *Harleian Miscellany*, ii. 248.

29. W. B. Devereux, *The Devereux Earls of Essex* (1853), i. 471.

30. Wright, op. cit. ii. 425.

31. H.M.C., *Salisbury MSS.* viii. 370. Thomas accepted his father's motto, *cor unum via una*, as descriptive of his father's character.

32. Lloyd, op. cit. i. 357; *The Political Works of James I*, ed. C. H. McIlwain (Harvard U.P., 1918), 329; P.R.O., S.P. 70–26–41.

33. Strype, *Annals*, iv. 330.

34. C. C. Weston, *English Constitutional Theory and the House of Lords, 1556–1832* (1965), 9–43; D'Ewes, op. cit. 350.

35. Camden, op. cit. 555; B.M., Cotton MSS., Caligula C, ii. 80; Peck, op. cit. 33.

36. Woodworth, art. cit. 15.

37. P.R.O., S.P. 12–41–75.

38. Harington, op. cit. ii. 136; Peck, op. cit. 45.

39. Ibid.; P.R.O., S.P. 12–193–90.

40. R. De Roover, *Gresham on the Foreign Exchange* (1949), 301; D'Ewes, op. cit. 244, 287; Scott, op. cit. iii. 487; T. S. Willan, *A Tudor Book of Rates* (Manchester, 1962), liii, liv; G. Unwin, *Studies in Economic History* (1927), 133–220.

41. Tawney and Power, op. cit. ii. 45.

42. P.R.O., S.P. 12–41–151; Tawney and Power, op. cit. ii. 124.

43. H.M.C., *Salisbury MSS*. vii. 497–8; ii. 251; H. Miller, 'Subsidy Assessments of the Peerage in the Sixteenth Century', *Bulletin of Institute of Hist. Research* (1955), xxviii. 15–34; L. Stone, *The Crisis of the Aristocracy, 1558–1641* (Oxford, 1966), 479; J. Hurstfield, *Queen's Wards* (1958), 281.

44. Camden, op. cit. 558.

45. *History of the Reign of Henry VII*, ed. J. R. Lumby (Cambridge, 1880), 72.

46. P.R.O. S.P. 12–201–31.

47. E. Hughes, *Studies in Administration and Finance, 1558–1825* (Manchester, 1934), 35, 59–60.

48. F. Raab, *The English Face of Machiavelli* (1964), 8–76.

49. *Harleian Miscellany*, ii. 278.

50. P.R.O., S.P. 12–203–152; *Sadler Papers*, i. 378; P.R.O., S.P. 12–203–132.

51. Fénelon, op. cit. iii. 188; Peck, op. cit. 170.

52. Clancy, op. cit. 168–9.

53. *Harleian Miscellany*, i. 493; Peck, op. cit. 33.

54. P. Munz, *The Place of Hooker in the History of Thought* (1952), ch. 4; Dickens, op. cit. 84–86.

55. *Harleian Miscellany*, i. 496–513.

56. W. G. Zeeveld, *The Foundations of Tudor Policy* (1948), 137–56; Murdin, op. cit. 666.

57. B.M., Lansdowne MSS. 1, 9.

58. *Advice to a Son*, ed. L. B. Wright (Cornell, 1962), 3–6; *C.S.P. Domestic, 1595–7*, 469; Peck, op. cit. 173.

59. B.M., Lansdowne MSS. civ. 2; Bacon, *Letters and Life*, ed. J. Spedding, i. 201; Camden, op. cit. 557.

60. Harington, op. cit. ii. 219; Wright, op. cit. i. 160; P.R.O., S.P. 12–200–51.

61. P.R.O., S.P. 12–203–34.

62. B.M., Cotton MSS. Vespasian cviii. 14; ibid. Galba C, xi. 79.

63. *C.S.P. Ireland, 1509–73*, 254; Peck, op. cit. 47; P.R.O., S.P. 12–266–5.

64. Wright, op. cit. i. 31; P.R.O., S.P. 12–168–5; H.M.C., *Salisbury MSS*. iv. 54–55; B.M., Cotton MSS. Vespasian, cviii. 14.

65. B.M. Lansdowne MSS. cii. 36; Lodge, op. cit. i. 435; H.M.C., *Salisbury MSS.* iv. 72.

66. D'Ewes, op. cit. 466; J. Dee, *Diary*, ed. J. O. Halliwell (Camden Soc., 1842), 9.

67. J. D. Kendrick, *British Antiquity* (1950); B.M., Cotton MSS., Caligula B, iv. 236.

68. W. Haller, *Foxe's 'Book of Martyrs' and the Elect Nation* (1963); B.M., Cotton MSS., Caligula B, iv. 236.

69. P.R.O., S.P. 12–27–151; Lodge, op. cit. ii. 373.

70. Strype, *Annals*, i. 150.

71. Hatfield MSS. cxlviii. 30.

72. B.M., Add. MS. 22925, f. 33.

Chapter Sixteen: Politician and Administrator

1. Bacon, 'Of Great Places', *Essays* (Everyman ed., 1925), introd. O. Smeaton, 33.

2. P.R.O., S.P. 63–18–44; T. Wright, op. cit. i. 30–31.

3. Wright, op. cit. i. 209.

4. Haynes, op. cit. 444; D. M. Loades, *Two Tudor Conspiracies* (Cambridge, 1965), 246–7; P. Williams, *The Council in the Marches of Wales* (1958), 229–31; C. Read, 'Walsingham and Burghley in Queen Elizabeth's Privy Council', *E.H.R.* (1913), xxviii. 34–58.

5. H.M.C., *Salisbury MSS.* viii. 152; Camden, op. cit. 152; E. Grindal, *Remains* (Parker Soc., 1843), 332; *Zurich Letters* (Parker Soc., 1845), ii. 198.

6. Peck, op. cit. 35; B.M., Add. MS. 22925, f. 29b; Lloyd, op. cit. i. 359.

7. Peck, op. cit. 35.

8. Bacon, 'Of Simulation and Dissimulation', *Essays* (Everyman ed. 1925), introd. O. Smeaton, 19; P.R.O., S.P. 70–26–59; Goodman, op. cit. i. 30–31.

9. P.R.O., S.P. 63–18–44.

10. H.M.C., *Ancaster MSS.* 298; Wright, op. cit. i. 103.

11. P.R.O., S.P. 12–203–119; B.M., Stowe MSS. cxlii. 21.

12. T. Smith, *De Republica Anglorum*, ed. L. Alston (Cambridge, 1906), 106; *Harleian Miscellany*, i. 513.

13. H.M.C., *Salisbury MSS.* iii. 294.

14. R. Dunlop, 'Sixteenth-Century Maps of Ireland', *E.H.R.* (1906), 309–37; *Unton Correspondence*, 87–88; J. Gillow, *Lord Burghley's Map of Lancashire 1590* (Catholic Record Soc., 1907), iv. 162–222; H.M.C., *Salisbury MSS.* v. 413; *Cabala*, 149.

15. W. B. Rye, *England as seen by Foreigners* (1865), 45, 135; Wilbraham, op. cit. 23.

16. *A.P.C.* ii. 312; G. Ungerer, *Anglo-Spanish Relations in Tudor Literature* (Bern, 1956), 50.

17. E. H. Miller, *The Professional Writer in Elizabethan England* (Harvard, 1959), 172.

18. F. B. Williams, *Index of Dedications* (1962), 35–36; S.T.C. 12745, 12746, 18270, 25357, 25358, 11862, 11869, 1523.

19. *Harleian Miscellany*, ii. 279; H. Ellis, *Letters of Eminent Literary Men* (Camden Soc., 1843), 9; B.M., Lansdowne MSS. cccxcvi. 4; T. Fuller, *Church History* (1842), iii. 34; J. Strype, *Whitgift*, i. 340–6; Strype, *Annals*, iii, pt. 1, 352–4; *C.P.R., 1560–3*, 64.

20. *Harleian Miscellany*, ii. 279; *Nowell's Catechism* (Parker Soc., 1853), vi; F. O. White, *Lives of the Elizabethan Bishops* (1898), 349; Becon, *Catechism* (Parker Soc., 1844), 480.

21. Hatfield MSS. clxxiii. 80.

22. H.M.C., *Salisbury MSS.* xvi. 380; Wright, op. cit. ii. 17–21, 438–9.

23. C. Read, 'William Cecil and Elizabethan Public Relations', *Elizabethan Government and Society*, ed. S. T. Bindoff *et al.* (1961).

24. J. M. Phillips, *Images of a Queen* (California U.P., 1964); Anderson, op. cit., *passim*.

25. B.M., Lansdowne MSS. cii. 108.

26. W. T. Maccaffrey, 'Place and Patronage in Elizabethan Politics', *Elizabethan Government and Society* (1961).

27. H.M.C., *Salisbury MSS.* viii. 240; Bacon, i. 37 n. 2; H. Ellis, *Original Letters illustrative of English History*, 3rd ser. (1846), iv. 52; B.M., Lansdowne MSS. cxviii. 23; H.M.C., *Salisbury MSS.* viii. 552; Stone, op. cit. 446.

28. Peck, op. cit. 33; Murdin, op. cit. 588; G. S. Thomson, *Lords Lieutenants in the Sixteenth Century* (1923), 74; H.M.C., *Rutland MSS.* i. 190, 155; H.M.C., *Salisbury MSS.* v. 128, 340; vi. 99, 294; xii. 435; Haynes, op. cit. 444; *Cabala*, 136; *C.S.P. Domestic, 1547–80*, 309; Peck, op. cit. 89–90, 167, 169; Strype, *Annals*, iii, pt. 2, 501.

29. E. Spenser, *The Ruins of Time*; *Leycester's Commonwealth* (1641), 43; Bacon, *Letters and Life*, ed. J. Spedding, i. 255.

30. H.M.C., *Salisbury MSS.* iv. 531; *C.S.P. Domestic, 1547–80*, 309; J. A. Froude, *History of England* (1864), viii. 410.

31. Peck, op. cit. 29–30; A. R. G. Smith, 'Sir Michael Hickes and the Secretariat of the Cecils' (unpublished Ph.D. thesis, University of London, 1962), ch. 5.

32. Bacon, *Letters and Life*, ii. 52; C. Read, *Sir Francis Walsingham*, iii. 384.

33. B.M., Lansdowne MSS. xxxi. 42; E. St J. Brooks, *Sir Christopher Hatton* (1946), 337; Collins, *Letters and Memorials of State*, i. 331.

34. B.M., Lansdowne MSS. cii. 108; H. E. Bell, *An Introduction to the History and Records of the Courts of Wards and Liveries* (Cambridge, 1953), 24, 25, 32, 33; J. E. Neale, 'The Elizabethan Political Scene', *Essays in Elizabethan History* (1958), 65; *C.S.P. Scottish, 1583-4,* 108; Bacon, *Letters and Life*, i. 200.

35. H.M.C., *Salisbury MSS.* ii. 125; viii. 33.

36. J. E. Neale, *The Elizabethan House of Commons* (1949), 205-6.

37. *C.S.P. Scottish, 1547-63,* 234; Peck, op. cit. 167; H.M.C., *Salisbury MSS.* viii. 552, 88; Peck, op. cit. 189; Strype, *Annals*, iii, pt. 1, 688.

38. Parker, op. cit. 454, 124, 202.

39. H.M.C., *Salisbury MSS.* ii. 184; Strype, *Annals*, i, pt. 2, 144; ii, pt. 1, 37, 510, 542; pt. 2, 53, 5, 600; iii, pt. 1, 37, 318; Strype, *Grindal*, ii. 282; H.M.C., *Salisbury MSS.* iii. 153; Strype, *Whitgift*, iii. 347, 349.

40. Parker, op. cit. 148; Strype, *Annals*, iii, pt. 1, 33, 138-9; Strype, *Parker*, i. 214; H.M.C., *Salisbury MSS.* ii. 367; Strype, *Whitgift*, iii. 106.

41. *Harleian Miscellany*, ii. 278; H.M.C., *Salisbury MSS.* ii. 532; xii. 142; iv. 67-68, 527; P.R.O., S.P. 12-28-4; H.M.C., *Salisbury MSS.* iv. 74-75.

42. B.M., Lansdowne MSS. cii. 37; Peck, op. cit. 39.

43. Tytler, op. cit. i. 228; H.M.C., *Salisbury MSS.* iii. 250.

44. Wright, op. cit. i. 160; G. R. Elton, *The Tudor Revolution in Government* (Cambridge, 1953), 298-315.

45. N. Faunt, 'Discourse touching the office of Principal Secretary', in C. Hughes, *E.H.R.* (1905), xx. 499-508; R. Beale, 'A Treatise of the Office of Councillor and Principal Secretary', in C. Read, *Walsingham*, i. 423-43.

46. Hatfield MSS. cxl. 40; F. M. G. Evans, *The Principal Secretary of State* (Manchester, 1923), 42, 50, 53-55, 308, 322; R. B. Wernham, 'The Public Records . . .', *English Historical Scholarship in the Sixteenth and Seventeenth Centuries*, ed. L. Fox (Dugdale Soc., Oxford, 1956), 15, 17-18, 20-22.

47. B.M., Cotton MSS., Vespasian F, vi. 131; Camden, op. cit. 293; Wright, op. cit. i. 159.

48. Hurstfield, op. cit.; Bell, op. cit.

49. Hatfield MSS. viii. 92.

50. Smith, op. cit. 120; Peck, op. cit. 20; Stone, op. cit. 739-40.

51. G. E. Aylmer, *The King's Servants* (1961), 15, 21, 37, 49, 161, 184; W. C. Richardson, *History of the Court of Augmentations* (Baton Rouge,

1961), 454–6; G. R. Elton, 'The Elizabethan Exchequer: War in Receipt', *Elizabethan Government and Society*, ch. 8.

52. Lehmberg, op. cit. 49–50, 111–12.

53. Naunton, op. cit. 261; H.M.C., *Salisbury MSS*. IV. 239–301; Woodworth, art. cit. 12–15, 41; B.M., Harleian MSS. 215, 62; B.M., Lansdowne MSS. xiv. 18.

54. Murdin, op. cit. 327; D'Ewes, op. cit. 496; Miller, art. cit. 22; F. C. Dietz, *English Public Finance 1558–1641* (1932), 54–55.

55. Camden, op. cit. 555.

56. R. B. Outhwaite, 'Studies in Elizabethan Government Finance: Royal Borrowing and the Sales of Crown Lands 1572–1603' (unpublished Ph.D. thesis, University of Nottingham 1964); Dietz, op. cit. 27.

57. Dietz, op. cit. 63–64; *Statutes of the Realm*, ed. A. Luders *et al.* (1810–28), iv. pt. 2, 924–5; Strype, *Annals*, iii, pt. 1, 43; Dietz, op. cit. 43–44, 63.

58. Ibid.; T. S. Willan, *A Tudor Book of Rates*, pp. xliii, xlviii–lv; Dietz, op. cit. 313–37, 73–74.

59. Scott, op. cit. iii. 514, 516–19; Dietz, op. cit. 27, 44–47, 55, 395; Woodworth, art. cit. 4–5.

60. Dietz, op. cit. 55.

61. P. Williams, op. cit. 127, 130; K. R. Andrews, *Elizabethan Privateering* (Cambridge, 1964), chs. 1, 2.

62. Collins, *Letters and Memorials of State*, i. 353; W. S. Holdsworth, *A History of English Law*, i (1922), 242–6; iv (1924), 255; H.M.C., *Salisbury MSS.* v. 493, 505; vi. 93, 108, 199; Williams, op. cit. 219–20; B.M., Lansdowne MSS. cxl. 85.

63. H. Ellis, *Original Letters illustrative of English History*, 3rd ser. iv. 54; *Journals of the House of Lords*, ii. 63–72; D'Ewes, op. cit. 338, 350; Peck, op. cit. 32.

64. Hatfield MSS. viii. 92; Wilbraham, op. cit. 51–52; H.M.C., *Salisbury MSS.* vi. 270.

65. Bacon, *Letters and Life*, ed. J. Spedding, i. 200; Peck, op. cit. 15, 19, 20, 31, 33; H.M.C., *Salisbury MSS.* iv. 196.

66. J. E. Neale, 'The Elizabethan Political Scene', *Essays in Elizabethan History* (1958), 59–84; Hurstfield, op. cit. 181–217.

67. H.M.C., *De L'Isle and Dudley MSS.* ii. 314; Peck, op. cit. 46; Wright, op. cit. ii. 425; P.R.O., S.P. 12–180–45.

68. Peck, op. cit. 22; Bagwell, op. cit. i. 123; Peck, op. cit. 32; H.M.C., *Salisbury MSS.* viii. 252; iv. 412.

69. Froude, op. cit. viii. 122; xi. 108, 404; *C.S.P. Spanish, 1568–79*, 668–9; H.M.C., *Salisbury MSS.* iii. 362.

70. Stone, op. cit. 533; A. R. G. Smith, 'Portrait of an Elizabethan', *History Today* (1964), xiv. 718–21; H.M.C., *Salisbury MSS*. iv. 497.

71. Tytler, op. cit. ii. 160; H.M.C., *Salisbury MSS*. iv. 370.

Chapter Seventeen: Lover of Learning and Patron of the Arts

1. H.M.C., *Rutland MSS*. i. 91; Bacon, 'Of Studies', *Essays* (Everyman ed., 1925), introd. O. Smeaton, 150.

2. Peck, op. cit. 48; Ascham, op. cit. 175.

3. H.M.C., *Rutland MSS*. i. 275; *Harleian Miscellany*, ii. 279.

4. *C.P.R., 1553*, 35–36; H.M.C., *Salisbury MSS*. i. 119–20; xi. 5; Ellis, *Original Letters illustrative of English History*, 2nd ser. ii. 268–71; *C.R.P. 1560–3*, 227.

5. Peck, op. cit. 257.

6. H.M.C., *Salisbury MSS*. i. 257; Porter, op. cit., *passim*.

7. J. Nichols, *The Progresses . . . of Queen Elizabeth*, i. 151–2; Porter, op. cit., ch. 6, 175–6, 385–6, 373; M. H. Curtis, *Oxford and Cambridge in Transition, 1558–1642* (Oxford, 1959), 313, 218–19, 176–77; *Leycester's Commonwealth* (1641), 69.

8. J. Nichols, *The Progresses*, i. 149–89.

9. Hurstfield, op. cit. 249; A. L. Rowse, *Shakespeare's Southampton* (1966), ch. 3.

10. P.R.O., S.P. 12–26–50; H.M.C., *Rutland MSS*. i. 283; Strype, *Smith*, 19–20; H. Peacham, *The Complete Gentleman*, ed. V. B. Heltzel (New York, 1962), 63; P.R.O., S.P. 12–77–10.

11. H.M.C., *Salisbury MSS*. ii. 119; Hurstfield, op. cit. 256; Murdin, op. cit. 301–2.

12. Hurstfield, op. cit. 255; Peck, op. cit. 24.

13. Strype, *Cheke*, 195.

14. Peacham, op. cit. 57; *Advice to a Son*, 4; Peck, op. cit. 37; H.M.C., *Salisbury MSS*. i. 118; *Cabala*, 125, 128, 130, 134.

15. Hatfield MSS. cxliii. 91; F. S. Fussner, *The Historical Revolution* (1962), 63–64; Parker, op. cit. 254.

16. A. Collins, *Life of . . . Lord Burghley*, 93; T. Bentley and B. Welford, *Bibliotheca Illustris sive Catalogus variorum librorum* (1687); S. Jayne, *Library Catalogues of the English Renaissance* (California U.P., 1956), 22, 132.

17. W. W. Greg, 'Books and Bookmen in the Correspondence of Archbishop Parker', *The Library* (1935), xvi. 243–79; Flower, art. cit. 54–55, 69; Strype, *Cheke*, 87; *C.S.P. Domestic, 1547–80*, 222.

18. Digges, op. cit. 148; Peck, op. cit. 41; J. Baret, *An aluearie or triple dictionarie in Englishe, Latin and French* (1573); T. Thomas, *Dictionarum linguae Latinae et Anglicanae* (1588).

19. Peck, op. cit. 32; H.M.C., *Salisbury MSS.* v. 100; iv. 44-45, 86, 91-97. Cecil wrote, 'But Civil Law only I covet in foliis ...'; *C.S.P. Foreign, 1561-2,* 403.

20. P.R.O., S.P. 12-205-112; Camden, op. cit. 165; *C.S.P. Spanish, 1558-67,* 218; *C.S.P. Foreign, 1561-2.* 486; H.M.C., *Salisbury MSS.* vii. 79; *Cabala,* 167.

21. *C.S.P. Ireland, 1509-73,* 189; H.M.C., *Salisbury MSS.* ii. 183, 199; Wright, op. cit. i. 235.

22. F. Wormald and C. E. Wright, *The English Library before 1700* (1958), 156; Parker, op. cit. 328; Camden, op. cit., 'Author to Reader'; H.M.C., *Salisbury MSS.* iii. 299; Hatfield MSS. clxiv. 120-35.

23. Flower, art. cit.; C. Read, *Elizabeth of England* (1951), 1-26; Parker, op. cit. 425; R. Grafton, *A Chronicle at large to the first yere of Queen Elizabeth* (1569).

24. R. Holinshed, *Chronicles* (1578); Strype, *Grindal,* 184-5; Ellis, *Letters of Eminent Literary Men* (Camden Soc., 1843), xxiii. 77; B.M., Lansdowne MSS. lxv. 166-9.

25. S.T.C., 3933, 4335, 5602, 12463, 20926, 3593, 20309, 4503, 18638; J. Aubrey, *Brief Lives,* ed. A. Clark (1898), ii. 28.

26. E. Spenser, *The Faerie Queene,* bk. IV. i; E. Spenser, *Ruins of Time, Tears of the Muses, Mother Hubberd's Tale*; E. H. Miller, op. cit. 105.

27. J. Lyly, *Euphues,* ed. M. W. Croll and H. Clemons (New York, 1964), 425-6.

28. T. Chaloner, *De Republica Anglorum Instauranda* (1579); *C.S.P. Domestic, 1566-79,* Addenda, 482; G. Peele, *Works,* ed. A. H. Bullen (1888), ii. 311; G. Puttenham, *The Arte of English Poesie,* ed. G. D. Willcock and A. Walker (Cambridge, 1936), 2.

29. The eight Tragedies of Seneca (1566), were dedicated to Cecil; B.M., Add. MS. 32091, f. 100; *C.S.P. Spanish, 1558-67,* 247; J. Nichols, *The Progresses . . . of Queen Elizabeth,* i. 153; E. K. Chambers, *The Elizabethan Stage* (Oxford, 1923), i. 167, 227; Wright, op. cit. ii. 88; E. Grindal, *Remains* (Parker Soc., 1843), 268-9.

30. Wright, op. cit. ii. 273; Strype, *Annals,* iv. 364; Strype, *Cheke,* 103-4; *C.S.P. Domestic, 1547-80,* 283.

31. Digges, op. cit. 152; C. F. Smith, *John Dee* (1909), 21; Strype, *Cranmer,* ii. 481; J. Spedding *et al., Collected Works of Francis Bacon* (1857-74), viii. 307; B.M., Add. MS. 22925, f. 34b.

32. T. Wilson, *The Three Orations of Demosthenes* (1570), Dedication; Puttenham, op. cit., 139-40; B.M., Lansdowne MSS. cccxcvi. 59; civ. 150, 62, 63; Peck, op. cit. 37.

33. W. Damon, *The former book of musicke conteining all the tunes of*

David's Psalms (1590); W. Damon, *The second book of the music* (1591); H.M.C., *Salisbury MSS.* xii. 143.

34. B.M. Add. MS. 32379; P.R.O., S.P. 12–26–50.

35. Peck, op. cit. 37, 49; B.M., Add. MS. 22925, f. 34b.

36. Ibid.; Peck, op. cit. 37; S.T.C., 25852, 1508, 3744, 3746; Ungerer, op. cit. 51; Strype, *Whitgift*, iii. 224; Strype, *Annals*, ii, pt. 2, 483–6.

37. B.M., Add. MS. 22925, f. 34.

38. Faunt, art. cit. 507; Lloyd, op. cit. i. 368; *The Elements of Geometrie* ... *translated* ... *by Henry Billingsley* ... *With a very fruitful Preface made by M. J. Dee* (1570). Cecil possessed a 'Euclid with figures', *C.S.P. Foreign, 1547–53*, 204.

39. C. Hill, *Intellectual Origins of the English Revolution* (Oxford, 1965), ch. 2; E. Worsop, *A Discoverie of sundrie errours and faults daily committed by Landmeaters* ... (1582), Dedication; J. O. Halliwell, *Letters Illustrative of the Progress of Science in England* (1841), 18, 19.

40. E. R. G. Taylor, *Mathematical Practitioners of Tudor and Stuart England* (Cambridge, 1954), 168; Halliwell, op. cit. 5; Naunton, op. cit. 280.

41. B.M., Lansdowne MSS. vi. 54; Ellis, *Letters of Eminent Literary Men* (Camden Soc.), 21–23; H.M.C., *Salisbury MSS.* vii. 459; J. Norden, *Speculi Britanniae Pars*, ed. H. Ellis (Camden Soc., 1840), ix. 3; S.T.C. 18638, 18635; Parker, op. cit. 424; 'Copy of a Manuscript addressed to Lord Burghley', H. Ellis, in *Archaelogia* (1829), xxii. 161; Dunlop, art. cit.; E. Lynam, *British Maps and Map-Makers* (1944), 17.

42. Peck, op. cit. 39; *C.S.P. Colonial, 1513–1616*, 35; Hatfield MSS. cxliii. 91; *Hakluyt's Voyages*, introd. J. Masefield (1927), vi. 119; H.M.C., *Salisbury MSS.* i. 260.

43. Cecil wrote, 'I fantasy of cosmographie ...', Wright, op. cit. i. 120; T. Digges, *Alae* (1573); J. Blagrave, *The Mathematical Jewel* (1585); J. O. Halliwell, op. cit. 30, 7; Rye, op. cit. 44; P.R.O., S.P. 12–105–111; S.T.C. 11445.

44. H. J. Webb, *Elizabethan Military Science* (Wisconsin U.P., 1965); Strype, *Cheke*, 170–1; Hatfield MSS. cxliii. 91; Taylor, op. cit. 321, 328, 319; Halliwell, op. cit. 37; *C.S.P. Domestic, 1566–79*, Addenda, 78–81; Ellis, *Letters of Eminent Literary Men* (Camden Soc., 1843), 56–62.

45. Strype, *Smith*, 101–5; H.M.C., *Salisbury MSS.* ii. 513, 523; *C.S.P. Ireland, 1509–75*, 209, 325; Strype, *Annals*, iii, pt. 2, 131; vi. 1–6; *Shakespeare's England* (Oxford, 1916), i. 472–3.

46. L. Stone, 'Elizabethan Overseas Trade', *Ec. Hist. Rev.* (1949), ii. 30–35; G. N. Clark, *Science and Social Welfare in the Age of Newton* (Oxford, 1949), 126; F. Bacon, 'Of the true Greatness of Kingdoms and Estates', *Essays* (Everyman ed., 1925), introd. O. Smeaton, 90.

47. Peck, op. cit. 38; Strype, *Cheke*, 180; Strype, *Annals*, iii, pt. 1, 272; Halliwell, op. cit. 35; Lloyd, op. cit. i. 369; Hardwicke State Papers, i. 178.

48. *C.S.P. Domestic, 1547–80*, 80, 100; Stone, op. cit. 312; H.M.C., *Ancaster MSS*. 25.

49. Rye, op. cit. 45, 213, 205; F. Bacon, 'Of Gardens', *Essays* (Everyman ed., 1925), introd. O. Smeaton, 139; *C.P.R. 1566–9*, 192–3; *C.S.P. Domestic, 1547–80*, 182; H.M.C., *Rutland MSS*. i. 150.

50. H.M.C., *Salisbury MSS*. ii. 225; *C.S.P. Domestic, 1547–80*, 198, 288, 97; C. E. Raven, *English Naturalists from Neckam to Ray* (Cambridge, 1947), 94, 95, 99, 205; *Catalogus Arborum* (1596); *General Historie of Plantes* (1597); F. R. Johnson, 'Thomas Hill: an Elizabethan Huxley', *Huntington Library Quarterly* (1952), 329–51; Peck, op. cit. 26.

51. P.R.O., S.P. 12–77–10; W. G. Hoskins, *Provincial England* (1963), ch. 7.

52. L.C.C., *Survey of London*, ed. G. Gates and W. H. Godfrey (1937), xviii. 125; Wilbraham, op. cit. 23; J. Summerson, 'The Building of Theobalds', *Archaeologia* (1959), xcvii. 107.

53. J. Summerson, *Architecture in Britain 1530–1830* (1953), chs. 3, 4; E. Mercer, *English Art 1553–1625* (Oxford, 1962), 12–14; Hatfield MSS. cxliii. 49; Nicolas, *Memoirs of the Life and Times of Sir Christopher Hatton* (1847), 126.

54. H.M.C., *Salisbury MSS*. ii. 111, 200; *C.S.P. Domestic, 1547–80*, 84; Summerson, art. cit. 113–15; Mercer, op. cit. 55; Rye, op. cit. 213.

55. Mercer, op. cit. 33; J. Buxton, *Elizabethan Taste* (1963), 47, 54, 57; H.M.C., *Salisbury MSS*. v. 360; *C.S.P. Domestic, 1547–80*, 409, 288, 189; Hatfield MSS. cxliii. 36; J. Summerson, art. cit. 113.

56. Ibid. 125–6; Nicolas, *Memoirs of . . . Sir Christopher Hatton*, 125–6; Buxton, op. cit. 71–72.

57. Holinshed, op. cit., ed. J. Johnson *et al.* (1808), i. 317; Summerson, op. cit. 110; Rye, op. cit. 44, 45.

58. J. Nichols, *The Progresses . . . of Queen Elizabeth*, i. 113, 114, 124, 128; ii. 52, 71, 81, 289, 388, 397, 420, 426, 451, 528; iii. 15.

59. H.M.C., *Salisbury MSS*. i. 236; Peck, op. cit. 236; Strype, *Smith*, 148.

60. Digges, op. cit. 21; *Shorter Elizabethan Novels*, ed. G. Saintsbury (Everyman ed., 1957), 49.

61. Wilbraham, op. cit. 23; Rye, op. cit. 163; H. M. Hake, 'The Historic English Portrait: Document and Myth', *Proc. Brit. Acad.* (1943), xxix. 139–40; H.M.C., *Salisbury MSS*. viii. 232; R. Strong, *A Catalogue of Sixteenth-Century Portraits in the National Portrait Gallery* (forthcoming).

62. Ibid.; J. L. Caw, 'The Portraits of the Cecils', *Lord Burghley*, ed. F. P. Barnard (1904), 91–97.

63. Goodwood Collection, no. 5.

64. This picture hangs in the Bodleian Library, Oxford. Peck, op. cit. 36.

65. A. M. Hind, *Engraving in England in the Sixteenth and Seventeenth Centuries* (Cambridge, 1952), i, pls. 36, 138; Flower, art. cit. 62; M. Whinney, *Sculpture in Britain, 1530–1830* (1964), 235 n. 26.

66. H.M.C., *Salisbury MSS.* xvii. 117–18.

67. E. Rosenberg, *Leicester, Patron of Letters* (New York, 1955); Brooks, op. cit., ch. 13; Strype, *Smith*, ch. 17.

68. Halliwell, op. cit. 6; Ellis, *Letters of Eminent Literary Men* (Camden Soc., 1843), 33.

69. Porter, op. cit. 113.

Chapter Eighteen: Lord and Dynast

1. Stone, op. cit. 98.

2. *C.S.P. Foreign, 1561*, 62, 44, 48; Anon., *An Advertisement written to a Secretary of my Lord Treasurer* (1592), 15.

3. Clancy, op. cit. 26–27; *Treatise of Treasons* (1572), 'Preface to the English Reader'; Camden, op. cit. 132, 558; B.M., Add. MS. 22925, f. 29.

4. H.M.C., *Salisbury MSS.* ii. 5; P.R.O., S.P. 70–17–127.

5. H.M.C., *Salisbury MSS.* ii. 225.

6. *Sadler Papers*, ii. 73.

7. Peck, op. cit. 28; Bacon, op. cit. i. 173; Murdin, op. cit. 340.

8. Peck, op. cit. 28, 45; Peacham, op. cit. 57; Becon, op. cit. 481.

9. Ascham, op. cit. 205; R. Pace, cited F. Caspari, *Humanism and Social Order in Tudor England* (Chicago, 1954), 150; Holinshed, op. cit. (1808), ed. J. Johnson *et al.* i. 273.

10. *C.S.P. Domestic, 1547–80*, 290; A. Simpson, *The Wealth of the Gentry* (Cambridge, 1961), 28; Holinshed, op. cit. (1808), iv. 317–19; H.M.C., *Salisbury MSS.* viii. 287; Anon., *An Advertisement written to a Secretary of my Lord Treasurer* (1592), 15.

11. Peck, op. cit. 48; C. Read, *Lord Burghley and Queen Elizabeth* (1960), 437; C. H. Warren, *Sir Philip Sidney* (1936), 56; H.M.C., *Ancaster MSS.* 288.

12. P.R.O., S.P. 70–17–130; *C.P.R. 1558–60*, 78, 336, 408; ibid. *1560–3*, 132, 165–6, 322–3, 369, 414–15, 439, 581; ibid. *1563–6*, 24–26, 45, 186, 196–7, 499, 512; ibid. *1566–9*, 37, 106–7, 192, 295, 438–9; H.M.C., *De L'Isle and Dudley MSS.* i. 248, 257; C. Read, 'Lord Burghley's Household Accounts', *Ec. Hist. Rev.* (1956), ix. 344; Peck, op. cit. 27.

13. T. S. Willan, *The Muscovy Merchants of 1555* (Manchester, 1953), 86; *C.P.R. 1566–9*, 211, 274; *C.S.P. Domestic, 1547–80*, 288; *C.S.P. Foreign, 1566–8*, 463; Williamson, op. cit. 113; *C.S.P. Colonial, 1513–1616*, 7, 11, 17, 37, 73; Collins, *Letters and Memorials of State*, i. 353; H.M.C., *Salisbury MSS.* ii. 320; H.M.C., *Ancaster MSS.* 320; Strype, *Memorials*, ii. 346, 349.

14. H.M.C., *Salisbury MSS.* xii. 70; Hurstfield, op. cit. 281.

15. Chamberlain, op. cit. 15–16; Peck, op. cit. 27.

16. Collins, *Life of . . . Lord Burghley*, 92; *C.P.R. 1553*, 39.

17. Peck, op. cit. 48.

18. Naunton, op. cit. i. 261; Stone, op. cit. 204; H.M.C., *Foljambe MSS.* 40; Lodge, op. cit. ii. 345.

19. H.M.C., *Foljambe MSS.* 62, 133; H.M.C., *Salisbury MSS.* iv. 5; B.M., Lansdowne MSS. cxviii. 54.

20. H.M.C., *Salisbury MSS.* xv. 137; Peck, op. cit. 24; H.M.C., *Salisbury MSS.* i. 127, 142; Strype, *Annals*, iv. 489; *C.P.R. 1553*, 42–43; *Harleian Miscellany*, ii. 76.

21. Tytler, op. cit. ii. 118; P.R.O., S.P. 12–253–88; B.M., Lansdowne MSS. cxviii. 54; P.R.O. S.P. 10–14–121; *C.S.P. Domestic, 1591–4*, 50; P.R.O., S.P. 12–141–39.

22. Dewar, op. cit. 56; *C.S.P. Domestic, 1547–80*, 133; H.M.C., *Salisbury MSS.* vi. 71, 220, 257; H.M.C., *Ancaster MSS.* 338–9.

23. H.M.C., *Salisbury MSS.* xii. 220; ii. 335, 107, 125; iii. 109; iv. 516; Peck, op. cit. 48; H.M.C., *Ancaster MSS.* 319; *Harleian Miscellany*, ii. 280.

24. Strype, *Annals*, iii, pt. 2, 126; *V.C.H. Lincolnshire* (1906), ii. 475; Peck, 49, 23, 26, 174–7.

25. Ibid. 24; H.M.C., *Salisbury MSS.* v. 293; Goodman, op. cit. i. 174.

26. P.R.O., S.P. 12–193–91; Bacon, 'Of Nobility', *Essays* (Everyman ed., 1925), introd. O. Smeaton, 40–41.

27. J. Nichols, *The Progresses . . . of Queen Elizabeth, passim*; B.M., Cotton MSS. Titus B, xiii. 174.

28. Stone, op. cit. 452; Peck, op. cit. 25.

29. Ibid. 49; Stone, op. cit. 562–6; E. M. W. Tillyard, *The Elizabethan World Picture* (1943), 7–15.

30. C. Read, 'Lord Burghley's Household Accounts', *Ec. Hist. Rev.* (1956), ix. 345.

31. Wright, op. cit. i. 160; Spedding *et al.*, op. cit. viii. 307; Strype, *Annals*, iii, pt. 2, 381; Peck, op. cit. 25; Wright, op. cit. i. 391.

32. Lloyd, op. cit. i. 369.

33. Peck, op. cit. 45.

34. M. Greaves, *The Blazon of Honour* (1964).

35. Camden, op. cit. 557.

36. B.M., Add. MS. 22925, f. 35; A. L. Rowse, 'The Cecils of Alltyrynys', *E.H.R.* (1960), lxxv. 54–76; Strype, *Cheke*, 138–9, 140–4; Haynes, op. cit. 755; P.R.O., S.P. 63–25–137; Ward, op. cit. 231–2; Strype, *Annals*, iii, pt. 1, 30.

37. B.M., Add. MS. 22925, f. 35; Peck, op. cit. 48.

38. M. St C. Byrne, art. cit. 356–63; Strype, *Annals*, iii, pt. 2, 126–8; B.M., Lansdowne MSS. cxviii. 54; Peck, op. cit. 6; B.M., Add. MS. 22925, f. 35b; *C.S.P. Spanish, 1558–67*, 78; *C.S.P. Foreign, 1547–53*, 231, 96–97; Brooks, op. cit. 335.

39. Haynes, op. cit. 293, 301, 350; *C.S.P. Scottish, 1547–63*, 391; Stone, op. cit. 492; Lodge, op. cit. ii. 100; *C.S.P. Foreign, 1547*, 53, 221.

40. Strype, *Annals*, iii, pt. 2, 125, 9; Lodge, op. cit. ii. 372.

41. Hatfield MSS. Legal, 22–25; Peck, op. cit. 25; Collins, *Life of . . . Lord Burghley*, 80–85; B.M., Add. MS. 22925, f. 30b; Peck, op. cit. 191; C. Read, *Lord Burghley and Queen Elizabeth*, 437.

42. *Advice to a Son*, 3–6; Peck, op. cit. 47; Becon, op. cit. 481.

43. Ellis, *Original Letters illustrative of English History*, 3rd ser. iv. 43.

44. B.M., Harleian MSS. 1107, f. 62; H.M.C., *Salisbury MSS.* xiii. 309; iii. 462; H.M.C., *Rutland MSS.* i. 271; Strype, *Annals*, iii, pt. 2, 129.

45. H.M.C., *Rutland MSS.* i. 200; B.M., Lansdowne MSS. x. 38; H.M.C., *Salisbury MSS.* ii. 64, 112, 527.

46. Peck, op. cit. 47, 48.

47. Fénelon, op. cit. ii. 304.

48. Devereux, op. cit. i. 43–44; Strype, *Annals*, iii, pt. 1, 86; Lady Stafford offered her son to Burghley for 'any of his blood' in 1582, H.M.C., *Salisbury MSS.* iii. 214.

49. Lodge, op. cit. ii. 52; Ellis, *Original Letters illustrative of English History*, 3rd ser. iv. 40–43.

50. P. M. Handover, *The Second Cecil* (1959), 67–69.

51. P.R.O., S.P. 63–25–137; H.M.C., *Rutland MSS.* i. 95; Ellis, *Original Letters illustrative of English History*, 3rd ser. iv. 90.

52. H.M.C., *Rutland MSS.* i. 95, 94; Ward, op. cit. 285.

53. H.M.C., *Salisbury MSS.* iv. 319; Peck, op. cit. 36; Warren, op. cit. 52; In 1597 Burghley wrote, 'I had at dinner of old and young 14 descended of my body', Wright, op. cit. ii. 485.

54. H. Foley, *Records of the English Jesuits* (1878), iv. 49.

55. H.M.C., *Rutland MSS.* i. 300; Ward, op. cit. 315–28; Bacon, *Letters and Life*, ed. J. Spedding, i. 205.

56. *C.S.P. Domestic, 1595–7*, 489–90; Collins, *Letters and Memorials of*

State, ii. 63; Ward, op. cit. 329–30; H.M.C., *De L'Isle and Dudley MSS.* 249, 297, 305; Collins, *Life of . . . Lord Burghley*, 97.

57. Wright, op. cit. ii. 440.

58. B.M., Add. MS. 22925, f. 31b; H.M.C., *Rutland MSS.* i. 282.

59. Collins, *Life of . . . Lord Burghley*, 84; H.M.C., *Salisbury MSS.* viii. 370.

Further Reading

THE standard work on the career of William Cecil is provided by Dr Conyers Read's two volumes, *Mr Secretary Cecil and Queen Elizabeth* (1955), and *Lord Burghley and Queen Elizabeth* (1960). They constitute a great quarry of information and furnish a guide to the sources. Professor Joel Hurstfield's *Queen's Wards* (1958) deals with Burghley's administration of the Court of Wards and has a valuable discussion of Burghley's conduct in the prevailing political conditions. The same author has written on Burghley's character in an article in *History Today* (1956), vol. vi.

Students can read sympathetic contemporary comment on Burghley in the biography included in Francis Peck's *Desiderata Curiosa* (1779), in John Clapham's *Certain Observations*, ed. E. P. and C. Read in *Elizabeth of England* (Pennsylvania U.P., 1951), in Francis Bacon's 'Certain Observations upon a Libel', printed in James Spedding's *The Letters and Life of Francis Bacon* (1862), and in William Camden's *Historie of the most renowned and victorious princesse Elizabeth, late Queene of England* (1675). The contemporary attack upon Cecil is expounded in T. H. Clancy's *Papist Pamphleteers* (Chicago, 1964).

Specimens of William Cecil's own writings are reproduced in the first two volumes of the *Harleian Miscellany* (1808). *Advice to a Son*, ed. L. B. Wright (Cornell, 1962), contains Cecil's advice to both his sons.

The following are a selection of biographies of those closely associated with William Cecil: J. Strype, *Life of . . . Sir John Cheke* (1821); L. V. Ryan, *Roger Ascham* (1963); Lady Cecilie Goff, *A Woman of the Tudor Age* (1930); M. Dewar, *Sir Thomas Smith* (1964); J. W. Burgon, *The Life and Times of Sir Thomas Gresham* (1839); F. G. Emmison, *Tudor Secretary* (1961); S. E. Lehmberg, *Sir Walter Mildmay and Tudor Government* (1964); J. Ridley, *Cranmer* (1962); B. W. Beckingsale, *Elizabeth I* (1963); V. J. K. Brook, *Archbishop Parker* (1962); N. J. Williams, *Thomas Howard,*

Fourth Duke of Norfolk (1964); J. A. Williamson, *Sir John Hawkins* (1927); P. M. Dawley, *John Whitgift and the Reformation* (1955); E. St J. Brooks, *Sir Christopher Hatton* (1946); A. C. Miller, *Sir Henry Killigrew* (1963); B. M. Ward, *The Seventeenth Earl of Oxford* (1928); A. L. Rowse, *Shakespeare's Southampton* (1966); P. M. Handover, *The Second Cecil* (1959).

The following are a selection of books on various aspects of the background of William Cecil's life: M. L. Clarke, *Classical Education in Britain 1500-1900* (1959); H. C. Porter, *Reformation and Reaction in Tudor Cambridge* (1958); M. H. Curtis, *Oxford and Cambridge in Transition 1558-1642* (1959); K. Charlton, *Education in Renaissance England* (1965); C. Hill, *Intellectual Origins of the English Revolution* (1965); E. R. G. Taylor, *Mathematical Practitioners of Tudor and Stuart England* (1954); F. Wormald and C. E. Wright, *The English Library before 1700* (1958); C. S. Lewis, *English Literature in the Sixteenth Century* (1954); F. S. Fussner, *The Historical Revolution* (1962); J. D. Kendrick, *British Antiquity* (1950); W. Haller, *Foxe's Book of Martyrs and the Elect Nation* (1963); P. Munz, *The Place of Hooker in the History of Thought* (1952); M. M. Knappen, *Tudor Puritanism* (1939); W. K. Jordan, *The Development of Religious Toleration in England* (1932); J. K. McConica, *The English Humanists and Reformation Politics* (1965); W. G. Zeeveld, *Foundations of Tudor Policy* (1948); F. Raab, *The English Face of Machiavelli* (1964); J. Buxton, *Elizabethan Taste* (1963); E. Mercer, *English Art 1553-1603* (1962); E. M. W. Tillyard, *The Elizabethan World Picture* (1943); R. Kelso, *Doctrine of the English Gentleman in the Sixteenth Century* (1929); L. Stone, *The Crisis of the Aristocracy 1558-1641* (1966); P. Ramsay, *Tudor Economic Problems* (1965); *Elizabethan Government and Society*, ed. S. T. Bindoff, J. Hurstfield and C. H. Williams (1961); J. E. Neale, *The Elizabethan House of Commons* (1949); A. L. Rowse, *The England of Elizabeth* (1950); R. B. Wernham, *Before the Armada* (1966); G. Mattingly, *The Defeat of the Spanish Armada* (1959).

INDEX

Achurch, Northants., 56
Admonition to Parliament (1572), 135
Africa, 116
Alae, seu Scalae Mathematicae (1573), 260
À'Lasco, John, 36
Alençon, Francis Valois, Duke of, 130,
    132, 133, 135, 137, 138, 140, 142, 143,
    144, 145, 146, 148, 149, 150, 155, 276
Alford, Roger, 44, 49, 50
All Souls College, Oxford, 35
Allington, Hugh, 24
Alltyrynys, Herefs., 4, 267, 283
Alost, 61
Alva, Don Fernando Alvarez de Toledo,
    Duke of, 115, 120, 132, 133, 134
Amadis de Gaul, 250
Amyce, Israel, 262
Anabaptists, 28
Anglo-Saxon Chronicle, 250
Anjou, Henry Valois, Duke of, *see*
    Henry III, King of France
Anne of Cleves, 58
Antiquaries, Society of, 251
Antwerp, 41, 57, 61, 83, 103, 116, 130,
    131, 135, 138, 140, 158, 206, 238
Apologie for Poetrie (1595), 253
Apology for the Church of England (1561),
    100
Apprentices, Statute of (1563), 100
Architettura (1566), 265
Aristotle, 273
Armada, the Great (1588), 164, 165, 166,
    167, 168, 169, 170, 172, 173, 214, 225,
    226, 276, 286
Arran, James Stuart, Earl of, 79, 80, 93,
    153
Art of Rhetoric (1553), 255
Art of Shooting Great Ordonance, 260
Arte of English Poesie (1589), 254
Arthur, King of Britain, 215, 253, 273
Articles, the Forty-Two, 41, 73; the
    Thirty-Nine, 112
Arundel, Henry Fitzalan, 12th Earl of,
    36, 37, 48, 49, 50, 82, 123, 125
Arundel's, Poultenay Lane, London, 63
Ascham, Roger, 16, 17, 29, 33, 35, 66,
    73, 209, 254, 255, 256, 266, 269, 272,
    276; widow of, 245

Ashley, William, 168
Ashton, Thomas, 246
Asia, 259
Association, Bond of (1586), 156, 157
Aubrey, John, 253
Audley, John Tuchet, Lord, 43; George
    Tuchet, Lord, 243
Audley End, Essex, 144, 265
Austin Friars, Stamford, 56
Aylmer, John, 73, 74, 203, 224, 231
Azores, the, 151

Babington plot, 162
Bacon, Anne (*née* Cooke), Lady, 23, 24,
    50, 100, 228; Anthony, 179, 183, 283;
    Sir Francis, 179, 180, 194, 199, 207,
    218, 220, 229, 255, 258, 261, 262, 265,
    272, 279, 283; Sir Nicholas, 24, 45, 59,
    69, 73, 74, 102, 126, 147, 192, 220, 232,
    256, 264, 268, 273, 279, 283
Baret, John, 251
Barholme, Lincs., 56
Barnes, Richard, 231
Baro, Peter, 247
Barrow, Henry, 224; Philip, 192, 257
Beale, Robert, 163, 172, 226
Beaufort, Margaret, Lady, 4
Becon, Thomas, 224, 272
Bede, the Venerable, 250
Bedford, Countess of, 59; Francis
    Russell, 2nd Earl of, 59; John Russell,
    1st Earl of, 31, 32, 48, 73, 231
Bellott, Thomas, 172, 187
Bereham, Lincs., 56
Berkshire, 9
Berwick, Northumberland, 82, 276;
    warden of, 220
Bess of Hardwick, *see* Shrewsbury,
    Countess of
Bible, the, 18, 46, 199, 212, 250; the
    Bishop's, 224, 255, 259, 268
Bill, William, 73
Billingsley, Sir Henry, 225, 258
Bilney, Thomas, 14, 77
Bilson, Thomas, 231
Blagrave, John, 260
Blois, Treaty of (1572), 131, 133, 134
Blundeville, Thomas, 262

Y

PRINTED IN GREAT BRITAIN BY ROBERT MACLEHOSE AND CO. LTD
THE UNIVERSITY PRESS, GLASGOW